# OXFORD GEOGRAPHICAL AND ENVIRONMENTAL STUDIES

General Editors

*Gordon Clark, Andrew Goudie, and Ceri Peach*

Editorial Advisory Board

*Professor Kay Anderson (United Kingdom)*
*Professor Felix Driver (United Kingdom)*
*Professor Rita Gardner (United Kingdom)*
*Professor Avijit Gupta (Singapore)*
*Professor Christian Kesteloot (Belgium)*
*Professor David Thomas (United Kingdom)*
*Professor Billie Lee Turner II (USA)*
*Professor Michael Watts (USA)*
*Professor James Wescoat (USA)*

# Pension Fund Capitalism

Gordon L. Clark

OXFORD

UNIVERSITY PRESS

# OXFORD

UNIVERSITY PRESS

Great Clarendon Street, Oxford OX2 6DP

Oxford University Press is a department of the University of Oxford.
It furthers the University's objective of excellence in research, scholarship,
and education by publishing worldwide in

Oxford New York

Athens Auckland Bangkok Bogotá Buenos Aires Calcutta
Cape Town Chennai Dar es Salaam Delhi Florence Hong Kong Istanbul
Karachi Kuala Lumpur Madrid Melbourne Mexico City Mumbai
Nairobi Paris São Paulo Singapore Taipei Tokyo Toronto Warsaw

and associated companies in Berlin Ibadan

Oxford is a registered trade mark of Oxford University Press
in the UK and certain other countries

Published in the United States
by Oxford University Press Inc., New York

British Library Cataloguing in Publication Data

Data available

Library of Congress Cataloging in Publication Data

Clark, Gordon L.
    Pension fund capitalism / Gordon L. Clark.
        (Oxford geographical and environmental studies)
        Includes bibliographical references.
        1. Pension trusts.  I. Title.  II. Series.
HD7105.4.C58  1999    332.67'25421—dc21    99-045918
ISBN 0-19-924047-7
ISBN 0-19-924048-5 (Pbk.)

1 3 5 7 9 10 8 6 4 2

Typeset by Best-set Typesetter Ltd., Hong Kong
Printed in Great Britain
on acid-free paper by
Biddles Ltd Guildford and King's Lynn

*For Peter and Shirley*

# EDITORS' PREFACE

GEOGRAPHY and environmental studies are two closely related and burgeoning fields of academic inquiry. Both have grown rapidly over the
past two decades. At once catholic in its approach and yet strongly committed to a comprehensive understanding of the world, geography has
focused upon the interaction between global and local phenomena.
Environmental studies, on the other hand, has shared with the discipline
of geography an engagement with different disciplines addressing wide-
ranging environmental issues in the scientific community and the policy
community of great significance. Ranging from the analysis of climate
change and physical processes to the cultural dislocations of postmod-
ernism these two fields of inquiry have been in the forefront of attempts
to comprehend transformations taking place in the world, manifesting
themselves at a variety of separate but interrelated spatial scales.

The 'Oxford Geographical and Environmental Studies' series aims to
reflect this diversity and engagement. Our aim is to publish the best original research in the two related fields and in doing so, to demonstrate
the significance of geographical and environmental perspectives for
understanding the contemporary world. As a consequence, its scope is
international and ranges widely in terms of its topics, approaches, and
methodologies. Its authors will be welcomed from all corners of the
globe. We hope the series will assist in redefining the frontiers of knowledge and build bridges within the fields of geography and environmental studies. We hope also that it will cement links with topics and
approaches that have originated outside the strict confines of these disciplines. Resulting studies contribute to frontiers of research and knowledge as well as representing individually the fruits of particular and
diverse specialist expertise in the traditions of scholarly publication.

*Gordon Clark*
*Andrew Goudie*
*Ceri Peach*

# PREFACE

THE title of this book refers to the remarkable size and significance of public and private pension funds in the Anglo-American (also known as Anglo-Saxon) economies, suggesting that there is something distinctive about the financial and institutional structure of these economies at the dawn of the twenty-first century. Pension funds have been a crucial catalyst in the transformation of the theory and practice of financial management; many of the new financial instruments which have come to dominate global securities' markets owe their invention to the burgeoning needs of large, sophisticated pension funds. In this respect, the point of departure for the book can be simply stated: pension funds and their agents in the investment management industry control enormous sums of money, profoundly affecting the structure and performance of nation-states and the global economy. At the same time, it is also apparent that many Western governments are retreating from the provision of 'public goods' once thought essential to the fabric of urban life. If we are to understand the long-term future of the Western economies (in general) and our communities (in particular), we need also to understand how institutional investors allocate assets, mobilize funds, and make investment decisions.

Drucker's (1993: 69) thoughts about pension fund capitalism have been varied and provocative. He suggests we should think of it as 'pension-fund socialism', referring to 'ownership of the means of production by the employees . . . through their pension funds'. Legally pension fund contributions are invested by trustees on behalf of their plan beneficiaries. Trustees are the agents of plan beneficiaries, as investment managers are the agents of trustees. To the extent that pension funds own stock in companies that produce goods and services, plan beneficiaries could be thought to 'own' those companies. But in the Anglo-American economies, company-sponsored pension plans cannot hold a large portion of stock in their sponsor. Nor do individual pension funds normally hold such large stakes in unrelated companies that they could directly control corporate managers' use of the means of production on behalf of their plan beneficiaries. 'Ownership' is actually incredibly diffused. While pension fund led campaigns over corporate governance are increasingly important, the fact that so many pension funds invest in, and rely upon, markets of all kinds and across so many

regions of the world suggests that beneficiaries' reliance on market capitalism is as profound as securities' markets reliance upon pension fund
assets.

The focus of the book is reserved for pension funds in the Anglo-
American economies. Empirically I report research on pension funds
in the USA, the UK, Australia, and, to a much lesser extent, Canada.
These countries and other historically related countries which share
the English common law tradition seem more alike with respect to the
nature, structure, and regulation of pension funds than most continental European or Latin American countries. Anglo-American countries
also host many of the same global finance companies including J. P.
Morgan, Schroders, and State Street Bank of Boston. These companies
offer similar investment management services to local pension funds set
within a web of regulations that have many commonalities between
countries. Of course, these are broad sweeping generalizations which
ignore diversity within the common law tradition, and significant statutory differences between these countries with respect to state social
security and private retirement provision. Also ignored are moves
being made in some regions of the world towards the Anglo-American
model; witness the transformation of retirement funding in Chile and
Argentina and the experiments underway in Eastern Europe. Nevertheless, my focus is reserved for the Anglo-American economies as a
group and the investment management industry which has come to
dominate those economies, with minor amendments made to distinguish
between specific countries' pension experiences.

The book begins with a brief analysis of the growth and status of
pension funds in the USA, the UK, and Australia. Very simply, I aim to
show the reader that pension funds matter. At times in the book I also
discuss related financial institutions like listed mutual funds and unit
trusts. In the USA, these have grown very quickly over the past
decade or so, in part because of a shift by pension fund sponsors
towards defined contribution plans and retirement options that often
come under the heading of 401(k) retirement plans. I do not analyse
these latter kinds of retirement savings vehicles in any detail. Rightly or
wrongly, it has proved difficult to cope with the full range of pension
funds, let alone retail sector mutual funds. Nevertheless, there are considerable overlaps between these sectors, evident in the fact that
firms like Fidelity have asset management groups which utilize and rely
upon expertise from their mutual fund investment programmes. In
fact, the largest investment management firms have sought to capitalize
on their functional scope by offering to large plan sponsors' participants

so-called retail services (personal mutual fund options) and wholesale services (pooled employer-sponsored retirement accounts).

The book moves on to an argument about the retreat of the state from the provision of public goods. Again, my focus is reserved for the Anglo-American economies. This time it is because we seem to have stumbled into an era in which raw elements of nineteenth-century liberalism have combined with post-cold-war doubts about the scope of the state to undercut the legitimacy of the inherited functions of government. This is particularly apparent in the Anglo-American countries affecting the agenda of politics, as well as the identity of political parties (witness the transformation of Blair's Labour Party in the UK, as well as the tumult in US presidential and congressional politics). It is perhaps less apparent in continental Europe, where social democratic parties retain considerable influence, given less than robust economic conditions and the upheaval occasioned by moves towards a single market. Basically, I would argue that if the urban fabric of the Anglo-American countries is to be sustained and enhanced, pension funds are the obvious and only likely sources of new investment over the coming years of the twenty-first century. When I refer to urban fabric, I mean urban infrastructure of all kinds, including housing, transportation, water and sewerage services, small and medium-sized enterprises, etc. In other words, I include the entire mix of public and private activities that make urban life possible. This is an element hidden in many governments' privatization programmes, and underpins new initiatives such as the UK's Private Finance Initiative.

The heart of the book is a set of six chapters about the structure of the investment management industry (two chapters), the logic behind pension fund trustees' investment decision making (two chapters), and the institutional mechanisms being developed to target pension fund assets to urban infrastructure investments (two chapters). I touch on issues such as economically targeted investments (ETIs), alternative investment products, and the scope of pension fund investment. I am interested in understanding the extent to which pension funds may actually be mobilized for urban economic development, given the structure of the industry and the nature of decision making by key players in the pension funds themselves. These chapters rely upon a great deal of fieldwork: interviews and discussions of all kinds with a wide range of professionals inside and outside of pension funds in the USA, the UK, and Australia. In the Introduction I go into more detail about my research methodology. The point here is that pension fund investment is an industry. Firms and financial institutions are basic to understanding how it works. Yet there is little in the literature which can help us understand the industry. While there are many learned papers on efficient markets, there are few on the structure of investment management firms in relation to their pension fund clients. In this respect, the book is also an attempt to map the economic organization of pension fund investment.

In the final two chapters, I deal with the regulation of pension fund investment. Here I have three concerns. One is about the extent to which government policy should in some way stimulate or direct the investment practices of pension funds, with respect to the needs of urban society. For some commentators this is anathema to beneficiaries' interests. And yet it is not so easily discounted as a policy issue, given the degree to which pension fund assets have come to represent the vast bulk of our nations' savings. Another concern is the extent to which a coherent case can be made for the community interest in pension fund investment decision making. And a third concern is the intimate connection between money and corruption. These issues are developed in relation to recent US debates over economically targeted investments and the recurrent concerns over the legitimacy of pension fund capitalism. In the final analysis, I ask how community solidarity can be squared with pension fund capitalism (if at all).

Throughout, I use separate but paired chapters to sustain my argument. In doing so, presentation of my argument revolves around questions of substantive knowledge of the pension fund industry juxtaposed against theoretical issues derived from finance and economic geography. In the main I aim to set the agenda and argue for my opinion. This is not a book which surveys and adjudicates between theoretical arguments. As a consequence, it is both broad ranging and agenda-setting. In this respect, I use chapter endnotes in a manner consistent with J. Hillis Miller's (1987: 15) sense of authorial proportion: to suggest additions or amendments about the scope of conclusions and to acknowledge opinions or related claims that are at a tangent to my own. In sum, the book is designed with this scope in mind.

# ACKNOWLEDGEMENTS

THE project started with my research on corporate restructuring in the USA over the 1970s and 1980s, and the role of pension obligations in labour–management negotiations over the restructuring process. I was introduced to these issues by the United Steelworkers of America and my wife Shirley who was a negotiator for the union. I was also aided by conversations with corporate executives from major manufacturing corporations, participants in seminars sponsored by Carnegie Mellon University's Labour Studies Centre. Thanks are due to Richard Cyert, Brian Berry, Angel Jordan, and Ben Fischer for making all this possible. Without a doubt, the special research environment of Carnegie Mellon enabled me to expand my intellectual horizons and enter the world of corporations and finance. From that research I learnt a great deal about the origins and evolution of US pension entitlements and the various institutions that have regulated the provision of pension benefits. I also learnt that what appear, at one level, to be firm liabilities are, at another level, assets which must be invested for the long-term benefit of eligible employees. Understanding the difference between liabilities and assets was a first step into finance. The next step was into the Anglo-American investment management industry. Again, I have been aided enormously by Shirley—this time by her experience in the funds management industry and her work for the asset management group of Norwich Union (Australia).

Through her contacts, I have been able to meet investment managers, consultants, and pension fund trustees. In this respect, I would particularly like to acknowledge the assistance and encouragement of John Evans and James Burkitt. They have been especially generous with their time and have made it possible for me to meet many others in the industry. One virtue of such close relationships in the industry is the opportunity to participate in industry briefings and related conferences. For instance, I had the privilege of meeting a group of trustees and consultants representing some of the largest US pension funds looking for private equity deals in Asia. Floating around Sydney harbour drinking white wine is always a pleasurable experience. On that occasion, it was made more so by the remarkable combination of people and institutions put together by Bell Resources and *Pensions & Investments*. These kinds of sessions are part and parcel of the investment industry;

networks and alliances involving pension funds and their advisers (actual and potential) are formed and reformed through briefing sessions in far-flung regions of the world. They are an essential ingredient in the social structure of money management—a fact that has paid dividends when making visits to fund managers in the USA and the UK.

While at Monash University, I was fortunate to play a role in establishing the Australian Housing and Urban Research Institute (AHURI). Michael Berry, AHURI's founding executive director, was a consistent supporter of the project. More recently, I have benefited from the resources of Oxford University's Transport Studies Unit (a research unit of the School of Geography). Along the way, various banks, investment companies, and financial service providers have supported the project through seed money for various projects. In this respect, I would like to acknowledge the early support of Wespac's asset management group in sponsoring a series of industry seminars in Australia during early 1996. These sessions allowed me a rare opportunity (for an academic) to talk directly with some of the most important firms and pension funds in the industry, and through them, appreciate the logic and significance of my work.

My research project really got going when I attended a conference at the AFL-CIO in Washington, DC in early 1993 on economically targeted investments. There I also met Richard Grant, a pensions benefits specialist at the AFL-CIO and now an investment consultant. He was very helpful in making links with union pension funds in the USA. We have also interviewed many investment managers, consultants, and trustees in New York, Boston, Washington, and Chicago. In this regard, I would like to particularly acknowledge the comments and advice of Dallas Salisbury and his colleagues at the Employee Benefits Research Institute in Washington, DC. While ETIs are very contentious in some quarters, the idea that pension funds could be mobilized and focused on areas of need in communities across America is less radical than it would appear from the rhetoric. It has become apparent from the leading investment houses in New York and London that whatever the politics of ETIs, the idea of urban economic development as an asset class has generated significant interest in the investment community. In this context, rekindling my friendship with Beldon Daniels at Economic Innovation International Inc. (Boston) has been very fruitful in helping me appreciate the possible connections between institutional investors, and state and local economic development programmes, which have had close relationships with venture capital firms for many years.

I have also benefited significantly from attendance at conferences sponsored by the Pension Research Council at the Wharton School of the University of Pennsylvania. Olivia Mitchell has offered advice and has welcomed my attendance. Likewise, I was very fortunate to participate in a conference on behavioural finance at Harvard University, sponsored by the Cambridge Centre for Advanced Study. Sherman Roberts made me welcome, while Richard Zeckhauser was especially helpful in making my participation possible. Through the Harvard conference I met a number of people including Mike Clowes, the Executive Editor of *Pensions & Investments*. Mike, Paul Barr, and Joel Chernoff in London have been important sources of unpublished industry information and material. Other important initial contacts were with Jeffrey Gordon and Mark Roe at Columbia Law School. More recently, I have benefited from the comments and advice of many academics and practitioners, in particular Keith Ambachtsheer, Patrick Atiyah, Bernard Black, Don Ezra, Maryann Feldman, David Hirshleifer, Ron Gilson, Jack Gray, the late Bennett Harrison, John Ilkiw, Bob Lake, Helen Lawton Smith, Andrew Leyshon, Ron Martin, Alicia Munnell, Werner Nussbaum, Carol O'Cleireacain, Michael Porter, Robert Reich, Adam Tickell, and Jennifer Wolch, and Julie Kast at Greenwich Associates. Unfortunately, I have not been able to incorporate all the advice I have been given.

More formally academic have been the opportunities to present my research to seminars and conferences inside and outside of geography. A first step in this context was made at a workshop of the Economic Geography study group, sponsored by the Institute of Australian Geographers. My colleagues were puzzled but supportive. Similarly, the audience at an Institutional Investment Marketing Conference sponsored by Burkitt (Australia) were curious but encouraging. I have also presented portions of this work at the annual meetings of the Royal Geographical Society, the Association of American Geographers, and the Regional Studies Association. Seminars on papers related to the project have been held at Manchester University, Bristol University, University College London, Oxford University, Southampton University, Leeds University, Leicester University, the University of Toronto, McMaster University, Cambridge University, and many other universities. Thanks to those who participated and the comments they provided.

Most importantly, I must acknowledge the support of Nigel Thrift, editor of the journal *Environment and Planning A* published by Pion Ltd., London. He has published three significant pieces from the project and has provided advice and encouragement in the face of considerable unease voiced by some who have neither appreciated the significance of the issues raised, nor understood the importance of understanding

xvi                            *Acknowledgements*

the logic and structure behind investment decision making in the finance industry. His journal remains a most important outlet for innovative research which is at the margins of a variety of disciplines, just as his judgement has been critical in encouraging new research which is neither hostage to the past nor subservient to the doctrines of the present.

Selected material from this project has been previously published in the following journals or books. Chapter 1, 'Stylized facts and close dialogue: methodology in economic geography': *Annals* of the Association of American Geographers 88 (1998), 73–87. Reproduced with permission of Blackwell Publishers. Chapter 2, 'The retreat of the state and pension fund capitalism': R. L. Martin (ed.) *Money and the Space Economy* (1999), 214–60 & 296–7. Copyright John Wiley & Sons Limited. Reproduced with permission. Chapter 3, 'Pension fund capitalism: a causal analysis': *Geografiska Annales B* 80 (1998), 139–57. Reproduced with permission of Blackwell Publishers. Chapter 4, 'The functional and spatial structure of investment management': *Geoforum*, 31/1 (2000). Reproduced with permission of Elsevier Science. Chapter 6, 'Why convention dominates pension fund trustees investment decision making': *Environment & Planning A*, 30 (1998), 997–1015. Reproduced with permission of Pion Limited. Chapter 7, 'The anatomy of corruption: the practice of pension fund trustee decision making': *Environment and Planning A*, 30 (1998), 1235–53. Reproduced with permission of Pion Limited. Chapter 8, 'Pension funds and urban investment': *Environment Planning A*, 29 (1997), 1297–1316. Reproduced with permission of Pion Limited. Chapter 9, 'The private provision of urban infrastructure: financial intermediation through long term contracts': *Urban Studies*, 35/2 (1998) 301–19. Reproduced with permission of Taylor & Francis. Chapter 10, 'Contested terrain: Republican rhetoric, pension funds, and community development': *Urban Geography*, 20 (1999), 197–225. Reproduced with permission of Bellwether Publishing. Chapter 11, 'Moral sentiment and reciprocal obligations: the case for pension fund investment in community development': *Ethics, Place, and Environment*, 3/1 (2000). Reproduced with permission of Taylor & Francis. I should also thank Wayne Marr, publisher of the Financial Economics Network, a division of Social Science Electronic Publishing (www.ssrn.com). He willingly published the abstracts from my research, circulating them to many thousands of subscribers around the world. I have learnt a great deal from comments received and material provided in return from its many subscribers. It has been a thrill to live in this virtual world with other researchers similarly concerned with the same issues if not the same disciplinary loyalties.

Finally, I should also mention the support I have received from closer to home. My personal assistant, Jan Burke, has been superbly efficient. Paul Bennett, Melanie Feakins, Mojdeh Keykhah, Terry Lumish, Dominic Power, Amanda Root, and Leslie Turano were very helpful research assistants. Peter Haywood, Neil McIntosh, and Ailsa Allen drew the diagrams. Andrew Goudie, Ceri Peach, Colin Mayer, Dominic Byatt, and my colleagues at Oxford have proven to be warm and congenial collaborators. And over the years I have benefited from kind words of encouragement and support from Elizabeth Prior Jonson, Meric Gertler, and Neil Wrigley.

The book is dedicated to Shirley and Peter who shared the vision, and saw it through to fruition.

G.L.C.
Oxford
September 1999

# CONTENTS

# LIST OF FIGURES

# LIST OF TABLES

# ABBREVIATIONS

AFL-CIO  American Federation of Labour and the Confederation of Industrial Organisations

AHURI  Australian Housing and Urban Research Institute (Melbourne)

AIP  alternative investment products

CAPM  capital asset pricing model

CRA  Community Reinvestment Act (US)

DB Plans  defined benefit or final salary (pension) plans

DC Plans  defined contribution or accumulation (pension) plans

DoL  Department of Labor (US)

EBRI  Employee Benefits Research Institute (Washington, DC)

ERISA  Employee Retirement Income Security Act (1974) (US federal statute)

ETIs  economically targeted investments

IFS  Institute of Fiscal Studies (an ESRC-sponsored research institute at the University College, London)

MPT  modern portfolio theory

PAYG  pay as you go

PFI  Private Finance Initiative (United Kingdom)

PPP  Public–Private Partnerships (United Kingdom)

PRC  Pension Research Council (of the Wharton School, University of Pennsylvania, Philadelphia)

# 1

# Introduction

THIS book is an exercise in political economy and economic geography.
It is about the structure and organization of pension fund capitalism
focusing upon the institutional framework of the investment process. I
explain the growing significance of pension funds in relation to the
limited fiscal powers of government, the changing balance of power
between banks and new non-banking financial institutions, and the
financial services industry. All this is set within the astonishing growth
of Anglo-American pension fund assets over the past thirty years
(Langbein 1995).[1] Not surprisingly, the project involves analysis of competition and innovation in the investment management industry as well
as analysis of the nature and mediation of agency relationships within
the industry, and between the institutions of pension fund capitalism. In
these ways, the book is more about the institutions of finance than it is
about the performance of financial markets compared, for example, with
Campbell, Lo, and MacKinlay (1997).[2]

In more detail, I am most interested in the investment decision
making process, being concerned to identify and document the protocols that are essential in understanding that process. Four of the ten
chapters of the book are focused on this issue starting with trustee decision making in the context of the market for financial services and
broadening out to the question of pension fund investment in urban
infrastructure and community economic development. Again, the focus
of this analysis is institutional, reflecting a widespread recognition in
the industry and in the academic literature that the trustee institution
is a basic, distinguishing characteristic of Anglo-American financial
markets. To do so has required detailed knowledge of decision making—
I have relied very heavily upon interviews with trustees and consultants
for that knowledge informed, of course, by theoretical insights gleaned
from the relevant economic and psychological literature attributed to
Tversky and Kahneman (1986) amongst many others. Indeed, the entire
project has relied upon what I call close dialogue with industry and academic respondents (see below).

There is considerable interest, of course, in the role of institutions in affecting and sustaining national and international financial and economic performance (see e.g. Roe 1994). One branch of political economy identifies this issue as central to its agenda suggesting that understanding the connection between institutions and wealth must rely upon the theoretical and empirical integration of transaction costs with property rights. In this vein Eggertsson (1996) suggested that the 'new' institutionalism is a form of conventional economics extended to a world characterized by significant transaction costs and path dependence. As will become apparent, this book is similarly concerned with the boundaries of institutions and their interactions with other institutions in a world characterized by risk and uncertainty. This perspective is at the heart of my analysis of relationships between trustees (Chapters 6 and 7), relationships between trustees and their service providers, and agency relationships within the investment management industry (Chapter 4). It is also very important in assessing the determinants of industry structure and performance (Chapters 4 and 5). Insights gleaned from Coase, Williamson, Richardson, and Storper and Salais amongst others underpin my analysis.

Political economy, however, is more than the economics of institutional analysis. This point was neatly illustrated by Anne Krueger (1996) in her study of the regulation of the American sugar industry. She began by surveying conventional models of regulation, noting their objectives and limitations. One important point she makes is that most models are static, once-and-for-all definitions of the relationships between known agents and their representative institutions. By contrast, her analysis of the regulation of the sugar industry was informed by the evolution of agents' interests and changing circumstances. Structure and agency count, so too does the contingency of power and influence. This is a broader view of institutional analysis, even if explicitly linked by Eggertsson to his agenda for political economy. Throughout I am concerned with the intersection between at least two parts of political economy: the economics of institutions and the role of public policy in the evolution of those institutions. This is obvious in the first two chapters of the book. But it is also embedded in the chapters devoted to institutional and industry relationships. Importantly it re-emerges in full force in the last two chapters where I analyse the politics of regulation. By my account, political economy should not be limited to the economic principles of the proper design of organizations.

My interest in pension fund capitalism goes back to earlier work on the geographical patterns of corporate restructuring in the United States (Clark 1993*b*). The economic geography of pension liability in large US manufacturing firms has preoccupied scholars, regulators, and unions for the last twenty to thirty years. As important, though much less studied, is the economic geography of pension fund investment. With the 1997 Asian financial crisis (the Russian crisis, and then the Brazilian crisis, etc.) there has been considerable interest in the international flows of financial assets (in general) and the spatial structure of pension fund asset allocations (in particular). So, in this respect, there is an emerging literature on the economic geography of finance dealing with questions such as whether Western financial institutions precipitated the Asian crisis or simply followed local circumstances and then exacerbated the flight to quality (see e.g. Choe, Kho, and Stulz 1998 and Edison et al. 1998). In this book, however, the international landscape of institutional investment is only briefly touched upon (Chapter 3). In terms of economic geography, my core empirical interest is in Anglo-American pension fund investment in urban infrastructure and community economic development. This is an important issue in its own right being related to the retreat of the state and the relative decline of first order intermediaries in the context of regional growth and decline (Chapter 2). It is also a reference point for assessing more general issues like the structure of the investment management industry, patterns of competition and innovation (Chapters 4 and 5), and the nature of investment decision making (Chapters 6 though 7).

Having introduced the economic geography agenda for the book, I should also acknowledge that my agenda is more related to political economy in the broad sense noted above than it is related to Paul Krugman's (1991) 'new' economic geography. There is no doubt that his entry into the field has brought a sharp edge to our understanding of issues such as spatial structure and agglomeration economies. His methods of analysis combined with trade theory have been welcomed by many seeking fresh insights into stubborn problems. Even so, this book has not focused upon the core problems of the 'new' economic geography. Rather, it reflects my continuing concern with another important theme in the field: the logic of urban economic development in relation to institutions and economic decision making practices. This theme is at the intersection between the institutions of finance, the structure and organization of the industry, the practice of investment, and the regulation of investment. The book is focused upon issues such as structure and agency in the context of variegated and differentiated economic landscapes in a manner consistent with my colleagues Storper and Salais (1997) and Scott (1998) rather than Krugman (1991).

One of the most important research themes in economic geography over the past twenty years has been industrial structure and corporate organization. Whereas issues such as optimal spatial structure domin-

*Introduction*

ated theory building for many years after the Second World War, a new generation of scholars have sought a different economic geography focused on spatial and economic restructuring—the study of economic geography through the actions of firms in the context of industrial competition. In many respects, the theoretical agenda has been dominated by two themes: agency and differentiation. The former has prompted a concern for understanding the economic landscape as the result of agents' actions rather than supposing those actions are always and everywhere overcome by market imperatives. The latter has brought to the fore new work on the persistence of heterogeneity in time and space. This type of work takes seriously institutions, codes of practice, and market forces. It does not, however, reduce these elements to market imperatives. These issues are deeply embedded in this book. It is, amongst other things, a book about the structure and organization of the financial industry (Chapters 3, 4, and 5).

## Codification of Practice

The proper focus of economic geography is one issue. Perhaps more problematic are the proper methods of economic geography. Whereas economists have a well-developed tool bag of techniques, recent work in economic geography and the geography of finance tends to be more empirical, being based upon in-depth interviews or close dialogue with industry respondents; see e.g. Leyshon, Thrift, and Pratt (1998), L. McDowell (1997), Thrift (1996: ch. 6), and Saxenian (1994). Unlike other forms of empirical research, close dialogue relies upon the intimacy or closeness of researchers to industry respondents. It is a mode of case study research that uses structured and unstructured interviews between nominal equals to reveal the actual logic of decision making. Close dialogue can involve complex relationships between interviewers and interviewees, a level of personal commitment at odds with the conventional notions of social science. By contrast, in the 'new' economic geography stylized facts dominate intellectual reasoning.[3]

In researching Anglo-American pension fund investment strategies, it has become apparent to me that understanding financial decision making has been unfortunately limited by the hegemony of one stylized fact: the claim attributed to Michael Jensen that the efficient markets hypothesis is the most well-established fact in the social sciences. This 'fact' has had far-reaching implications for what are legitimate questions of research (e.g. the role of geography in financial markets), what are legitimate assumptions about individual decision making (e.g. the significance of local context in investment decision making), and what are legitimate arguments about regulation (e.g. the prospects for directing pension funds to urban needs). Likewise, Krugman's stylized facts threaten the hard won work of the past twenty years aimed at integrating spatial heterogeneity into the theoretical core of economic geography. We have inherited a body of theory that is at once extraordinarily idealistic about the efficiency of markets, and quite removed from the actual practice of investment decision making. If we are to escape the shadow cast by the efficient markets hypothesis in the geography of finance, and if we are to sustain a rich geographically informed economic geography, we need to be clear about how and why close dialogue is a plausible mode of analysis.[4]

The goal of the book is not so much to dispute the market efficiency hypothesis, so much as to indicate that its widespread acceptance has led many researchers to ignore the decision making practices of agents and institutions. Embedded in the theory is an expectation that the practice of decision making is irrelevant in the face of structural, market imperatives. The arbitrage process should systematically strip out of markets sub-optimal behaviour, leaving only market-consistent behaviour (for an early statement, see Alchian 1950). Missing in the literature are explanations of apparent local trends in decision making, the process of product innovation in 'thin' (incomplete and missing) markets, and an understanding of the interaction between the prejudices of investment institutions with respect to the urban economy in all its variety. Not surprisingly, the stylized facts claimed to be relevant to the geography of finance are often lacking in content—cutting against their abstraction is one object of geographers' research (Thrift 1996). Close dialogue is useful in this context because of the potential richness of substantive observation, the opportunity it promises for intellectual innovation, and its relative scepticism about the doctrine of market efficiency.[5] Close dialogue can be used, as it is used in the industry, to document and assess the actual practice of investment decision making, given the extraordinary variety of practice and the decentralized nature of market behaviour (see Greenwich Associates 1996*b*).[6]

Therefore one goal of this book is to systematically identify, describe, and analyse the structure of pension fund capitalism given a more general concern about the potential for pension fund investment in urban infrastructure and community economic development. There are few, if any, related studies in the literature. Indeed, apart from O'Barr and Conley's (1992) anthropological study of institutional behaviour in the finance industry and more general studies of pension fund investment (see Davis 1995 and Blake 1995), it has proved difficult to identify relevant research against which to assess the logic of analysis. Inevitably an important goal of the project is the codification of practice: to formalize through a set of more general terms and concepts economic behaviour that is otherwise tacit and hidden in the play of customary practice. In this respect, my aim is to suggest coherent, theoretically informed accounts of financial decision making, recognizing that my account is inevitably partial and subject to a degree of indeterminacy and uncertainty which is hard to specify a priori (Bourdieu 1990: ch. 4).

Codification is a process of classification, of distinguishing what are important attributes of a system from those that are unimportant and properly treated as background detail. Classification relies upon judgement, analysis, and perception, all of which must begin from some external reference point—a theory or set of principles that can order the process of codification. In each chapter, the assumptions and threads of theory used to structure analysis are developed in conjunction with the problem studied. In doing so, I do not mean to suggest that codified practice matches precisely how industry participants and respondents understand the overall structure of their world. In the main, trustees and industry consultants have found it difficult to offer a coherent, integrated account of the bases of their decision making. In this respect, codification may elide the gaps and blur disjunctures in practice, suggesting a level of integration that may not be evident to individual players. Still codification has a significant virtue: codification 'bring[s] out into the open, make[s] visible, public, known to all' (Bourdieu 1990: 81) and hence codification allows for the external scrutiny of a whole institution, something which is essential given the increasing importance of pension funds to all citizens.

Although a focus on investment institutions is interesting in its own right, some theorists might argue that agents' behaviour is not particularly relevant for understanding the macro economic and geographic patterns of investment. It may be argued that all agents should be assumed to be rational decision makers, whose behaviour is conditioned by an apparent and external objective world. By such an account, behaviour should be best understood as being simply a reflection of profound economic imperatives, supposing that deviations from optimal behaviour would be rigorously policed by market arbitrage processes. This school of thought dominates the theory of finance and is embedded in many arguments about the structure and performance of efficient markets (Houthakker and Williamson 1996). But it is not the only story. In fact, research by Shleifer (1998) and Cochrane (1999*a,b*) and their colleagues has sought to show that arbitrage processes and market performance are systematically not efficient in the strong sense assumed by many financial analysts. It is arguable that reading off (micro) behaviour from (macro) economic imperatives would miss significant and relevant information about the actual practice of decision making.

More directly, Simon (1986) is scathing in his criticisms of the empirical foundations of conventional models of behaviour. He suggests that these models are too often based upon unfounded axioms, justified by weak and superficial evidence, and ignorant of the scope and determinants of actual behaviour. Most significantly, he suggests that people are not, and cannot be in a cognitive sense, utility maximizers; economic agents operate in a world of limited knowledge with a complex array of goals and objectives, and have a limited capacity to assess and organize the available knowledge. This is the world of the financial agents. It is a world characterized by considerable risk and uncertainty, requiring a variety of strategies of accommodation and management in the context of legal obligations and past commitments. This is a world in which the practice of decision making counts. It is also a world in which behaviour can be understood only by direct observation or by 'interrogating the decision maker about [his or her] beliefs, expectations, and methods of calculation and reasoning' (p. S211). Simon's perspective underpins the structure and empirical design of this project.

## Choreography of Close Dialogue

A serious charge could be levelled at close dialogue: that it is vulnerable to systematic and random 'errors', relying, as it does, on respondents telling the truth about themselves and their industry. For those skilled in questionnaire design and survey techniques this kind of vulnerability may be countered in a number of ways. Interviewees' responses can be cross-checked against disguised control questions, designed to test the veracity of respondents. Informants may be told in advance that they are part of a larger survey implying a form of cross-checking involving their peers. And informants may even be rewarded, or promised a reward, if the interview 'goes well'. These strategies and others are part of the tool kit of any survey researcher who relies on the opinions of respondents. They are not, however, foolproof as Lewontin's (1995) critique of Laumann et al.'s (1994) study of sexuality in America has shown. There may be questions which respondents are uncomfortable in answering and there may be reasons, hidden from researchers, for systematic misrepresentation by individuals and whole groups. Close dialogue is an art as much as it is a science.[7]

While relevant to my argument, there is another dimension to the problem of research. Much of social science survey research presumes that expertise resides with the researcher, and that the proper design of questions in the light of anticipated right and wrong responses can cope with the possible 'errors' noted above. Implied by this logic is an asymmetrical distribution of power: metaphorically speaking, social scientists hold the cards and deal them out to respondents in a pre-established pattern. Respondents can only respond. They cannot reshuffle the deck and deal them back to social scientists. This may be the case in opinion polling and perhaps focus group interviews about pre-arranged topics. But it does not accurately capture the intimacy and intrigue involved in close dialogue in the finance industry. Recent research on finance has made it clear that few academics appreciate the scope of intellectual innovation in the higher reaches of financial institutions. This makes academics involved in close dialogue with industry specialists vulnerable to analysts' concealment and obfuscation. It has also become clear that knowledge of the industry is valuable to both sides in close dialogue. Academics moving between respondents are part of a complex web of information flow. Information is the object of research and the medium of exchange for the industry as a whole (see Daniel et al. 1998).

Researchers who rely upon methods such as close dialogue to understand social phenomena feel they have an obligation to just record and report their respondents' views (see Emerson et al. 1995 on ethnographic fieldwork methods). The asymmetry of power suggests an ethical obligation to voice the opinions of those who are ordinarily not important members of institutions of authority. But in the finance industry, where the social status, education, and salary of respondents are at least equal to (and sometimes significantly higher) than academic researchers, power is more equal and contested between the parties to close dialogue. Indeed, the possibility that respondents may deliberately represent issues in a manner beneficial to their or to their institution's interests, and in a manner not easily detected by academic researchers, suggests that we should be wary of invoking any ethical obligation to simply record and report. Once we recognize this possibility, it is apparent why critics of idealized versions of social science like Lewontin are so effective. He asked whether we can trust what we are told. And if we cannot, we should be careful of claiming the truth of our knowledge.

If information is both the object of research and the medium of exchange, why are finance industry informants so willing to engage in close dialogue? There are a variety of likely motivations. For some respondents, being interviewed is an affirmation of status, an external validation of importance which may, or may not, be indicative of their actual standing in the firm or industry. Not surprisingly, some respondents exaggerate the importance of their positions and functions, at one level depending upon the interviewer to confirm their importance and, at another level, demanding respect if they are to help research. It is also true, of course, that the apparent knowledge and experience of the interviewer (advertised prior to the interview as part of the strategy of gaining access) can also be a significant inducement to cooperate. Implied here is a reciprocal relationship: access is made possible by an informal agreement to exchange information, sometimes involving an elaborate and highly choreographed process of sequential revelation, joining both sides of dialogue. This is particularly true of industry informants who are experienced interview subjects. It is also possible that access is offered in the hope that the interviewer will pass on inter-viewees' versions of events and circumstances, the significance of his/her firm, and related 'information' to other respondents.

Interviewees may adopt one or a variety of roles over the course of an interview. To illustrate, five common types of roles were identified in my own research on financial markets. To begin, there is *the conversa-tionalist (and tester)*. Here, the interviewee opens dialogue in an expan-sive manner talking about what he/she knows, the current situation in the industry, and the importance of research for a better appreciation of the nature of finance and investment. There may be other topics. Favourite restaurants may be identified, hotels queried, and personal-ities discussed. In many instances, the interviewee's expansive manner conceals an interest in the interviewer's own knowledge of the indus-try—who they know, and the level of their appreciation of apparent symbols of status and income. In this respect, the conversationalist is also testing the interviewer. The trick in this situation is to simul-taneously indicate an appropriate knowledge and appreciation of the interviewee's circumstances without capitulating to his/her charms.

Having dealt with the conversationalist, the next interview may bring us face to face with *the seller (and buyer)*. Here, dialogue opens with a quick burst of information which you (the interviewer) are seeking. This may be prompted by the interviewer, having been given an early oppor-tunity to set out the nature of the project and the kind of information sought. Or the interviewee may seize upon the material provided by the interviewer prior to the interview to demonstrate the fact that you really need their advice. From there on, information becomes harder and harder to wrinkle out of the interviewee as he/she reverts to the alter-native game of selling information to the interviewer in exchange for more information from the interviewee. Once understood, this exchange relationship may be very fruitful, obviating the need for the exchange of personal information and confidences. But it may also prove to be quite frustrating. The type of information he/she is seeking may not overlap with the information you have. And the more apparent this becomes, the more likely the interview is interrupted and terminated prematurely, ultimately by the interviewee invoking his/her other commitments.

In large part, we tend to assume that the interviewee is representative or illustrative of his/her firm. And yet it is not uncommon to talk with respondents who take the opportunity to criticize the firm and dispute other senior managers' versions of the current circumstances of the firm and the industry. More often than not, the respondent will demand assurances that he/she will not be directly quoted. Such assurances have to be credible. Thus, there is an incentive for the interviewer to exaggerate the confidentiality of interviews, while casting the respondent in an important role of truth-teller: the ultimate check on reality. In these ways, the respondent introduces us to a world of conspiracy, silences, and denials. Both sides of close dialogue collaborate in the fiction that the respondent is the person who really knows what is going on, and going wrong in the firm. This is the world of *the insider (and critic)*. In many respects, the insider welcomes the chance to tell his/her side of the story. And he/she hopes that his/her side of the story will hold sway in the writing-up of the case.

Then there is *the player (and enemy)*: a person who is the ideal respondent given their place in the firm, a person who understands very well what you are looking for, a person who is willing to engage in close dialogue. He/she can provide new information, and can be an important check on the information collected. Their virtue is their place in the industry, the fact that they know key elements of the project and have access to firms and respondents not available to the interviewer. The player is the ultimate wheeler-dealer. This may be demonstrated by the hectic nature of the interview, being coincidentally included in on-going commentaries and conversations with the respondent's employees, friends, and acquaintances. It also may be demonstrated by the urgency of the interview, the need to get the issues out into the open before a real, approaching deadline (the New York market's opening, the Singapore opening, etc.). But appearances are deceptive. He/she may also be the enemy of truth. Just as he/she wheels and deals on the phone, calculating advantage and disadvantage with every move, so too may our conversation be integrated into the player's chess board. The player does not discriminate between us and the rest of the financial world. While it is flattering to imagine that we may be that important to the player, the fact is that he/she treats everyone this way.

And not least of all there is *the interviewer (and confidant)*: the person for whom dialogue has a rather different goal than that commonly acknowledged in the initial stages of discussion with the targets of research. For some, the interviewer is naively presumed to be neutral, almost invisible.[8] But experience shows that one's gender, age, ethnicity, and status may all (together or separately) matter a great deal in establishing contact and encouraging the exchange of confidences (see Pierce 1995). Interviewers may be very skilled, using their identity (identities) to justify common interests or beliefs. Naturally, the skilled interviewer may 'change' as the interviewee changes, at the limit becoming a chameleon in the interests of his/her empirical agenda. It is also possible that genuine rapport develops, and that one interview becomes the opening for further interviews and, at the limit, a long-term relationship. Here, there can be real dilemmas: information provided may, if publicly identified, compromise respondents' professional careers.

There are other kinds of respondents, many of which are friendly and cooperative, concerned to help rather than hinder research. As well, there are others (perhaps fewer) who are hostile or extraordinarily devious.[9] The point in identifying respondent types in close dialogue is simple but profound. Like Lewontin, I do not believe that respondents tell us the truth if truth is defined as neutral, uncommitted observations about the given world. Just as I am interested in close dialogue as a means of world-making, so too are respondents committed to constructing worlds through their dialogue with researchers. This is not only because all people have their own life-projects which require articulation (and concealment) from others. In the finance industry, where information is both the object of analysis and the medium of exchange, respondents are skilled and calculating informants. It does not make sense to deny this fact of life. Nor does it make sense to retreat from close dialogue, given the 'subjectivity' of respondents. Rather, scepticism should be recognized as a most appropriate response to a world which is made and re-made by the interpretations of ourselves and our respondents.

## The Research Programme

Economic geography is a growth industry on both sides of the disciplinary divide. Economists and geographers are increasingly talking about related issues, if not in similar ways or for the same purposes. It may be that, in fact, there are many overlaps and commonalties. It may be that any search for real difference may founder on the remarkable variety of research strategies within both disciplines. In that case, while we may criticize some economic geographers for their stylized abstraction and their presumption in favour of particular analytical methods, I hope this project shows that there are alternative approaches amenable to the finance industry.

Close dialogue is not like conventional social scientific models of research. It denies the most obvious tenet of positivism: the claimed difference between objectivity and subjectivity. It also goes beyond distinctions made between quantitative and qualitative research methods. It cannot be tamed in the same way that qualitative research is thought by some to be complementary with quantitative research (see Morrow and Brown 1994). Being focused upon the derivation of knowledge through, and out of, social relationships, close dialogue is very much related with contemporary feminist research. Close dialogue, like Stanley and Wise's (1993) feminism, begins with the personal, relies upon contested social relationships, and demands a level of reflexivity that is unusual in science.[10] But it is not so unusual compared to the actual practice of decision making inside and outside of financial institutions. As I show in the book, close dialogue is an essential ingredient in the industry; the exchange of information (including individual interpretations of common data) and the management of networks of information (especially those that rely upon reciprocity) are vital social processes that are ignored only at the peril of the institutions concerned. These observations go to the very heart of the financial industry and the patterns identified by Shleifer and his colleagues.

If there are significant and important connections to be made between close dialogue and contemporary feminist methodology, there are also commonalities to be recognized between close dialogue and the so-called behavioural finance literature. According to Thaler (1993), the stylized facts that have dominated economic theorizing and financial economics, in particular, are often unjustified—the empirical evidence does not support rudimentary assumptions made by efficient market theorists about agents' rationality and attitudes to risk and uncertainty. Close dialogue is a means of understanding better the actual practice of decision making. It is a means of reintroducing geography (and history, sociology, etc.) into a world that seems to have been invented for the benefit of theorists. Through close dialogue, our goal must be to reintroduce the texture of local circumstances evaded by theorists more concerned with the simplicity rather than the diversity of economic life.[11]

At the same time, there are reasons to be concerned about the intimacy of close dialogue. It can be indulgent, even isolating given the special knowledge suggested by shared confidences. Worse, close dialogue may promise unique insights into the closed world of industry organization and relationships, but, actually, only ever deliver information tainted by suspect motives. How can we avoid indulgent isolation? In a sense we must be simultaneously committed to the relationships essential to close dialogue, and yet willing to 'betray' our informants by reference to the scepticism of cold-hearted theory. This does not mean that theory-enslaved stylized facts are the ultimate test of close dialogue. Rather, we need an external check on our enthusiasm, a sense of scepticism that works both ways: from theory to close dialogue, and from close dialogue back to theory. In this sense, my philosophical stance has much more in common with Hume's reflective and evaluative scepticism, than perhaps with recent postmodern developments that tend to emphasize the impossibility of knowing (compare with Gibson-Graham 1996 and Righter 1994).[12]

Close dialogue is used in this book as a means of promoting conceptual and theoretical innovation. In recent years, social scientists have used this strategy very effectively becoming more sensitive to both the spatial and temporal components of the turbulent global economy. Given the potential rewards for conceptual innovation, stylized facts and related methods of research may give way to our fascination with spatial differentiation. But we must be always cautious of the integrity of information, whether information is formal or informal. The problem with close dialogue is its lack of cross-referencing with other cases, other instances. While it is a powerful strategy for interrogating the claims of stylized facts, it is hardly adequate as a strategy for coalition building. Whereas stylized facts may be shared by analysts sitting, quite literally, at their PCs any attempt to cross-reference and integrate sets of separate cases from individual researchers becomes a problem of collective action. The pluralism inherent in close dialogue is a threat to building intellectual coalitions which will ultimately affect political action and policy choices. In this respect, my goal is always aimed at codification: the translation of observation into claims about agents' actions and objectives.

## Notes

1. Throughout the book, I refer to the Anglo-American system of pension fund capitalism and finance. While there are some significant differences between countries like the USA, the UK, Canada, and Australia with respect to the

regulation of pension funds, funding, and administrative structures, in the main
I assume that these differences are less important than their overlapping commonalities (see Ch. 3). In a related context, G. P. Miller (1998: 51) noted that
'[w]hen viewed against the backdrop of corporate governance systems worldwide, the similarities between England and the United States are more pro-
nounced than the differences' (compared to Germany and Japan). He noted
also that whatever the apparent differences between the USA and the UK,
these 'are often matters of degree rather than kind'.

2. My approach can also be related to Samuel Hayes' (1993) edited book on the
   various dimensions of the financial service industry as well as Crane et al.'s
   (1995) larger Harvard Business School project on the financial infrastructure of
   Anglo-American economies.

3. By contrast, Kaldor (1985: 8) thought stylized facts could be used to subordin-
   ate 'deduction to induction'. He argued that stylized facts may well be created
   through 'a study of statistics or through special inquiries that include "informal
   conversations with the owners or executives of small business" (and I presume,
   the executives of large businesses as well)'. But his notion of stylized facts has
   been thoroughly displaced and lost. I was reminded of Kaldor's contribution by
   John Agnew and Trevor Barnes.

4. See Martha Nussbaum (1990) on the connection between the form and substance of intellectual reasoning. I have also been encouraged by her recent argument to the effect that we can use all kinds of resources (including literature)
   to liberate our economic imagination. She makes this point with reference to
   the sterile models of famine and deprivation that dominate the economics literature (see Nussbaum 1996). As will become apparent, I also agree with her
   that 'the literary imagination' is no more anti-scientific or anti-economic than
   the closed imagination of many theorists obsessed with the reigning conventions that rely upon stylized facts in economics and geography.

5. My arguments for and against conventional economic theory are shared by
   many critics within and without the discipline. While simplifying may reveal
   basic principles underlying observed economic patterns, too much of economic
   theory assumes away the most compelling problems faced by individuals, firms,
   and other organizations in an uncertain world. In a paper published about 50
   years ago, A. D. Roy (1950) made a similar argument, consistent with Simon's
   (1986) argument of the current day. Therein, Roy noted: 'a valid objection to
   much economic theory that it is set against a background of ease and safety.
   To dispel this artificial sense of security, theory should take account of the often
   close resemblance between economic life and navigation in poorly charted
   waters or manoeuvres in a hostile jungle' (p. 432). Roy goes on to develop the
   notion of risk aversion, as we would term it. In his case, however, he was concerned with the notion of 'safety first' in relation to potential disasters. I return
   to this point in the book, and refer to the risk aversion tendencies of trustees
   (see Ch. 6).

6. Thrift (1996: 101) refers to this kind of knowledge building as 'practical knowledge', an informal type of knowledge 'that is learnt from the experience of
   watching and doing in highly particular context in direct mutual interaction'. It
   is a necessary step towards creating 'empirical knowledge' which 'is not only

cumulative but systematic and co-ordinated over vast tracts of space and (time)'.

7. A point which is made nicely by Schoenberger (1991) in her assessment of the opportunities and dangers of corporate interviews for research in economic geography.

8. Here, I basically disagree with Lamont (1992). In her study of upper-class American and French men, she made considerable efforts to appear anonymous, to be someone with a 'blurred professional identity' (p. 20). She believed that such blurred identity 'was essential to decontextualize the "impression management" [strategies] conducted by the men . . . interviewed' (p. 21). She sought neutrality in inconspicuous dress, a low-key approach to conversation, and an average car. But, equally, she was a Princeton (assistant) professor, a woman professional in her early thirties, someone at home with French conversation and culture, and a person of considerable intellectual ability. Was she really anonymous? Did she really control the conversations as she claimed? I doubt that any senior respondent in the finance industry would be seduced in such a manner.

9. I have not set out to interview anyone I either suspected of treachery or believed responsible for unethical or morally wrong actions. Even so, this does happen. On such occasions one is struck by the nature of the game: the topics discussed and the topics not acknowledged lurking just below the surface. Often it seems that the respondent is intent on demonstrating his/her reasonableness, charity, and consideration as if he/she can convince us of their ordinariness. But equally, one is suspicious looking for signs of cunning and evil subtly. In this regard, Alice Kaplan's (1993: 189–90) account of her interview with a French Nazi sympathizer is germane to the issue.

10. Of course, there are many versions of feminism inside and outside of geography (compare McDowell 1992*b* with Bondi 1997).

11. My concern with the world of market agents and the practice of decision making is one shared by others in the financial literature. For some, of course, this is anathema; building theory is believed to require a commitment to widely shared intellectual templates focused upon standard notions of rationality notwithstanding their questionable relevance for the world of finance. See the paper by Daniel et al. (1998) in a recent issue of the *Journal of Finance* which is somewhat akin to my strategy.

12. An excellent summary of philosophical pragmatism, including the classics and recent commentaries is to be found in Goodman (1995). Sunley (1996) has a useful discussion of the topic related to economic geography.

# 2

# The Retreat of the State

ERIC HOBSBAWM (1994) refers to the twentieth century as a 'short century', dating its onset with the First World War and its conclusion with the 'end of the Soviet era'. He suggests that the early years of this century were dominated by events that owed their origins to nineteenth-century European imperialism, while the last decade of the twentieth century seems to be best understood as the beginning of a new era whose features and logic will only be fully revealed next century. Between 1914 and 1989, wars, revolutions, economic catastrophes, and economic growth engendered extraordinary experiments in social and economic organization, many of which are now thoroughly discredited by virtue of the lives lost forcing through their implementation.

What, if anything, has this to do with pensions, the state, and the private provision of urban infrastructure? The answer to this question is hard to summarize simply and precisely. Recognizing that the chapter is devoted to explicating the argument, I believe that many responsibilities and functions collected together under the banner of the welfare state are either being returned to the private sector, or are being systematically discounted in terms of their real value as governments under-invest or fail to maintain budget-to-budget the original value of those functions and entitlements. To illustrate, a recent report of the UK National Institute of Economic and Social Research (Pain and Young 1996) demonstrated that previous Conservative governments failed to maintain the inherited stock of infrastructure, suggesting a policy of deliberate disinvestment in the basic capital goods of society. In a similar vein, it is also apparent that the value of state social security has declined in many countries. In the UK, this is largely the result of a switch in benchmarking the value of state-provided pensions from wage growth to changes in the cost of living.

It has been suggested that the change of a Conservative to Labour government in the UK, and a possible shift from a Republican-controlled to a Democratic-controlled Congress could reverse these trends. This is unlikely, notwithstanding the stakeholder society espoused by Hutton (1995) and others. For some, it is difficult to believe that the policies and institutions of the past fifty years or so could wither and die. The welfare state was conceived in the darkest moments of the Great Depression, and forged as an institution in the aftermath of the Second World War. At its peak, its many functions and responsibilities literally institutionalized the social relations of Western societies. For many, the state was both *the proper provider* of public infrastructure, and, given the vagaries of the market, the only institution *capable of providing* a comprehensive system of public goods. But events of the past two decades across the Western world have shown that neither the normative nor the positive claim justifying the state provision of infrastructure are now compelling. Recent moves to radically reform (UK) and even dismantle (US) welfare programmes suggest, in fact, that the post-war consensus that legitimized state intervention in market capitalism is in tatters. The state is in retreat on many fronts, from providing the most obvious forms of infrastructure like bridges, roads, etc., through to the less obvious forms of urban development, including employment, housing, etc.

Set against these trends is another, equally compelling trend. Since the early 1980s, Anglo-American private pension assets have 'attained stupendous size and importance' (Langbein 1997: 168), eclipsing all other forms of private savings, and transforming the nature and structure of global financial markets.[1] This phenomenon is not found, however, in most continental European countries; there government-funded social security systems remain the central pillar of retirement planning, albeit threatened by bankruptcy (discussed in Chapter 3). In the Anglo-American economies the growth of private pension assets reflects, in part, the rapid post-1950 expansion of employment and increased participation in employer or multi-party-sponsored private pension plans. The fact that private plans must be fully funded, the fact that pension benefits have come to be an important component in many employees' wages, and the fact that those of the baby boom generation have moved into their peak earning years means that the net flow of assets to pension funds has become a tidal wave.

What are the prospects for urban infrastructure and development funding given, on one hand, the retreat of the state and, on the other hand, the rise of pension fund capitalism? The chapter documents and accounts for the retreat of the state, the phenomenal growth in pension assets, and the prospects for pension fund investment in urban development. In essence, I suggest that the retreat of the state has been accompanied by a variety of displacement strategies shifting responsibility for many inherited nation-state functions to market agents and other tiers (higher and lower) of governmental authority. In the case of urban infrastructure and development, in part, the state has displaced responsibility for its financing and provision to the financial sector (its institutions and decision making systems). In this respect, two issues are emphasized in the later sections of the chapter: (1) pension fund trustee investment decision making, and (2) increased social and geographical polarization and the likelihood of greater accountability applied to public and private pension funds. Note that the chapter makes wide-ranging connections between countries, abstracting from particular institutions and economic trends.

## State Income and Expenditures

To set the scene, Figure 2.1 summarizes patterns of state receipts and liabilities for the four principal Anglo-American countries (the UK and Australia, the USA and Canada), and Germany and Sweden over the period 1980–1996. I have argued elsewhere that Anglo-American countries are closely related in terms of their financial markets and the inherited common law tradition which is the basis of their regulatory institutions (Chapter 3; see also La Porta et al. 1997). The other two European countries are included for the purpose of contrast. Over the past couple of decades, it appears that the Anglo-American states have had very similar flows of receipts as a proportion of gross domestic product. In this respect, these countries are different from Germany and significantly different from Sweden. However, with respect to the USA, it is apparent that the state's share of receipts has slightly increased for Australia, decreased for the UK, and significantly increased for Canada. A second observation is that state indebtedness, having stabilized and even declined during the 1980s, surged in the early 1990s as a consequence of the global recession.

Perhaps not surprisingly, three of the four Anglo-American states' shares of national income are either constant or declining. The exception is Canada, which increasingly appears more like Sweden in terms of its expenditure profile than the other Anglo-American countries. Indeed, its recent poor economic performance is more akin to the continental European countries than its Anglo-American cousins. See Drache and Gertler (1991) on the recent performance of the Canadian economy and the threats to domestic policy occasioned by the emergence of meta-regional trading blocs. In all cases, as the flow of state revenue closely tracks national economic performance, economic downturns tend to add significantly to states' indebtedness, as state

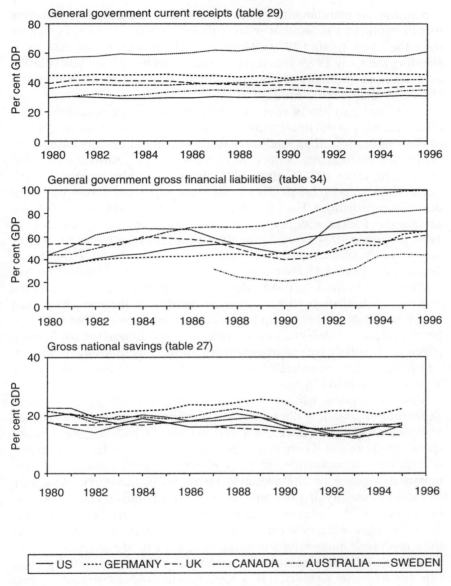

FIG. 2.1. Fiscal constraints and national saving (1980–1996)
*Source*: OECD 1997.

expenditure is maintained or even increased. Comparing state receipts to expenditures, the latter is more volatile than the former, especially over the early to mid-1980s. More recently, however, and not withstanding the early 1990s recession, expenditures have been less volatile, as states have gradually cut into the rate of growth of their revenue and especially their expenditures.

The macro patterns of revenue and expenditure are revealing. Even more revealing is the decreasing discretion of nation-states with respect to their allocation of expenditures to competing budgetary categories. Figure 2.2 summarizes budget outlays for the UK, Australia, and the USA, comparing 1980 against 1994. Where possible, categories have been merged and relabelled to facilitate comparison across time and between jurisdictions. For the UK, three trends are apparent. First, the categories of social security, health, and education, while important in 1980, dominate 1994 expenditure allocations. Entitlement expenditures are similarly of increasing importance for Australia and the USA. Second, defence and 'other functions' have taken the brunt of budget reallocations in the UK, just as defence has been squeezed in Australia and the USA. If there was a peace dividend from the end of the cold war, it has been swallowed up by burgeoning entitlement expenditures. Nevertheless, US defence expenditures are still important when compared to the other two countries. Third, in the UK, housing, transport, and public safety practically consume what is left of the public purse. This is also the case in Australia.

Much has been written about the rapid growth in entitlement expenditures, and how their growth in the context of limits on revenue and total expenditure have conspired to radically reduce governments' spending discretion. There is no need here to belabour the point. But it is important to acknowledge an implication which follows from the apparent squeeze on the available resources in the Anglo-American world. The capacity of governments to switch significant resources from current committed expenditures to new needs is small, and often only symbolic. Inevitably, government departments and the public services they represent must campaign year-to-year to hold their past budget allocations, let alone maintain the real value of those allocations. Their capacity to garner significant new resources to fund investment in areas of need like transport, employment, housing, and urban infrastructure is caught in a cruel vice affecting all government expenditures. In the UK, at least this has resulted in a long-term decline in infrastructure investment, and has greatly contributed to the wholesale privatization of many government enterprises and services. Furthermore, there is no evidence that the underlying financial constraints will change in the near

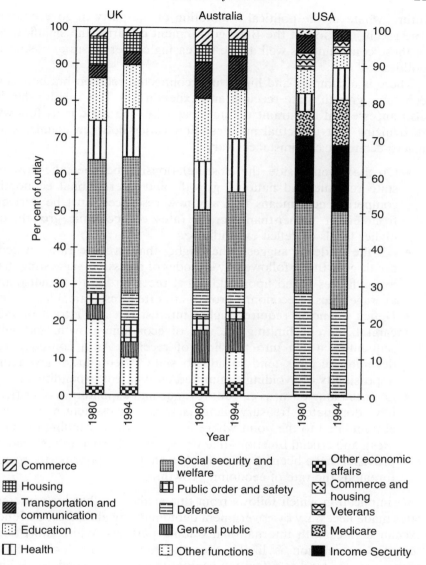

FIG. 2.2. Where it goes: changes in budget outlays

*Source*: OECD for UK and Australia, US Budget for USA

future, whatever the political orientation of the party in government. The recent election of the Blair government confirms the significance of these constraints as well as the increasing conservatism of electoral politics.

There is a complex and highly interconnected relationship between economic growth, state receipts, and expenditures. This relationship is also an essential constraint on state capacity. The logic is as follows, recognizing that its actual manifestation varies between countries as macro-economic circumstances vary.

- On the revenue side, the close relationship between the flow of state revenue and national growth, and international economic competitiveness means that any new resources must be derived from either higher-than-average rates of economic growth, or higher levels of deficit expenditure.
- All the evidence suggests that higher-than-average rates of economic growth are followed by episodes of recession, suggesting that expenditures based upon additional receipts due to higher-than-average rates of economic growth are often unsustainable.
- Deficit financing requires higher interest rates to attract private capital, thereby limiting the rate of economic growth, and subsequently cutting into the flow of receipts. As a consequence, declining receipts tend to add to state indebtedness, given the impossibility of avoiding committed entitlement expenditures.
- Over the long term, as current revenue and expenditure objectives have dominated Treasury planning, unmet investment needs have accumulated to the point where whole sectors (including the utilities), and crucial functions like transport and urban infrastructure provision have been so impoverished that their poor performance threatens the rate of economic growth.

One implication which follows from this analysis is that high interest rates made necessary by government debt financing also affect currency exchange rates with international trading partners. While short-term currency speculation is likely, over the longer term, high relative exchange rates tend to affect the competitiveness of traded goods and services, setting in motion the possibility of a slowdown in the rate of domestic economic growth. Thus, in this context, massive urban infrastructure investment projects like rebuilding and re-equipping the London Underground can be seen as too expensive for any government to finance over the long term. The alternatives are disinvestment, user charges, privatization, or some form of private investment and public partnership: the Keynesian state we inherited from the Second World War is increasingly the 'pauper state' (Froud et al. 1997).[2]

## The Cold-Hearted Voter Problem

A simple-minded argument would be that the state is in retreat because of declining resources in relation to contemporary needs. But this seems to imply that state resources have actually declined, where, in fact, state receipts have expanded step-by-step with economic growth. In some instances, states have gone beyond available resources, expanding expenditures to either sustain inherited functions and/or gain short-term political advantage. But increased indebtedness has been one consequence. Another consequence has been global financial markets' speculation regarding government budget policies, interest, and currency exchange rates. As I suggested above, there are longer-term economic limits to state indebtedness. In this respect, the hard political lesson of the 1970s and 1980s has been that '[e]xcept for the briefest of periods, in conditions of dire crisis or brief and dramatic opportunity, the fulcrum of political realism for any modern society is always an understanding of the conditions for its economic flourishing' (Dunn 1990: 7).

The retreat of the state is a product of three interlocking forces. Notwithstanding the growth of state income, politically inspired attempts at expanding state expenditures beyond that justified by the rate of growth often sets in motion macro-economic forces which ultimately threaten the stability of national economic performance. Significant changes in budget priorities, including new budget expenditures on urban infrastructure, must be found more often than not in the reallocation of current and expected resources. This uncomfortable fact has been exacerbated by the rapid increase (compared to the rate of economic growth) in resources allocated to entitlement programmes. Many states have been unable to limit the rate of increase in social security and health expenditures which are driven, in part, by the ageing of their populations. Furthermore, the priority assigned in many countries to recurrent programme-related expenditures as opposed to long-term investments has led to significant shortfalls in infrastructure provision and even disinvestment in the basic infrastructure of Anglo-American economies. The retreat of the state is a combination of reduced fiscal discretion and narrowed functional scope.[3]

Reduced fiscal discretion and functional scope are also profoundly related to the current practice of democratic politics. For many voters accustomed to a paternal and relatively resource-rich state, reduced fiscal capacity has translated into declining standards of public services, increased loads on the available services, and even the abandonment of public service provision in favour of market provision and individual responsibility. At every turn, when service deterioration has been seen to be driven by disinvestment, it seems that the only available option has been privatization. In the UK, this is evident in the energy sector, the water sector, railroads, airports, and many other related infrastructure dependent public services (see Martin 1999*a*). In some cases where privatization has proved impossible, secondary markets have been created to allow those with more income to bypass the existing state-based rationing system to directly purchase services. While this is clearly a policy that leads to gross inequalities in terms of the timing and quality of overall service provision, for previous Conservative governments it was a step towards greater competition within the state sector and the possibility of declining or, at least, constant per-unit service costs. The experience of the UK National Health Service over the last ten years exemplifies this argument.

Twenty years ago, analysts debated the causes of the fiscal crisis of the state (see O'Connor 1973). Invoked were various left of centre and right of centre explanations of the overburdened state. Some analysts on the left focused upon the necessary, increasing functions of the state in relation to the crisis-ridden nature of capitalist economies. This argument was justified, more often than not, by reference to the Great Depression and the immediate post-World War II era of economic reconstruction. Those on the right tended to focus upon rent-seeking behaviour, arguing that there was a close, even exploitative (in relation to the taxes paid by voters) relationship between state apparatuses and their 'clients' in the private sector.[4] The increasing scope of state functions, coupled with the close relationship between the state and private sectors by virtue of the increasing significance of state expenditures, encouraged theorists to suppose there was a near equivalence or balance between the state and markets. When linked with widespread use of long-term planning and management in the state and private sectors, Shonfield (1965) heralded the advent of a new era of 'corporatism'.

If corporatism represented the Anglo-American world of the 1960s, Reagan and Thatcher attacked and destroyed its legitimacy. In Clark and Dear (1984: ch. 3), I suggested a different logic, working from Type I consensus-oriented functions through Type II economic reproduction functions and Type III social integration functions, and finally Type IV executive functions. I supposed that each type of function had its own clients and institutional forms by virtue of the resources and powers associated with those functions—an argument not dissimilar from those who have focused upon rent-seeking behaviour. While not specifying a hierarchy of functions, I emphasized those related to consensus building, arguing that the nature and status of democratic politics plays a crucial symbolic role in legitimizing the unequal distribution of resources. I assumed that functions related to economic reproduction were essential for the maintenance of state power, and argued that social integration functions came after satisfying consent and economic reproduction. Reassessing this logic in the light of recent history, it seems me that the state remains preoccupied with consensus and the conditions of economic reproduction. The most vulnerable functions, however, have been those related to social integration.

Dispute about the legitimacy of the state presupposed an alternative, even if idealized with respect to the communist world of the time. It is now apparent that the end of the cold war has both legitimized the capitalist state in relation to any alternative, and discounted the claims of many poorer voters for state resources. Consensus can be sustained without a wide range of social integration functions. While many state functions were inherited by current governments from the post-war welfare state, rationalizing and discounting the value of those functions dominates democratic politics. The historical legacy of the Great Depression and the immediate post-World War II era has been forgotten by the ascendancy of a new generation of middle-class voters with little knowledge of those circumstances. In fact, many of those living in the major centres of the Anglo-American countries believe that the state as an economic agent has become a long-term burden on the international competitiveness of the private sector.[5] Even though privatization has been often prompted by unmet capital needs, governments of all political persuasions suppose that privatization is necessary to improve the performance of the private sector itself. Thus, states' economic functions have been redefined, in part, in relation to the imperatives of the emerging global economy (compare with Boyer and Drache 1997).[6]

There are, of course, some who argue for increased nation-state taxes to sustain the inherited range of state functions, or at least those functions that are able to garner the support of a broad spectrum of voters. And yet, notwithstanding the force of their argument (see Hutton 1995 in the UK, and Kuttner 1997 in the USA), they have had little success in counteracting the movement towards the narrowing of states' functional scope. At the most general level, arguments for general tax increases in order to support the inherited scope of state functions have been discounted by counter-arguments regarding the probable negative effects of tax increases on long-term economic growth. At the same time, polling data suggests that many voters do not trust governments to use new revenue in ways that would enhance the standards of existing public services. And given chronic shortfalls in operating revenue in state sectors such as health and education, it is apparent that any new revenue derived from a general tax increase would simply be absorbed into current expenditure. Furthermore, in an era of low inflation and low rates of individual income growth, many middle-class voters look upon taxes as a burden on their real income. There is a political presumption against general tax increases, recognized as such across the political spectrum (see Glyn 1996).[7]

It is also obvious that middle-class voters tend not to support state expenditures except in areas that directly affect their well-being. In part, middle-class voters increasingly perceive themselves to be 'consumers' of public goods and expect a level of service consistent with the quality of service available in the market for related, even competing goods. But also, in part, middle-class voters are increasingly hostile to cross-subsidies or transfers of state revenue to other groups of public service consumers. In this respect, the functional coherence of the welfare state is profoundly under attack from the fragmentation of the electorate into rival groups of 'public goods' consumers, all of which seek to maximize their share of existing resources, while discounting the claims of those perceived to be net costs to the state. Accentuating this trend has been the emergence of the identity politics of multiculturalism and post-modernism, as opposed to the politics of class (the origins of the welfare state). See Sennett (1998) on the dilemmas posed by contemporary capitalism for social and community mobilization, and compare his argument with Peterson (1997), who believes that identity politics are a necessary step towards emancipation from the state.

In this new world of the cold-hearted and isolated voter, the functional scope of the state is dependent upon spontaneous issue-based coalitions rather than collective solidarity sustained by long-term class alliances. Political fragmentation threatens the coherence of state functions, replacing the substance of social cohesion with the symbolism of consensual agreement. In this new world of post-cold-war politics, the nation-state has actively sought ways to displace inherited responsibilities to the market, or to higher or lower tiers of governmental organization. If state legitimacy is threatened by these displacement strategies, such threats are, more often than not, fractured by deep divisions in civil society about the proper conception (let alone design) of state responsibilities and institutions. State legitimacy is secure.[8]

## Rise of Pension Fund Capitalism

Writing in 1965, Shonfield argued that 'modern capitalism' was dominated by large economic organizations, some public and others private. He described a world in which collaboration was common between the public and private sectors, and dispute resolution was managed between nominally equal partners (including unions). In comparison with the economic world prior to and immediately after the Second World War, modern capitalism was, as a consequence, believed to be more stable and predictable. Economic volatility had been tamed by state macro-economic policy making, and the increased significance of planning and management in all large enterprises. By his account, the modern state could claim equal standing with industry by virtue of its control of banking and finance (in some cases), or 'the existence of a wide sector of publicly controlled enterprise' (p. 66) in other cases. And he argued that the state was a major economic agent because 'government's expenditure has been enormously enlarged,' therefore directly affecting 'a large segment of each nation's economic activities' (p. 66).

Thirty years later, and notwithstanding political rhetoric to the contrary, the modern state is a much smaller fraction of Anglo-American economies. In part, this is because of the economic and political limits imposed upon state revenue and expenditures. In some cases, like the UK, the smaller role of the state reflects the significance and scope of privatization since the mid-1980s. At the same time, the economic structures of all the Anglo-American economies have been more or less altered by the relative decline of employment in national industrial and manufacturing sectors, set against the rise of firms in international information-intensive industries. For some, this is the new world of post-Fordism; a common, global movement towards flexible production and accumulation.[9] For others, including Webber and Rigby (1996), the transformation of Anglo-American economies over the past thirty years reflects the inevitable capitalist dynamics of capital accumulation and uneven development. Here, however, I wish to emphasize a distinctive aspect of the transformation of Anglo-American economies over the

TABLE 2.1. *Personal sector gross financial assets for the United Kingdom, 1980, 1990, and 1996 (31 December) (in current £ billion)*

| Financial asset | 1980 | 1990 | 1996 |
|---|---|---|---|
| Bank deposits | 37.4 | 157.3 | 219.6 |
| Building society deposits[a] | 57.6 | 160.0 | 210.0 |
| Government securities and debt | 13.8 | 10.4 | 12.3 |
| Miscellaneous instruments | 4.4 | 15.3 | 24.0 |
| National savings | 12.1 | 35.6 | 61.3 |
| Notes and coins | 8.3 | 13.6 | 18.9 |
| Overseas investments[b] | 4.5 | 12.0 | 15.9 |
| Pension/life assurance | 106.6 | 528.0 | 1,080.3 |
| Trade credits (DOM) | 14.8 | 42.0 | 51.8 |
| Unit trusts | 3.0 | 18.2 | 60.0 |
| UK securities | 38.4 | 171.1 | 336.4 |
| Accruals adjustments | 5.0 | 24.4 | 36.0 |

[a] Includes deposits with other financial institutions.
[b] Includes direct investments and securities.

*Source*: *United Kingdom National Accounts—The Blue Book* (London: HMSO, 1997), table 12.2 (p. 138).

past twenty years often only accorded the briefest of mention: the rise of pension fund capitalism and the world of finance with which it is intimately associated (detailed in Chapters 3 and 4).

To illustrate, Table 2.1 summarizes UK personal financial assets in nominal terms for 1980, 1990, and 1996.[10] Absolute values are less important than the relative changes between categories over the entire period. In this respect, three retirement and investment categories stand out in terms of their relative growth rates: pension/life assurance assets (tenfold increase), unit trust assets (200-fold increase), and UK securities (tenfold increase). By contrast, bank deposits (sevenfold increase), building society deposits (fourfold increase), and national savings (fivefold increase) registered significantly lower rates of increase. These patterns are also apparent in the USA for household assets (Table 2.2). Through to the end of 1994, US retail deposits increased less than threefold, bonds of various kinds fivefold, corporate securities about threefold, pension/life assurance assets more than sixfold, and mutual fund assets by an amazing 300-fold. Mutual funds are important tax-preferred option for individual retirement savings, in some cases replacing existing employer-sponsored pension schemes (the 401(k) option).[11] Similar trends can be identified for Canada and Australia; the former is more like the USA, and the latter is more like the UK, in terms of the distribution of assets between savings categories.

TABLE 2.2. *US households' financial assets 1980, 1990, and 1996 (31 December) (in current $ billion)*

| Financial asset | 1980 | 1990 | 1996 |
|---|---|---|---|
| Deposits | 1,490 | 3,239 | 3,531 |
| Credit market instruments (including bonds) | 423 | 1,494 | 1,961 |
| US government securities and bonds | 491 | 1,418 | 2,358 |
| Municipal securities | 104 | 574 | 432 |
| Corporate and foreign bonds | 31 | 195 | 390 |
| Mortgages | 84 | 147 | 217 |
| Open-market paper | 38 | 63 | 47 |
| Mutual fund shares | 46 | 467 | 1,491 |
| Corporate and non-corporate equities | 2,806 | 4,382 | 7,514 |
| Life insurance/pension fund reserves | 1,176 | 3,788 | 7,003 |
| Personal trusts | 265 | 522 | 834 |
| Security credit | 16 | 62 | 158 |
| Miscellaneous assets | 74 | 224 | 376 |

*Source*: *Statistical Abstract of the United States* (Washington, DC: US Department of Commerce, 1997), table 777. Derived from Board of Governors Reserve System, *Flow of Funds Accounts*, March 1997 diskettes.

In the Anglo-American world, bank deposits and related financial institutions are of declining significance, relative to market transactions and related financial institutions. This trend has been widely noted, and is considered a major difference between the Anglo-American financial systems and the banking-based financial systems of continental Europe (see Allen and Gale 1994b and Boot and Thakor 1997). The available evidence on European pension fund assets as a proportion of gross domestic product (GDP) suggests that most continental European countries have small to negligible assets. French, German, and Italian pension fund assets are each only about 5 per cent of GDP, compared to 93 per cent for the UK. Notice that pension fund assets are 89 per cent for the Netherlands, 87 per cent for Switzerland, and 57 per cent for the USA.[12] In this respect, three observations can be made about the distinctiveness of Anglo-American pension fund capitalism. First, the three largest continental European economies have very modest pension assets. Second, governments' restrictions on investment options used by existing continental European pension funds have constrained the rate of growth of these funds over the past twenty years (especially important in Switzerland). In combination, the size and scope of many European equity markets are much smaller than that predicted by the size of their economies. Not surprisingly, the nature and rate of financial innovation is also significantly less than the Anglo-American economies (La Porta et al. 1997).

Two other observations should be made about national variations in retirement financing and likely long-term liabilities. Data from the OECD (1997) on national savings show that the advanced economies, except Germany, experienced marked declines in savings rates over the period 1980–96 (see again Figure 2.1). For example, Australia's savings rate declined from 21.6 per cent in 1980 to 16.8 per cent in 1995. Over the same period, UK and US savings rates declined from approximately 17 per cent to 14 per cent, and 20 per cent to 16 per cent, respectively. Even in the case of Germany, the 1995 savings rate was slightly less than the 1980 savings rate (22 per cent) despite significant increases during the 1980s (peaking at 32 per cent in 1986). The OECD also estimates that by 2010 the elderly dependency ratio will be 18.6 per cent for Australia (compared to 16.0 in 1990), 20.4 for the USA and Canada (respectively 19.1 and 16.7 in 1990), 25.8 for the UK (24.0 in 1990), 29.1 for Sweden (27.6 in 1990), and 30.3 for Germany (21.7 in 1990) (see Leibfritz et al. 1995). By the year 2020, the dependency ratios of Germany and Sweden will be about 35.0, compared to an expected European OECD average of 30.8.

The early 1980s recession and subsequent slow growth rates, and then the early 1990s recession, which continues in one form or another in continental Europe if not in the Anglo-American countries, have, in combination, limited the capacity of many nation states to accumulate public savings. In this respect, the recent growth of pension assets in the Anglo-American economies may have profound positive consequences for their future economic performance relative to much of continental Europe. Not surprisingly, these trends have prompted significant debate inside and outside of the academic world about the long-term funding of state social security programmes, and the status and significance of pension schemes now and in the future.[13] In response, many countries are contemplating the introduction of mandatory pension systems based upon employer and employee contributions to sponsored pension funds. Such systems have been introduced in Australia and Chile, and are the object of discussion in Western and Eastern Europe including Germany (see P. Diamond 1994 on recent developments).[14]

## Urban Infrastructure and Economic Development

If the state is in retreat with respect to urban infrastructure and development, and if financial institutions and markets are now the dominant sources of capital, how are those resources to be mobilized? And what is implied by the private financing of public infrastructure? These are significant, and far-reaching questions not easily answered in the space of just a few paragraphs.[15] These questions are, in part, the object of academic scholarship as well as being of practical concern to pension fund trustees and their investment advisers. Here I identify the dominant logic underpinning the pension fund investment process. This is the basis for a brief overview of recent moves towards pension fund investment in urban infrastructure and development. The first part of the story is common to many Anglo-American countries. The second part necessarily draws upon recent US experience.

To set the issue in context, consider Figure 2.3. There, annualized rates of return are reported for commonly traded market investment products over the period 1947–1996, set against their measured risk or volatility as indicated by standard deviations. The data is for the USA, but is indicative of other Anglo-American countries' experience, including the UK, Australia, and Canada. Embedded in this figure are a series of theoretical propositions that currently underpin pension fund investment strategies.[16] Based upon the pioneering work of Markowitz (1952) and Sharpe (1964) on modern portfolio theory, analysts and practitioners expect that rates of return are commensurate with their risks. The higher the risk, the higher the expected return. As indicated by Figure

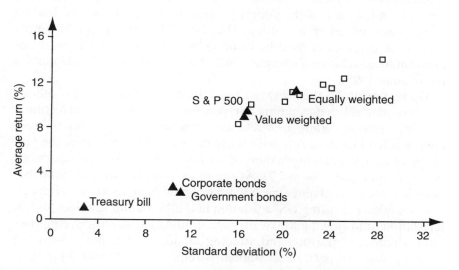

FIG. 2.3. Mean vs. standard deviation of real returns, 1947–1996

*Source*: Cochrane 1997, p. 5. Triangles are equally weighted and value weighted NYSE; S & P 500; three-month Treasury bill; ten-year government bond; and corporate bond returns. Unmarked squares are NYSE size portfolios.

2.3, this relationship can be 'mapped' over a set of asset classes: from Treasury bills (practically risk-free investments) through to small stock portfolios (high-risk investments). Notice also that the larger the stock portfolio, the more likely it reflects the performance of the whole market. In this sense, diversification is a valued strategy because it spreads the risk of poor performance of selected stocks over the performance of all stocks.

Many theorists assume the market is efficient in the sense that investments are properly priced in accordance with all the available information. There are two implications which follow from this assumption. One is that it is impossible to systematically beat the market. While some investment managers may by happenstance or by virtue of 'local' information perform better than average, this kind of performance is very difficult (even impossible) to sustain over the long run. The other implication is just as drastic. Active investment strategies are, more often than not, less rewarded than passive investment strategies. Indeed, it is apparent that once the costs of investment management are factored into the analysis of net returns, the majority of managers do not perform as well as the standard benchmarks like the S&P 500 or the FT-SE 100. This does not mean that all investors are equally rational. Nor does it mean that all investors are equally informed. It is also apparent that some investors, especially those with significant institutional resources, may take advantage of the poorer judgement, information, and trading competence of other investors (Shleifer 1998). The point is simply that active investment must be justified by reference to benchmarks of performance, relative expertise, and the availability of information (Grossman 1995).

Modern portfolio theory (MPT) and the efficient markets hypothesis are essential reference points for pension fund trustees' investment decision making. While it would be surprising to find that trustees always acted in accordance with these theoretical propositions, the language of decision making is thoroughly impregnated with related terms and concepts (see Chapter 7). At the same time, the flow of contributions and the current and expected flow of paid benefits are also important variables. Following US legislation in the 1970s and revisions to UK legislation following the Maxwell scandal, all Anglo-American countries have rigorous reporting and funding standards for most forms of pension plans. In part, these standards require the current funding of expected liabilities and the diversification of investment strategies. With respect to Figure 2.3, this means that trustees first allocate assets amongst asset classes like equities, bonds, and cash equivalents, and then choose amongst competing investment managers in accordance with their past performance and expertise. While it seems that stock portfolios are more desirable than other types of investments, bonds (for example) do offer trustees greater certainty with respect to the rate of return. Even cash equivalents may be desired by trustees concerned to meet short-term liabilities. These are especially important considerations for plan sponsors that offer defined benefit plans.

Now let us return to the issue of urban infrastructure and economic development. And in order to give the analysis specificity, let us assume that two kinds of investments are contemplated: one in infrastructure (for instance, a link-road or hospital emergency unit) and one in development (for instance, a start-up firm with close links to a particular community). Where in the past the state may have contemplated both kinds of 'investments' as part of its urban and regional strategy, fiscal and functional constraints make both impossible. Let us also assume that the first is offered as a bond promising a twenty-year rate of return net of inflation, whereas the second is offered as a share of ownership (equity) with no contractually agreed rate of return, but a proportionate share in any profit with the option to sell-out after five years to other partners. For the sake of argument, let us also assume that pension fund trustees and their investment advisers seek opportunities to diversify their portfolios with no special conditions imposed by the state.[17]

So one issue facing trustees is how best to assess the value of the investment options. With respect to the infrastructure option, the obvious benchmark is the risk-and-return profiles of other competing bonds. But how should we assess the particular risk of this kind of investment? This issue is explored in depth throughout Chapters 6, 8, and 9. Lacking a well-established market in urban infrastructure bonds, and lacking experience in the performance of such investments, trustees may draw an analogy with existing cases and assign a relevant risk somewhat higher than traded bonds, or retreat from the option altogether. If the risk is higher, then the contractually agreed rate of return would have to reflect that risk. With respect to the development option, the obvious reference point would be a small portfolio of venture capital investments (the upper right-hand corner of Figure 2.3). But, again, the fact that the investment would be a private placement with no option for short-term trade means that the pension fund would be locked into the project. Therefore, a higher risk would be attached to the investment, implying a higher expected rate of return.

Notice, though, that the annualized rate of return on a small portfolio of traded equities hides considerable temporal specificity. Apparent high rates of return identified in Figure 2.3 for US equities (of all kinds) are the product of the accelerating run-up in all Anglo-American markets over the past seven, five, and three years leading up to mid-

1997. Since rates of return are almost impossible to predict over the short term, and because downturns are likely after bull markets, to make an investment decision with respect to the immediate past performance of equities (on the upside) or bonds (on the downside) runs the risk of rejecting investment options that at another time would seem entirely compatible with the broad range of expected risks and returns. It is also clear that the accelerating markets of the 1990s attracted assets from other investment classes, notably bonds, as well as more specialized investment options because of a perceived lack of short-term risk and a perceived opportunity cost of not being 'in the market'. The implication is stark: the infrastructure bond may find few takers because of a more general shift towards equities, and the development equity may find few takers because of the significance assigned to immediately past high rates of return on traded securities.[18] Herd behaviour is very common in financial markets, and in investment decision making in general (see Zeckhauser et al. 1991).

Other trustees may pursue contrarian investment strategies relying upon expertise and special knowledge to discriminate between 'good' and 'bad' urban investments. Expertise is expensive. Therefore the investment management industry is highly differentiated with, at one end of the spectrum, large international and multifunctional investment firms controlling vast amounts of traded assets, and at the other end of the spectrum, small highly specialized firms offering product-specific and project-specific expertise based upon their access to non-traded information. At one end of the spectrum, dis-intermediation is the order of the day, whereas at the other end of the spectrum, especially designed intermediaries are crucial for mobilizing assets and transferring them to investments that fall outside of the accepted conventions of the industry. For large firms specializing in market-related investment products, efficiency is a product of the design and management of markets and the capacity of firms to identify and take advantage of short-term asymmetries. For small firms specializing in custom-designed intermediation, management efficiency is a product of scale economies with respect to transaction costs and reporting mechanisms that allow investors to verify the veracity of their partners. Not surprisingly, both kinds of firms have to be close to the markets for finance expertise. The industry is remarkably spatially and functionally centralized (see Clark 1997*b* and Martin and Minns 1995).

An aspect of financial intermediation, in relation to urban infrastructure and economic development, concerns the role played by public sector pension funds. The available evidence from Greenwich Associates (1996*a,b*) suggests that only the largest private defined benefit plans in the USA have a significant interest in so-called alternative investment products such as infrastructure and venture capital. As is the case in so many other issues including proxy voting and corporate governance, private pension plans tend to rely upon their investment managers, rather than take an interest in the active assignment of pension fund power. In the USA, at least, perhaps one reason for this particular difference is public funds' reliance upon local economic performance for the continuing flow of participants and the flow of pension fund contributions. It also seems that defined contribution plans are preoccupied with the short-run returns. Therefore, we should accept that some types of pension funds are more likely to invest in urban infrastructure and development, and that the increasing preference of private employers for defined contribution plans and the like may mean that urban investment is largely a public sector pension plan phenomenon.

However, there has been considerable criticism of public pension funds investment in the urban realm. In part, it has been observed that many pension funds have neither the internal expertise nor the resources to hire the external expertise necessary to discriminate between competing development options. While it seems that the demand for alternative investments is rapidly expanding amongst many of the largest pension funds, the supply of viable projects remains limited because of the high level of transaction costs involved. See the recent report of Goldman Sachs and Frank Russell surveying the rapid growth in private equity deals, compared to the situation a couple of years ago (cited as Goldman Sachs 1995, 1997). Other critics contend that the often close relationships between pension fund trustees and the providers of non-traded urban investment options leaves trustees open to charges of recklessness and even corruption when deals go wrong. Because of the public significance of many large urban infrastructure and development projects, and because of the inevitable long-term commitments implied by such deals, the motives and actions of pension funds are often open to public scrutiny. The prospect of scrutiny has made trustees even more risk-averse, reinforcing the perceived high risk nature of such investments.

One result of scrutiny has been a shift away from long-term investment relationships to project-by-project assessments ruled by the law of contract. Another result of scrutiny has been the development of third party urban investment trusts where pension funds remain distant from the actual development and management of particular investments. In this model, pension funds can be thought of as partners in investment clubs (Chapter 8). To my mind, at least, these criticisms of pension funds and their investment in urban development projects are entirely

warranted. But it would be misleading to suppose that these criticisms
are only applicable to investment in urban infrastructure and development projects. While no doubt often attached to particular projects and
pension funds, these criticisms are indicative of the extensive nature of
agency relationships in the pension fund investment industry and the
decentralized nature of government regulation of the relationships
between trustees and plan beneficiaries. It is very rare for plan participants to have a voice in trustee investment decision making. And Anglo-
American governments have relied upon the trustee institution to
regulate the interests of beneficiaries. The principal–agent problem
(Pratt and Zeckhauser 1985) is deeply embedded in the whole system
of Anglo-American pension fund management.

In general, urban infrastructure and development are a very small
fraction of even the largest funds. Nevertheless, those funds with either
a close attachment to an industry or a place have become more interested in community investment. As noted above, some large US public
sector funds do participate in a range of development options including
venture capital. There is a significant number of specialized investment
consultants that design and broker these investments for public sector
funds. In the USA, at least federal pensions legislation does not apply
to states' government-sponsored pension funds, allowing for, some
might contend, a wider range of investment options (as well as the
possibility of under-funding!). Industry-based jointly trusteed pension
funds that are concentrated in certain segments, sectors, or regions are
also increasingly interested in what are termed 'economically targeted
investments', or ETIs. While regulated by federal law and related expectations regarding the ultimate value to beneficiaries, these investments
have flourished even if their relative significance remains minor and disputed (see the recent report of Levine, (1997) on the experience of
Wisconsin).

## Implications for the Project

It is clear that Thatcher and Reagan and their notional ideological allies
around the Western world have made a lasting difference to the structure and size of Anglo-American governments, relative to their national
gross domestic product. But my argument goes beyond ideological war-
riors: the post-cold-war era will be a 'cold-hearted era' in which the functional scope of government spending is squeezed by a combination of
political limits imposed by the middle classes on state income, reduced

discretion in the spending of the available state income, and economic limits imposed by financial markets on state deficit spending. In other words, forces already at work in the 1980s have combined in the last decade of the twentieth century to de-legitimize the welfare state. Implicated in this story is the baby boom generation whose fealty to the axioms underlying the welfare state has been undercut by the collapse of the enemy without and by threats to the stability and predictability of national economic performance.

The rise of pension fund capitalism as a set of Anglo-American market-based financial institutions is also an important reference point in understanding the full extent of the retreat of the state. While previous sections emphasized limits on the state's functional capacity, the rise of pension fund capitalism has undermined the nation-state's status as a significant economic agent. Compared to the 1960s, when Shonfield could reasonably argue that the state and markets were balanced in terms of their respective sizes and financial resources, new market institutions now dominate the state in terms of their command over global finance. Thus, any understanding of the likely topography of urban infrastructure and development over the coming decades must begin with the financial industry in general, and with the pension fund investment decision making process in particular. This is a real and profound change in what we have believed to be the proper status of the state. As a consequence, we must better understand how and why trustees make investment decisions, as well as the incentives and impediments to financial innovation in the urban and non-urban realms.

With the advent of pension fund capitalism, urban structure will be increasing as an investment good managed with respect to the interests of pension funds and their beneficiaries. If Figure 2.3 were to remain as the essential reference point for pension fund investment strategy, it is likely that the urban fabric of Anglo-American societies will be systematically discounted by under-investment over the coming generation, with selective private investment replacing comprehensive investment by the state. There need be no connection between the goals of funds' investment strategies and the economic and social coherence of urban society. Indeed, as I have suggested above, the very idea of social integration as a necessary element in the legitimacy of the state has been lost with the collapse of an (albeit primitive) alternative. This does not mean that the state is irrelevant as a regulatory institution. Financial institutions are neither benign in effect nor systematically self-organizing in ways consistent with one another's interests or the interests of communities. This much has been recognized by the union movement in the USA, reflected in the controversial but largely failed

push to encourage ETIs. The apparent centralization of funds and the
investment management industry in the major urban centres of Western
economies may have far-reaching implications for urban and regional
inequality.

If urban investment is to be a private responsibility, and if individual
decision makers are to be responsible for urban structure in the twenty-
first century, it is possible that new political movements may want to
regulate the scope of pension fund investment. The manner in which
such movements may appear over the coming years is not obvious at
this time, notwithstanding the AFL-CIO's ETI strategy. Nor is it obvious
how such movements would so affect the polity that the state would be
mobilized to regulate pension funds in these ways. Most nation-states
have generally lagged behind market-based financial innovations preferring to idealize market and trustee decision making, rather than
develop a centralized regulatory response. But it is clear that pension
entitlements are not evenly spread; the middle classes are its principal
beneficiaries. As a consequence, over the coming decades, gross inequalities in retirement welfare between the middle classes and others will
likely appear just as there will be increasing evidence of gross inequalities in terms of urban infrastructure. Pension funds may reasonably
argue that their responsibility is simple and exclusive—plan participants' welfare. In this respect, any argument to the effect that pension
funds generally owe society more than what the state is now perceived
to owe society may be quite problematic. Even if particular types of
pension funds may believe the interests of beneficiaries are related to
sustaining urban development, there are many who dispute the legitimacy of any investments that take into account the wider context of
members' interests.

At the same time, as the investment industry becomes more concentrated in terms of the management of pension assets, and more and
more divorced from particular jurisdictions as the flow of resources
pushes them out into the global economy, plan beneficiaries who
together do have particular jurisdictional loyalties may come to see their
interests and the interests of the industry opposed at every turn. As
pension funds offer more investment choices to their members and
presume that members should assume greater responsibility for their
welfare, the politics of community loyalty may be internalized into
the finance industry through coalitions of beneficiaries and non-
beneficiaries. The responsibilities of trustees may be perceived as wider
and more comprehensive than heretofore imagined in law (compare
with Langbein 1995): the trustee institution may be integrated into the
regulatory structure of the nation-state and the supra-nation-state, even

if political debate about its status is muted by the displacement strategies of the state. Here, perhaps, are the rudiments of an intellectual strategy: '[w]e must then rediscover in the small variations on which legal thought has traditionally fastened the beginnings of larger alternatives we can no longer find where we used to look for them' (Unger 1996: 2).

## Notes

1. Making the connection between the state and global finance is an urgent theoretical and practical task. There are many issues to be considered. While I am not convinced that mobile capital is the ultimate 'enemy' of nation-state capacity, I do agree with Gill (1997: 21) and others that a profound 'shift is occurring away from the socialisation of risk provision . . . towards a privatised system of self-help'. Pension funds are deeply implicated in this process.
2. Froud et al. (1997: 366) define the pauper state in the following terms (italics deleted): it is a state 'whose revenue problems and liberal economic ideology encourage it to run down nationalised industries, privatise utilities, squeeze provision of high quality public services and, through deregulation, strip-out the floors under competition even in sheltered sectors'.
3. In this respect, I am not convinced that the state has been, or is being, 'hollowed-out' if that is interpreted to mean fewer resources. Compare with Jessop (1994). He tends to see the hollowing-out process as a result of increased constraints on nation-state functional capacity due to 'internationalisation.' He is also more optimistic than I am with respect to the opportunities for other tiers of the state to grasp the 'powers' given up by the nation-state.
4. In Clark and Dear (1984) we provide a summary of the literature referencing both left of centre and right of centre perspectives before developing a neo-marxist account of the capitalist state in relation to democratic politics.
5. There have been many assessments of the recent transformation from mixed economies to liberal, free market economies in the West. One by Edward Luttwak (1998) both praises the new resulting capitalism and, at the same time, raises questions about the damaging scope of 'freedom' involved in this process. For example, he wonders in one section what is meant by the notion of 'free market'? In a short passage, he summarizes his basic concerns: 'what they celebrate, preach and demand is private enterprise liberated from government regulation, unchecked by effective trade unions, unfettered by sentimental concerns over the fate of employees or communities, and restraint by customs barriers or investment restrictions, and molested as little as possible by taxation' (p. 27). In effect, free market capitalism is a capitalism short of constraint. Whether or not this is the best description of current circumstances is open to debate. Nevertheless he captures threads of argument and policy making which have profoundly undermined inherited assumptions about the proper nature and role of the state.

6. See also Rosecrance (1996) on what he describes as the 'virtual state'—that state left as a consequence of the demands of mobile capital, and the new sites of productive value found in knowledge and information (not land). By his account, the state 'no longer commands resources as it did in mercantilist yesteryear' (p. 46).

7. At a June 1997 conference in Oxford hosted by the Institute of Fiscal Studies (a UK Economic and Social Research Council funded research institute), many speakers from the Institute and from the Social Market Foundation noted three related trends in taxpayer attitudes: (1) an unwillingness to pay more taxes; (2) distrust of the state with respect to its ability to spend efficiently the available revenue; and (3) an increasing demand for higher quality services. Tyrie (1996) provides a useful overview of UK public expenditure, and a social market perspective on the political forces which shape spending priorities.

8. Analytically, a useful treatment of the issue of fragmented voter solidarity is to be found in Ordeshook (1986: ch. 5). There he uses game theory to demonstrate how and why the lack of voter solidarity may make it so difficult to get public agreement on increased public spending and why it may lead to outcomes that are undesirable for all voters even if on an issue by issue basis clusters of voters are advantaged by non-cooperation. This is the logic, of course, of the prisoners' dilemma.

9. See Hollingsworth and Boyer (1997) on Fordism, and see Hirst and Zeitlin (1997) on post-Fordism and related notions of flexible accumulation. There is now a massive literature on this issue overlapping and intersecting with geography, economics, political science, and sociology. See Amin (1994).

10. Data for the UK comes from the Office on National Statistics (ONS), and refers to the personal sector which is made up of individuals, unincorporated businesses, and other organizations relying upon particular individuals. No direct measures are taken to estimate the data recorded in Table 2.1. The ONS makes estimates based upon information provided from other sectors and assumptions made about the allocation of financial assets between various sectors. In general, data on pension coverage, individuals' assets and liabilities and net worth are not as reliable in the UK compared to the USA.

11. The rapid growth of mutual funds over the past twenty years in the USA has been remarkable (compared to other Anglo-American countries) (see Blume 1997). While institutional investors dominate US and global securities' markets by virtue of their command of large tranches of assets, individual investors through their mutual funds have maintained a significant presence in these markets. Much of their growth can be traced to the success of companies like Fidelity and Massachusetts Financial Services in the retail market for investment and retirement planning. It might also be argued that the systematic misrepresentation of mutual funds' performance has led to consumers overestimating long-term returns (see Carhart 1997*a* on the issue of survivorship bias in estimating mutual fund performance). See Martin (1999*b*) more generally for a cross-country comparison of share-holding.

12. The data on European pension fund assets are less reliable than one might hope. In this chapter I have used industry sources (Deutsche Bank AG 1997). Other rather different estimates can be found in Davis (1995) and Harrison (1995).

13. Disney (1996) has a very useful treatment of the demographics and economics of retirement in the twenty-first century. Of course, the issue is more complex than simple dependency ratios would suggest. We should also take into account the likely financial implications of social security pension values recognizing that some countries' benefits are more lucrative than others. Disney suggests that the UK government's decision to sever the link between social security benefits and real wage increases once a person is retired has, in effect, significantly discounted the long-term financial burden of social security in Britain (compared, for example, with Italy and Germany).

14. Vittas (1996) and Vittas and Michelitsch (1995) provide useful overviews of the current and evolving situation in Eastern Europe. Ploug and Kvist (1996) provide an overview of the role and status of social security in Europe situating the welfare state provision of pensions in the context of the fiscal crisis of the state.

15. Spence (1992) provides a useful introduction to the relevant issues concerning infrastructure and urban and regional development.

16. The data represented in Figure 2.3 finishes in the year 1996. Since then there has been global market turmoil, being buffeted by the Asian and Russian crises. However, notwithstanding these two crises, 1998 was the fourth year in a row in which the Standard and Poor's 500 index gained more than 20% for the year. For many market analysts this has been an extraordinary turn of events. A year-end report in the industry newspaper *Pensions & Investments* (7 Dec. 1998) indicated that the four years ending 1998 had an average compound annual rate of return of nearly 30%. And over the twenty-year period 1978–98 the compound average annual return was 17%. While not standardized as Cochrane's figures in Figure 2.3, this represents extraordinary rates of return. In effect, the equity risk premium has moved substantially in favour of equities. In fact, so much so that in the same issue of *Pensions & Investment*, an editorial argued against re-allocating pension fund assets to alternative investments. While we should not imagine that these kinds of rates of return need continue into the future, few market commentators are able to suggest when the run up in (Western) stock markets will finish. For the average pension fund, these data reinforce long-term allocations towards equities.

17. An essential feature of pension fund investment decision making in the Anglo-American world is its decentralized nature: trustees are ultimately responsible for the allocation of assets, the choice of investment products and the management of the investment process. Over the past few decades, Anglo-American governments have systematically eliminated restrictions on trustees' investment options, and have been concerned to narrow responsibility to trustees rather than any other related or unrelated group (Langbein 1995).

18. It is possible that pension fund investment strategies not deliberately aimed at a particular sector or community may have distinctive geographical outcomes. So, for example, it is possible that a passive or an active traded equities strategy may carry with it a distinctive spatial 'footprint' affecting the cost of capital in some areas while neglecting other areas. But we should take care not to over-estimate the significance of such 'footprints'. Most pension funds hold relatively small amounts of any individual company's stock and are diversified across large numbers of companies; their apparent 'footprint' would be trivial in the face of

the total volume of traded securities. Even when pension funds attempt to exercise their 'powers' through corporate governance campaigns, the publicity associated with such actions belie the common lack of impact of such strategies. See Del Guercio and Hawkins (1999) on the issue and the mixed evidence on the success or otherwise of a sample of campaigns.

# 3
# Pension Fund Capitalism: A Causal Analysis

THE rise and significance of pension funds has been described in various ways. Drucker (1993) thought that their growth presaged an era of 'pension fund socialism': because pension plans own large tranches of corporate equities, workers now own the means of production by virtue of their status as the beneficiaries of pension plans. This is an intriguing idea, one that reappears every so often in debates about the proper scope of pension fund investments. But the idea of 'pension fund socialism' is an exercise in political rhetoric rather than reality. Pension funds depend upon the performance of national and international markets for their accumulated wealth. Their assets are the product of the employment relation, and agency relationships with the investment management industry. The concentration of financial assets in pension funds, coupled with the fact that trustees and their investment advisers have considerable autonomy from plan beneficiaries, is analogous to the separation of ownership from control characteristic of modern corporations. Some types of plan beneficiaries are just creditors, many resemble individual stockholders, and only a much smaller fraction have the capacity to decide their investment strategy. Pension fund capitalism is a further stage in the evolution of capitalism, rather than a profound break with the past; see Minns (1980) on the UK, and R. C. Clark (1981) on the USA.[1]

Western advanced economies are not equal partners in pension fund capitalism. It is principally an Anglo-American phenomenon. The three largest European economies—France, Germany and Italy—have weak, even non-existent (Italy) pension fund sectors; the value of their pension fund assets are low relative to other much smaller countries like the Netherlands and Switzerland, and the values of those assets relative to GDP are modest except when compared to Belgium and Portugal.[2] By all accounts, the German, French, and Italian economies have few important indigenous market-based investment management firms. Their pension assets are trivial in relation to the Anglo-American

## Pension Fund Capitalism

economies, and there are very few pension funds in these economies that could rival the size and growth potential of the larger Anglo-American funds. Inevitably, the rate of market-based financial innovation is very different between these economies (see La Porta et al. 1996, 1997). At the same time, the burgeoning growth of Anglo-American pension assets has had, and will have in the future, significant implications for the global economy.

While many countries have employer-sponsored pension systems operating in parallel with state-funded retirement systems, the growth and significance of pension assets in the Anglo-American countries is a qualitatively different process compared to most continental countries. Indeed, so distinctive is the Anglo-American experience that some developing countries and the transitional economies of Eastern Europe have sought to emulate the institutional structure and design of Anglo-American systems rather than other continental systems. Even in countries long dominated by the German financial model of state-funded social security and integrated banking and corporate relations, questions have been raised about the future of this model in the face of the burgeoning financial assets of the Anglo-American pension-driven economies. Likewise, there have been proposals in the Anglo-American economies to privatize state security systems, or supplement those systems with private contributions to take advantage of the perceived virtues of private pensions and the institutional investment management industry (see Mitchell and Zeldes 1996 on the prospects for privatizing US social security, and Clark et al. 1996 on the Australian system of compulsory pension contributions).[3]

Why have pension funds become so important in the Anglo-American economies? What are the causes of pension fund capitalism? And what distinguishes the Anglo-American economies from continental economies (especially Germany) in this regard? These three questions are the focus of this chapter. The chapter begins with a brief history of pension fund capitalism, and moves on to consider the issue of spatial heterogeneity—the putative persistence of different institutional systems like the German and continental economies (excluding the Netherlands and Switzerland) compared to the Anglo-American economies. This is the basis for a discussion of the causes of pension fund capitalism. While this chapter is concerned with national and international comparisons, a spatial perspective quite different from that of Graves (1998), Green (1995), and Martin and Minns (1995), who are all similarly interested in the geography of pension fund capitalism (and its various manifestations), it should be apparent that spatial differentiation is one of the building blocks underpinning this chapter. I would argue that understanding the causal logic which has created and sustained gross differences between financial systems is a necessary research project for all social sciences including geography (see also Laulajainen 1998).


## A Brief Historical Perspective


State-sponsored, pay-as-you-go (PAYG) social security pensions have been very important in Germany, France, and Italy over much of the twentieth century. The close relationships between corporations and banks in Germany are another important difference between the Anglo-American market-based financial systems and the financial structures of continental Europe (see Roe 1994). And yet, invoking these types of differences is an ad hoc, partial, and even circular explanation of the differences between the major financial systems of the global economy. In any event, notwithstanding the significance of state-funded retirement pensions for German workers, many workers participate in employer-sponsored pension plans. German coverage rates are not so different from the UK and USA, all being between 45 to 50 per cent.[4] So what has caused the extraordinary growth of pension fund assets in the Anglo-American world? And what is distinctive about that experience? To answer these questions requires some history informed, in part, by Roy Goode's (1993) report *Pension Law Reform*. This is followed with an analysis of causality.

As far as we know, the first mention of 'pension' in English statute is to be found in 1285 (Ed I. St 4), where it was simply noted that if a prelate of the Church were to demand a pension, all such demands were to be made in a special court (paraphrasing the early English). It is not known how such a court would have been constituted, nor do we know how a court would have dealt with such a demand. By the seventeenth century, it was well established that the Crown would reward and compensate soldiers and sailors, or their widows and orphans, with a pension for service to the Crown. Eligibility was determined by military service, by physical disability (loss of limbs, etc.), by financial ruin, or by death. A 1662 statute (14. Cha. 2) provided for weekly payments to those eligible administered at the local level. By the conclusion of the war with France, Parliament had voted lifetime annuities not only for military service, but also for help in raising the money necessary to sustain the war (6 & 7. Will. 3, c. v, 1694). Such pensions were to be paid by levies on excise taxes and the like. A century later, Parliament was also voting individuals ex gratia pensions. For example, in 1790 Parliament voted, on behalf of the Crown, the Revd Francis Willis (a physician) an annuity of £1,000 per year, clear of any 'deductions whatsoever' (30 Geo. III, c. 44). These pensions were paid at the end of an individual's service to the government and/or the Crown at the discretion of their employer. Ex gratia pensions were a form of patronage.

As early as 1793, Parliament used its powers to promote friendly societies whose purpose it was to provide for members' 'mutual relief and maintenance' in case of sickness, old age, and infirmity (33 Geo. III, c. 54). The purpose of such statutes was to encourage private provision for retirement and infirmity, given that people were living longer. A Report of the House of Commons in 1827 on friendly societies noted that the available data suggested that one-half of all people alive at age 25 would live to age 65, and more than one-third of those alive at 65 would live through to 80 years of age (p. 5). Throughout much of the nineteenth century, governments sought to encourage the growth and development of friendly societies by regulating their organization, the role and responsibilities of trustees, and the financial security of con-tributors' assets (see 59 Geo. III, c. 128, 1819 and 18 & 19 Vict., c. 63, 1855). Over the century, coincidental developments in the common law of trusts, including judicial determinations concerning trustees' duties, were slowly incorporated into the regulation of friendly societies (see Phillips 1957). While of limited significance in terms of their total mem-bership, the promotion of friendly societies reflected governments' interests in focusing the financial burden of old age on individuals, and an ideological commitment to voluntary action (see Blake 1995).

With respect to its own employees, through much of the nineteenth century, UK governments provided superannuation schemes for significant groups of the Civil Service. In 1809 (49 Geo. III, c. 96), an act was passed providing excise (tax) officers with a superannuation scheme, reputedly one of the first of its kind in England, although a limited scheme had been proposed for customs in 1686. Whereas gov-ernments had previously allocated pensions as compensation for mil-itary service and had provided select individuals with ex gratia pensions, the excise officers' superannuation scheme was designed to sustain the administrative efficiency of the revenue collection process. Many excise officers held their positions for life. Others paid a weekly levy for the retirement of their predecessors, and some officers and their local authorities levied extra charges to pay for the retirement of the frail and infirm. The 1857 Report on the Operation of the Superannuation Act noted these ad hoc arrangements had been both objectionable and unsustainable. Thus, the 1809 Act provided a means whereby excise officers could routinely retire by reason of age or infirmity, having been 'rendered incapable of executing or performing their duty'. The Act specified eligibility criteria, benefit levels, and investment guidelines for the Commissioners of Excise. It became the model for many public and private superannuation schemes through the nineteenth and twentieth centuries.

However important this scheme was for the design of modern super-annuation schemes, it was not immediately applied to all civil servants. In fact, by 1821 it had become apparent that the scheme was a significant financial burden on government revenue. A series of reforms followed tightening up eligibility, limiting benefits according to years of service, introducing standards of employee performance, requiring participants to make their own contributions (salary deductions), and limiting the portability of pension contributions if excise officers were to leave their jobs. By the passage of the 1840 Act establishing county and district con-stables, Civil Service superannuation had become a compulsory con-tribution system, tightly controlled in terms of promised benefits and, where possible, administered at the local level (including the respons-ibility for any fund liability and its investment management) (3 & 4 Vict., c. 88). Alternative funding sources were also sought, including, in the case of police superannuation schemes, the option for local Justices of the Peace to assign revenues from fines for drunken and disorderly conduct to local police superannuation funds (see 13 & 14 Vict., c. 87, 1850).

Notwithstanding the 1834 Act (4 & 5 Will. 4, c. 24) establishing a contribution-based system of superannuation schemes for the Civil Service, many other public servants were not covered by pension schemes. In the case of teachers, successive governments encouraged teachers to contribute to friendly societies and generally rely upon the individual virtues of thrift and economy. Rhodes (1965) suggests that the case of teachers illustrates just how slow the transition was in society at large from patronage-based ex gratia pensions to general pension schemes. Governments were reluctant to offer teachers the option to contribute to pension schemes, believing, apparently, that such commit-ment would, in effect, commit government to the general provision of pensions. Nevertheless, the same administrative pressures that had prompted Parliament to streamline customs and excise pensions slowly overcame government inertia. A series of reports and commissions of inquiry over the last half of the century concluded that the quality and efficiency of teaching would be greatly enhanced by the provision of superannuation schemes. Even so, it was only in 1898 that the Act estab-lishing 'a universal, compulsory scheme for elementary school teachers' was passed; 'other school teachers had to wait still longer' (Rhodes 1965: 24–7).

While essential to the development of modern superannuation and pension fund management, government superannuation schemes were of limited impact. Hannah (1986: 9) estimated that government employees were a very small proportion of the labour force (less than 3 per cent in 1891). Over the last decades of the nineteenth century, public debate focused less on the nascent superannuation industry and more on old-age poverty. Not only were the costs of the inherited system of poor relief increasingly onerous for government; the number of people living through to 'advanced age' in penury was increasingly seen as an important moral and political issue. Commentaries at the time stressed over and over again that many of the aged were destitute despite having planned for retirement. Distinctions were drawn between undeserving 'tramps', and the deserving old-aged poor who had been thrifty throughout their lives (see Alfred Marshall's evidence to the Royal Commission on the Aged Poor, 5 June 1893). By 1892, when the first Act was passed providing means-tested age pensions for the destitute (55 Vict.), the political will had been mobilized to create a system of state-funded pensions.

Notwithstanding the political movement towards universal, state-funded social security in Britain, friendly society, trades union, and government superannuation schemes were to be remarkably important for the development of independent pension funds over the twentieth century. They provided legal and administrative templates for the design of private superannuation schemes. Dependence upon actuarial expertise inside and outside of government for assessing long-term liabilities promoted the development of needed pension management expertise. Their reliance upon bond and equities markets for the investment of funds prompted the development of government and non-government institutions to regulate those markets, and their reliance upon trust law and the judicial process for regulation was widely copied throughout the Anglo-American world. Sass (1997) reports, for example, that early twentieth-century US corporations and governments relied heavily upon English superannuation plans to design their own pension funds. English trust law concepts have had a profound influence on Anglo-American conceptions of trustee responsibilities and autonomy (see Jobling 1994 for an exposition linking English, US, and Australian experience). As Chancellor Bismarck led Europe with the introduction of state contribution-based old-age pensions in 1889 (the law on invalidity and old-age insurance), German and continental European occupational pension institutions have remained relatively underdeveloped over the twentieth century (see Nottage and Rhodes 1986).

## Modern Industrial Society

In evidence before the Royal Commission on the Aged Poor (5 June 1893), Charles Booth noted that 'modern times' had fractured employment relations. By his account, rural–urban migration, the system of day labour in London, and the residential separation of the employed from their employers had destroyed the traditional system of pension entitlements.[5] It was almost impossible for a labourer to 'get his old employer to take an interest in him as a human being' (p. 544). A 'charitable middleman' was necessary to sustain the welfare of the old aged. For Booth, the solution was to be found in state-funded retirement pensions and the passage of the 1908 Old Age Pensions Act (18 Edw. VII, c. 40).[6] For much of the twentieth century, the state has been seen as the most important institution guaranteeing old-age well-being. At the same time, to understand the growth and development of employer-sponsored pensions and superannuation over the twentieth century also requires a better appreciation of other, less charitable middlemen. It was the growth of the modern corporation and the concomitant growth of the state as an employer over the first fifty years of the twentieth century that re-established the employment relation so necessary for the growth of pensions (as opposed to social security).

The history of social security has been widely studied; it is hardly necessary to rehearse the arguments of so many other scholars.[7] However, a couple of points are worth making for understanding the political forces behind the evolution of state-funded social security. At the time of the passage of the 1908 Pensions Act, the inherited nineteenth-century system of voluntary contributions to sickness and death-benefit schemes sponsored by friendly societies and trades unions was wholly inadequate with respect to the scope of old-age penury. Notwithstanding liberal sentiment in favour of individual responsibility, and the attempts of governments to shore up and expand the voluntary schemes, Booth and his urban middle-class allies overwhelmed opposition inside and outside of Parliament to state-funded pensions: witness the critical response that greeted the Rothschild Report of 1898 which advocated no new pension policies (see Sires 1954). In effect, nineteenth-century liberalism was challenged by twentieth-century social democracy *before* the First World War and the Great Depression. In this context, the Beveridge Report of 1942 which set out the logic for the UK welfare state could be seen as the culmination of a political movement forged together in the last years of the nineteenth century (cf. Abel-Smith 1994).[8]

In between, the First World War and then the Great Depression both challenged the legitimacy of inherited institutions and profoundly undercut the plausibility of nineteenth-century liberalism. While no doubt contested and disputed, the Great Depression, in particular, redefined the scope and responsibilities of the modern state (evident, of course, in the debate led by Keynes 1936 over government macro-economic policy). In the USA, however, the Great Depression was to be the first opportunity to frame a national response to the problems of old-age social security. Previous attempts had foundered on a presumption in favour of states' welfare legislation. Nevertheless, poverty was widespread, and there were gross inequities between the states in the treatment of the old aged. The Social Security Act of 1935 was an attempt to stitch together a national retirement policy based upon mandatory contributions. But it was compromised by funding problems, and little knowledge of the long-term consequences of the system (cf. the assessment of the Institute of Economics in 1936 with Berkowitz 1991, 1997). Only in 1950 did the USA finally enact a coherent public retirement system that surpassed the states' welfare systems.

As a consequence of the Great Depression, nineteenth-century regulatory agencies were swept away and new institutions created which relied upon centralized bureaucratic planning and control. These institutions were then added to and developed during the Second World War as economic planning and political integration became national priorities. Inevitably, the modern state's share of national income rapidly expanded, matched by greatly increased numbers in the Civil Service. With UK state sector employment about 3 per cent of the labour force in 1890, and US government employment about 2 per cent of the labour force at the turn of the century, by 1950 public sector employment had grown to be more than 25 per cent of the labour force in both countries (ignoring employees in the UK nationalized industries). Growth in public sector employment had two effects on pensions. The growth of employment, combined with stability of job tenure, greatly expanded the numbers of employees eligible for existing retirement benefits. At the same time, the nature and value of retirement benefits due to government employees were liberalized, including the addition of cost-of-living adjustments in many countries. As the demand for managerial labour increased, public sector pension benefits became essential reference points for the expanding number of private sector pension funds.[9]

Just as government had become a bureaucratic institution, so too had much of the private sector. Writing in the 1960s with respect to the US economy, Galbraith (1967: 74) noted '[n]othing so characterises the industrial system as the scale of the modern corporate enterprise'. He cited data that corporations (not owner-managed firms) dominated production and employment as well as the control of productive assets. For instance, in the 1972 revised edition Galbraith reported that in 1970 the 500 largest industrial corporations controlled 74 per cent of 'all assets used in manufacturing', and that 'the 11 largest manufacturing, mining, retailing, and wholesaling corporations employed 10% of the workers in these fields' (pp. 74–5). It is apparent that Galbraith's vision was true for many other advanced Western economies and was to become the model of industrial growth for Japan and Korea. Essential to Galbraith's argument were two propositions: the modern corporation was more focused upon growth in the flow of revenue rather than short-term profits, and the management of the corporation was the product of the application of technology to planning, and the routinization of decision making in groups rather than by individuals.

Galbraith wrote as if the modern corporation was an organic whole, conceived and developed as an economic institution in response to the inefficiency and instability of the market. Like Chandler (1977), he believed that the modern corporation both required and created a new managerial class, replacing the unquestioned authority of owner-managers with managers whose power was a product of their place in the functional hierarchy of a priori defined tasks and their need for cooperation from similarly placed managers in the organization. Not surprisingly, the management of managers was itself routinized and their eligibility for pension benefits generalized rather than personalized. With the growth of corporations as the dominant form of industrial organization came stability of employment, job tenure, and the development of internal labour markets. In the twenty years after the end of the Second World War, employer-sponsored pension plans proliferated, and coverage of the private workforce greatly expanded. In the USA, coverage went from 22.5 per cent in 1950, to 48 per cent of the workforce around 1970. In Britain, coverage went from less than 15 per cent immediately before the Second World War, to peak at about 50 per cent in 1965. Of course, rates of coverage have been much higher in the public sectors of both countries when compared to their private sectors.

In many corporations, managers were required to participate in their employer-sponsored pension plans. In effect, benefits were treated as deferred compensation and given preferential tax status. While Galbraith writes as if the imperatives of corporate management generalized and equalized the treatment of workers within and outside the corporation, labour unions and governments on both sides of the Atlantic played important roles in broadening the participation of waged workers, women, and minorities in employer-sponsored pension plans. Specifically, the 1949 decision of the US Supreme Court in *Inland Steel*, which ruled that pension benefits were a form of wage compensation, empowered US unions representing production workers to negotiate pension benefits with the major industrial corporations.[10] The United Steelworkers of America, the United Auto Workers, and other leading (and competing) industrial unions began a long campaign to make pension benefits a customary part of workers' compensation. This campaign, as were other related campaigns in Britain, Australia, and Canada, was only partially successful. Even now, the continuing importance of defined benefit pensions more often reflects the historical power of the industrial unions rather than national solidarity. In 1991, British coverage rates were highest in those sectors with a long history of union representation, such as coal-mining (84 per cent) and heavy manufacturing (67 per cent), compared to sectors such as retailing and services (34 per cent), that have had weak union presence.[11]

Furthermore, in the USA the industrial unions played major roles in the passage of the first comprehensive federal legislation guaranteeing workers' pension rights and pension funding. The Employee Retirement Income Security Act of 1974 (ERISA) became the benchmark for many countries around the world seeking mechanisms to regulate and broaden the coverage of private pension schemes.[12] The political context of its passage is described in detail in Sass (1997). Two points should be kept in mind, however, about its underlying logic. At one level, it sought to establish in statute funding principles and standards so that workers' pensions would not be lost in the case of corporate bankruptcy or the like. It took the English common law heritage and built a regulatory framework around notions such as fiduciary duty relevant to the new industrial state (Langbein 1995). At another level, though, it imported notions such as 'workers' rights' from civil rights legislation, the goal being to generalize pension entitlements in the workplace and protect those 'rights' from arbitrary corporate decision making. Coincidentally, Britain also passed legislation dealing with discrimination in the provision of private pensions (the Social Security Pensions Act of 1975). However, it was to take another fifteen years and the intervention of the European Court of Justice before UK legislation had the same force on this issue as the US legislation.[13]

Arguably, Galbraith caught the new industrial state at its zenith. Since the mid-1970s, corporate restructuring has been the operative strategy in much of the Anglo-American world. In its initial stages, corporate restructuring sought to escape the boundaries imposed by the inherited configuration of production. Growth in the flow of revenue was to be achieved by diversification and conglomeration. Corporations were to become diverse portfolios of income, ideally structured so as to balance risks against one another in the interests of sustaining the stability of corporate growth. These plans were never quite realized. As Hamel and Prahalad (1994: 5) have noted, Galbraith's pantheon of the leading industrial corporations have been attacked in their core markets. They have failed to 'keep up with the accelerating pace of industry change'. The form, functions, and ownership of the modern corporation have become essential variables in the search for competitive advantage; and for many managers, cost-efficiency has been an important driving force behind corporate restructuring.

Not only have many hundreds of thousands of workers lost their jobs as corporations have sought to simultaneously downsize and increase labour productivity, recurrent waves of mergers and acquisitions have drastically affected job tenure in manufacturing through to the highest levels of corporate life (B. Harrison 1994). In this context, the employment relation and pension benefits have taken the brunt of corporate re-engineering.[14] There are many instances where corporations have sought legal (and not so legal) ways of discounting their pension liability or creaming off so-called 'excess' reserves. In addition, the nature and design of employer-sponsored pension plans is also significantly changing. Defined benefit plans were once the standard model, wherein employers bore the burden of liability. New models of pension plan management, such as defined contribution plans, have come to rival defined benefit plans, reallocating risk to beneficiaries. Furthermore, there is increasing evidence that (in the USA) 401(k) plans have been introduced to shift the apparent administrative burdens of defined benefit and defined contribution plans to beneficiaries.[15] Rates of private employer-sponsored pension plan coverage have either plateaued or declined in many countries, as the nature of work begins to change and contingent contracts become more common for the male unionized employees.

## Causes of Pension Fund Capitalism

I have argued that the growth of pension fund assets in the Anglo-American economies can be traced back to: (S1) the development of English pension-related institutions during the nineteenth century; (S2) the re-establishment of long-term employment contracts in the first half of the twentieth century, and their expansion immediately after the Second World War; and (S3) the latent political significance attached to private, market-based solutions for retirement planning. In making these claims, I suggested that English pensions institutions were profoundly important in shaping and affecting subsequent developments in pension provision in the rest of the Anglo-American world. It is also apparent, however, that the diffusion of pension-related innovations has not been unidirectional. In particular, US pension legislation has been an important reference point shaping other countries' anti-discrimination policies, and was very important in reshaping UK regulations in the wake of the Maxwell scandal (Goode 1994a, 1994b). Likewise, the new Australian system of mandatory pension contributions may have long-term consequences for retirement policy in the UK and elsewhere.

Here I will refer to the historical roots of the current Anglo-American pension system as *structural determinants* (S). In my judgement, however, they are not equally important. Their identification (S1) through to (S3) reflects a deliberate order of importance beginning with the design and regulation of private pensions in the nineteenth century. Having established a pension system which could be relied upon, continuity of employment was an essential requirement for the long-term accumulation of pension contributions. While I have emphasized the employment relation between employers and employees, it is apparent that other models can deliver the kind of continuity necessary to sustain asset accumulations. For instance, the multi-employer, jointly trusteed pension funds established by unions and employers in US craft industries in the early years of the twentieth century achieved a kind of continuity that survives to this day. Even though members often switch employers, as long as they remain with employers who participate in the industry pension scheme, continuity is maintained. Furthermore, it seems that the slow adoption of state-funded social security systems in much of the Anglo-American world sustained, perhaps by default, the private pension institution. Even in the UK and Australia, which both embraced the principles of the Beveridge Report (1942), governments of the day failed to rationalize the overlap and interrelationships between social security and private pension provision.

The *pension institution*, the *employment relation*, and the *latent preference* for market solutions are structural determinants of Anglo-American pension fund capitalism. The notion of causality implied by this argument is quite particular and, perhaps, unusual with respect to common practices in the social sciences. Causality is often equated with generality and laws of nature (systems or regimes of institutions). Humean causality first establishes general propositions and then uses specific instances to either illustrate or test those general propositions (Ehring 1997). For example, it might be supposed that there is a (general) necessary relationship between pension fund accumulation and the employment relation, and that what I have suggested by way of historical examples are evidence in support of that proposition. By this logic, causality is an abstract property of whole systems (like capitalism). This is not really my argument, as I have tried to suggest by a brief reference to US craft union pension plans. Ehring (1997: 15) captures the spirit of my analysis in the following manner: '[c]ausal inquiry is a matter of providing first a breakdown or analysis of the constituents of the relevant trope [or determinant] at a time $t$, then a history that indicates how these components came to be realised in their incarnation at $t$ through property persistence, fission, and fusion.' This is the basis of Figure 3.1.

These structural determinants of pension fund capitalism have persisted for many years, even if their influence has varied over time (events) and space (nations). The structural determinants have set the broad parameters of pension fund capitalism, distinguishing in the aggregate the Anglo-American financial system from the German and continental European financial systems. But also embedded in the previous historical analysis are a set of what might be termed second-order (SO) determinants or causes of pension fund capitalism. These determinants have amplified and extended the boundaries of the inherited pension system in the following ways: (SO1) post-war economic and demographic growth greatly increased the numbers of workers eligible

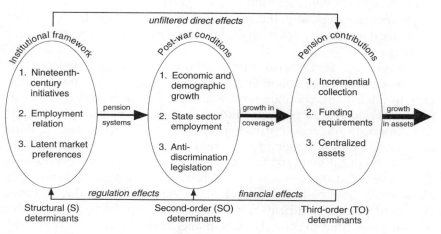

FIG. 3.1. Causes of pension fund capitalism

for private pension coverage; (SO2) just as the rapid growth of government employment automatically extended the volume and rate of coverage of all workers; while (SO3) government anti-discrimination legislation mandated eligibility for private pensions of groups of workers previously arbitrarily excluded by corporate fiat. In essence, *post-war growth*, the *state sector*, and *government policy* together profoundly affected the numbers and rate of actual and potential pension coverage. The structural determinants provided a framework for the second-order determinants to promote growth in coverage, rates, and numbers.

In this respect, it is difficult to rank in importance the second-order causes of the growth of coverage. There was clearly considerable interaction between the first and second determinants. Competition for labour between the industrial and state sectors in an environment of economic growth both promoted coverage and extended the scope of benefits and the costs of private pension coverage to employers. In those industrial sectors with strong union representation, the value of pension benefits continued to increase well after the economic vitality of those sectors had been eclipsed by new competitors (domestic and international), and long-term shifts in the global and local market configuration of demand. Indeed, it could be argued that government policy mandating equality of eligibility and benefits came after the peak in employment in the industrial and state sectors that had led post-war economic growth. In the US context, anti-discrimination legislation has significantly affected the pension coverage rate of full-time women employees, increasing from 38 per cent in 1972, to 48 per cent in 1993. Even though the numbers and relative significance of unionized male employees are declining, the extension of pension benefits to women has tended to stabilize (even to slightly increase in the USA) the overall coverage rate.

Whereas La Porta et al. (1996, 1997) distinguished between the Anglo-American and continental European financial systems by reference to the English common law tradition, I have argued that the structural determinants of pension fund capitalism can be found in English and American financial institutions and their regulation. For La Porta et al. these kinds of structural determinants drive contemporary differences in financial markets' forms and functions. Here, however, I have also argued that the second-order determinants of pension fund capitalism have amplified and extended the boundaries of the inherited system of pension fund capitalism. In this respect, I would argue that invoking inherited structural determinants as the causes of systems' differences is an inadequate explanatory strategy, given the extent to which the identified second-order determinants have played a major role in promoting the growth of pension fund capitalism. Clearly, workers' entitlements to pensions remain quite vulnerable to changes in the underlying employment relation, yet growth in the system itself has gone beyond the logic of the employment relation.

Identification of the structural determinants and second-order causes of pension fund capitalism has allowed us to better appreciate the connection between the inherited institutional framework and the growth in pension coverage after the Second World War. But this connection remains silent on a crucial issue: the enormous growth of pension assets in the Anglo-American economies since the late 1960s. The combination of structural determinants and second-order conditions is insufficient as a complete explanation of the differences between the Anglo-American economies and the German and continental European economies. Why? German and many continental economies have shared most of the previously identified causes of pension fund capitalism. Even if they did not begin the twentieth century with the same pension-oriented institutional and regulatory structures, many German corporations have provided pension plan options for their employees. Even if state-funded social security has dominated retirement planning in Germany, economic and demographic growth, state employment growth, and anti-discrimination legislation could be argued to have had similar effects on the potential to expand pension coverage rates.

And yet, notwithstanding similar pension coverage rates, the growth in pension assets has been astonishingly different. The final step, then, is to introduce a set of third-order causes of pension fund capitalism that can account for this most important aspect of the Anglo-American system. Three separate but mutually reinforcing elements of the Anglo-American system have converted stable, or even declining, coverage rates into a profoundly different financial system: (TO1) the incremental collection and accounting of individuals' pension contributions; (TO2) customary and then legally enforced requirements to fund private, employer-sponsored pension liabilities; and (TO3) the fact that many larger plan sponsors centralized collected pension contributions in pension funds as opposed to outsourcing individuals' pension dues to the insurance sector. In combination, TO1 to TO3 have promoted the formation and maintenance of larger pension funds, distinct from, and in competition with, the inherited insurance systems of the Anglo-American economies.

By custom and convention, and later by virtue of judicial rulings to the effect that pension benefits are a form of remuneration, pension plan sponsors in the Anglo-American economies have organized the collection of pension contributions as part of their normal wage and salary payment systems. So, for example, corporate pension plans that were either based upon employer contributions, or a combination of employer and employee contributions, collect those contributions as workers are paid (hourly, daily, weekly, and monthly). Indeed, many of the major industrial union contracts for 'blue-collar' workers in the USA, Canada, the UK, and Australia have specified in great detail the hourly contribution rate by class and status of worker. Since many employers provided defined benefit (final salary) plans, it was possible for plan sponsors to forecast their long-term liability and adjust (with the agreement of their unions) incrementally the wage- and salary-based contribution rate. This does not mean that pension plans were necessarily fully funded. For many years, plan beneficiaries relied upon the inherited common law tradition of trustee duty to ensure that sponsors lived up to their obligations. However, celebrated instances of corporate bankruptcy and malfeasance prompted the passage of legislation like ERISA, setting standards for the funding of private pension plans and, in most Anglo-American countries, establishing regulatory bodies to monitor funding arrangements.

Many pension plans are still relatively immature, the product of post-war economic and demographic growth. Thus *incremental collection* combined with the *ongoing funding* of expected liabilities has sustained a massive long-term inflow of assets to invest. More often than not, the larger plan sponsors have centralized the flow of assets and liabilities into sponsored pension funds and have relied upon the burgeoning investment management industry to manage the investment process (see Chapter 4 on the functional and spatial structure of the industry). Whereas the insurance sector has played a significant role in the past in managing firms' pension obligations, since the Second World War, the sector has seen its share of assets systematically decline and become increasingly reliant upon small firms and plan sponsors for their business. The concentration of larger pension plan sponsors' assets into separate pension funds is a distinctive and profoundly important aspect of the Anglo-American world. There are hundreds of thousands (even millions) of pension plans in the Anglo-American world. Only a small fraction have more than fifty participants. Only an even smaller fraction have more than £10 million in assets. But those that do exert enormous influence on the structure of Anglo-American capitalism.

The contrast with the German pension and financial system is stark. At a time when Anglo-American corporate and government pension funds were rapidly expanding their coverage (numbers and rates of employees), in the late 1950s West Germany (as it was) completed the social security system begun by Bismarck in the late nineteenth century. Participation was made mandatory for all private, non-professional employees, with close links established between the rate of contributions and the level of promised benefits. It was originally designed to accumulate assets, but quickly became just a PAYG system. As Queisser (1996: 5) notes, with respect to the current system, it 'has practically no funding, apart from a liquidity reserve amounting to one month's expenditure'. At present, the more than 2.5 million state sector employees do not participate in this system; their retirement plans are based upon employer contributions also funded on a PAYG basis (by local, state, and federal governments). There are, as well, a large number of retirement schemes for a small number (relatively speaking) of professionals separate from the social security system. Only 20 per cent of these schemes are fully funded. Very simply, the potentially important postwar effects of economic and demographic growth and state sector employment growth have been muted in Germany by the promotion of PAYG public sponsored social security systems.

Of course, the rate of employer sponsored pension coverage is significant, compared to the Anglo-American world. As noted above, the 1990 German occupational pension coverage rate was about 46 per cent of all employment, with about 33 per cent of covered-employees in company-sponsored schemes. However, the growth of pension assets in those pension plans has been very low compared to the Anglo-American world. Why? Principally because more than half of the covered employees participate in plans that use the book reserve method of accounting for pension liability. Much has been written about this system of corporate accounting. According to Edwards and Fischer (1994: 55), this means that the 'enterprise makes pension provision for its employees by investing its contributions to employee pensions within the enterprise itself.' There are complicated accounting standards and requirements regulated and guaranteed by the government, and there has been considerable debate about the consequences of this arrangement for corporate banking relationships and the long-term development of German industry (see Roe 1994). By contrast, the right to self-invest is closely regulated in the Anglo-American world, and in any event, even when firms do self-invest a small portion of contributions, these funds must first be removed from the corporate accounting system as a deduction, and full account taken of the implied long-term liability.[16]

The book reserve system internalizes pension assets (in the context of a historically limited equity market). While it accounts for the majority of pension 'assets' in Germany, it is not a particularly popular mode of pension provision for the average German firm. Queisser believes that less than 14 per cent of firms manage their plans in this manner, and those that do are large not small firms. The vast majority of firms (nearly 70 per cent) still prefer to arrange direct insurance for their employees outside of the firm. As Edwards and Fischer note, the insurance companies that offer such services more often than not invest pension contributions in long-term corporate and government bonds. The obvious alternative model, and second in significance to the book reserve system in terms of covered employees, is a separate employer-sponsored pension fund (the Anglo-American model), but this is also relatively unimportant. Queisser reports that about 28 per cent of firms have sponsored pension plans involving about 20 per cent of covered employees. The majority of these plans are offered by larger firms and are typically underfunded (comparing assets against expected liabilities). In fact, as the industry newspaper *Pensions & Investments* (15 Sept. 1997, Vol. 25, No. 19) has noted, of the world's 300 largest pension funds only seven German funds qualify for inclusion, and four of the seven have less than US $6 billion in assets, even though most are major, global corporations.[17]

By this account, the German and continental European financial systems are different because they share neither the structural determinants, nor the third-order determinants of Anglo-American pension fund capitalism. There are reasons to suppose that the gap between these systems is not so significant with respect to the second-order determinants. It could be argued, for instance, that post-war economic and demographic growth, state sector growth, and European initiatives to equalize the treatment of men and women with respect to pension entitlement have tended to increase the numbers and rates of pension coverage in Europe and the Anglo-American world. But just as significantly, the processes whereby pension contributions are collected (or not collected) are accounted for within firms, and held against the net worth of firms in the market, have conspired to drastically curtail the rate of growth of pension assets. In this respect, it might also be argued that these financial practices are, themselves, directly attributable to basic, structural differences between these economic systems. In a sense, these financial practices derive from very different financial and institutional traditions already apparent in the last years of the nineteenth century and persisting through much of the twentieth century and beyond.

## Pension Funds and Global Capitalism

So far I have dealt with the structural and contingent causes of the growth of pension assets in the Anglo-American world, remaining largely silent about the status of pension funds as institutions. Here I reintroduce the funds into the narrative, indicating how and why they are so important in the world of finance. In doing so, I begin with a set of observations about the nature and scope of pension coverage noted previously, but hitherto not brought to the centre of discussion. While many workers belong to very small plans (sponsored by firms with ten employees or fewer), the larger the sponsor, the bigger the coverage rate. The US Department of Labor (DoL) (1994) reported very low coverage rates for the smallest firms (13 per cent) but also showed that coverage rates rise in proportion with firm size (53 per cent for firms with 100–299 employees, and 73 per cent for firms with more than 1,000 employees). Historically, it is apparent that larger firms have tended to offer defined benefit plans. This is changing, of course, as medium to large firms increasingly come from industries that have not experienced significant levels of unionization. Even so, these firms dominate the coverage of workers and have accumulated large reserves of pension assets to pay for promised benefits.

With the introduction of compulsory contributions, the pattern of coverage by firm size in Australia is more complicated. Large numbers of new plans have been created over the past few years, predominately by small firms having to comply with federal regulations. In many cases, small firms have joined large industry-sponsored pension plans, while others have sought the assistance of insurance industry-sponsored master trusts and the like.[18] Throughout the Anglo-American world, the increasing volume and complexity of government-mandated reporting requirements, and closer scrutiny of plan sponsors and trustees with respect to the interests of plan beneficiaries, have all added significantly to the costs of operating pension plans. Small and medium-sized enterprises have found such regulations and reporting requirements a costly burden on owner/managers. There are significant economies of scale in the management of pension funds, especially in processing and accounting for the flow of contributions and benefits in and out of the fund. Data on plan economies of scale are, however, notoriously difficult to obtain. Nevertheless, industry commentators believe administrative costs are better managed if there are at least 1,000 plan participants (about US $100 million in assets) and there are considerable economies of scale with larger numbers of plan participants (more than 10,000 participants represents about US $1 billion in assets).[19]

Given the limitations of data, it is difficult to take this point much further. In any event, the economic structure of the pension fund investment industry is dealt with in more detail in Chapter 4. However, it is important to acknowledge that industry research suggests there is a close correlation between the size of a fund and the demand for sophisticated financial products. Greenwich Associates (1996*a, b*) have conducted wide-ranging questionnaire surveys and interviews of a stratified sample of large and small, public and private US pension funds. They show that the larger private funds use financial futures, stock index futures, hedge funds, and derivatives. This is especially the case for funds with more than US $1 billion in assets, although they also note that a significant, but smaller, proportion of private funds (US $250 million in assets or more) also use these products. Their data also suggest, however, that only the largest public funds use these products, despite the general interest of all public funds in venture capital investments. On the question of corporate governance, one of the most contentious issues in the Anglo-American financial world (and one which threatens continental European practices), the Greenwich data reinforces the point: the largest public and private funds take the most interest in corporate governance. Smaller funds leave the issue to their investment managers.

There can be little doubt that the larger funds have played important roles in Anglo-American financial markets. They have been consumers of financial services, promoting the development of global financial flows management and accounting. They have also been the consumers of sophisticated financial products, thereby promoting the process of product innovation. They have been the consumers of trading systems, playing significant roles in promoting the efficiency and reliability of third-party markets and trading institutions. Furthermore, they have been an essential component in the massive increase of traded capital in Anglo-American securities' markets over the last couple of decades. In the USA, households have become less and less important as owners of equities; institutional investors have, in effect, squeezed their significance. In 1950, households owned 91 per cent of all equities, whereas in 1994, they owned 48 per cent of all equities. Public and private pension funds owned less than 1 per cent of all equities in 1950, whereas they owned more than 25 per cent of all equities in 1994. Combining pension funds with other institutional investors (mutual funds), these institutions now control more than 45 per cent of all equities. Furthermore, pension funds and institutional investors more generally defined control the majority of stock of the largest 1,000 US corporations. Similar patterns have been observed for the UK, Canada, and Australia.

In these ways, the connection between finance and economic growth in the Anglo-American economies has been realigned around new institutions and modes of financial intermediation (cf. King and Levine 1993).[20] In this context, La Porta et al. (1997: 1131) ask a simple question: '[w]hy do some countries have so much bigger capital markets than others?' Their answer has a basic, unidirectional causal logic. They begin, as I have done in Figure 3.1, with the legal-cum-institutional framework of financial markets distinguishing between various traditions including English common law and continental European models. Their next step in the causal chain is to argue that as a result of those inherited frameworks, identified groups of countries have very different rules and enforcement procedures regarding the protection of investors' equity. The last step in their analysis was to suggest that because of these differences, countries' markets vary in terms of their size (the number and diversity of stocks offered for sale) and volume (the trading of companies' stocks). Comparing various European traditions, they conclude that apparent differences in countries' size and significance of equity markets can be explained by the underlying legal framework. Clearly, their argument is related to my own concerning the causes of growth in Anglo-American pension assets. But it is also possible that the size and significance of capital markets can be explained by the demand for securities—the product of the structural and contingent causes of pension fund capitalism.

Anglo-American pension funds are also active participants in global securities' markets. On average, UK pension funds allocate 80 per cent of their assets to equities, including 20 per cent allocated to international equities. This will change as the recent pension funding regulatory reforms force funds to shift towards a more balanced asset allocation formula. Nevertheless, emerging markets and other significant international markets will remain an important part of UK pension portfolios. In the USA, most funds have had quite limited allocations to international equities (often less than 5 per cent). This depends, somewhat, on the nature of pension plan benefits. Defined contribution plans tend to allocate a larger portion of assets to higher risk, short-term investments. Defined benefit plans, on the other hand, tend inevitably to balance short-term equities against long-term bonds given their expected long-term liability.[21] Notwithstanding these different patterns of investment, Anglo-American pension plans are inevitably participants in the global economy. The integration of the principal securities markets over the

past twenty-five years via advanced telecommunications has enabled
small markets such as Hong Kong to have significant short-term effects
on the performance of the largest markets in London, New York, and
Tokyo. Even the most parochial US public pension fund has a stake in
the performance of global and national markets.

Recurrent market crises have affected pension funds' capital accumulations. The most recent example is, of course, the Asian 'meltdown'
precipitated by the Hong Kong market in the last third of 1997. Yet,
notwithstanding the negative consequences of this crisis for Asian
economies, the magnitude of its short-run effects for Anglo-American
markets was smaller than expected. While the timing of the crisis was
not predicted, it had been apparent for some years that the Asian
growth economies were burdened by highly leveraged and inefficient
corporate and financial systems. Consequently, they had been subject to
long-term discounting by Western financial institutions.[22] For the period
ending 30 September 1997, the Salomon Brothers EMI World Index of
international equities recorded a third-quarter decline of −4.04, a year-
to-date gain of just 0.97, translated as an annualized gain of 0.35 and a
three-year annualized gain of just 3.31. Up to the 'meltdown', Japan and
the emerging markets had dominated the poor performance of global
market indices. The Russell index for Japan recorded a third-quarter
decline of −15.21, a year-to-date decline of −8.33 annualized as −19.57,
and a three-year annualized decline of −9.28. The J. P. Morgan fixed
income emerging markets index recorded a third-quarter decline of
−9.17 and a year-to-date decline of −4.60, against a three-year annualized increase of 4.15. Anglo-American pension funds had already
responded to emerging markets' weaknesses, and hence only exacerbated those weaknesses by shifting liquid assets towards core markets
in the hope of reaping the rewards of Western bull markets.

We should be careful, moreover, not to overestimate the significance
of non-Anglo-American securities' markets.[23] While the Japanese
market is important in terms of its share of global traded volume, the
US and UK markets, together, far outweigh its volume and have enormous significance for the performance of related markets in Canada and
Australia, as well as Europe. In fact, while the Japanese market recorded
a three-year annualized decline of −9.28, over the same period the
Salomon Brothers US Treasury Bill (three-month) index recorded a
three-year annualized gain of 5.41. In other words, simply holding assets
as convertible cash was a far superior strategy to investment in Japanese and emerging market equities for some years. At the same time,
Anglo-American equity markets recorded extraordinary three-year
gains: 14.77 for Australia, 18.66 for Canada, 22.48 for the UK, and 28.75

for the USA (to September 1997). Few would contend that this extraordinary performance is 'normal' when compared over the entire post-World War II period, and few suggest that it is sustainable over the next few years. Many commentators have recalled the circumstances leading up to the 1987 crash. Herd behaviour in the market can easily switch from reinforcing a bull market to precipitating a bear market.

Whatever the doubts regarding the current bull markets' sustainability, and notwithstanding doubts about the desirability of 'playing roulette' with the global economy (see Kuttner 1997: 160), the recent strong performance of Anglo-American financial markets is part and parcel of a long-term structural economic transformation in the financial sectors of many Anglo-American economies. Through to the early 1970s, many pension funds' assets were relatively small, compared to banks and other related financial institutions. The post-war expansion in plan participation had not, at that time at least, translated into huge holdings of assets. Moreover, many US funds had conservative investment policies, often preferring to hold government bonds rather than equities, while typically holding rather than trading its equity portfolio.[24] As time has elapsed, however, the gap between the returns of market equities and government bonds has been the subject of considerable investment speculation and arbitrage. While equities have, on average, outperformed bonds over the past twenty-five years, periods of high inflation in the major economies have episodically advantaged bonds over equities. More recently, as equities have been seen as the 'winning' asset class of the 1980s and 1990s, Anglo-American pension funds have slowly switched more assets towards equities. In periods of market run-ups, the switching process has dramatically accelerated.

As a consequence of the rapid growth in assets and the claimed value of more active investment strategies, pension funds have developed their own internal expertise or have purchased related services from the market. In recent years, the burgeoning volume of many larger funds' assets, coupled with the need to provide more complex services to fund participants, including, in the USA, 401(k) options, has overtaken many pension funds' internal accounting and flow-of-funds management practices. At the same time, the growth of financial service companies specializing in these functions, and the development of sophisticated real-time accounting software among some of the leading mutual fund companies, together, have promoted the development of an external market for plan management. Reinforcing these trends has been the need of pension funds for expert advice on investment strategy and specialized investment management services. This has been especially important for smaller funds, unable or unwilling to invest, given the costs of hiring and maintaining staff and the opportunity costs of poor market information (compared to specialized managers). Even larger funds now outsource many investment and flow-of-funds functions. In combination, over the last twenty-five years a global investment management industry has been formed around the needs of the Anglo-American pension funds—an industry that now challenges the banking institutions of continental Europe in their own markets.

## Conclusions

In this chapter, I outlined a causal framework which accounts for the growth of pension assets in the Anglo-American world, and distinguishes that experience from the German and continental systems, excluding the Netherlands and Switzerland. The causal framework is both hierarchical in order and additive in effect: structural determinants inherited from English initiatives during the nineteenth century set the basic parameters of the Anglo-American pension system during the twentieth century; second-order determinants particularly significant after the Second World War have amplified and extended pension coverage rates in the private sector; and third-order determinants relating to the funding of pension liability have, in combination with the other two sets of determinants, generated an enormous flow of assets into pension funds. While the German and continental European systems share in some of these determinants (like economic and demographic growth after 1950), and appear to share similar levels of pension coverage rates, in the end, the systems are remarkably different. Pension fund capitalism is very much an Anglo-American phenomenon.

In part, differences will persist because, as Hollingsworth and Boyer (1997: 3) put it, '[m]arkets and other mechanisms for co-ordinating relationships among economic actors place constraints on the means and ends of economic activity to be achieved in any society.' The particular mix of markets, social institutions, and state regulations that are the basis of the Anglo-American pension system are different from the German system. To suppose that there are simple solutions for funding German retirement liability in the near future by replicating aspects of the Anglo-American pension system surely ignores the inherited ensemble of causal determinants that create the whole. This does not mean that change is impossible, or that economic systems are impervious to the adoption of external initiatives. Such propositions are manifestly implausible in the face of the possible bankruptcy of many continental European state social security systems. Nevertheless, the framework outlined above, which combines structure and contingency, suggests that simple, partial solutions are bound to be problematic to implement, and inevitably unpredictable in effect.

On the other hand, to imagine the Anglo-American system is far superior or necessarily more efficient, would be to ignore the fragility of some of the major elements that make up the whole system. In particular, stable or declining coverage rates and changes in the nature and scope of pension benefits illustrate just how vulnerable the Anglo-American system is to the employment relation, and to the economic and institutional environment in which it is negotiated. So much has changed over the past thirty years to directly threaten private-sponsored arrangements for retirement saving. Whereas Galbraith (1967) could write with assurance about the rise of the 'new industrial state' and the array of large corporate and state institutions that underpinned the associated employment relations, the new world of the twenty-first century is one of increased insecurity of employment tenure, increased mobility (voluntary and involuntary) over a lifetime of work, and heightened competition between firms caught up in the increasingly global market for corporate control. We have not returned to the dark world of Victorian London; history does not simply repeat itself as if bound by a never-ending cycle of given causes and events (Carr 1961). But it is clear that the whole Anglo-American institution of pension fund capitalism is vulnerable to the stability of second-order causal determinants.

There is, however, another important point to be made about the persistence of systems and their differences. If the Anglo-American system is vulnerable to disruptions in second-order determinants, it may also be thought vulnerable to itself. Even though coverage rates are stable or slightly declining, the net inflow of pension assets continues unabated. Over the past few years, the run-up in Anglo-American security markets has been nothing short of phenomenal; notwithstanding significant differences between markets' performances, institutional investors have fuelled an extraordinary increase in stock prices, reinforcing pension funds' reliance upon these markets as their primary focus of investment. The run-up in stock prices has had many effects. One important effect has been to lower the effective cost of mergers and acquisitions. Another related effect has been to increase the relative value of private placements (investments in leverage positions). In combination, a new round of corporate restructuring is underway. This time, the market for corporate control will reach into the heart of Europe. In effect, the speculative forces unleashed by the massive net inflow of pension assets in the Anglo-American economies can be increasingly seen as antagonistic to the corporations that sponsor pension plans.

By this logic, the rise of global finance as a system of institutions and economic agents, rivalling the better understood institutions and agents of production, is closely related to pension fund capitalism. Even so, some writers appear to imagine that global finance is a rootless creature, somehow spatially and functionally disembodied from the world that has given it life. For example, Hirst and Thompson (1997) identify a set of causes of increased international capital flows, emphasizing 'features' such as floating exchange rates, OPEC funds, Third World debt, and currency and trading liberalization. They suggest that while these features of the international capital system have overtaken systems of real production, these features are ephemeral rather than structural, and therefore reversible rather than endemic. Now it may be the case, as they suggest, that the re-regulation of currency speculation and the management of trading blocs in relation to exchange rate fluctuations may dampen global financial volatility, but Hirst and Thompson have only identified the immediate objects of institutional investors and their client funds. They fail to recognize the origin and growth of financial flows in the Anglo-American economies and the extent to which the related institutions have (or do not have) an interest in spatially bounded, as opposed to spatially unbounded, investment strategies.[25]

Historically, it would seem that pension funds and the related investment institutions have been quite myopic (geographically speaking). Until very recently, and in contrast with the Australian and UK experience, few US pension funds have had significant international equity portfolios. Of course, it is arguable that by simply investing in US blue-chip securities, pension funds have achieved international exposure, given the reliance of large US companies upon their international markets. And it is also the case that many public sector pension funds have been limited in their ability to invest in traded securities, let alone international securities. Likewise, many European governments have closely regulated their pension funds' international investments, claiming a national interest in the geographical destination of assets, as well as an interest in the nationality of the firms managing the investment process. And yet, even with these restrictions, the volume of internationally mobile Anglo-American pension assets is increasingly affecting whole nations' economies and the international system of debt management. As is the case domestically, the separate interests of plan sponsors and those who control and manage pension assets conspire in the international context to put in play the interests of the Anglo-

American economies, in relation to other global economic interests and opportunities.

## Notes

1. See also Ambachtsheer and Ezra (1998) who use the same terms. Hawley and Williams (1996) argue that the late 20th cent. is best understood as an era of 'fiduciary capitalism'. There are others, of course, who have made some more assessments about the transformation of modern capitalist economies. See also a recent paper by Robin Blackburn (1999) on pension fund capitalism from a rather different perspective.

2. Latest estimates from Deutsche Bank in 1997 suggest that German, French, and Italian fund assets were about 5% of GDP. By contrast, the value of pension fund assets for the Netherlands were estimated as 89% of GDP, for Switzerland as 87% of GDP, and for the UK as 93% of GDP (cf. Davis 1995) and D. Harrison (1995). Davis uses a restrictive definition of pension fund assets for Germany to suggest a 1990 figure of just 3% of GDP, whereas Harrison suggests a figure of 16% of GDP. The rank order of assets and percentage of GDP is not in dispute.

3. See Vittas (1996) and Vittas and Michelitsch (1995) for a review of the current and evolving circumstances in Eastern Europe.

4. I use the term 'coverage rate' to refer to the proportion of workers participating in sponsored pension plans. The UK Government Actuary (1994) estimated that pension coverage is about 50%, having peaked in the late 1960s. This means, of course, that private pension coverage is significantly less than 50% (about 40%). In the USA, the data are similar with an overall coverage rate at about 50% with the public pension coverage rate at around 80% and the private rate at around 43%. See the 1994 report of the US DoL and compare with Reno (1993). For Germany, Queisser (1996) reports an overall coverage rate at around 46% for all employees.

5. According to Jones (1971) and others, there were significant differences in working-class life between London and the northern industrial cities. In London, the labour market was dominated by casual employment, being driven by the comparative costs of production and the nature of demand in the local market for immediate supply. Jones (pp. 22–3) argues that employers 'off-set the disadvantages of high rents, expensive fuel, high wages, and scare skills' by 'sweating' the abundant supply of unskilled labour. He also argues that compared to London, northern industrial cities tended to be more amenable sites for the old, inherited customs of employer paternalism and workers' self-organization with respect to old age and pensions.

6. See Stead (1909) for a detailed, personal account of the passage of the Act beginning with the early moves towards social security in the 1890s. He emphasizes the role played by the New Zealand social security legislation of 1898 in overturning the entrenched conservatism of the government and the Treasury (see his caustic comments on the Rothschild Report of 1898).

7. See e.g. Orloff (1993) comparing the political evolution of social security in Britain, Canada, and the USA; Esping-Anderson (1990) on the various forms taken by the welfare state in modern capitalist economies; Skocpol (1990) on the evolution of social security pensions in the USA; and Hannah (1986) on British pensions and social security.

8. Interestingly, there is evidence that Beveridge was influenced by Bismarck's model of social security, albeit revised and crafted according to the circumstances of the mid-20th cent. (see Grundger 1994). The Beveridge Report was also very influential in framing social security and employment policy in many countries immediately after the Second World War. Witness the UK White Paper on Employment Policy (1944), the White Paper on Social Insurance (1944), the Australian National Welfare Fund Act of 1943 (as amended 1945), and the US Employment Act of 1946. Whether or not the promise of the Beveridge Report was ever attained is open to debate (see Smith 1997).

9. By the mid-1970s, however, public employee pensions had become a significant political issue in the USA and elsewhere. One major study on US state and local government employee pension funds reported that in 1967 the overall coverage rate of such employees was around 60%, and that in 1972 more than 8.5 million workers were involved (Tilove 1976). It was noted that union negotiations were an essential aspect of the expansion of coverage, and that benefit levels were often guaranteed by state constitutions. A latter study of the costs of public pensions by Fogelson (1984) noted that apparent rapidly rising costs of local government pensions had as much to do with the introduction of automatic cost-of-living adjustments as with the nature of work and the associated early retirement benefits enjoyed by some emergency service workers.

10. *Inland Steel* v. *United Steelworkers of America*, 77 NLRB 4 (1948), 170 F.2d 247 (7th Cir. 1949), *cert. denied* 336 US 960 (1949). Immediately after this decision, the federal government faced severe pressures on prices and sought to encourage unions and management to use pensions as a means of deferring negotiated wage increases (see Clark 1993b for more detail). More recently, this strategy was used in Australia as a means of managing wages and prices; see Marden and Clark (1994) on the ACCORD between unions and the previous Labor government.

11. This observation is also relevant to the USA. The recent 1994 Report of the US DoL observed (for the private sector) that '[c]overed workers were most likely to be employed by large firms in high wage, unionized industries' (p. 8).

12. Note, however, that there remains considerable unease both in the USA and elsewhere about the advisability of government guarantees for private plan sponsors' pension liabilities. In the British context Roy Goode (1994a) has argued that this is a fatal flaw in ERISA, pointing to accumulated debts incurred by the PBGC. While clearly an issue, recent US data suggest that the PBGC's debts are far less than many analysts have argued in theory ought to be the case.

13. See the decision of the European Court of Justice in *Barber* v. *Guardian Royal Exchange* [1990] 2 CMLR 513, where the Court ruled that pensions are to be treated as a form of pay and are therefore subject to equal pay principles. Craig and de Burca (1995: 820–3) have a detailed treatment of this important case. Note that I do not mean to suggest that US ERISA legislation 'solved' the

problem of sex discrimination in the provision of pensions. A late 1970s report from the Civil Rights Division of the US Department of Justice identified many unresolved issues relating to women's pension rights that would have been familiar and equally significant to the UK situation (cf. the 1976 report of the UK Occupational Pensions Board).

14. While recent evidence suggests that the impact of these policies of displacement on income and benefits are sensitive to the business cycle, the downwards trend in coverage associated with restructuring seems unmistakable (Aaronson and Sullivan 1998). Also important, however, may be what some analysts have identified as a structural shift towards 'flexible specialisation' (Piore and Sabel 1984)—the systematic replacement of long-term job tenure with contingent employment relationships based upon the externalization of risk and commitment from the employer to the individual. It is difficult to gauge at the moment the extent to which this transformation in work relationships will depress coverage rates. But I do not doubt that it will have a significant impact.

15. See Paine (1993) on the US situation. He reports data showing that while the number of defined contribution plans have always been larger than defined benefit plans (since 1970), only in the late 1980s did the number of participants in defined contribution plans begin to match in absolute numbers the number of participants in defined benefit plans. In essence, the growth of participants in defined contribution plans can be explained by (1) the decline in employment in large, industrial corporations with long histories of union representation; (2) the growth of smaller firms in non-industrial sectors, and (3) the desire of many employers, large and small, to shift the burden of risk to their employees. These are issues of great significance in the UK and other Anglo-American economies.

16. There are, however, exceptions to this general rule. Public pension plans often invest a significant portion of assets in their jurisdiction. More troubling are the US 401(k) plans; there is no federal law or regulation restricting self-investment. As noted above, 401(k) plans are growing quickly in terms of their share of all types of US plans. In cases where workers are only covered by such plans, self-investment is a real threat to workers' retirement welfare. For example, when Color Tile (a Texas-based home flooring company) petitioned for bankruptcy in 1996, it was revealed that the plan trustees had allocated as much as 90% of workers' 401(k) contributions to the purchase of Color Tile showrooms around the country with a lease-back arrangement to the company. With the closure of more than 200 of its over 380 showrooms, and then the failure of the company in 1997, many workers lost their retirement savings. This, and other celebrated cases have prompted Congress to consider the introduction of legislation like ERISA to regulate 401(k) plans.

17. These are: Siemens (ranked 88, with US $13.9 billion), Deutsche Bank (No. 95, 13.1 billion), IBM (Germ.) (No. 160, 7.1), Bayer (No. 193, 5.8 billion), Hoechst (No. 221, 5.1 billion), BASF (No. 281, 3.9 billion), and Baugewerbe (No. 282, 3.9 billion). Note that Siemens, Bayer, and Hoechst are global industrial firms whose shares are widely held outside of Germany, IBM is a US firm, and Deutsche Bank is also a major global financial services firm (see Grant 1997: 325 on shareholdings data). One could reasonably surmise that the extent to

which these firms have sought Anglo-American finance they have had to
conform to US and UK accounting practices that take into account unfunded
pension liability.

18. The Australian industry is rapidly changing. Data on the formation of new
    funds and the relative success of industry funds and related competitors can be
    found in the quarterly *Bulletin* of the Insurance and Superannuation Commis-
    sion (AGPS, Canberra).

19. See the comments of Keith Ambachtsheer in the 7 Sept. 1997 issue of *Pensions
    & Investments* comparing the operating costs of different sizes of pension plans
    in the US and Canadian context. Giant plans like some of the public sector plans
    and plans sponsored by global corporations have even greater economies of
    scale, enabling considerable internal capacity on the investment management
    of pension plan assets.

20. Just as there have been attempts to redefine and identify the scope of the new
    financial structure of Anglo-American economies, there has been wide-ranging
    debate about the nature of capitalism in general. For example, there has been
    considerable attention focused upon change in production processes, chart-
    ing the transformation of Fordism to post-Fordism (Amin 1994). In this vein,
    Luttwak's (1998) book attempts to link up changes in the nature of produc-
    tion to changes in the organization of capitalism under the heading 'turbo-
    capitalism'. What he means by that phrase is difficult to pin down precisely.
    However, in the following passage he comes close to giving a summary picture
    of the new world we have entered. 'What is new about turbo-capitalism is only
    a matter of degree, a mere acceleration in the pace of structural change at any
    given rate of economic growth. But that, it turns out, is quite enough to make
    all the difference. Structural change, with all its personal upheavals and social
    disruptions, is now quite rapid even with zero growth, becoming that much
    faster when economies do grow. The machine turns faster, grinding down estab-
    lished ways and the human relationships even when the economy is not growing
    at all; and it reaches Ferrari–like acceleration even when the economy advances
    at steamroller speeds' (p. 37).

21. I have resisted the temptation to document in detail the asset allocation models
    apparent in the Anglo-American world. More details on the USA can be found
    in Chapter 6; Davis (1995) has a valuable international comparison, and De
    Ryck (1996) compares asset allocation formulae in Europe. Note that with
    respect to Europe, there is considerable variation between countries in terms
    of their pension funds' asset allocations. Many countries' funds are heavily
    weighted towards fixed income bonds. This is particularly apparent for the
    Netherlands (58% of assets) and Switzerland (64%).

22. The data presented below come from a report on market indexes by Frank
    Russell Co. made available through *Pensions & Investments*, 25 (22) (27 Oct.
    1997), 50.

23. Notwithstanding the economic significance of Indonesia and Korea (for
    example) for international trade, they are small fractions of the total global
    market for traded securities. Moreover, there is a vibrant market for financial
    products in the West which discounts Asian market volatility.

24. For many years, the allocation of public sector pension fund assets to equities
    was regulated by the federal and state governments. In fact, there remain a

number of states that limit public funds' investments in domestic equities and international equities. Reforms have been made, particularly since the opportunity costs (lost returns) of such regulations have been very high. Similar kinds of restrictions were in place in the UK, Canada, and Australia until recently. Attempts to liberalize domestic and international equity allocations in continental Europe, however, have generally met with limited success (see the report by the European Commission 1997).

25. See also the argument by Appadurai (1996: 19) to the effect that just as globalization has transformed how we ought to conceptualize culture and ethnicity (the building blocks of anthropology), we are also witnessing the end of the nation-state as a crucial element in the organization of human societies. While cautiously sympathetic to his argument about the increasing transnational character of culture, if not the transnational character of identity, I am convinced that in terms of finance nation-states are essential components of the global capitalism.

# 4

# Functional and Spatial Structure of Investment Management

IT IS widely recognized that pension funds are major players in global financial markets. It is also recognized that Anglo-American pension funds, in particular, are essential to the rapidly growing international investment management industry which involves firms such as J. P. Morgan, State Street Global Advisors, Frank Russell & Company, and Merrill Lynch/Mercury Asset Management, as well as less well-known national and regional service firms. Useful discussions of the development of the international and national money management industries, including reference to both the retail (mutual funds and the like) and wholesale (pension funds) sectors of the industry, can be found in Lakonishok, Shleifer, and Vishny (1992) and Pryke (1994). At the same time, the determinants of the structure and pattern of relationships between pension funds and their service providers are less well understood. At issue here is the scope and logic of funds' delegation of managerial responsibility to external service providers, as well as the resulting geographical configuration of the industry.[1]

The Anglo-American pension fund industry is remarkably concentrated on both sides of the industry. In the USA, Canada, the UK, and Australia, a relatively small proportion of big pension funds dominate the flow of funds; in the USA, the largest 200 funds dominate the structure of the industry, notwithstanding the fact that there are many, many thousands of very small funds with fewer than ten participants. On the other side of the equation, a relatively small number of large international and domestic investment managers dominate the provision of services in each country, notwithstanding the fact that there are many small specialized and not-so-specialized investment firms that co-exist with the global and national firms in these markets.[2] In effect, large pension plans and their service providers sustain the national and international financial service industries of London, New York, Toronto, Melbourne, and Sydney, even if contracted services are provided to pension funds and their beneficiaries at their 'home' addresses (see

Clark et al. 1996 on the origins and structure of the Australian pension fund industry).

Explanations of the apparent structure of the industry typically invoke two variables: scale economies and agglomeration economies (two variables which are at the core of Krugman's 1991 economic geography). So, for example, the former provide a rationale whereby pension fund assets are allocated to competing investment managers, while the latter provide a rationale for the clustering of investment managers close together in specific financial trading centres around the world (see Houthakker and Williamson 1996). In combination, these two variables may be thought to 'explain' the functional and spatial concentration of the investment management industry. But appearances are deceiving— all that is 'explained' is the *state* of the industry not the structure of transactions and the *flow* of assets that, together, drive competition in the industry. These two variables are also silent about a variety of crucial issues, including the decision to delegate (or outsource) asset management; the decision about how many external managers to employ (*intensive* as opposed to *extensive* delegation); and the decision to switch assets between managers. Understanding the logic and determinants of these decisions in relation to the functional structure of the industry is essential if we are to appreciate the significance of pension funds in the dynamic world of regional and urban economic development.

The chapter begins with the functional structure of the Anglo-American investment management industry. Based upon industry sources and interviews in the USA, Canada, the UK, and Australia over the past five years, the flow of services are generally sketched, and crucial relationships within and between funds identified. The empirical logic of my research strategy was first set out in Clark et al. (1996). This is the basis for a summary set of problems or patterns to be explained in subsequent sections of the chapter. For the purposes of analysis, four models or types of pension funds are used to work through the logic for and against delegation, and for and against alternate forms of delegation. The analysis reveals important limits to claims made for the explanatory powers of scale economies and agglomeration economies as important components funds of delegation and switching decisions. Implications are then drawn for the spatial and functional structure of the industry.

My analysis yields three important conclusions. First, any generalized claims made about the spatial configuration of Anglo-American pension fund systems must be sensitive to the particular model of delegation that underpins the functional arrangement of a pension fund. To imagine that the institutional structure of investment management and services is the same for all funds runs the risk of ignoring substantial differences between models of management. Second, the reliance of many funds upon consultants as the nexus between internal decision making and external service provision presumes the existence of highly developed markets for financial services. Inevitably, these markets are in the most important regional, national, and international financial centres. Third, the reliance of some funds upon internal managers presumes the existence of stable employment relations, and a form of insulation from the apparent benefits (to employees) of being close to the major markets for investment managers. Sustaining such employment relations is a difficult task, especially in situations where expertise is vital to sustain fund performance. Ultimately, I am sceptical of arguments that suggest funds can remain decentralized (local) in relation to the (centralized) markets for financial services and labour.

As indicated, the chapter begins with the functional structure of the industry and then discusses its spatial structure. It might be argued that the priority assigned to functional logic is at the expense of its spatial structure and that a better analytical strategy would be to begin with the 'home' locations of the funds themselves, and then articulate the functional structure of the industry at large. This is the type of analytical strategy preferred by Graves (1998), Green (1995), and Martin and Minns (1995). If the industry was 'local' fifty years ago, reflecting a settled corporate and public geography of pension plan provision, in all Anglo-American countries national regulatory regimes now dominate the financial landscape, just as national and international financial firms dominate industry. The industry has changed remarkably over the last twenty years, becoming dominated by sets of transactions between institutions and markets, rather than remaining sets of independent self-sufficient organizations. In this sense, the functional structure of transactions (services in general) tends to dominate the geography of finance. At the same time, it should be acknowledged that there is no settled functional arrangement or model of transactions. Not surprisingly, it is difficult to read off from the functional logic a settled spatial configuration of pension fund capitalism. This point is noted again in the conclusion.

## Structure of the Industry

The pension fund industry is now the largest single source of savings in Anglo-American economies. In an era in which first-order financial intermediaries (banks) are of declining relative significance for managing personal assets and mobilizing capital, pension funds and their market representatives (second-order intermediaries) are at the very core of national and international securities' markets. These institutions distinguish the Anglo-American financial system from continental European systems, where financial intermediation is often internalized and concentrated in the banking system (Allen and Gale 1997).[3] These institutions dominate day-to-day financial flows, far outweighing the power and influence of multilateral regulatory agencies. At the same time, there are remarkable commonalities between the Anglo-American countries in terms of their underlying regulatory frameworks. They share the heritage of English common law and the trust institution, and they share similar tax regimes, designed to enhance the full-funding pension contributions through deferred income. More recently, as the USA has led pension regulation in the Anglo-American world, they share a common commitment to notions like modern portfolio theory and fiduciary duty now embedded in countries' statutory provisions. The regulatory framework underpinning Anglo-American pension fund capitalism was considered in Chapter 3; I look at the process of investment management and the underlying determinants of product innovation in Chapter 5.

There are a variety of ways in which the structure of the industry can be analysed. Martin and Minns (1995) used a simplified set of states and flows to show the origin of funds, and how funds flow between regions and to fund managers. While I am critical, in part, of their analytical logic, their chapter is an important beginning for understanding the spatial configuration of the industry. A more complex realist perspective is provided by Pryke, who was concerned to show the causal links and mediating influences affecting the organization of money flows in the economy. Following Harvey (1982) amongst others, Pryke's institutions are the mobilizers of money, the means by which money flows from one part of the system to other parts and back again. In this regard he has a useful summary of the process of investment management, assuming that the identified process is invariably internal to the institution. In large part, he is concerned to demonstrate the connection between the institutions of finance and property investment.

In this chapter, a fund-centred functional perspective is used to map the principal nodes in the networks that link initial pension fund contributions to beneficiaries' pension pay-outs. Merton and Bodie (1995) use a similar starting point, supposing that the core functions of the global financial system, including the clearing and settling payments, as well as the managing of risk, determine the role of institutions, and drive the relationships between different components of the financial system. While they essentially begin with a blank slate and fill in the institutions as functionally necessary, my perspective is more circumspect. In the main, it is assumed that the types of funds and firms identified have had historical roles to play in the flow of funds, and that the choice of institutional structure (delegation as opposed to non-delegation, for instance) is not the necessary consequence of unambiguous imperatives. It is shown in the next sections that the choice of structure is highly contested and unresolved in favour of one particular model. As Allen and Santomero (1996: 7) note, '[i]nstitutions have come and gone, evolved and changed, but functional needs persist while packaged differently and delivered in substantially different ways.' Richardson (1972) has a similar intellectual agenda.

The basic map of functions is set out in Figure 4.1 (redrawn from Clark et al. 1996). It is assumed that the ideal unit of analysis, the pension fund, is sponsored by a single employer and is, by industry convention or by legal requirement, jointly trusteed (see Langbein 1997 on the trust relationship). At present, it does not matter if the employer offers a defined contribution, a defined benefit plan, or a combination of both. It is sufficient to assume that trustees must manage pension fund contributions for beneficiaries' interests in a manner consistent with overall expected liabilities and returns. In this respect, it is assumed that the plan is relatively immature with many more active plan participants than retired beneficiaries. It also does not matter for the moment whether the fund is big or very big. But it is assumed that the plan is sufficiently large to manage its own assets if so desired. In other words, pension fund trustees have a real choice between internal management and external delegation of some or all functions, just as they have ultimate responsibility for asset allocation and investment management. Related schematic structures are described in Light and Perold (1987), and Ambachtsheer and Ezra (1998).

A first step in the management process is the routine collection of contributions to the fund from the employer and employees, and the electronic transfer of those contributions appropriately tagged or identified through the fund administrator to a bank and/or custodian. Unless the employer is a financial institution, few plan sponsors have the capacity to hold and account for the flow of contributions, or, on the other side, the flow of paid benefits to retirees. Having collected and tagged pension fund contributions, the fund administrator is responsible to plan trustees for the allocation of those funds in accordance with the terms and conditions of the plan, as well as the investment decisions of the trustees. In this respect, there are a variety of specialized services either maintained

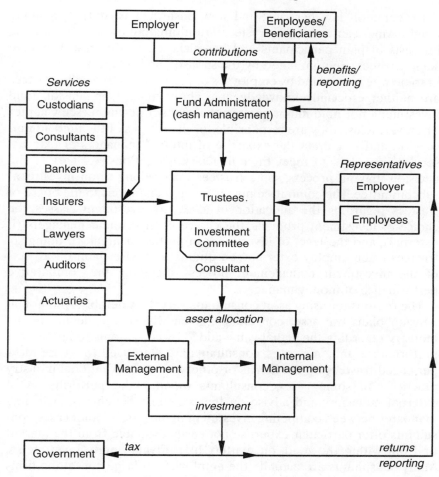

FIG. 4.1. Pension fund investment management: institutions and services

internal to the fund, or obtained from outside the fund. In some cases, services must be obtained from outside the fund *and sponsor* so as to ensure plan integrity and independence: external auditors are often mandated by statute, just as funds often utilize independent advice on plan management and entitlements to sustain their reputations. The Maxwell scandal in the early 1990s, as well as other highly publicized instances of financial fraud and malfeasance, have prompted legislative initiatives in the UK and Australia to shore up the integrity of private pension fund management. In particular, the role of external auditors has been considerably enhanced (see Goode 1994*a,b*).

By common law heritage, and now enshrined in statute in many Anglo-American countries, trustees are ultimately responsible for the interests of plan participants and beneficiaries. In this case I assume some trustees are nominated by the sponsor, and others are elected or in some way nominated by employees or their unions. Typically, trustees are neither especially knowledgeable about finance or pension fund investment, nor hold major posts in the sponsor or union (see Chapter 7). Nevertheless, they are responsible for the actions of the fund administrator, and rely upon the expertise of internal managers or external service providers to meet their fiduciary obligations. As part of the decision making process, some trustees may belong to an investment subcommittee. The committee makes recommendations to the board of trustees regarding the allocation of assets to investment classes, the choice of investment products, the choice of investment managers (if external), and the level of investment in particular areas. In doing so, trustees often employ external consultants to advise them on aspects of the investment management process, including the comparative performance of money managers.

The reasons for using asset consultants vary considerably. And not all pension plans use asset consultants, given widespread debate in the industry regarding the actual value added by consultants to investment performance. In some cases, consultants are employed to advise inexperienced trustees on the merits or otherwise of conventional industry practices. In some cases, consultants monitor the performance of external managers and advise on the costs and benefits of switching mandates between competing investment managers. In other cases, consultants offer particular expertise not easily available from the market or from within the fund, on matters like private equity investments. Many consultants are actually the employees of large consulting firms like Frank Russell and William Mercer, which offer a wide range of services from accounting through to strategic asset allocation. Indeed, the largest consulting firms can practically offer all the management skills necessary to sustain the system of services identified in Figure 4.1.

Having allocated assets and carried through an investment programme, the resulting returns on investments then flow back to the fund administrator, and are simultaneously reported to the investment committee and trustees. Note, of course, investment performance is commonly evaluated against a set of benchmarks or comparable industry performance standards and the costs of the current management of investment, including, perhaps, reference to the likely costs on alternate management systems (Ambachtsheer and Ezra 1998). With respect to the plan's assets, the administrator, in conjunction with the sponsor, reports annual returns to plan beneficiaries, adjusts benefits if appropriate, and ensures that legal and actuarial obligations are met. Depending upon the jurisdiction, pension plans may pay taxes on investment returns, or individuals may pay taxes upon their benefits when paid those benefits upon retirement. Some jurisdictions, like Australia, tax the flow of funds (including investment returns) into and out of the pension plan, whereas other jurisdictions, like the USA, tax beneficiaries' income. Others also tax transactions.

With respect to the spatial structure of the industry, it is apparent from industry interviews that large pension plans which rely upon external service providers tend to use firms that are able to provide services close to the plan sponsor and fund administrator. This does not mean that service firms are necessarily 'local'. More likely, it means that successful service providers are those able to decentralize client support, even if those firms are headquartered in the major global financial centres. On the other hand, given the intimate relationships between large plan sponsors, and the administration and management of their pension plans, to the extent to which plan sponsors rely upon external service providers and are located in major metropolitan areas, there are significant agglomeration effects. Of course, given the specialized nature of these services, it is often the case that the local service industry is closely related to national and international service firms. This is especially apparent in areas such as custodial services, and is also reflected in the market for pension management expertise.

## Management of Investment

Most pension plans use basic benefit formula, offer few (if any) options, and are administered by financial intermediaries like insurance companies. Given the increasing complexity of legal requirements with respect to fiduciary duty, and the high transactions costs of small investments, the vast majority of plan sponsors rely almost entirely upon the financial industry for the management of their assets and liabilities.[4] At this level, scale economies are harsh and unforgiving. The assets of many participants in small pension plans are consumed by high administration fees and charges. At the same time in the USA, Canada, the UK, and Australia, a small number of large pension plans hold the vast majority of pension fund assets and have an enormous influence upon the structure of the international investment management industry. There is considerable competition for investment mandates, even if at any point in time, pension fund assets are concentrated in the hands of a fraction of investment management firms.

The functional configuration of the industry is one aspect of the investment management problem. Just as important, however, is the management of investment inside and/or outside of the fund. In this respect, there are many issues to be considered, including the scale economies and diseconomies of investment management, as well as the role of consultants. In this section, I concentrate on three related 'management' problems: (1) coping with uncertainty (the context problem); (2) monitoring the process of investment (the information control problem); and, (3) sustaining the goals of the fund (the constraints problem). Each of these problems has implications for the institutional organization of the investment management process, and each relates to a series of decisions that fund trustees must make time and time again in managing the investment process.

The context problem is simply stated. Whereas much of the financial literature is about the risk-and-return relationship, pension fund trustees are also very concerned about coping with uncertainty. To illustrate, consider the 'two-colour' problem owed to Keynes (1921), Ellsberg (1961), and others. Imagine there are two colours (black and red) of balls in an urn containing 100 balls. If we know how many there are of one, we know the distribution of both. The risk of drawing one as opposed to the other can be specified using standard probability theory. If we do not know the number of one or both a priori, repeated draws will help approximate the distribution. While small samples may suggest quite different underlying distributions, over repeated draws, it should be easy to converge on the underlying distribution (assuming trustees are sensitive to sample size; for the classic argument against this presumption, see Tversky and Kahneman 1974). The problem for trustees, is that they may never really know the underlying process driving the distribution of outcomes, and approximations may be subject to sudden and unpredicted 'errors' (massive loses or unanticipated gains). Many decision makers have a preference for certainty (see Fox and Tversky 1995); but the more certain the environment, the lower the likely returns.[5]

The control problem flows from the context problem. In a world of uncertainty, pension funds have an interest in either directly controlling or, in some way, understanding the process of investment. To illustrate, imagine two investment managers with similar mandates have very different rates of return one year to the next. Now imagine that one is internal (the lower return), while the other is external (the higher return) to the fund. Should trustees rely upon the apparent difference between these managers in making their allocation of assets over the subsequent period of time? Perhaps. The switching decision may depend upon the reputation and track record of each of the managers. It will also depend upon trustees' fiduciary obligations of due diligence. One implication from this argument is that performance alone is often an insufficient measure of desirability. Given uncertainty, performance from one time period to the next may be unpredictable, even grossly misleading. Therefore, trustees may also prefer to monitor the process of investment, whether internal or external to the fund. Just as clearly, investment managers like to represent their performance in the best possible light and obscure the contingent nature of performance. Knowledge of the investment process in the light of the incentives facing (internal and external) managers is the essence of this problem (see also D. W. Diamond 1984).

Having discussed the significance of uncertainty, and having recognized the importance of knowledge of the investment process for pension fund trustees, the third management problem is entirely obvious: the management of fund assets within pre-specified cost constraints. This is a means of stabilizing or at least partially controlling a fund's annual net rate of return. The available interview evidence suggests that this issue is very important in trustees' assessment of investment managers' performance. Where investment performance may be subject to great uncertainty, many fund administrators believe the internal and external costs of management should be specified prior to the allocation of an investment mandate, and managers should be held to those parameters over the course of the investment programme. There are a variety of ways of achieving performance within cost constraints. One is to reduce the costs of investment management (including trading) by utilizing advanced technologies. Another is to flatten the management hierarchy and minimize the costs of services like consultants and actuaries. Both are important strategies in investment management and the mutual fund industry more generally.[6] The industry is highly concentrated. Nevertheless, the industry is easy to enter and exit, indicating a continuing squeeze on incumbents' profits and cost margins.

In this context, the trustees of large pension plans face a set of four closely related decisions with regard to the management of assets. Assuming funds are of sufficient scale, the most obvious decision is whether to manage funds internally or externally (decision 1—a dichotomous choice), and if externally managed, what proportion of funds and for what goals (decision 2—a conditional choice). Having decided on the mix of internal and external management, the next decision (3) is about *intensive* as opposed to *extensive* delegation. At issue here is whether to use a few managers and all that implies for long-term contractual dependence, or to use many managers and all that implies in terms of short-term contractual relationships. Related to decisions 1, 2, and 3 is the decision (4), whether to switch mandates either between competing investment managers or to bring the mandate back into the fund. Some funds are almost entirely internally managed. They only use external managers for new areas of investment, or for investment options trustees believe they have insufficient internal expertise to cover their obligations with respect to due diligence. Other funds are almost entirely externally managed, using a vast array of specialized and not-so-specialized investment managers and products.

There are a variety of functional resolutions apparent in the industry with respect to these types of decisions. However, in theory at least, pension funds and investment managers ought to converge on a single optimal relationship or a set of optimal organizational structures, perhaps differentiated according to plan size and 'local' differences in regulation. One implication of the efficient market hypothesis is that observed variations from industry best practice must be unsystematic and inevitably disciplined by the imperatives of market competition (the flow of plan beneficiaries away from high-cost plans, and the flow of mandates away from expensive and poorly performing investment managers). Decisions 1 through 4 could be thought unproblematic given these imperatives. And it could be argued that this is one role that asset consultants play: by virtue of their place in the industry, they are able to identify what works and what does not work, and bring this information to their clients who should act accordingly. While firms and institutions cannot instantly and costlessly change their configurations, it is presumed that arbitrage works over the long run to sustain organizational efficiency. See Carlton and Perloff (1994) for a textbook treatment of the issue, referencing the question of industrial structure and its evolution.

As an empirical matter, however, there are few who would dispute the co-existence of quite different, even competing modes of industry (pension fund investment management) organization (Emmons and Greenbaum 1996). Few analysts hold to the strongest version of the efficient market hypothesis. Even Alchian (1950), an often cited reference on the supposed efficiency of arbitrage, and hence the evolution of institutional forms, was more circumspect than often assumed. The issue is really the effectiveness of competitive imperatives in driving the arbitrage process. Here two kinds of claims can be made against theoretical expectations. There is an empirical claim that can be made against the efficiency of arbitrage in financial markets. Shleifer (1998) and his colleagues have systematically undercut assumptions about the efficient order of financial markets, demonstrating that so-called pricing anomalies are more pervasive than hitherto supposed (see Shleifer and Vishny 1997). A behavioural claim can also be made about the impossibility of optimal decision making. Simon (1984) argues that cognitive limits, unreliable information, and past commitments conspire to bound decision making. This does not mean that economic agents are irrational. Rather, economic agents are *'intendedly* rational but only *limitedly* so' (Simon 1961: p. xxiv cited in Williamson 1985).

## Models of Investment Management

While the four decisions identified above appear particular to the finance industry and its institutions, these decisions are actually representative of a more general theoretical question identified by Coase (1937). How do we account for the existence of the firm? Specifically 'why [does] a firm emerge at all in a specialised exchange economy' (p. 40)? As there are 'alternative methods of co-ordinating production' (markets and hierarchies, using the terms made popular by Williamson 1985), there must be a reason (or reasons) why some or all functions are internalized and, in other cases, externalized. In our context, Coase's question can be translated as: what drives pension funds to internalize or externalize investment management and the many other specialized functions essential to the operation of pension funds? In other words, why are some pension funds complex, hierarchical organizations, and others are simply the nexus of market-based contracts for particular services? This is, of course, a topic of considerable importance in economics, and economic geography (see the recent paper by Beyers and Lindahl 1997, and the earlier study of Taylor and Thrift 1983).

The answer provided by Coase to this type of question is well known. He suggested that the 'main reason . . . it is profitable to establish a firm would seem to be that there is a cost of using the price mechanism' (p. 40). In fact, Coase identified a series of different types of transaction costs including the search costs of establishing market prices for services, the *ex-ante* negotiation costs of contracts, and the *ex-post* compliance costs of contracts. Of course, Coase did not use these precise terms. It was Williamson who codified the concepts. Nevertheless, Coase argued that firms are not burdened by these transaction costs because coordinating entrepreneurs use their employees and the 'system of relationships' essential to the operation of the firm across the functions that would be otherwise subject to separate service contracts. His rationale for externalization was as follows. There comes a point where the internal costs of management of an additional function outweigh market costs for the equivalent transaction. At this point, decreasing returns to scale (of the firm) begin to adversely affect the costs of management so that market-based transactions become more desirable than internal management. He also observed, however, that short-term contracts may be quite 'unsatisfactory' when there is considerable uncertainty about the future. In this respect, firms are a better means of accommodating the costs of uncertainty than contracts.

In what follows, Coase and Williamson appear and reappear in many different guises. There can be no doubt as to their relevance and significance with respect to understanding the functional structure of the investment management industry. On the other hand, agency issues are also vital in understanding the choice between alternative organizational forms. Coase avoided the agency issue by integrating the manager (coordinator) with the owner (entrepreneur). In investment management, however, there are many agents with considerable responsibility but few, if any, active principals.[7] Likewise, the substantive issues of uncertainty, knowledge, and cost control have a variety of solutions, more so than those implied by Coase and Williamson (compare with Storper and Salais 1997). It is my contention that unresolved agency issues in relation to the three identified management 'problems' are essential in understanding the functional structure of the industry and the persistence of competing models of management.

*Model A (Small Funds)* is the dominant model (in terms of the number of funds rather than pension fund assets) in the industry. Uncertainty, fiduciary duty, and cost constraint problems are resolved, first, by delegating the entire management of the fund to a single firm in the insurance industry, and second, by offering simple types of benefits like accumulation benefits, instead of more complex defined benefits. The assets of small funds are pooled with other small funds, investments are conventional and often relatively unsophisticated, and cost accounting is the crucial 'performance' criteria. As noted above, notwithstanding the benefits of pooling assets, in this model management fees are a significant constraint on the growth of individuals' retirement funds. Even so, there are few options, except perhaps individuals may opt out from the offered fund and place their retirement planning with the mutual fund sector. Opting out has the perceived advantage of higher potential rates of return and the reporting systems of the sophisticated mutual funds. In the USA, this is an increasingly significant option, given the run-up in equity markets over the past decade. Even so, for the unsophisticated investor mutual funds represent a long-term trap: many individual investors seem committed to funds with high relative management costs and low relative performance, with apparently little consistent ability to discriminate between funds (Gruber 1996).

*Model B (Large Funds, Internally Managed)* is an important type of pension fund. It is commonly associated with defined benefit (or final salary) schemes, can be found in the public and private sectors, and may be sponsored by a single employer or industry group. In Australia and the USA, it has also been associated with industrial unions and the collective bargaining process. In this model, the problems of uncertainty, knowledge of the investment process, and cost constraints are resolved through the internal employment relationship. Control over the essential management problems is centralized, and investment tasks and functions allocated up and down the management hierarchy, according to authority and expertise. While uncertainty cannot be eliminated, the combination of conservative investment products and internal control of the investment process provides a mechanism for close scrutiny of costs and performance. Model B is rarely an innovator. The stability imposed by the employment relation means that new kinds of investment products must be imported into the fund or slowly evolve within the fund in accordance with the sponsor's particular needs. If plan assets are significant in relation to expected liabilities, switching out is an unlikely strategy.

Model B appears consistent with Coase's logic. But there are significant limits to its match. Whereas Coase presumed that management could direct employees to perform a variety of tasks and functions, relying upon the discretion embodied in the employment relation which is not available in discrete contracts, investment management requires specific skills and expertise. Many tasks and functions have exacting standards of performance, reinforced by external legal obligations. Given the importance of cost controls for the management of overall investment performance, the internal flexibility of Model B may be tightly constrained by the available expertise. At this point, consultants may be the only option: they can have three important functions. First, they may provide information on external expertise, including information on market prices and reputations. Second, they may select service providers. And consultants may also act as conduits between the fund and the rest of the industry reporting on industry innovation, and standards and practices of management. Consultants' advice can be rejected, and service providers fired. In this model, the fund–consultant relationship is controlled by the fund.

In Model B, the decision to outsource tasks and functions is less related to the tipping point between increasing and decreasing returns to scale (Coase's determinant of firm size) than it is related to skill specificity and the low rate of substitution between the internationally available but separate professional skills. This is more obviously Williamson's (1985) world of asset specificity and sunk costs, although for Williamson asset specificity drives the persistence of organizations, rather than prompting the outsourcing of selected functions.

*Model C (Large Funds, Extensive Delegation).* While operating at arm's length from their sponsor, Model B funds often match the organizational competence of their sponsor. But there are other types of large funds, ones that rely upon *extensive* delegation of investment management. There are a variety of reasons for extensive delegation. For some large public funds, unable to compete in terms of salary and conditions with corporate funds for the best investment managers and administrators, delegation is a way of gaining access to needed expertise without having to violate mandated compensation guidelines. For some funds, dominated by inexperienced and cautious trustees, well-known and respected external investment managers are thought to provide a quality of competence not available from internal managers. And for other large funds, wary of the uncertainty inherent in investment performance, and wary of making commitments to any managers, let alone internal managers whose motives and competence they may suspect, external extensive delegation is a means of managing distrust. In combination, these three reasons for delegation presuppose the existence of a mechanism or agent to manage delegation: here, then, is a vital role for the asset consultant.

Consultants may have a number of functions in Model C funds. They may act as the interface between the fund trustees and the industry, introducing them to one another without requiring any commitment from trustees. This is, at once, a social function and a management function, being simultaneously the catalyst for trustee–investment manager connections and the sorting mechanism rank-ordering in importance of those connections. There are a variety of variables used to rank-order connections: investment managers' reputations, year-to-year performance, scope of expertise, and the costs of services. Many consultants delegate the collection of this data to either their own company or to third-party data providers. There is a large and highly differentiated industry in financial and performance data, involving huge conglomerates through to specialist pension fund consultants and many other small companies and individuals. Another function of the asset consultant is to advise on strategy and timing: where assets ought to be allocated, and when assets ought to be shifted from one class to another, and between one investment manager and another. This function involves data processing. But it also involves packaging and presenting insider-information gleaned from consultants' industry sources. Implicitly or explicitly, consultants promise special knowledge and a quality of judgement superior to the flow of daily unprocessed financial information.

Model C funds use consultants to handle uncertainty, spread trustees' fiduciary responsibilities, and manage the costs of service provision. In doing so, the model relies upon competition between service providers and the loyalty of consultants to the objectives of the fund. One consequence of this model has been the proliferation of service providers, and the fragmentation of investment mandates into relatively small units. So, for example, to sustain inter-firm competition of investment performance and management costs, it is common for consultants to recommend overlapping mandates and differentiated mandates, spread over a range of time periods. Model C funds may then use quite a large number of firms to manage their assets. To illustrate, Figure 4.2 summarizes a common equities strategy involving as many as fifteen different managers with different components of the equities' universe. The distinction between styles of management (growth and value), as well as the segmentation of the equities universe into different segments with

| Equity Products | Total Market | Growth | Value |
|---|---|---|---|
| Blue Chip | Manager A | AA | AAA |
| Large Cap | B | BB | BBB |
| Mid Cap | C | CC | CCC |
| Small Cap | D | DD | DDD |
| All Stocks | E | EE | EEE |

FIG. 4.2. Model C extensive delegation—investment managers and products
*Source*: *Pensions & Investments*, 25: 13 (23 June 1997), 26.

their own benchmarks is a common and often desired strategy. With comparative overlapping managers coordinated by funds' asset consultants, it is obvious that some funds could have more than thirty equities portfolio managers involved in the investment process (Greenwich Associates 1998). The implication is clear: Model C funds are, by choice or by default, active investors.

In this model, service contracts are short, and carry with them the threat of cancellation if performance standards and agreed management costs are not met. Switching is a real possibility, sustained by the power of consultants and competing managers in the market. The threat of contract termination is 'credible' in the sense that funds can choose between a large number of actual and potential service providers who offer, for all intents and purposes, much the same products. While managers and products can be distinguished from one another on the basis of cost and performance, no firm can plausibly promise a certain level of future performance. The threat of switching undermines the power of incumbent managers, and uncertainty over future performance discounts claims of distinctive skills and expertise (compare Williamson 1985: 167). Hence the contractual relationship between consultants and trustees is a very important aspect of Model C. Designing a contract which clearly separates consultants from investment managers, sustains the loyalty of consultants to trustees and yet limits the possibility of 'capture' by one or the other party is an important task. Not surprisingly, trustees may employ consultants to hire other consultants. There may be a hierarchy of Model C consultants all subject to the tests of performance imposed upon other kinds of service providers. Extensive delegation is a Model of investment management which can explode into a vast array of short-term service contracts, all competing for favours. Coordination costs may, in the end, paralyse trustee decision making.

*Model D (Large Funds, Intensive Delegation).* Model C remains the dominant model of the industry, affecting the practice of external investment management, and promoting the proliferation of many small, speciality investment houses. While the largest investment firms have continued to hold market share in the USA, UK, and Australia, there are enough new or switched investment mandates around to justify the entry of small groups (often spin-offs from large firms) into an already crowded market. In this context, market segmentation has become common, buttressed by data management companies that have introduced a wide variety of benchmarks and reference points to complement the variety of investment products. Model C also has had considerable influence on the retail market for equity funds. Amateur investors have come to believe that switching between mutual funds is a necessary element in any equities strategy, a point of view reinforced by the almost random performance of many funds year-to-year and the preoccupation of the investment media with 'beating the market'. On the other hand, it is also apparent that individual investors are rarely able to capitalize on market opportunities; arbitrage costs are significant and often a real barrier to efficient market pricing (Pontiff 1996).

For pension funds, concerned with overall fund performance, the proliferation of investment managers and products has not always been viewed as favourably as asset consultants have argued its virtues. A variety of problems have been identified with Model C extensive delegation. For funds actively pursuing short-term year-to-year performance, switching between managers has come to dominate the process of investment management. Industry commentators have noted that transaction costs have often cancelled out any apparent gains in fund performance from switching. Moreover, while the rhetoric of Model C emphasizes investment performance, fewer investment managers have been willing to match the rhetoric with performance-based fees, as opposed to volume and transaction-based fees. Worse, Model C has tended to empower asset consultants, rather than fund managers and trustees, leading to the relative isolation of the latter, with respect to the former, from the investment process. By some accounts, asset consultants have become the gatekeepers standing between clients and service providers while clawing back significant fees for the privilege. Most importantly, it is increasingly clear that the crucial decision, with respect to overall fund performance, is asset allocation to asset classes, rather than the choice between investment managers and products within classes (Chapter 5).

Model C continues to hold sway. But some larger private funds have shifted towards intensive delegation: what is termed in the industry as 'The New Paradigm' (Model D). According to Greenwich Associates (1996a), Model D is characterized by long-term relationships between the pension funds and select groups of investment firms. Rather than asset consultants being the nexus of service contracts, there is a direct and ongoing relationship between trustees and investment managers. Instead of a wide variety of service providers, Model D pension funds rely upon a small group of firms to provide most services. Intensive delegation is about bundling together what are otherwise separate but complementary tasks and functions (Richardson 1972). Not surprisingly, only the largest investment firms can provide the range of services desired, leading one commentator to remark that the New Paradigm manager is 'a multimarket, multiproduct organisation, with strong

capabilities—in both investment management and relationship development—that centre on professional investment counselling' (Greenwich Associates 1996*a*: 1).

Model D delegation still has a role for specialist investment managers
and service providers. But the numbers of service providers are much
smaller, and the competence and distinctive skills demanded of specialist providers much more significant. Notice that the threat of termination is less important in this model than the long-term provision of
services at standards of performance which reap the benefits of lower
transaction costs and scale economies. Instead of asset consultants being
at the nexus of service contracts, Model D relies upon close collaboration between the principals of funds and firms. In general, it may be supposed that in some cases market transaction costs (including agency
costs) become too large relative to Model D which, in effect, prompts
the internalization of many of the functions of pension fund management, even if, in the last resort, those functions are provided externally
to the fund through a small number of closely related (to the fund) firms.
Compare with Coase (1937) where he suggests '[a] firm is likely therefore to emerge in those cases where a short-term contract would be
unsatisfactory' (p. 41).

Notwithstanding the importance of Model C, why has Model D
gained acceptance amongst larger funds? In terms of the problem of
uncertainty, some trustees have come to realize that the virtues of
diversification and specialization do not necessarily solve so much as
complicate the management of uncertainty. Given that the asset allocation decision is so important in driving overall fund performance, it is
apparent to some trustees that understanding the larger context in
which such allocations are made is more important than trying to
closely manage the seemingly unmanageable. This perspective places a
premium on wide-ranging market information and longer term strategic decision making. It also means that one individual or function, like
the asset consultant, cannot be relied upon to process and distribute the
complex array of information necessary to make such decisions, especially if there are doubts about consultants' motives.[8] Moreover,
strategic decision making with respect to asset allocation is seen as a
sequential process, building upon expertise over the longer term rather
than the short term, implied by switching between investment managers
for momentary advantage. The implication is that long-term relationships are a better mechanism for coping with uncertainty than the other
options.

In exchange for pension funds' long-term commitment, investment
managers are required to bring trustees into the process of corporate

decision making.[9] As a consequence, pension fund trustees may become very informed about the logic and process of investment decision making. In this respect, Model D supposes that investment firms become the nexus for market information, rather than simply providing a service under contract. There are risks in such arrangements. One side or the other may exploit commitment. Therefore, tests of sincerity and value are either formally or informally applied by parties to these relationships. In addition, there is a risk that trustees will take firm-specific information and use it against the firm in staged competitions between similarly placed firms. There is also a risk (for the industry at large) that pension funds will become more knowledgeable about the industry than any single firm. In this model, there are obviously contracts which specify terms and conditions. But these contracts are *relational* contracts not discrete exchange contracts, and rely upon mutual interest and solidarity, as well as self-interest (see MacNeil 1980).[10]

## Spatial Structure of Investment Management

There are other models of investment management. We have not exhausted the scope of management organization, nor have we fully described and analysed the ways in which the identified models might vary by pension fund type, jurisdiction, and governance. As Richardson (1972: 887) suggested in a different setting 'we must not imagine that reality exhibits . . . sharp line[s] of distinction, what confronts us is a continuum' (compare with Beyers and Lindahl 1997). Nevertheless what emerges from this typology is a set of four models that represent a tangible and differentiated world of investment management. What also emerges from this discussion is a realization that the significance of variables such as scale economies and agglomeration economies, the reference points for much contemporary theorizing in economic geography, must be seen in relation to other crucial management problems, like coping with uncertainty, understanding the nature of investment decision making, and managing within constraints. That being the case, the next step is to assess each management model with reference to the spatial and network structure of the investment management industry.

Martin and Minns' (1995) study of the UK pension fund system and its attendant investment management industry is about the spatial structure of the industry and its concentration in London and the South-east. They note that many funds are located in the South-east, matching the headquarters locations of their sponsoring institutions (public and private). They also note that as most large funds outsource investment management (Model C), assets are concentrated in the hands of just a handful of managers located in London. When combined with UK funds' overwhelming emphasis on traded equity products, an asset allocation strategy, which is slowly changing in response to recent government policy initiatives, Martin and Minns suggest that the UK pension system is systematically spatially concentrated to the detriment of the rest of the country. In their words, 'the private occupational pensions system undermines the regions' (p. 139). And they go on to suggest alternatives, including a UK version of the German stakeholder model which, they believe, would counter the short-term focus of funds, and broaden the responsibilities of pension funds to include respect for beneficiaries' communities.

I am uneasy about their argument for a stakeholder model of pension fund capitalism (although it should be acknowledged that Hutton 1995 was a powerful advocate). While I agree that there are many interests embedded in pension funds, it is hard to sustain an argument that those interests are necessarily and specifically local. At the same time, their argument is made at a time when the German stakeholder model is clearly under pressure, in part because of the underfunding of German company pension plans and state security. Bankruptcy looms, and will result in profound institutional changes to many continental European financial systems. Moreover, it is arguable that German reliance upon first-order intermediaries such as banks and closely-related holding companies will have to give way to Anglo-American financial institutions which are dependent upon market intermediation as opposed to institutional intermediation. In this respect, the institutional structure of the European finance industry is in flux (and will be significantly affected by current negotiations over the harmonization of European finance industries).

Other Anglo-American countries are more or less like the UK. In Australia, pension funds and the investment management industry are basically shared between Melbourne and Sydney. While few Australian funds are so skewed towards traded equities, there is no doubt that the management and location of funds are highly concentrated. This is less apparent in Canada, with the industry being split between Montreal, Toronto, and Vancouver. Of course, there is an added spatial competitive dimension: the close existence of New York and the USA, in general. By contrast, the US pension management industry is far more decentralized. In part, this is because many state and local government public sector funds have had, until recently, relatively low-risk investment strategies, relying upon government bonds and constrained by limits on equity allocations. Local management (either Model B or Model C) has been viable in these cases even if 'local' has meant the employment of managers and consultants from large, regional financial centres such as Boston, Chicago, Philadelphia, Atlanta, Dallas, San Francisco, and Los Angeles. Even though the political constituency for local investment is relatively weak, witness the debate over ETIs, the enormous variety of public and private funds with diverse investment strategies, combined with an incredible array of service providers, have conspired to sustain a more decentralized investment management industry, compared with other countries.[11]

Notwithstanding these important differences, there is little doubt that Anglo-American pension funds have had difficulty recognizing local interests in their investment strategies. With respect to the UK, Martin and Minns' contend that one response should be to decentralize 'economic and political power to the regions', thereby reducing 'their dependence on the decision making and investment strategies of institutions and organisations located in the Southeast' (p. 142). They would force the decentralization of the financial system in the interests of promoting local management and investment decision making. While no doubt consistent with stakeholder principles, as a policy it would seem to be limited in several respects. Most importantly, it is an argument about political institutions and decentralized democratic representation, rather than the functional structure of the Anglo-American investment management industry. And just as importantly, they are silent about the different models of the investment management process preferring, for arguments' sake it seems, to treat all funds alike. In a sense, their ideal solution is profoundly at odds with the functional structure of the industry and its various spatial manifestations.

To illustrate, let us return to Model A. The vast majority of small funds contract out the entire administration, management, and investment of their assets to insurance companies and the like. These companies are really siphons. They collect small amounts of assets from widely dispensed individuals and small companies, and pool them together in investment products before disbursing benefits back to contributors. Concerns with uncertainty, the investment process, and managing within constraints are transferred to the firms. To the extent that these firms offer a range of investment products, the most conventional and least risky products have dominated the industry. Thus, at the level of the plan sponsor, uncertainty and a concern for the investment process have been accommodated by limiting exposure to risk. Like banking, many insurance companies provide local store-front operations to service individual clients or use very inexpensive telephone networks to centralize the processing of decentralized demand. However, as mutual fund companies and discount stock-broking companies have increasingly penetrated this market, they have offered similar kinds of distributed services, but a wider range of investment products with differentiated risk profiles. The extent to which these firms offer local investment options depends upon the demand for such options set against the *net* returns of other less tailored and more spatially generalized investment options.[12]

Model B may be more consistent with local interests. Large internally managed private pension funds located in regions outside of the major financial centres may have a stake in their local community. But realizing value from such loyalties may be more problematic than often acknowledged. Over the past few decades, industrial restructuring has resulted in many plant closures and the rationalization of productive capacity in many industries. Mergers and acquisitions have, more often than not, led to the consolidation of previously separate pension funds, focused upon managing their inherited liabilities rather than developing innovative local investment strategies (Clark 1993*b*). Indeed, an essential ingredient in the recurrent waves of mergers and acquisitions has been a deliberate shift in corporate loyalties from local communities to financial markets. A not unrelated issue, therefore, has been the shift of many corporate headquarters and their sponsored plans closer to the financial centres of the global economy. The concomitant integration of pension fund investment management with corporate financial management has also tended to shift internal managers' loyalties from the pension plan and its relationship with local beneficiaries to their career paths, internal and external to the plan sponsor. Not surprisingly, internal fund managers, like their external counterparts, have a personal stake in being close to important financial markets.

Because some funds are jointly trusteed and, therefore, reflect broad political and institutional commitments, and because of the close connection between the economic performance of the host region and tax revenues that sustain the size and scope of the public sector, US experience suggests that Model B public sector funds may be significant local investors. In the USA, of course, local pension fund investment is made palatable by the large and diversified state and local government bond market—a market which does not exist in the UK and Australia. Even in Canada, the capacity of local governments to raise bonds is very limited, notwithstanding the vibrant markets in traded Provincial bonds. State and local government bonds carry either an explicit or implicit government guarantee, thereby limiting risk and practically excluding uncertainty from funds' calculations. The fact that these types of investment products are transparent, and their returns entirely predictable in relation to funds' long-term liabilities, enables public Model B funds to sustain a geographical investment strategy without significant internal expertise (Clark and O'Connor 1997). Even so, state and local government bonds may not be the best type of local investment strategy or the most appropriate investment products, given the rates of return from equity and other related types of products.

What are the implications of short-term investment management contracts (Model C) for regional economic development? One answer is to be found in Scott's (1988) work on the spatial configuration of transaction costs. Having recognized that many routine service functions can be efficiently produced and provided at a distance from the point of consumption, Scott goes on to argue that '[p]roducers who operate in disintegrated and uncertain economic environments are very likely to be tied together in high-cost linkage networks in which transactions are numerous, small in scale, unstandardised and unstable over space and time' (p. 53). With respect to the pension management industry, and notwithstanding the enormous sums involved, the premium placed on short-term contracts and the switching of mandates in Model C funds is such that instability dominates much of the industry. Transactions may be, of course, large in scale and quite standardized, despite the efforts of service providers to differentiate themselves from other actual and potential competitors. In this respect, Scott's conclusion has considerable merit: '[t]hey are therefore also likely to be found in mutually beneficial locational symbiosis with one another' (p. 53). Model C implies a world in which service providers locate with respect to one another and with respect to the location of pension funds. While this may be important for the flow of transactions, it is also true, however, that the benefits of spatial agglomeration in the investment management industry may flow to individual employees more than their employing firms. Celebrated instances of defection reflect the rewards of intra-industry mobility, and mobility benefits all kinds of employees, from the lowest technical support personnel through to the well-known fund managers.

Given the dominance of Model C in the industry, and the growth of large multi-functional and multi-task oriented service companies, a two-tier spatial structure has emerged in the industry. At the highest level, in the most important financial centres of the world, investment management service firms follow the kinds of imperatives sketched by Scott. For investment firms concerned about sustaining their reputations, being at the centre of the market is vital in attracting and retaining the best employees. The largest financial markets are also the most

98 *Structure of Investment Management*

cost-efficient bourses. C. Cao, Choe, and Hatheway (1997) have shown that there are significant cost advantages in trading on the New York Stock Exchange as opposed to the other competing US exchanges, let alone the small regional centres. And given the reliance of initial public offerings (IPOs) on those markets, there is little doubt that investment firms must have a significant presence in the most efficient markets if they are to be competitive in providing investment services. Therefore, even in cases where funds rely upon a few long-term service providers (Model D), there seem to be compelling reasons for spatial concentration. Indeed, Model C and Model D service providers normally rely upon the efficiency of international markets for their long-term cost competitiveness.

At the other end of the spatial structure, at the lowest level of the spatial hierarchy, the investment management industry is simply a conduit for financial and information flows. Put another way, it provides individual plan participants services in accordance with plan specifications, using high-quality communication networks to reach dispersed beneficiaries in ways that are both cost-effective and informationally efficient. At the limit, service providers may have no 'local' presence at all—storefront sites may be eschewed in favour of telecommunication networks which provide 24-hour services nationally and internationally. Just as importantly, central telecommunication services need not be located in the major (expensive) financial markets. With the systematic discounting of telecommunication costs, the service side of the investment management industry can be spatially divorced from the imperatives driving the centralization of investment management.

## Conclusions

In essence, my argument in this chapter is twofold. First, any map of the functional structure of the pension investment management industry must take into account the various ways in which funds are organized and services provided. Second, conventional notions of scale economies and agglomeration economies are of limited value, recognizing other important issues driving the organization of the industry. Here I identified three crucial management issues particular to the pension funds industry and finance industry, in general. These issues are very important in pension fund investment and include coping with uncertainty, understanding the investment process, and managing within constraints. But these issues are probably not unique to the world of finance and investment. Recent studies of non-axiomatic decision making have also identified similar types of issues, even if they are based on different terms and examples (see Radner 1997). Throughout I have sought to suggest that there is no uniquely efficient or dominant model of the investment management process. This is empirically obvious. Moreover, I doubt the likelihood of such an eventuality, even in the long run. There are many reasons why the arbitrage processes are not rigorously efficient selectors of the 'best' institutional forms.

Underlying this analysis is an unresolved tension between the economics of distrust and the virtues of commitment. Those models of investment management which rely upon extended networks of service providers coordinated by asset consultants on behalf of their clients tend also to be networks of discrete exchange contracts, framed with reference to competing profiles of costs and performance. Basically, in this model of the investment management process trustees distrust service providers more than they distrust their agents of coordination. Their sense of vulnerability to uncertainty (risk aversion), and their sense of missed opportunities (regret), if committed to particular investment managers, means that the investment process is often a vast array of competing and overlapping service providers. This is the world of vertical and horizontal disintegration identified by Scott (1988) and others in another context (production and supply systems). It is a world in which it pays industry participants to collect together in space and time, not so much for the benefits of spatial proximity as for the pressing need to be close to the volatile market for services and the chance to benefit from third-party switching decisions.

There are other models of investment management. By contrast, some models rely upon the virtues of commitment: the reduced transaction costs and coordination costs of relying upon a limited set of investment managers, either internal to the pension fund or external to the fund and found in the investment management industry. In the case of internal commitment, the employment relation is the core conceptual apparatus and contractual device that sustains the relationship between pension fund trustees and their investment manager employees. The employment relation at once describes the scope of the relationship between trustees and employees and provides the means by which that relationship is given formal status through the terms and conditions of employment. As in all models of the investment management process, aligning the interests of the parties (agents all) is at the core of the model. But, unlike other models, the alignment of interests may be more or less precise, relying as it does upon the continuity of the employment relation rather than its formal characteristics. This is also an important aspect of the long-term relationship linking service providers to pension funds. In this case, however, I have argued that there is a dilemma embedded in this kind of relationship: an inherent conflict between personal and corporate interests.

Much of the literature on economic organization including recent research in economic geography tends to focus upon the most efficient form of organization. This is apparent in the finance literature (see Emmons and Greenbaum 1996), and is reflected in more general debate about Fordism and post-Fordism in economic geography over the past decade. The supposition lurking behind this debate is that form determines action; that there is a close connection between the structure of an industry, its firms, and spatial configuration which allows us to economize (theoretically speaking) on the study of individual and organizational decision making. While there are many insights to be gleaned using this approach, in this chapter I have argued that the functional and spatial configuration of the industry cannot be neatly partitioned into self-contained, mutually exclusive models. Just as functional needs can be met in a number of ways, so too may regions bear a variable and differentiated imprint of the industry. At the same time, it should be clear that I believe there is a strong case for approaching the issue from the top of the national and international spatial hierarchy. In part, this is because of the overlapping and reinforcing map of Anglo-American financial regulation, which provides the largest firms and funds an international arena in which to plan investments. It is also the case that crucial functions have centralized locations, even if their actual delivery is decentralized. How and why this is the case is at the heart of the models identified and explained above.

But if it is true that there is no settled functional and spatial configuration of the industry, and that there are rival models of management, rather than settled relationships and functional structures, we have to look more carefully at decision making within these institutions. That is, understanding the urban and regional implications of pension fund capitalism ought to proceed from the micro-economic foundations of decision making, rather than assuming there is a magic formula to be found in macro-economic imperatives. This is important for the study of financial markets, and economic geography, in general (compare Ellison and Glaeser 1997). In particular, we need a better understanding of trustee decision making, with respect to the allocation of assets between asset classes, and the choice amongst investment products that may, or may not, have certain inherent spatial biases. In this sense, the geography of pension fund capitalism could be understood to emerge from the decisions taken about the nature and focus of investment, rather than assuming an inevitable spatial preference or, more concretely, an inevitable spatial fix. Indeed, the premiss behind the pensions project is that the spatial consequences of pension fund investment management can only be understood by linking the process of decision making with the context of those decisions (in all its complexity).

## Notes

1. See the Goldman Sachs report (Moon et al. 1998) on the evolving patterns of concentration in the Anglo-American investment management industry. They compare the US situation 1986 with 1996, showing that 'the top 20 asset managers have grown the share of assets under management . . . to 49% from 43%' (p. 22). Moon et al. (1998) also have interesting comments on the increasing importance of size and scope for minimizing the costs of management. In this respect, firms that are able to combine the retail side with the wholesale side of the business may have a significant long-term advantage over specialized asset managers.

2. In their survey of the international funds management industry *Pensions & Investments* (7 July 1997, 18–19), the industry newspaper, reported that the top 300 money managers in the world held $21.2 trillion in assets and although these managers are spread around the world, more than two-thirds of all assets are managed by firms from just three countries: the USA, Japan, and the UK (in that order). Recent mergers has concentrated further the control of pension fund assets notwithstanding doubts raised by plan beneficiaries, consultants, and managers about the efficiency of such concentration for investment performance.

3. There is considerable research on the reasons for differences between the continental European systems and the Anglo-American systems. Boot and Thakor (1997) argue that the former are dominated by banks because of the high costs of agents' separate attempts to gather information on firms' prospects combined with banks control of the innovation process in existing financial markets. On the other hand, financial markets have come to dominate the Anglo-American economies because of the low costs and widespread availability of third-party information about firms' actual performance. Boot and Thaker conclude that, if left to themselves, financial markets come to dominate banks as sophistication increases with respect to the collection and dissemination of financial data.

4. It is also true that the increased burden of reporting requirements mandated by government regulation has encouraged plan sponsors of all kinds to move towards simpler pension plan benefit systems like defined contribution plans. This is an issue of considerable significance in the USA where defined benefit plans have dominated the large pension plan sector and the nature and structure of the investment management industry. This kind of shift in benefit structure may have significant consequences for retirees' long-term welfare (see Paine 1993).

5. There has been considerable interest in recent years in the ways in which people make decisions under uncertainty. While decision theory has been dominated by subjective expected utility models that, at most, assume measured risk or certainty equivalents, recent literature has sought to understand both the nature of uncertainty and the ways in which people cope with and adjust to uncertainty. For a very useful beginning on this literature, see Einhorn and Hogarth (1986).

6. It is apparent from industry studies and studies of mutual fund performance that the cost structures of investment management can have significant effects on net returns. Indeed Carhart (1997*b*) has shown that differences in costs are very important in explaining differences in mutual funds' net performance from one year to the next. In the main, expensive funds under-perform the relevant benchmarks. Likewise, expensively managed pension funds also appear to under-perform their peers.

7. There is a subtle issue embedded in these observations which distinguishes the pension fund investment management from many other kinds of economic activity involving delegation (compare with Garud and Shapira 1997). Social scientists typically suggest or imply that failure to perform in relation to market imperatives is a cost borne by owners and/or managers and employees. Profits and management salaries may decline, shareholders' equity be extinguished and employees lose their jobs. Although it is reasonably believed that managers are delegated the task of managing by shareholders, this notion of delegation does not seem to capture the strength of the underlying paternalistic relationship between trustees and beneficiaries. Not far from the inherited common law meaning of trustee fiduciary duty is a moral obligation to protect the welfare of beneficiaries. Agency relationships are fraught with all kinds of imperatives, legal and moral (see Black 1992).

8. Many pension fund trustees are conscious of the difficulties of monitoring consultants' actions, recognizing the possibilities of hubris and opportunism. See Roll (1986) for an early treatment of hubris, referring to corporate decision making and see Williamson (1985) on opportunism.

9. Whereas Williamson (1985: 167) believes credible commitments necessarily involve 'irreversible, specialised investments' in funds management, such investment seems less significant than other, more relationship-based signals of commitment. Notice, however, that there is a dilemma embedded in such relationships: at one level, relationships involve personal commitments while, at another level, the continuity of such personal commitments are undercut by mobility in the industry and firms' interests in sustaining the institutional links between organizations rather than personal loyalties which may evaporate in the future.

10. In the economic sociology and economic geography literature, trust is perceived as the core principle which functionally integrates economic agents in long-term exchange relationships (see generally Misztal 1996). There is no doubt that this is an important thread, allowing us to see beyond the standard neo-classical ideal of discrete exchange. But it runs the danger of leaving behind the world of exchange relations dominated by decision variables such as costs and profits. MacNeil's notion of relational contracts retains the world of commerce while recognizing '[r]elations involve a flow of exchanges, or often many flows at the same time, occurring in complex patterns not lending themselves to divisions

into discrete periods' (p. 86). It should be acknowledged that this model of inter-firm relations is thought to be more consistent with Japanese corporations than Anglo-American finance firms (see Milhaupt 1995). We should take care not to exaggerate its importance.

11. In this Chapter, I am not concerned with the city–suburban dynamics of the industry (compare with Bodenman 1998). From industry sources, it remains an open question whether the city–suburban split is a significant issue with respect to the investment process. Face-to-face contact can be episodic, rather than continuous and still be very effective. On the other hand, to the extent that suburban locations affect cost constraints then the city–suburb split may be more important.

12. This has become an important option in Canada. There the federal government has encouraged the development of provincial and national investment trusts (Labour-Sponsored Investment Funds) (LSIF) some of which are sponsored by unions and community development groups. The Canadian government has used tax provisions to stimulate individual retirement savings and an indigenous investment trust industry through LSIFs. The previous NDP Ontario Provincial Government established under their Labour-Sponsored Venture Capital Corporations Act of 1992 the option for union-sponsored investment funds to take advantage of the federal tax benefits. One such fund is the Ontario Investment and Growth Fund launched in early 1995 by a group of unions including the United Steelworkers of America. In part, the objectives of the fund include earning 'a satisfactory long-term rate of return' and promoting 'job creation and economic development in Ontario'. More information on LSIFs can be found at <http://www.workingventures.ca/libr.html>.

# 5

# Competition and Innovation in Investment Management

WHILE this issue is much debated, understanding the imperatives driving pension fund investment, especially in relation to the nature of investment strategies and products, requires a better appreciation of the financial services industry and, in particular, the investment management industry.[1] There have been, of course, many studies of money management and mutual funds. However most address competitive inter-fund financial flows, rather than the production of investment management services.[2] It is a remarkable industry on a number of counts. Most obviously, it is highly concentrated. In the USA, about fifty or so large firms dominate the management of pension and insurance assets (see Gompers and Metrick 1998). Likewise, a handful of firms dominate the Australian and UK industries (see Clark et al. 1996). These firms are increasingly international, often controlled by vast holding companies, and compete with one another in these and other overlapping Anglo-American markets.[3] At the same time, there are many, many other smaller firms in the industry offering services and products similar to the larger, successful players (Noyelle 1991 has a similar discussion of the patterns of concentration in other advanced service industries). It is relatively easy for small firms to enter local markets for investment services, particularly if those firms are formed by the exodus of managers from larger firms. There are significant and persistent differences between firms with respect to their structure and organization.

This chapter is a theoretical treatment of the investment management production process, focusing upon three crucial issues: management costs, investment performance, and product innovation. For the most part, I deal with the costs of management in the next section, reflecting recent studies of industry competition (Armstrong 1997; and Helm and Jenkinson 1997). Subsequently, I show that producing investment services is quite unlike other production processes; any analogy with manufacturing production processes that relies upon a priori defined standards of production would be quite misleading. Theoretical inspiration is drawn from evolutionary economics, although modified to reflect important aspects of the industry not captured by importance attached to the Darwinian ethos which underpins many models of economic arbitrage, dominance, and succession (compare Dosi and Orsenigo 1988, with Shleifer and Vishny 1997). This is followed by an analysis of the relationship between regulation and competition in the industry, emphasizing the economic geography of the industry. In the penultimate section, the chapter draws together the previous threads of argument with a discussion of the innovation process in the industry.

There are many reasons for being interested in the competitive structure of the Anglo-American investment management industry. Most obviously, our analysis complements related studies of the investment management industry, and its economic geography (nationally and internationally; Chapter 3). This particular chapter focuses upon aspects of the industry that are essential in understanding its apparent current preoccupation with short-term performance. Just as importantly, the chapter aims to contribute to a better understanding of claims made about the distinctiveness of the Anglo-American financial sector, an issue of considerable policy relevance (witness recent attempts of the European Commission to harmonize the European market for financial services; see European Commission 1997) and theoretical relevance (witness recent arguments about the possible persistence of geographically and sectorally differentiated regimes of accumulation; see Storper and Salais 1997). Most importantly, the chapter is a further step in understanding the scope of pension fund capitalism, with respect to mobilizing finance for other sectors of the economy and, in particular, investment in urban infrastructure (a topic of special concern to economic geography).

I must be clear at the outset, however, about the limits of the chapter. Being about theoretical issues, it has a limited empirical agenda. I am conscious that there are no tests of the propositions advanced in the chapter. For the most part, the chapter seeks a better conceptualization of a complex and variegated industry. To the extent that I refer to data, this is for illustrative purposes. At the same time, it should be acknowledged that the analysis reported in this chapter is based upon industry interviews and open-format discussions with UK, US, and Australian firms, consultants, and trustees. The logic of argument underpinning the project relies upon this raw material to construct general propositions regarding competition and innovation. In doing so, I am also conscious that the theoretical logic is explorative rather than definitive, engaging conventional notions of market efficiency and arbitrage so as to redefine the scope of the industry. If stylized facts can be thought to result from this strategy, those facts have at least the virtue of being derived from experience.

## Structure of the Industry

The investment management industry is global in scope. Being intimately linked to the financial services industry, it is found in every major financial centre. At the same time, it is dominated by Anglo-American firms. In part, their dominance can be explained by close contractual relationships with the large Anglo-American pension funds—over the last couple of decades, the burgeoning assets of these funds have transformed the structure of national and global securities' markets (see Moon et al. 1998). As well, the Anglo-American investment management industry has been at the cutting-edge of managing money and promoting product innovation. The combination is now formidable, rivalling the established banking and insurance sectors of many European countries. As a consequence, investment management has become an essential component of financial holding companies; mergers and acquisitions between the banking and insurance sectors and the investment management industry has transformed the industry during the 1990s (Jackson 1997).

Basically, the investment management industry has two functions. It manages the flow of money between the various institutions that make up the pension and insurance systems of most advanced economies. For example, specialized custodians such as State Street Bank of Boston collect, tag, and distribute the flow of contributions to service providers and, in return, distribute the flow of returns back to their client pension funds' beneficiaries. I describe the flow of money with respect to pension plans in more detail in Chapter 4. Here, it is sufficient to observe that managing the flow of money carries with it heavy administrative and, in most countries, statutory obligations. It is an aspect of the Anglo-American pension system which has attracted the close scrutiny of regulators and fund administrators. The investment management industry also manages the investment of assets for most pension funds and insurance firms. In this respect, the industry is organized around collecting, sorting, and valuing information relevant to the desired investment objectives of their clients. The industry is also a massive siphon, collecting money from all kinds of sources to be managed in relation to investment opportunities from around the world.

Competition in the industry revolves around three issues. *The cost of management* is defined as the percentage share of the investment mandate taken by the manager as its fee. This varies a great deal. A recent survey by Greenwich Associates (1996*a*) of US pensions funds put the mean fee at about 39 basis points (0.39 per cent) and ranging between 5 to 80 basis points. The costs of management are high for the first tranche of assets, but rapidly decline with increasing volumes of assets. There are apparent economies of scale in managing money, particularly if desired investments are conventional, market-based traded products.[4] Economies of scale are not, however, infinite. With respect to the mutual fund industry, for example, there are dis-economies of scale that can profoundly affect funds' rates of return. The larger more successful funds tend to close-off the entry of new money to those funds in order to maintain their flexibility in relation to market volatility. Where tranches are relatively small, it is common practice for investment firms to 'pool' assets from various sources into well-defined investment products so as to minimize the costs of management for individual clients. While it is not uncommon for funds to demand exclusive 'tailored' investment products, reflecting the specific objectives of funds and, sometimes, the preferences of pension plan beneficiaries. Tailoring can be expensive.

The costs of management are continuously under pressure. Ease of entry into the industry combined with the conventional investment tastes of pension fund trustees means that all firms are strongly affected by this issue. But also vital is the *investment performance of managers* measured as the net annual rate of return of the manager for a specific product set against an appropriate benchmark agreed to by both the fund and manager *prior* to the commencement of the mandate. This kind of competition could be referred to as 'yardstick' competition, although the term has been used in the context of regulated firms (Shleifer 1985). I analyse this competitive dimension at length in subsequent sections of the chapter. Note that performance-dependent fees are relatively unknown in the industry.[5] Greenwich Associates (1996*b*) noted that only the largest pension funds use these kinds of incentives, and even then only relatively rarely. The size of an investment mandate typically determines managers' fees subject to prior agreement on a tranche of money consistent with the underlying economies of funds management.

At the margin, the third competitive dimension is *product innovation*. Most pension funds choose conventional, well-recognized asset allocation formula determined, in part, by other related funds in the industry. Trustees are risk-averse, and are very conscious of industry practice

(Chapter 7). But, in general, large corporate funds tend to have more similar asset allocation formula than similarly sized public pension funds. The large private funds tend to avoid venture capital investments and related urban infrastructure investments while the larger public funds are more diversified in this regard. Nevertheless, product innovation is important for all funds. Larger corporate funds, especially those sponsored by multinational firms, have sought new kinds of products that can protect them against currency fluctuations. Similarly, some public pension plans have promoted the development of alternative investment products relevant to economic development. Unlike conventional products dominated by relative costs and performance, innovation commands higher fees for complex, non-replicated expertise. Having sufficient expertise may be a significant barrier to entry.

With respect to the costs of management, variable costs are more important than fixed costs which are more important than sunk costs. For many firms, variable costs dominate the internal management of the firm and ultimately determine the rate of profit. Collecting, sorting, and valuing the information necessary to make investment decisions is both labour intensive and often dependent upon third-party information providers. At the top of the compensation scale are the investment manager 'stars' of the firm—successful investment managers who, sometimes, attain a cult following in the industry. At the bottom of the salary scale are the clerical/electronic information processing staff. Celebrated instances of defection from one firm to another by 'stars' keen to maximize their annual bonuses has reinforced the income gap while adding pressure on firms' individual and collective costs of management. In-between are support-staff which are fixed costs in the sense that they are necessary for meeting the accounting and reporting requirements of clients and regulators. Fixed costs have become more important as regulatory oversight has strengthened often lax and inadequate internal supervision systems (see Goode 1994*a* and *b* on the UK Maxwell debacle). On the other hand, these functions have been increasingly outsourced as investment firms have concentrated on more limited, higher-value functions.

Ten years ago, sunk costs were quite unimportant. But this has changed as leading firms increasingly rely upon highly specialized software, information technology, and computer systems to manage information and money processing systems. Not only are systems highly complex, they are also vulnerable to rapid obsolescence by virtue of competitors' investments and the rapid pace of exogenous technological change in software engineering. If an investment firm is to be competitive in the core product markets of the finance industry, high levels of recurrent expenditure in information processing is essential. The entry of large mutual funds into the funds management market has added further pressures in this regard. But the combination of capital specificity and high turnover means that any investment in information technology is more than likely to become a sunk cost. Therefore the options are either to merge with large financial services holding companies or retreat to skill and expertise niches which are based upon judgement and experience rather than large-scale information processing.[6] This second option is the domain of new market entrants, and small boutique firms.

## Firm-Specific Production Routines

The next step is to draw out the distinctive characteristics of the investment management industry and the necessary heterogeneity of firm behaviour in the industry. All industries are different one from the one another if the focus is upon the 'rich' detail of particular industries. The trick is to identify the crucial differences with respect to a common theoretical framework (Schmalensee 1982). In this section, the particular attributes of the investment management industry are sketched out by comparing an idealized investment management firm and an idealized manufacturing firm (compare Allen and Gale 1994).

Let us begin by narrowing the potential scope for difference by identifying two firms (*a* and b) who are representative of their industries A and B. Industry A is the fund investment management industry and industry B is a manufacturing industry like the auto component parts industry. It is assumed that there are no significant differences between *firm a* and b with respect to their ownership, objective functions, and constraints: firms *a* and b are assumed to be privately held, profit maximizers whose flow of net revenue per unit increases with the volume of output. Being profit maximizers, both firms strive to maintain and expand market share (market share determines output which determines the rate of profit). To make the argument simple, it is also assumed that both companies face potential new entrants or existing rivals for contracts. That is, competitors must meet industry standards with respect to minimum costs of production or else lose their contracts (and market share) at year-end when all contracts are reviewed by the purchasers of services. In these ways, I assume (for the sake of convenience) that both firms are entirely conventional with respect to standard industrial organization theory (see Scherer and Ross 1990).

Having assumed firms *a* and b to be alike in all practical respects except for their industry affiliation (and hence the products they produce), let us set out the contractual process. Assume that at time *t* both firms write contracts with their clients to provide services over the period *t* to *t + 1* ( a year), assuming each firm specializes in one kind of product. Let us also assume that *firm a* provides managed domestic fixed income products and firm b provides headlights and auto-related lighting equipment. By convention, firms *a* and b win their contracts at time *t* on the basis of their past performance relative to their competitors and that the determinants of their performance are imperfectly understood by their competitors. Put slightly differently, it is assumed that over the short run competitors cannot exactly match or mimic the two firms' somewhat hidden qualities as service providers. Now, we can introduce a crucial difference between the industries: competitive advantage in industry A is based upon, *ceteris paribus*, achieving higher-than-average rates of return at the end of the period *t* to *t + 1*, whereas competitive advantage in industry B is based upon meeting a priori agreed design and output specifications of the product. By industry custom, purchasers of services roll-over contracts at *t + 1* for the period *t + 1* to *t + 2* (another year) if service providers can meet these standards.[7]

What does this difference between industries mean? Unlike firm b, *firm a* has to achieve a moving target—a standard which is generally identified at the beginning of the contractual period but whose exact resolution is only known at the end of the period.[8] By contrast, the general and exact specifications of firm b's standards are known at the beginning of the period and both parties (the buyer and seller of the service) are continuously aware of firm b's performance with respect to that standard throughout the contractual period. *Firm a* produces an end-of-period outcome and, given the time-dependent comparative measure of that performance, how it achieves (if it achieves) a better than average performance is essential in distinguishing itself from other firms. Not surprisingly, *firm a* has an interest in keeping information from other competitors about how it achieves better than average results. Firm b's expertise is not so contingent. It may develop special routines for meeting set standards but the processes by which its product is produced are well known in the industry and are often determined by buyers. Firm b's expertise is one of managing production systems, coordinating inputs and controlling costs within well-defined parameters. By contrast, *firm a* relies upon its expertise to *out-perform* other competing firms.

If both firms are successful in their different ways, and if that success is rewarded by the roll-over of contracts from one period to the next, it is easy enough to imagine that internal administrative routines are established in both firms which capitalize on the identified ingredients of each firm's success. Here, I use the term *routines* in much the same way as Nelson and Winter (1982): the term refers to systematic behavioural practices or customary modes of organizational response integrated into the management of the firm. For *firm a*, the kind of routines referred to here are most likely related to the real-time process of investment management including the timing of trades within and between portfolios of government securities. For firm b, the relevant routines may involve coordination between parts of the production process including, for example, the determination of where in the production process quality assurance is best sampled. For both firms, these routines may be treated over the short term as fixed costs. Over the long term, of course, these routines may also become identified within each industry as successful routines, so successful in fact that other firms seek to emulate them as a means of enhancing their own relative competitiveness. Here, then, is a glimpse of Alchian's world of inter-firm and intra-industry competitive selection—convergence upon efficient industry routines.

This apparent theoretical presumption in favour of the convergence of routines around industry standards depends, however, upon suppressing crucial differences between the two industries. If convergence on industry-based routines is typical of firms in industry B, in industry A it is fleeting over the short term, and unstable over the long term. To demonstrate how and why this is the case, I return to the point made above: that *firm a*'s end-of-period performance is temporally dependent and inter-firm contingent. Imagine that *firm a* did out-perform most firms over the period $t$ to $t + 1$ and imagine that, as a consequence, routines are put in place within the firm to institutionalize the investment protocols used during $t$ to $t + 1$, over the period $t + 1$ to $t + 2$. Should *firm a*'s past purchasers and recently attracted purchasers of its investment services be confident of achieving the same level of performance over the next period of time? Having got their control protocols right, firm b could reasonably guarantee to match or even improve on the past period's results. Should *firm a* make such a guarantee? *Firm a*'s clients should not be so confident, nor is it credible for *firm a* to simply extrapolate past performance into the future.

To illustrate we analysed the 'average' investment manager's performance for five common asset classes (domestic and international fixed interest, domestic and international equities, property, and cash) in Australia over the period 1988–1997 (Figure 5.1).[9] Data was provided by Rainmaker Information Services using reported monthly rates of return for Australian and international investment managers providing services to Australian clients. Our objective was to determine the predictability of relative performance month-to-month, and over yearly and three-yearly moving periods. In doing so, I sought to identify the 'value-added' of the average manager and the stock selection and management skills of the average manager set against common benchmarks used by industry analysts, consultants, and fund trustees. Value-added was measured as the difference between the monthly compounded rate of return, and the asset class' annual return as indicated by the relevant index. The indices chosen were entirely conventional, including the All Ordinaries Accumulation (domestic equities) and the MSCI World Accumulation (international equities).

In Figure 5.1, I present the yearly data on the annual value-added of the average manager. There are considerable differences between the five asset classes. For instance, with respect to domestic equities, the average manager produced positive value-added over the period, whereas the average manager often produced negative value-added for international equities. Value-added for international fixed interest was also quite variable year-to-year, whereas the average manager's value-added for domestic fixed interest was negligible after 1991. Significantly, it is shown in Figure 5.2 that on a year-to-year basis (with the exception of 1990), the average manager's value-added was dominated by the combination of the five asset classes' indices, with managers' asset allocation decisions making a minor positive contribution to average returns, and active stock selection making a negative contribution to average returns. That is, the average balanced manager's performance was dominated by the passive index component. Active management (represented by stock selection and asset allocation) had, overall, a negative effect on average returns. Notice also the second graph in Figure 5.2. The difference between the best and worst balanced manager over the entire period was often very small: the difference between the two was sustained by a few episodes of relatively poor performance cumulating over the entire period.

In summary terms, it was found that month-to-month performance *relative to the relevant benchmarks* was virtually random, and that year-to-year performance of the average manager simply tracked the relevant class indices. Consequently, on average it would seem that a passive stance was better than an active stance once management fees were taken into account. Over longer periods of time, it was apparent that an important determinant of the average managers' performance

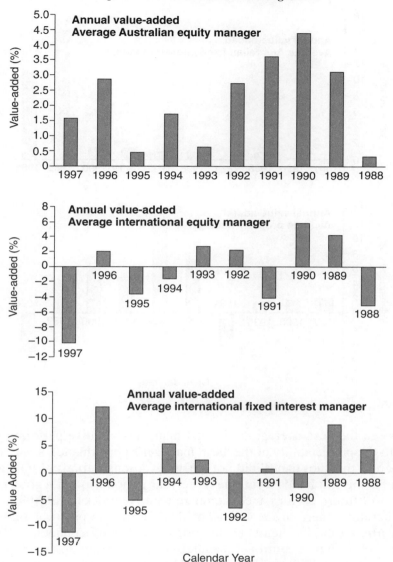

FIG. 5.1. Annual value-added

was the allocation of assets between classes, as opposed to either stock selection and/or management skills. Furthermore, the best manager's performance was, overall, more volatile than the average manager's performance and, as a consequence, worse than average, once I took into account compounded rates of return. There were significant differences

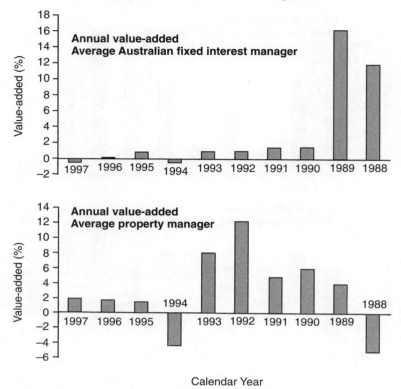

Fɪɢ. 5.1. (*Cont.*)

between the best, average, and worst managers' relative performance. As to the predictability of the 'best' manager's performance, it was also apparent that 'hot hands' did not persist over long periods of time and that having 'hot hands' over one three-year period was not a good predictor of future performance (compare with Hendricks et al. 1991).

Therefore, there are a variety of theoretical-cum-practical reasons why *firm a* (and its clients) should not share firm b's confidence. First, quite apart from its control of the internal management process, *firm a*'s control over its end-result is quite unlike firm b's. In fact, *firm a*'s performance is actually contingent on anticipated and unanticipated economic events, and others' anticipated and unanticipated actions with regard to those events. These others, their competitors, are, for all intents and purposes, uncontrollable (even unknowable). Second, *firm a*'s performance depends, in large part, upon the contemporaneous match between its understanding of the significance of economic events in relation to others' understanding of those events, their understanding

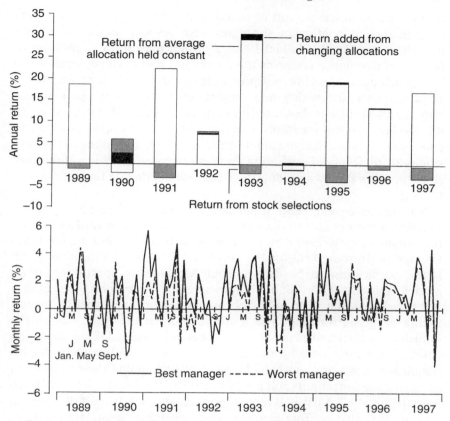

FIG. 5.2. Return analysis for average balanced manager

of *firm a*'s likely response, and so on. To be systematic, to establish and routinize investment protocols, requires *firm a* to develop a model of the world which can be used to assign value to events and thereby predict the behaviour of the economic system and the expectations of those who make decisions about the significance of events. If the economic world and the actions of others are measured accurately, and if others act consistently with respect to the identified logic of *firm a*'s model, then it may be possible to replicate past relative performance (Grossman 1989).

But knowledge about the world and others' actions may be unreliably compromised by uncontrollable noise (F. Black 1986). Others' actions may be profoundly unpredictable because of their unobserved heterogeneous expectations—search costs being too significant in relation to the potential pay-off of search. And others may have different models, indeed contrarian strategies with respect to others' known models of the world (Malkiel 1990). Another reason for caution about *firm a*'s performance concerns the contingent nature of performance—it depends upon applying past protocols to current and forecast events. If the circumstances which made that match efficient in the past change, only time will show if those routines remain efficient. By then, however, it is too late to cover shortfalls in performance. Knowing that, even firms committed to a particular model of the world are conscious of the possibility of their model exploding. In these circumstances it is quite possible that *firm a* may abandon their base model *during* the period *t + 1* to *t + 2*.

Now imagine by the end of period *t + 1* to *t + 2* it becomes apparent that *firm a* was not able to out-perform its benchmark or yardstick. Does this mean that its client base would switch to another higher-than-average performing firm for the period *t + 2* to *t + 3*? Presumably this is the implication to be drawn from Alchian's competitive survival model. Actually the available empirical evidence suggests that clients are slow to switch from relatively under-performing firms to higher-than-average performing firms. For evidence on the retail side of the industry, see Sirri and Tufano (1993). It could be argued that transaction costs of switching are a barrier to mobility, and it could also be argued that search costs are another barrier, notwithstanding the existence of performance consultants and publications (on the retail side) like *Morningstar* (in the USA), which reports performance along a set of common criteria. It is also entirely plausible that, assuming clients are aware of the contingent nature of performance, and assuming their interest in minimizing transactions costs, switching is a slow process because, *ceteris paribus*, one, two, or three periods of poor performance may be insufficient to make a decision about the long-term *pattern* of comparative performance. Unanticipated events, aberrant behaviour, noisy information, and the like can all be reasonably invoked to explain poor short-term results.

But convergence is unlikely for another reason. To consistently perform better than average requires a competitive edge relative to other firms in the industry. That edge may be technological (computer power and especially designed software), it may be specialized expertise (a group of traders and asset managers who are knowledgeable about how markets function), and it may be intellectual (theories of market behaviour, etc.). To perform better than average requires differentiation; distinguishing the firm by virtue of its investment protocols. So to converge on an industry standard, a recognized mode of investment practice would mean accepting (at best) an average rate of return and, most likely, a lower-than-average rate of return once transaction costs are fully accounted. And since there are significant economies of scale involved in managing funds, defections from *firm a* will likely affect its profitability and the average costs borne by remaining clients. At this point, active portfolio management routines may be less efficient than passive index instruments. But if passive instruments are preferred, there is no reason to contract asset management services from specialty firms like *firm a*.

## Competitive Strategy and Industry Structure

To this point, though, little has been said of inter-firm competition and the effects of strategic interaction with respect to industry structure. All that has been assumed is a type of firm which is procedurally rational to the extent that it chooses amongst the available options so as to maintain and increase its market share (and maximize profit). Such goal-oriented decision-making need not be conscious. Modern biological theory emphasizes the incremental nature of evolution, whereby step-by-step moves towards functional efficiency are rewarded, while moves away from efficiency are penalized. In the economic world, according to Alchian, firms that, for whatever reasons, move towards efficiency survive, and firms that move against efficiency perish (Alchain 1950). Here, though, let us assume strategy matters and conscious choice amongst strategic variables is important in firm decision making (Doyle 1989). The next step is to consider the effects of deliberate, inter-firm oriented competitive strategy.

Imagine that, by virtue of the particular history and geography of the market, *firm a* competes against two other firms in industry A, each of whom has a distinctive and different product. For argument's sake, we can assume that *firm a* offers a fixed interest product and the other firms offer, respectively, a domestic equity product and a property portfolio product. Assuming that the number of firms in industry A is fixed over the short term ($t$ to $t + 1$) but subject to change over the longer term (beyond $t + 1$); assuming a fixed market in terms of the volume of pension funds to be managed; and, assuming the importance of increasing economies of scale for lower per-unit service charges, we can identify a set of likely inter-firm competitive strategies. In essence, it is presumed that inter-firm competition is a zero-sum non-cooperative game, sustained by the threat of new entrants to the market and the continuing demand of pension fund trustees for lower per-unit service fees.

The first strategy *firm a* may consider is a strategy of product diversification by *modifying* its existing product to include, for example, an international fixed income option. Modification has two virtues. It uses the current expertise of *firm a*'s investment managers, and it allows the firm to process investment funds using its existing technology. If it costs more to offer a modified domestic fixed income product, these costs may be more than offset by the scale economies of additional funds managed. Of course, other firms may also modify their existing products in an attempt to attract more pension funds (the firm offering a domestic equity product may offer, as well, a blended international equity product). Alternatively, given the possibility of attracting few additional funds, each firm might *align* itself with a partner from another market which has the capacity to manage extra funds at a very low marginal (comparative) price. A more aggressive strategy may be to *match* other competitors by introducing products that add to *firm a*'s capacity to attract funds from other firms which offer similar products. Fund trustees might switch funds from one firm to another if *firm a* could sustain the argument that superior performance in its core product would flow over to the performance of other unrelated products. Over time, then, *firm a* may offer a range of related products which overlap one another, thereby attracting or maintaining scale economies, and which overlap the mix of products offered by close competitors.

The most aggressive strategy would be to *mimic* the investment style of leading competing firms.[10] To mimic another firm is, in effect, to draw upon the superior reputation of that firm, and display to pension trustees and their consultants a commitment to a style of investment that is apparently generally successful over the long term (beyond $t$ to $t + 2$). There are two ways of accomplishing such a strategy. One way would be to hire the other firm's principal investment managers, buying both their reputations and, presumably, the other firm's performance in one hit. Another way would be to obtain information about the other firm's investment style and package that information in a manner designed to represent a distinctive approach to investment management. Notice that this kind of information is not particularly difficult to obtain over the long term. Industry networks and the mobility of labour between firms is such that inter-firm information sharing is very common. As well, the formal process of bidding for contracts to manage pension funds encourages the articulation of investment styles and the flow of information about those styles throughout the industry. Each firm has an interest in keeping information about investment routines secret, so as to protect their performance advantage if successful and allow for adaptation if unsuccessful. On the other hand, if each firm is to be credible, it must share information with fund trustees and their consultants.

Assuming a fixed volume of pension funds to be managed and a fixed number of competitors and product types, would pension fund investment management firms tend to converge around a common portfolio of products (the modification and matching strategies), and even converge around common investment styles (the mimic strategy)? With respect to the mimic strategy it is easy enough to imagine that this occurs, at least in the short run. But this scenario is implausible over the long term for a variety of reasons. For a start, in the previous section of this chapter it was argued that investment routines are unstable because investment performance is unpredictable. To converge on one industry style may be to converge on a lower-than-average standard of performance. In this situation, pension fund trustees would have no incentive to shift funds to competitors who simply mimic the investment style of an average performer, whatever the reputation of that firm. The analysis is also misleading because of the assumed fixed nature of competition. For potential competitors, entry into the investment management market is easy. Asset allocation and investment performance consultants often have superior knowledge about the market and the vulnerability of incumbent firms. These firms are commonly the source of new entrants promising new products, superior performance, and advanced investment management styles. By virtue of their position, they are able to exploit gaps in the market and profiles of performance (see Van Horne 1985). Their initial competitive advantage may be slight, but so too are their start-up costs (compare Tufano 1989).

There is a troubling aspect to this analysis. It seems to imply that markets are informationally efficient—that is, convergence is likely because of the easy availability of knowledge about investment routines to potential and incumbent market participants. It seems we have stumbled back into conventional finance theory, despite having queried its robustness in the previous section, and having ignored serious questions about its viability evident in the folk lore of the industry, if not the academic literature, for many years (as suggested by Summers 1986, compared with Jensen 1978). The analysis does suggest there are limits to the use of available information—matching and mimicking strategies may simply divide the available pension funds for management so that no firm is able to achieve sufficient scale economies to reach their target rate of profit. There are important objections to this kind of analysis which attack the possibility of informationally efficient markets (Grossman and Stiglitz 1980).

Information about investment routines is treated above as an unencumbered commodity, as if information can be exchanged between firms without reference to the structure of firms. New entrants, firms that hire employees from other firms, and investment managers (as opposed to firm principals) all have an incentive to claim that information is mobile. But the value of information may be firm-specific if, hidden from view, are company-based administrative processes which determine the quality and flow of information and its strategic application in the market. The way information is produced, assigned to investment managers, and used in relation to the investment behaviour of other firms in the market is, more often than not, quite particular to individual firms. This can mean that one firm's investment routines are not easily replicated in other firms despite their apparent transparency, and it can also mean that the performance of individual managers is so firm-reliant that their performance is actually representative of firm-specific endowments, rather than just their own information and expertise (compare D. Hirshleifer and Welch 1994). It is also possible that the value of information is created at the intersection of the firm's endowments and the talents of its investment managers. Thus, the defection of investment managers to new firms can cripple the performance of their previous firms; equally, their own performance in new firms may not meet their previous levels of performance.

The idea that information is fully mobile throughout the industry is sustained in the literature, at times, by reference to the ease of entry of new competitors into the market and the limited duration of first-mover advantage (as Tufano suggests). However, just because set-up costs are low for new entrants does not necessarily mean that incumbent firms are able to switch investment routines at will. Incumbent firms not only provide investment returns, they also often provide investment services like information to plan beneficiaries. Indeed, as firms develop in the industry in terms of size and complexity, their accumulated sunk costs (compared to new entrants' set-up sunk costs) become very important for maintaining long-term relationships with plan trustees and consultants. As sunk costs accumulate, the relevance of information about other firms' routines may actually decline in the sense that *firm a* (for instance) is neither able nor willing to discard accumulated sunk costs in the interests of mimicking other firms' investment routines. Such information may be relevant, though, in structuring inter-firm competitive strategies. Firm-specific accumulated sunk costs are a means of market differentiation, a means of signalling difference, recognizing that few other firms can actually match *firm a*'s combination of investment performance and service structure.

It is also important to realize that the type of information discussed here appears to be technical and known. At issue is the mobility of information (and hence the convergence of firms around industry standards) related to the process of investment management. Firms may be able to make risk-related decisions about the potential value of information, recognizing the possibility that information is not as unencumbered as sometimes supposed, and firms may be able to modify information, given their own internal configurations. In these ways, firm-specific market and investment routine information could have social value (in J. Hirshleifer's 1971 terms). At the same time, there is another class of information which may be private, even proprietary. This kind of information is that which relates to identifying (in Hirshleifer's terms) or discovering market value. In particular, investment firms may develop methods of determining market value which rely on theoretical insights that are specific to firms and their employees, and, as such, are less about the process of investment and more about the design of investment. It may be very difficult to trade or mobilize design-related information. If it is exchanged between firms, either intentionally or by default, such information may attract a price. Likewise, firms' investment managers may also be able to attract an explicit or implicit market premium.

The distinction between process and design information may seem vague. To illustrate, imagine *firm a* establishes a team of financial analysts whose task it is to discover a robust relationship between risk-and-return. Recognizing that this relationship is at best an ideal rather than a practical reality, any firm which discovered a foundation for that relationship in a manner which could be integrated into investment decision making could claim a large share of the relevant market. Such information could also attract a significant market premium. And firms would be differentiated according to both the use-value of that information and their capacity to pay for the information. In this respect, inter-firm rivalry would be influenced as much by the financial resources of the firm and its holding company, as by the relative expertise of its employees. Differentiation would occur within the industry as firms sought to rearrange their relative positions according to the relevance of that information to their particular investment products and their capacity to adjust. In these ways, the industry would be internally ordered and differentiated between large firms and small firms, between resource-rich firms and resource-poor firms (see Shleifer and Vishny 1997 for a related argument with respect to arbitrage).

## Regulatory Regimes and Competitive Advantage

The analysis so far provides a logical framework for understanding why convergence in investment routines is unlikely over the long term. Even so, one consequence of this analytical strategy has been to emphasize the internal organizing logic of inter-firm market competition thereby excluding from the analysis more formal regulatory mechanisms structuring market organization. Here, I add an explicit appreciation of the role and status of jurisdiction-specific mechanisms of market regulation and firm behaviour thereby 'creating' the economic geography of the industry (compare with Arthur 1986).

Assume *firm a* and its immediate rivals are located now, as in the past, in a particular jurisdiction. Assume that jurisdiction is differentiated from others by virtue of a set of statutes, rules, and regulations which codify legal and illegal behaviour by investment management firms, with respect to the design and processing of pension fund investments. Also assume, for the moment, that those rules are unique in the sense that they are particular to the jurisdiction. Three implications immediately follow from this idealized economic geography. First, firms located in other jurisdictions cannot easily enter the local market using generic products and investment practices. Second, as a consequence, there are significant local set-up costs for any firm from another jurisdiction. Third, assuming widespread compliance with local rules, local firms' investment products and practices reflect the particular configuration of local rules. For example, there may be no market for international equity or fixed income products because regulations do not allow pension funds to invest outside the local jurisdiction (a common stance of continental European countries; European Commission 1997).

With respect to the evolution of the local industry in relation to other jurisdictions, its particular attributes (structure and performance) could be understood to have been set by two basic organizing mechanisms: *sanctions* and *screens* (see Brennan and Pettit 1993). Sanctions are defined as a set of rewards and penalties imposed by either a centralized (non-market) agency or by decentralized, market-driven imperatives. Simply illustrated, if *firm a* were to offer an international fixed income product to local pension funds it would be penalized in a decentralized manner by fund trustees who, conscious of their legal liability, would refuse to invest in such a product, whatever its apparent (or potential) virtues. Likewise, if *firm a* diverted investment funds from one portfolio (domestic) to another (international), it may be penalized by the industry regulator. At the same time, *firm a* may well reap great rewards (market share and profit) from offering a domestic fixed income product which performs consistently better than average. For many firms, especially those local firms who entered the market after the regulatory regime was set in place, the system of sanctions would seem natural. In these ways, the configuration of competitive firms are likely to reflect the boundaries implied by those sanctions. It may also be the case that the regulatory regime reflects the desires of a select group of competitive firms (see Kane 1988, 1991).

Screens are a little different and are best understood as mechanisms which sort by virtue of the fit, or otherwise of firms in relation to market demand. For example, a pension fund administrator may call for tenders to manage a particular tranche of funds in accordance with certain specifications. Some firms will be willing and able to meet those specifications, those that are not will be screened out of the competition for the management contract. To illustrate, given the configuration of *firm a*, it may only be willing and able to bid for fixed income management contracts which are more than $100 million and less than $500 million. If the contract is for a fixed income management contract of greater than $500 million, *firm a* may be, in effect, screened out of the competition while other firms with more congenial configurations are screened into the competition for the contract. Typically, screens are decentralized and market-based. But it is possible to think of centralized screens like rules and regulations which require firms to have specific skills or insurance coverage when managing different kinds of products or different levels of investment. Sanctions and screens thus affect the scope and application of inter-firm competitive strategies, affecting the value for each firm (or type of firms) of modification, matching, and mimicking strategies.

In combination, sanctions and screens operate to differentiate firms (or types of firms) one from the other. In this respect, they function like systematic sieves, sorting and ordering firms into different market segments according to their attributes. The boundaries between segments may be blurred and permeable. But they may also be hard, monitored and policed by government agencies. In this context, then, changing regulations which affected the boundaries of segments may be an important stimulant for innovation in the pension fund investment industry. Thus, deregulation of the financial services industry could be understood as an instance of changing the sanctions and screens of a market which, in the past, served to structure the boundaries of the local industry (see Kane 1988 and M. Miller 1986). But notice that the effects of changing regulations would not be random. Since the location of local firms in the industry is not random, a change in regulations will benefit some firms and leave others relatively untouched (although, perhaps, relatively disadvantaged). The historical legacy of operating in a particular market segment will both structure firms' capacities to respond to new opportunities, and structure the choice amongst available strategic options. By this analysis, local firms are neither omnipotent nor epiphenomenal.

Imagine, however, industry A's regulatory agency is convinced by non-industry interests that product innovation has been stymied by the overwhelmingly parochial character of pension fund investment regulations. As a consequence, it begins a process of regulatory reform designed to harmonize local rules and regulations in relation to the rest of the Anglo-American world. Since many of these countries share an English trust law heritage, and share common conventions regarding the status of statutes in relation to common law, harmonization may be relatively straightforward at least at the level of formal public institutions. Harmonization may, however, be less clear-cut at the margins of imported or adapted local rules and regulations. Case-by-case adjudication of the meaning and application of those rules and regulations often depends upon jurisdiction-specific political values which are not as easily rationalized as formal statutory systems. For local firms like *firm a* which have specialized and have limited their competitive strategies to inter-firm competition in the local market, harmonization could be a significant long-term threat to their place in the local industry.

To appreciate why this may be the case I must return to the assumptions made about the nature of the industry and *firm a*. A vital assumption of the analysis has been that there are significant scale economies in managing pension fund investments (see also Davis 1993). Scale economies are important for minimizing the cost profile of *firm a* with respect to other firms competing for management contracts. Let us assume, again, that the volume of pension funds to be managed are fixed in the short term so that any successful new product or new entrant to the local market would reduce the absolute share of other firms' managed funds (adversely affecting their costs of management). Also imagine that a new entrant to the market offers a new product (international fixed income) which has not been allowed prior to a change in local rules by the industry regulator. And if we assume that the new entrant has an existing international fixed income product which can be simply modified to incorporate local funds, then the new entrant may be very cost competitive with respect to local firms. Since the new entrant has expertise and experience as well as a documented track record of performance in managing their international fixed income product it may be impractical for *firm a* to match or mimic the new entrant over the long term.

Whereas previous to the change in local regulations their idiosyncratic nature protected local firms from outside competition, acting in effect as an exclusionary sieve, harmonization of local regulations within the Anglo-American system would act to reduce the effectiveness of exclusionary sieves and would also attack the relevance and significance of past inter-firm competitive strategies. In these circumstances, long-term relationships between local firms and trustees could help local firms protect their market, and concern about the predictability of new entrants' performance could also limit the potential for switching funds over the short term. At the same time, the possible introduction of more exacting external benchmarks and the scope for new products with existing (but outside) benchmarks could conspire to encourage a higher-than-expected rate of funds switching. Recognizing this possibility, it would not be surprising if firms like *firm a* lobbied the regulatory agency to slow the rate of harmonization and in other ways use existing rules and regulations to limit the introduction of modified products from outside sources. Another firm-based regulatory strategy may be to prompt the industry regulator to require new entrants to provide services to pension funds which require significant start-up costs or at least, joint ventures with local firms.[11]

In combination, sanctions and screens act as sieves sorting and ordering potential competitors into geographically structured product markets. But it is also clear that the existence of overlapping and harmonized regulatory regimes allows larger investment management firms to spread the costs of managing investment products across the Anglo-American world. To the extent that one jurisdiction is or becomes the leading regulatory innovator (even deregulator), whose rules and regulations are incorporated over time into other jurisdictions, a significant presence in the leading jurisdiction could be vital for firms in their competition with other firms across the world. In this kind of world, the costs of developing new products and of demonstrating their performance can also be spread between markets thereby lowering management costs and enhancing the competitive profile of such firms against industry standards. In this context, convergence is unlikely not because other firms wish to maintain their distinctiveness but because most firms are unable to keep up with leading firms in the race to develop and trial the performance of new products. Matching and mimicking strategies would be thereby reduced in value; local firms may have to retreat to market segments which remain, for whatever reason, relatively small and specialized.

## Paradox and Progress (Innovation)

The analysis of firm behaviour and strategy sketched in previous sections began with a set of quite restrictive assumptions: that *firm a* and like firms are unitary organizations, that they optimize objectives functions with common elements, that service provision in the pension fund investment management industry is characterized by increasing returns to scale, and that firms may have informational advantages over the short term if not over the long term. Also assumed, for clarity sake was an environmental condition: that the short-term volume of pension funds to be competitively managed is fixed. Underlying the analysis, of course, was an even stronger assumption that the industry analysed is the Anglo-American industry. From those assumptions, and the previous analysis, we were able to better understand the significance of potential and actual new entrants to the market. Here, we summarize the most important findings or propositions to be derived from our analysis, and assess their sensitivity to changing the initial assumptions.

Having assumed that firms aim to maintain and expand market share and hence maximize profit, our initial finding is that (1) competitive advantage in the industry is sustained by minimizing the costs of managing investment funds while maximizing returns on funds invested over and above the industry average or some appropriate benchmark. It was recognized, of course, that investment performance is at best unreliable and subject to considerable risk and, at worst, subject to unquantifiable and uninsurable uncertainty. In play here is the distinction emphasized by Frank Knight (1921). Even if the past were an adequate proxy for the future in terms of providing a risk profile of the investment product, there remains a significant element of uncertainty which could dramatically effect investment performance. This leads to finding (2) that because of uncertainty regarding the performance of investment routines, and because of the competitive need to achieve higher-than-average returns, differentiation of investment routines is a continuing impulse. If there is convergence upon an industry standard, convergence is fleeting.

With respect to inter-firm competitive strategy, three different types of strategies were analysed ranging from the simplest and least expensive in terms of new resources (product modification) through to more aggressive strategies like mimicking the investment routines of competitors. Finding (3) is that inter-firm strategy is profoundly affected by the need to enhance firms' competitive advantage recognizing the existence of potential new competitors and existing competitors in the industry. Of course, because of the impulse to differentiate investment routines inter-firm competition may, at times, unravel into competition between sets of apparently unrelated firms. Firms have an interest in limiting the universe of apparent competitors, they also have an interest in limiting the applicability of common benchmarks to firm-specific products. Thus our next finding (4) is that given the costs of introducing new products without an initial large pool of investment funds across which to spread management costs, innovation tends to be product modification rather than product invention. And because of the lack of performance records of new products, product adaptation is desired, more often than not, by pension fund trustees.[12]

We could imagine that, on the basis of these findings, the industry is practically chaotic. The lack of stable standards might be thought to encourage a cacophony of competition. But I would argue that (5) by virtue of the operation of non-firm-specific sanctions and screens firms have particular locations (or market niches) inside jurisdictions and distinctive market expertise between jurisdictions. Firms are neither omnipotent nor epiphenomenal—vertical and horizontal sorting is typical of the industry. In this context, I believe that (6) differences in rules and regulations between jurisdictions within the Anglo-American world and between Anglo-American jurisdictions and Europe reinforce the sorting process. Strong differences between jurisdictions in terms of rules and regulations may provide local firms with a distinct advantage in meeting client needs. On the other hand, as rules and regulations are harmonized between jurisdictions the major international firms tend to gain competitive advantage by virtue of their ability to cross-over common products between jurisdictions and thereby reap the rewards of lower costs of service provision.

From these findings there are two paradoxes at the heart of the process of product innovation in the industry. First, while the impulse towards differentiation may encourage innovation, the adoption of new innovations may be limited by virtue of the imperatives of building and maintaining competitive advantage. Second, the larger international firms which have the most well-established investment products and investment routines as well as the most articulated performance records, have the least incentive to promote product innovation other than product modification whereas the smaller companies, most often tied to particular markets, have greater incentives to promote product innovation but the shallowest expertise in designing and implementing new innovations. In this respect, perhaps the industry is not so different from others where the structure of competition and the system of institutionally centred sanctions and screens combines to create a distinctive pattern of innovation which favours smaller than larger companies.

It is reasonable to ask, however, how sensitive these findings are to the initial assumptions which could be thought to drive competitive practice in the pension funds investment management industry. What if we were to drop the assumption of unitary investment firms and introduce the possibility of different interests between agents (investment managers) and principals (investment firm owners)? Here, I suspect the impulse towards differentiation would be enhanced. As suggested in the previous section, the mobility of investment managers is a function of their performance and the market for distinctive investment routines. Whereas firms have an interest in standardizing investment routines inside their firms so that firms are recognized as the source of performance, if investment management employees are successful they have an interest in personalizing performance. Similarly, if the assumption of procedural rationality was relaxed in favour of satisfying behaviour or bounded rationality one could imagine that differentiation would become more entrenched. A comprehensive maximizing behavioural imperative would, in effect, protect differentiation. The initial behavioural assumptions were chosen because of their common acceptance. Relaxing these assumptions would seem to match the impulse towards divergence.

What of the assumptions behind competitive advantage? The assumption of scale economies and the emphasis on performance over time are empirically plausible. But there is some evidence of negative returns to scale which can make funds management unwieldy, difficult to manage in relation to the target market, and subject to enormous processing costs if flows in and out of the funds are unpredictable. If the size of investment pools can be strategically managed then, perhaps, economies of scale can be protected. Otherwise, economies of scale could evaporate enhancing the competitiveness of smaller, more tailored investment funds managed by smaller competitors. It is also the case that emphasis on investment returns matches industry prejudices. If risk was the crucial decision variable, as some would argue is more appropriate, then perhaps the pressure to differentiate products and investment routines would be replaced by a closer scrutiny and analysis of the determinants of risk per se rather than possible explanations of different returns. Even so, there are limits to this argument. In the end, uncertainty could be thought more important than risk. In that case, there is no stable reference point for comparing performance; thus industry practice necessarily emphasizes returns.

## Conclusions

More than twenty years ago, Robert Clark (1975: 1606) suggested that 'financial intermediation is one of the most significant institutional facts about advanced economic systems as they have developed this century'. He distinguished between financial intermediaries that obtain most of their funds from households (first-order institutions) and those that obtain most of their funds from other financial entities (second-order institutions). He chose to concentrate on the former, believing those were the most important institutions for mobilizing capital. At the turn of the twenty-first century, however, second-order intermediaries dominate first-order intermediaries. Thus, with respect to mobilizing capital (generally) and the financing of urban and regional development (in particular) it is essential to better understand the competitive structure and imperatives of innovation in the investment management industry. This has been recognized by writers such as Martin and Minns (1995); the challenge has been to articulate and sustain a model of competition and innovation in the industry relevant to this kind of interest.

If the essential task of financial intermediation is to mobilize capital for investment, the ultimate goal of pension funds is to invest contributed assets so as to enhance beneficiaries' welfare. To do so requires, more often than not, firms with expertise and competence in the investment process. Whereas some of the largest pension funds internalize the investment process, most large funds and almost all small funds rely upon the investment management industry for such services (Chapter 4). It is a very competitive industry, marked by high levels of concentration but, as well, large numbers of actual and potential competitors. Having developed an analytical understanding of the forces of competition in the industry, including reference to cost competition and performance competition, I then focused upon competition with respect to product innovation. At first sight, this is an important issue; the extent to which innovation is a crucial dimension of competition will determine the extent to which the industry is able to offer investment products beyond the conventional traded securities that currently dominate pension funds' asset allocations. But as I explained, innovation is often limited to matching and mimicking strategies and is limited by the capacity of firms to develop the expertise necessary to sustain the innovation process.

To get to this point required a detailed and idealized treatment of competitive practice in the industry. In general, the analytical structure of the chapter was based upon conventional assumptions of firm behaviour and industry structure. Even so, there were distinct departures from convention. By linking the analysis and conceptual apparatus to concepts congenial to evolutionary economics an attempt was made to emphasize the temporal contingency of firm behaviour and inter-firm strategy. While not dealt with in any detail, this analysis presumed that firm investment in routines and practices over time is, in effect, a form of cumulative investment. Firms have particular paths of development, firms learn-by-doing and may even fail by making mistakes about the putative efficacy of their choice of investment routines they also constrain their capacity to switch between routines. Thus, strategy matters as does the capacity of firms to anticipate the actions of others and respond to events (and the actions of others) which were not anticipated. Here, there are loose connections to be made between the approach of this chapter, and that of others like Doyle (1989), Nelson (1994), Zysman (1994), and Storper and Salais (1997) who are, in their different ways, conscious of the historical and geographical specificity of economic decision making.

Clearly, the theoretical approach taken in this chapter does not have the well-defined boundaries of conventional models of firm behaviour, industry structure, and the 'new' economic geography. But this is necessary if we are to integrate in a comprehensive manner the nature and structure of competition with the apparent dimensions of industry structure including the dominance of large, Anglo-American investment firms. Furthermore, this strategy is important if we are to identify the distinctive characteristics of the industry. Here, I emphasized the fact that relative performance is highly contingent, resolved only at the end of contractual mandates. In this respect, the industry is quite unlike manufacturing industries where the production process can be managed with respect to ongoing standards of performance. This is a particularly important aspect of the industry, one that has profound implications for product innovation. Therefore our analysis is related in substance, if not in precise analytical style, with other writers like Hahn (1989) who are prepared to sacrifice analytical precision in the interests of capturing the real time performance of firms and their strategic actions in competition with other firms.

## Notes

1. Porter (1992*a*) argued that institutional investors hold stocks, more often than not, for short-term stock market gain rather than being interested in the long-term dividend value of those stocks. Whole sectors may be starved of the 'patient' capital necessary to see innovative ideas translated into long-term

economic growth. But Wahal and McConnell (1997) argue that the presence of institutional investors allows managers greater discretion with respect to investment in research and development. Porter and Wahal and McConnell use very different methods of analysis, and have different views as to the effectiveness of competing systems of investment. This kind of debate is very relevant to that of Martin and Minns (1995) and others who contend that institutional investors' dominance of capital markets results in spatial polarization.

2. The most comprehensive treatment of the money management industry is to be found in Lakonishok, Shleifer, and Vishny (1992). Many studies of the mutual fund industry focus upon the relative 'efficiency' of asset switching by retail customers on the basis of fund performance over time. See also Hendricks et al. (1991). For those interested in a geographical approach to the money management industry, the reader is referred to Pryke (1994). Pryke's paper is a theoretically informed paper about the status of the money management industry in market economies and the institutions of capital focused upon urban property markets.

3. In this chapter we do not analyse the interrelations between parent holding companies and investment managers. This is an increasingly important research topic, but under-studied. See Berlin and Mester (1998) for a theoretical treatment, focusing upon the vertical integration of financial intermediation, and Jackson (1997), focusing upon the institutional and regulatory structures affecting such holding companies.

4. Data on the costs of management, and data on the administrative costs of pension funds and social security programmes are rare. Few funds disclose their costs, and very few plan beneficiaries have any idea of the relative costs of their funds and the managers they employ. The available academic evidence is slight indeed. One exception is Mitchell's (1996) study which reports on the cost structures of US pension funds (public and private), and different social security programmes around the world. She also reports on the apparent scale economies of funds management.

5. Goetzmann et al. (1998) have an interesting study of performance-based fees in the context of hedge funds. They note that most performance fees are 'high water mark' fees in that there is a financial incentive to reach a priori agreed portfolio share values (net returns); in many cases exceeding those values results in the application of a formula that shares 'excess' returns between the client and the manager. An example cited by the authors is the Soros Quantum Fund. They argue that this kind of compensation system is very sensitive to the size of assets managed; negative returns to scale set-in rather quickly.

6. In this respect, competition between investment firms may be more about the resources of their parent firms than, necessarily, about the immediate costs and prices of their investment services. For the sake of argument, we do not deal with this issue in the rest of the chapter. But it may be very important in partially explaining the recent international wave of mergers and acquisitions amongst complementary financial services firms. See Zingales (1998) on the consequences of 'deep pockets' for competitive survival in US industry (in his case, transportation).

7. We do not accept a common assumption made in the literature that the financial industry is just another version of all other industries. In particular, we do not accept most of Anderson and Harris's (1986) analytical-cum-theoretical

assumptions that (1) competition in the industry is best represented as an oligopolistic game; and (2) delayed entry is a problem for firms that imitate market leaders. As will become clear, we also dispute an implied assumption that financial products have a determinate (predictable) performance profile.

8. The temporal contingency of financial firms' economic performance has been recognized by other writers on service industries. Barcet (1991) argues that service provision is an act (or process) as opposed to a physical product. She goes on to suggest that the 'output notion traditionally used in economic theory would not be directly applicable' when conceptualizing production (p. 60).

9. The analysis reported in this section, draws upon the work of my colleague John Evans. Note, that the discussion is focused on investment managers' performance, not the performance of their pension fund clients. One of the rare studies of pension fund performance found little evidence of significant persistent differences between larger UK pension funds' performance over the period 1986–94 (Blake et al. 1997). Of the variation found, the overwhelming proportion of such variation was attributed to differences between funds in their allocations between asset classes—a finding consistent with our results reported in this chapter. They also found that larger funds tend to be over-represented in the under-performance group. It appears that they did not check for variation between types of funds (public, private, industry, etc). In the US and Australian cases, some analysts argue that there have been significant differences in performance between types of funds, although these differences are thought to have declined over the 1990s.

10. These kinds of matching strategies are common in all kinds of industries, not just investment management. For Bikhchandani et al. (1998), imitation is a fundamental human trait important in the explanation of the evolution of whole populations and economic organizations. From this perspective they develop a series of models that explain how and why imitation may translate into herd behaviour (a feature of financial markets and competitive strategy in investment management). To do so, they rely upon the notion of information cascades, wherein individuals learn (process information) by observing the actions of others. This idea is reintroduced in Ch. 6 to help understand trustee decision making.

11. The choice of regulatory standards, and the process of deregulation, are very important aspects of the contemporary European scene, affecting the likely long-term 'place' of the Anglo-American investment industry in the continental European economy. As Sobel (1997) shows in a theoretical context, yardstick setting can have significant implications for the timing of investment by firms in competitive markets, and can have significant implications for the competitiveness of existing capital endowments.

12. This is an important finding which may have ramifications across a variety of interests. For instance, it may help explain why it has been so difficult to develop alternative investment products relevant to urban and regional economic development. As well, it may have significant implications for those seeking to promote the introduction of new kinds of retirement savings products that are designed to cope with the risks associated with defined contribution pension benefits (see Bodie and Crane 1998).

# 6

# Pension Fund Trustee
# Decision Making

PENSION funds invest the vast bulk of their assets in stocks and bonds, hence their significance for Western stock markets and emerging markets. Even so, the allocation of assets between asset classes (stocks, bonds, property, etc.) as well as the choice of investment managers and products within classes are important decisions, repeatedly evaluated and revised by fund trustees in accordance with past and expected investment performance. In fact, the apparent stability of funds' asset allocations to stocks and bonds at any point in time hides an enormous flow of funds over time between asset classes and between investment managers and investment products. Why should we be interested in trustee decision making? Why should we analyse seemingly arcane issues like asset allocation and the choice of investment manager? Very simply, trustees control enormous financial resources. How they allocate those resources has had, and will have in the future, profound implications for cities, regions, and nations. This is only now being recognized in the geographical literature (see e.g. Martin and Minns 1995); understanding trustee decision making is an essential step in making sense of the macro, spatial patterns of economic development.

The available evidence suggests that trustees are quite conventional with respect to their allocation of assets to asset classes. Alternative investments (the terms used in the industry to refer to investments in urban and related projects) are a small proportion of all pension fund investments. While there are some investments in urban and related projects, it is common to observe amongst pension fund trustees both ignorance of the available opportunities and considerable resistance to any suggestion of altering the allocation of assets outside the conventional parameters of the industry. Understanding whether alternative investment products will gain a larger share of pension plan assets, if pension funds will make a significant contribution to urban infrastructure and community development needs, and if pension funds will encourage product innovation in the financial services industry, requires a better understanding of trustees' investment decision making. My goal here is to describe and explain the dominance of convention in trustee decision making.

The chapter is based upon detailed interviews with pension trustees, investment consultants, and managers. In the next section, the context of trustee decision making is sketched using a set of assumptions to focus the subsequent analysis. This is followed by a discussion of the frames which are structured upon trustee decision making. Here, my analysis is inspired by Kahneman and Tversky (1979).[1] But John Maynard Keynes (1921) is also important, especially in the penultimate section dealing with methods of analogical reasoning with respect to new types of investments relevant to urban needs. The chapter closes with a discussion of the significance of my analysis with respect to standard notions of rationality and optimality. Note that my 'map' of trustee decision making is tentative. It is based on detailed discussions with many in the finance industry, but it has not been formally tested. To do so would take us into the realm of experimental psychology.

## The Prototypical Trustee

The analysis of trustee decision making presented here reflects the Anglo-American world, a shared heritage of English common law and trust law. Of course, within those broad parameters there is a wide variety of pension plan types, legal requirements with respect to the funding plan liabilities, and formal arrangements regarding trustees' powers, all of which can be attributed to the distinctive characteristics and evolution of different political jurisdictions, industries, and firms. Here my goal is to sketch the prototypical trustee leaving aside, for the moment, differences between institutions, and the like so we can focus on crucial issues regarding the process of decision making. Inevitably, there will be a number of important issues that will be ignored using this strategy.

Let us assume our prototypical trustee is appointed to a board of trustees which is jointly trusteed. That is, there is an equal number of plan sponsor representatives and plan beneficiary representatives. This assumption has the advantage of suppressing the significance of the plan sponsor or sponsors in the decision making process and matches in substance a common formula of representation in the USA, as well as recent legislative initiatives in the UK and Australia (Blake 1995). Let us also assume that the plan sponsor operates across a variety of jurisdictions so that trustees are not necessarily loyal to any particular local constituency. This is, at times, an important issue in state and municipal public pension plans (in a subsequent chapter, this assumption will be dropped). And with respect to the age and experience of the trustee let us assume the trustee is neither especially endowed by intelligence and education nor especially ignorant. In essence, our trustee is just like the average plan beneficiary.[2] Plan trustees have hardly ever heard of the efficient markets hypothesis before being appointed and rarely are so important to the plan sponsor that their absence from their employer is missed in the management of the organization. I will refer to these assumptions as *identity assumptions*.

With respect to the pension fund there are a number of related assumptions which are essential to the analysis. Let us assume that the plan is primarily a defined benefit plan which promises to provide a certain level of pension benefits for retirement. Increasingly, defined benefit plans also offer voluntary contribution options for individual plan participants over and above their mandatory participation in the defined benefit plan. This issue will be considered later in the chapter. I also assume that the plan is relatively immature in that it has a net inflow of contributions relative to payments. Of course, over the long term the plan will likely experience a net outflow as an increasing number of plan beneficiaries retire. Two implications follow from these assumptions. First, the fund must estimate its long-term flow of liabilities and revise those estimates as basic parameters change over time (e.g. interest rates). Second, the likelihood of a net outflow of funds in the future means that trustees cannot be complacent regarding the current investment performance of the fund. Notice, however, no trustee remains at the fund until its obligations are exhausted. Trustees are appointed for an initial period of five years and may be reappointed for a further term of five years. Finally, it is assumed that trustees are paid for their membership of the board, although their renumeration is modest compared to their salary. I will refer to these assumptions as the *benefit assumptions*.

What are the goals of our trustee? Principally to ensure that the investment performance of the fund is sufficient to meet current and expected plan obligations (the flow of liabilities). In doing so, our trustee recognizes that there may be significant short-term fluctuations in investment performance and, hence, the extent to which fund assets are 'sufficient' relative to liabilities. Reinforcing this goal is a statutory or regulatory constraint that the fund maintain a volume of invested assets valued at least at the level of 95 per cent of its projected liabilities. By these assumptions our fund could be a private fund given the fact that many governments do not require such funding of their own pension obligations (GAO 1996*b*). Notice that the fund will have its own estimates of future liabilities and returns, and hence aim at a level of funding consistent with those estimates. It is possible that the fund may accumulate 'excess' assets relative to projected liabilities. If so, such excess assets are treated as a windfall for the plan sponsor and/or the plan beneficiaries. This issue—the ownership of 'excess' funds—is very contentious. But I do not believe it is particularly important in the management of funds or for the actions of trustees notwithstanding the public policy issues involved (see Bodie and Papke 1992).

From these three sets of assumptions, we have a preliminary sketch of the trustee, the fund, and the imperatives facing the trustee. Notice, there are other 'players' involved in the management of the fund including the fund administrator, custodian, and chief investment officer. For the sake of simplicity it is assumed that there are no *internal* agency problems; that is, the other 'players' act in accordance with the instructions of the trustee board.[3] Focus on the board of trustees does hide a myriad of functions, agents, and services. In some cases, where pension funds are of sufficient size, pension plans are literally financial institutions. Clark et al. (1996) provide a detailed analysis of the services and functions of the pension fund investment management industry, noting the extraordinary range of services which may be provided external to the fund (their analysis was based upon the Australian pension fund system but can be related to the Anglo-American financial services industry in general; see Hayes 1993). For the sake of simplicity, it is assumed that the fund contracts for investment services from the market.

## Logic of Trustee Decision Making

So far, I have treated the trustee as an individual, appointed to the plan to represent plan beneficiaries' interests. This is consistent with the historical antecedents of trust law and fiduciary duty (see Nobles 1993). Trustees are very much aware of their fiduciary responsibility, particularly since most trustee's wealth is trivial in relation to beneficiaries' total claims on the pension fund. But, of course, the trustee is also a member of a board which, by law, manages the fund and makes investment decisions in a collective manner. It is not my intention, here, to discuss the precise details of the process of collective decision making— there are, no doubt, many formal and not so formal mechanisms used to arrive at collective decisions including voting, consensual polling, and bargaining. However, it is important to acknowledge the fact that while individual trustees are responsible for pension plan investment decisions, those decisions are made by trustees together in conjunction with the fund administrator and consultants. The social fabric of decision making is essential to consider if we are to understand how decisions are actually made (see the next chapter). In this section, I set out the logic of decision making focusing on three identified types of decisions which will be the basis of subsequent analysis of the 'framing' of decision making.

As mentioned above, it is assumed trustees have two related goals: (1) to satisfy current and expected plan liabilities, and (2) to maintain funding of expected liabilities at proscribed levels set by pension plan regulators (the 95 per cent rule). Do trustees maximize or optimize pension investments in the sense which dominates much of financial economic analysis (owed to von Neumann and Morgenstern 1944)? That is, do trustees maximize their expected utility in a manner consistent with rational expectations? Here, we must be careful not to idealize pension fund trustees' decision making prowess. For a start, it is not possible to specify 'a complete set of rules of behaviour [for] all conceivable [contingencies]' (von Neumann and Morgenstern 1944: 33). There is a great deal of uncertainty about future circumstances, including the flow of plan liabilities, as well as great uncertainty about the investment performance of managers. While it is possible (and normal) to set investment targets according to historically derived risk profiles of liabilities and returns, uncertainty is a pervasive feature of financial markets (Knight 1921). More generally, it is not clear that trustees and other economic agents, perhaps more importantly, can be reliably characterized as Bayesian forecasters (De Bondt and Thaler 1994). It seems more realistic to suppose that trustees make the best decisions they can given the immediate context in which they find themselves as members of a board of trustees and the risk and uncertainty inherent in the financial markets (Anand 1993).

These issues of context and uncertainty will be analysed in more detail in later sections. For the moment, however, it is important to acknowledge a set of implications for pension investment decision making that flow from these issues. With respect to uncertainty, it is clear that it is impossible to a priori specify the most efficient investment strategies given the goals of the pension plan trustees. This does not mean, though, that trustees are paralysed, unable and unwilling to act until the current uncertainty is resolved (and replaced by more uncertainty). Trustees do not have the luxury of sitting-out uncertainty;

the opportunity costs of such a strategy can be extremely high. Rather it means that any 'rules of decision making' must be adaptive, recognizing the contingency of actions and outcomes as opposed to the presumed stability and optimality of investment algorithms in conditions of certainty. Tversky and Kahneman (1986) have a more extensive treatment of this issue, pointing out that any normative claim for optimal decision making is compromised if *dominance* (the choice of the best option over inferior options) and *invariance* (the application of a standard interpretation of options) are systematically violated. This means that trustees must learn to cope with uncertainty, and develop routines for decision making which can be justified internally (to themselves and their plan beneficiaries) and externally (to other plans' trustees and regulators).

For the purposes of this chapter, it is assumed that trustees make, and remake, three types of decisions. In order: (1) they must allocate assets between asset classes (stocks, bonds, property, etc.); (2) they must evaluate and choose types of investment products (for example, index funds, growth funds, etc.) that match their needs in each asset class; and (3) they must evaluate and choose investment managers who will manage the allocated tranche of assets in accordance with the goals and a priori determined standards of performance agreed by the trustees. In the main, investment performance is measured and reported to trustees on a quarterly and yearly basis although management contracts are often set for longer periods of time, even up to five years (assuming performance standards are consistently met). At this point it is worth reminding the reader that the performance standards of investment managers often involve pre-specified benchmarks (for example, a composite stock index like the Dow-Jones or FT-SE100) against which managers are evaluated and, sometimes, performance-related bonuses set in accordance with some a priori standard relative to the benchmark. Switching between managers on the basis of short-term fluctuations in returns is unusual, given the liquidation costs of withdrawing assets and the transaction costs of establishing a new mandate (evaluating competing managers). Just as there is inertia (status quo bias) in individuals' holdings of mutual funds (see Samuelson and Zeckhauser 1988), there are significant costs involved in pension fund investment decision making.

Figure 6.1 summarizes the structure of these three decisions. Using industry publications and sources, and interviews, Figure 6.1 sets-out the typical ('conventional') and not so typical ('unconventional') parameters of such decisions.[4] There is, of course, a great deal of variety not captured by this summary. For instance, public pension plans typically

## Decision 1: asset allocation

| percentage share | | | | |
|---|---|---|---|---|
| 48 | 40 | 7 | 5 | 'conventional' |
| equities | fixed income | property | other | |
| 55 | 25 | 15 | 5 | 'unconventional' |

## Decision 2: product type within asset class

| product type | | | | |
|---|---|---|---|---|
| national | government | pooled | cash | 'conventional' |
| stocks | bonds | property | other | |
| emerging markets | junk | private | SME | 'unconventional' |

## Decision 3: investment management by asset and product

| manager | | | | |
|---|---|---|---|---|
| Merrill Lynch | JP Morgan | Schroders | Mellon | 'conventional' |
| stocks | bonds | property | other | |
| spin-off | specialist | regional | venture capital | 'unconventional' |

FIG. 6.1. Three trustee investment decisions

invest in fixed income products rather than equities because some political jurisdictions still restrict pension plans' national and international holdings of equities. Likewise, some union-sponsored pension plans are very cautious about equities, referencing recurrent but unpredictable stock market crises as a reason for their caution. For simplicity's sake, Decision 1 is assumed to involve three principal asset classes, weighted by convention to equities but with a significant percentage share allocated to fixed income. Property is an important asset class, whose share is often determined by the plan's liquidity needs with reference to cash holdings and related 'other' types of assets. With respect to product types (Decision 2), the equities' asset class is normally managed as national securities' products, fixed income are normally government bonds products, and property are normally set-up as pooled and traded investment trusts. With respect to the choice of managers (Decision 3), pension plans tend to distribute significant tranches of their assets to well-known investment managers. Here, I refer to four globally recognized managers while acknowledging that companies like Merrill Lynch and J. P. Morgan offer a wide array of products across all kinds of assets and products.

Notice that in parallel with the conventional parameters of these decisions, there are a set of unconventional parameters. For instance, with respect to Decision 1 some plans have a very aggressive (relatively speaking) asset allocation mix preferring to weight their allocations to so-called 'higher risk' classes (equities and property) than the conventional mix. With respect to product types, the unconventional model can include emerging markets, junk bonds, and private placements and perhaps even venture capital investment with small and medium enterprises (SMEs). With unconventional investments comes specialized and less recognized investment managers hired for their distinctive expertise. Conventional investment decision making is the norm; unconventional investment decision making the exception. More often than not, when faced with a decision which could mean departing from convention, trustees err on the side of convention. For trustees making conventional decisions there are independently managed, detailed, and wide-ranging databases structured around these parameters. For trustees seeking to make unconventional decisions data is less available, less reliable, and more dependent upon particular investment managers (Chapter 10). It is commonly argued that better, more reliable data and independent data is a necessary condition for a wider acceptance of unconventional investment strategies by trustees. But I would also argue there are aspects of the decision process which sustain convention, whatever the availability of information.

## Three Frames of Decision Making

In discussing the two phases of 'prospect theory' (framing and editing), Tversky and Kahneman (1986) observed that '[f]raming is controlled by the manner in which the choice problem is presented as well as by norms, habits, and expectancies of the decision making' (p. S257). In this section, I use their logic to 'frame' the trustee decision making process paying particular attention to the set of decisions sketched above. As will become clear, my analysis will focus on habits, rules, and norms. In this respect, it is important to understand how the 'choice problem' (the allocation of assets, choice of products, and investment managers) is oftentimes presented to trustees. Formally, and now enshrined in statute in many countries, the problem is often presented to trustees in terms of modern portfolio theory; the virtues of portfolio diversification with respect to risk-and-return. Less formally, and consistent with the common law traditions of trust law, the choice problem involves distinguishing between risk and uncertainty.

To illustrate, let us begin with a variation on Ellsberg's (1961) 'two colour problem' (owed to many others including Keynes 1921). Suppose an urn contains 100 balls, equally divided between black and white balls. Assuming that after every draw the drawn ball is returned to the urn, the probability (risk) of drawing a black (white) ball is 0.50. If we vary the proportion of black and white balls, the probability (risk) varies accordingly. We can say, in fact, that the risk of drawing a white ball is $1-\text{Pr}(b)$. We can extend the story by adding other coloured balls (say yellow and red) and attributing a different value to each colour of ball. For instance, imagine there are 45 black balls each worth $100, 35 white balls each worth $120, 15 yellow balls each worth $150, and 5 red balls each worth $200. If the players (trustees) have to make a bid (investment) on each draw, and if they have limited resources (assets) and an expected flow of liabilities over a given time, it is apparent that the most obvious strategy, and that recommended by consultants, is to invest according to the plan's long-term liability profile. Even so if trustees have, in effect, only four bets in which to achieve $500 over ten draws and may lose their bet if their expected ball is not drawn, we can readily see that even in a situation where the distribution of risks and returns are known trustees could end up with an underfunded pension plan.

Investment managers and consultants commonly present the choice problem in these terms: risk-and-return is the dominant language of the industry (and finance in general; see Sharpe and Alexander 1990). Claims for pension funds to manage emphasize the expertise of investment managers in 'disciplines' like picking the colour sequence of drawn balls, managing a balanced portfolio of bets, and minimizing the risks of poor bets relative to fund requirements. But unfortunately for trustees, the choice problem is also subject to a great deal of uncertainty. For instance, while trustees may know the range of colours available, they may not know their true proportions or their total numbers. That is, they may not know how many red balls there are relative to the other balls nor may they know the total number of balls. Indeterminacy can mean that the appearance of a red ball is treated as a discrete event rather than an event that could be expected to be repeated over a given set of draws. Worse, even if repeated draws help in approximating the underlying distribution of red in relation to other colours trustees have no way of knowing if the process which determines the distribution of colours is stable or unstable. This may be because the process is unstable or it may be because trustees' understanding of the true process is incorrect. Adding to uncertainty is the possibility that others' actions are unpredictable, informed by unknown theories and mistaken about others' motives (the 'noisy trader' phenomenon; see De Long et al. 1990).

In essence, the actual world in which trustees must decide investment strategy is a world of risk and uncertainty.[5] It is a world in which normative theories about efficient markets, rational expectations, and optimal decision making sit uneasily with the limited capacity of trustees to make informed decisions about the available set of investment options. At one level, the normative power of these theories is such that trustees often believe they ought to behave 'more rationally' but are unable to do so given the pervasiveness of uncertainty. Rules structuring the decision making process have been one response. At another level, recognizing uncertainty has encouraged the formation of ad hoc habits and norms to cope with uncertainty and manage the decision making process. In combination, habits, rules, and norms frame trustee decision making.

Before considering Figure 6.2 in detail, it may be useful to briefly explain my perspective on framing relative to Kahneman and Tversky's (1979) canonical version. Clearly, their prospect theory is useful in suggesting a distinction between normative models of decision making which idealize agents' rationality, and more descriptive models which tend to emphasize the actual behavioural traits of decision makers. I begin with a commitment to a descriptive approach to trustee decision making framed in three ways, one overlapping the other with each being a partial frame as opposed to a complete frame. However, Kahneman and Lovallo (1993) suggest that internal frames dominate decision

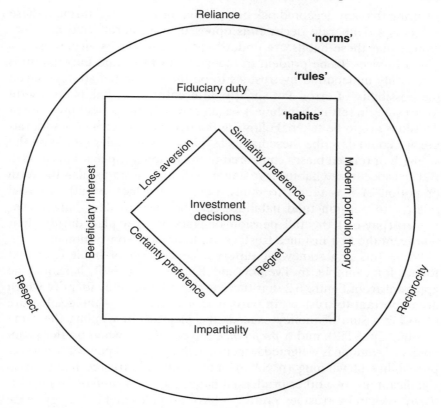

FIG. 6.2. Framing trustee decision making

making, I suggest below that while trustees may begin with an internal view, they are required (for a variety of reasons) to work out to an external view (including rules, and then norms). Accepting that habits are very important, I am uncertain about their status; they are behavioural traits, with considerable functional value. But I am not prepared to accept the idea that they are psychologically profound in the sense of being *innate* to all humans, let alone all organisms (compare with Nevin 1995 with Loewenstein and Prelec 1992).

*Habits of prudence* are systematic and ingrained. They are commonly practised and accepted by trustees as the immediate response to risk and uncertainty. In effect, they regulate trustees' burdens of risk and uncertainty in relation to their obligations to beneficiaries. As a conservative force, habits of prudence minimize trustees' exposure to risk ensuring that any accepted risk beyond that incorporated through these habits is a deliberate decision as opposed to an unreflected decision. Notice that these habits are understood by trustees as virtues, as opposed to vices. To be prudent in the context of risk and uncertainty is commonly understood by trustees to be the best initial strategy given the possibility of error. Put slightly differently, these habits are useful for trustees in setting benchmarks against which subsequent investment decisions are to be taken. Following the behavioural economics literature, we could describe these habits as 'biases'. See Thaler (1993) on the strength of related biases compared to the rational expectations model. But I suspect these habits have a more affirmative status than the term or notion of bias seems to imply. Because trustees' wealth is trivial relative to pension fund liabilities, and because trustees hardly ever realize (pay-off) the full pension obligations of a plan during their tenure, in the first instance trustees are habitually conventional.

While this is a somewhat different conception of habit than that found, for example, in Tversky and Kahneman (1986), it should be apparent from Figure 6.2 that there are two habits they identify which are important to trustees. In particular, *loss aversion*—'the displeasure of losing a sum of money exceeds the pleasure of winning the same amount' (p. S258), and a *preference for certainty*—whereby the probability of winning is weighted larger than the potential pay-off of a lower probability of winning (p. S266)—are significant trustee habits. Also significant are two other prudential habits. One is a *preference for similarity*—whereby trustees prefer to have an investment strategy more like other trustees at other funds even if similarity means lower potential returns, and the other is *regret*—whereby trustees tend to regret a lost opportunity for realizing higher returns more than they value making a current investment decision for a higher-than-average return *given* the risk of not realizing that return and being dissimilar in their investment strategy relative to other funds and trustees. Regret has been recognized by other writers who analyse financial decision making (see Thaler 1993), as having the preference for similarity, although it is often-times referred to as the practice of 'barn-door closing' (following others in making an investment decision after the value of that particular kind of investment has been lost) (see Zeckhauser et al. 1991). In part, I have described these habits in terms of trustee decision making, thereby making them more specific. But it is also clear that they are aspects of the more general virtue of prudence.

Habits of prudence have two consequences for trustees' investment decisions. At one level, they sustain the practice of conventional decision making. Whatever the potential value (return) of an unconventional asset allocation strategy (for example), trustees tend to err on the side of convention. While they may regret a lost opportunity for higher-than-average returns, they value certainty and convention more than they value achieving a higher-than-average return. Put slightly differently, again, on average they value certainty more than episodic or momentary 'excess' returns. This does not mean that trustees are unwilling to make unconventional investment decisions. All the evidence is that, despite the dominance of convention, trustees are willing to step away from prudential habit. But to do so, to deny habit by choosing an unconventional product or investment manager, requires an affirmative case which overcomes (if only momentarily) the virtues of habit. Thus, our second implication is that trustees tend to choose unconventional investment strategies in situations that encourage them, or require them, to deliberately suspend habits of prudence.

*Rules of proprietary conduct* regulate the process of collective decision making by trustees, referencing external (to the fund) standards of behaviour. These rules define in general ways the 'correctness' of behaviour recognizing that, internal to the fund, trustees may be tempted to follow ingrained prudential habits as well as engage in corrupt practices which are unrelated to plan beneficiaries' interests. Like Schauer (1991), it is presumed here that these rules are prescriptive in nature (rather than simply descriptive), embedded in specific principles (rather than being subject to negotiation and change at the local level), and formal (in the sense of institutionalized). However, it is also important to recognize that the set of rules identified in Figure 6.2 is more often standards for behaviour rather than detailed and comprehensive guidelines for the trustees' actual decision making processes. As well, while Schauer is principally concerned with formal rules which have a legal mandate, not all rules need have an immediate legal image. Nevertheless, it should be clear that rule-based decision making is often valued by trustees wary of the external status of prudential habits. In this sense, 'following the rules' in investment decision making is a means of limiting the legal burden that attends the actions of pension fund trustees.

Whereas prudential habits have a certain coherence (one with each other), some rules of proprietary conduct originate from the common law while others do not. For example, *fiduciary duty* is a rule setting the standards of trustee conduct which has a long history in the common law, shared and incorporated into many countries' statutes over the past thirty years or so. As a rule, it is the cornerstone for trustees' understanding of their obligations and liabilities. Connected and immediately related is the rule that trustees respect and pay due regard to *beneficiary interests* though it is less a legal rule like fiduciary duty and more a formal requirement whose status is directly attributable to the structure of the pension plan itself. In recent years, *modern portfolio theory* has also been incorporated into trustee decision making, in some cases becoming a legal requirement that trustees pursue their investment decisions paying particular attention to the virtues of portfolio diversification. Perhaps most importantly, though perhaps less formally than the other three rules, trustees believe that their decision making should be *impartial* in the sense of respecting the merits (risk-and-return) of alternative investment options as opposed to other, less formal, bases of decision making. For many, impartiality requires the use of rules for decision making; it is hoped that rule-based decisions meet trustees' obligations and responsibilities. Rule-based decision making is perceived to be a virtue in itself.

For trustees' investment decision making, rule-based behaviour has a number of virtues. For a start, it is a means of justifying past investment decisions, even if the consequences of those decisions for the fund's investment performance are unacceptable if simply viewed as an issue of performance, relative to some established benchmark measure (perhaps the S&P 500 index). Since so many trustees are relatively ignorant, and since the likelihood of even expert investors making poor decisions with respect to the future performance of an investment product is so significant, to be able to appeal to an independent rule to 'explain' a prior decision is an attractive option. Another valuable aspect of rule-based decision making is its apparent generality. In a sense, trustees are required to apply these rules to particular cases, thereby discriminating between an enormous variety of investment options which have competing (and difficult to understand) claims regarding their merits. Rule-based decision making is a means of ordering and classifying these options, thereby reducing the range of options to those that, in all likelihood, overlap with their prudential habits. Even so, we must also recognize that rules are, more often than not, vague and ambiguous. They are typically defined by reference to exemplary cases, but often require skilled interpretation in their application to normal cases. Rule-based decision making is hardly ever conclusive; rather it is typically indicative.

*Norms of relationships* regulate trustees' interaction with others outside the plan, particularly consultants and investment managers. Of course, norms may well be important in trustees' relationships with the plan sponsor and even plan beneficiaries. For present purposes, however, I am most concerned with trustees' relationships with those who advise on their investment decisions and those that manage their assets (service providers). Norms are variously defined in the literature. For some, norms are like rules in that they set out in a deliberate fashion, standards of behaviour expected and mandated by society. The difference is that norms are informal, non-legal, and non-binding, even if there are well-understood social sanctions and rewards for, respectively, violating and observing their imperatives (see J. S. Coleman 1990 with Majeski 1990). In the pension fund industry, at least, norms are not so well defined. While norms are social customs and conventions internalized by individuals, they do not have the power of rules of propriety conduct, nor do they have the immediate significance of prudential habits. Their significance is to be found in the fact that trustees *necessarily* rely on others for expertise in managing risk and uncertainty, recognizing that others' interests may not be consistent with trustee responsibilities and may be deeply (but concealed) antagonistic to those responsibilities.

There are three norms peculiar to the relationship between trustees and service providers. The most contested norm is *reliance*: the realization that trustees must trust individuals and institutions in carrying out the investment process. For instance, trustees must choose a plan custodian, i.e. an institution that will manage the disbursement of benefits and the flow of contributions and allocations to investment managers. There are huge sums involved. Likewise, trustees cannot, normally, actually invest plan assets; the mechanics and expertise needed is quite outside the scope of the average trustee. They must rely on others. Knowing this, trustees use all kinds of tests of commitment and sincerity. It is also the case that relationships with service providers typically involve *reciprocity*: that trustees owe service providers in some rough approximation to the benefit (or burden) received (Becker 1990). This expectation goes beyond simply standing by the terms of a service contract. Loyalty is an important aspect of the relationship, particularly since there is a widespread recognition that higher-than-average returns (given risk) may carry the likelihood of periods of lower-than-average returns. And buttressing reliance and reciprocity is the norm of mutual *respect*: that trustees carry an enormous burden of responsibility and rely upon expert advisers for professional services. All three norms sustain longer-term relationships, overlapping rules of proprietary conduct and prudential habits. Indeed, these relationships may come to dominate trustees' interpretations of those rules and habits.

One of the most compelling aspects of the pension fund investment is the extent to which the decision making process has been penetrated by service providers. For many trustees, wary of the consequences of trusting habits, and terrified of the possibility that their conduct may be scrutinized by external agencies (of all kinds), to involve service providers with established reputations in their decisions is a form of sharing the burden of risk and uncertainty. Not that they are any less liable if their conduct were scrutinized. Rather, risk-sharing relies on the apparent superior expertise of major investment companies. Not surprisingly, major companies whose expertise is often concentrated in particular asset classes, products, and sectors dominate the investment process. Moreover, given trustees' prudential habits and the formal rules of proprietary conduct, major companies tend to emphasize conventional investment strategies—strategies in which they have established reputations and economies of scale. The combination of habits, rules, and norms in the context of risk and uncertainty is a combination which is inherently conventional rather than unconventional.

## Analogical Reasoning and Investment Innovation

In the previous sections, I developed a comprehensive description of the logic behind pension fund investment decision making. As described, convention dominates decisions; habits, rules, and norms conspire to narrow the scope of asset allocation, investment products, and managers. However, we must be careful not to exaggerate the dominance of convention. There is a great deal of interest in alternative investment products, even if the rate of adoption is relatively low, and the share of assets allocated to this category (normally designated 'other'; see Figure 6.1) is commonly very small (Chapter 8). Moreover, with the decline of public sector fiscal capacity in many Anglo-American countries, increasing levels of public debt and stringent political limits on revenue, many commentators believe that mobilizing pension funds is an essential ingredient in any private response to apparent needs for urban infrastructure investment.

Assuming that governments will not mandate pension funds to invest in urban infrastructure, and assuming any related investment would be assessed by trustees as they assess other kinds of investment options, how do trustees innovate? What modes of reasoning are used to overcome convention? Here, I suggest innovation can happen in two ways. One way is to use analogical reasoning to extend the boundaries of what are designated as conventional investment options to include opportunities otherwise excluded if past decisions are the reference point for evaluation. A second way of innovating is to suspend or in some way violate (in a deliberate fashion) the habits, rules, and norms that sustain convention. Not surprisingly, I would suggest that trustees prefer to extend options by analogical reasoning, rather than directly challenge those habits, rules, and norms which are so important in managing the apparent burden of risk and uncertainty. However, while trustees prefer analogical reasoning, it would seem that advocates of alternative investments often argue for the suspension of relevant habits, rules, and norms. In this sense, there may be considerable conflict between trustees and advocates of alternative investments about the process of decision making, rather than about the virtues or otherwise of specific alternative investments.

To illustrate, let us return to Ellsberg's (1961) two-colour problem. Assuming a given number of balls in an urn, successive draws from the urn (assuming also that after each draw, the ball is returned to the urn) allow observers to estimate the distribution of black and white balls, and predict the probability of the next draw turning up a black or white ball. For Keynes (1921) repeated draws, or repeated experiments, are a process of induction. The more experiments, the better the prediction and the more likely the estimated distribution matches the real distribution. Of course, in reality, trustees rarely have the luxury of repeated experimentation, and may face a great deal of uncertainty about the stability of the underlying process, as well as uncertainty about the consequences of investments. Given the limits of induction (conceptual as well as financial; see Knight 1921), trustees also reason by analogy: they make assessments of investment options by comparing them to what they know—the likeness of an option compared to other investment strategies with which they may be more familiar. Ellsberg's two-colour problem is not especially useful in this context. Balls are either black or white. They are either exactly the same or categorically different. Neither attribute is especially useful for trustees trying to make sense of the commonalities between possible investment options and their experience.

For Keynes, the goal of analogical reasoning is generalization: to establish the degree of likeness between objects or categories. While he recognized in others the temptation to determine the exactness of any match between objects, analogical reasoning was, for Keynes, an economical mode of reasoning, by virtue of its focus only on the relevant characteristics and ignorance of the irrelevant characteristics of different objects. There were a series of steps identified by Keynes as essential to analogical reasoning, beginning with the identification of crucial characteristics, the search for likeness, and the search for the limits of an analogy's application. Instead of repeated experiments using exactly the same objects and conditions (induction), Keynes advocated extensive tests of an analogy's power across all kinds of objects and conditions. In a sense, the wider the scope of application (or at least tests of the scope of application), the greater the confidence of those who would wish to use the analogy to sort between alternative investment options. To the extent that trustees are averse to ambiguity, tests of the power of an analogy may be wide indeed (compare with Fox and Tversky 1995).

To illustrate, I note elsewhere that trustees (and many other kinds of investors) tend to prefer investment products that have at least the following characteristics: the option for liquidity (being able to enter and exit a position at will), risk pooling (diversifying risk across a range of positions or circumstances), and risk-sharing (having a small stake or share in the investment relative to the total investment required) (see Chapter 8). Many traded equity products have these characteristics as well as other desirable characteristics like economies of scale. Beginning with these desired characteristics, the next step is to evaluate other investment options to determine the likeness or not of those options, set against the risk-and-return profiles of those products. For many trustees, traded real estate investment trusts (REITs) are quite like traded equity products and desirable for their categorical diversity (compared to stocks and bonds). Thus, accepting the value of the analogy, trustees may reallocate assets towards property, thereby moving the pension fund from the conventional side of the equation, to the unconventional side. This is entirely possible without having to compromise or violate trustee habits, rules, and norms. Indeed the virtue of analogical reasoning is that categorical extension occurs within those initial conditions. It is not difficult, then, to move from a balanced portfolio manager to a specialty manager; the virtue of the analogy is that it demands respect for its implications.

For the investment industry, moreover, analogical reasoning by trustees is not particularly threatening to established relationships. In fact, if trustees begin with products and managers they prefer, and if they seek specific characteristics derived from those products and managers in other investment options, it should not be surprising to learn that existing managers often move with their trustee clients to those investment options, applying their particular expertise in ways that match trustee expectations. Alternatively, joint ventures are established and mergers and takeovers occur as the larger investment managers acquire a wider range of options within the general terms of their expertise. This strategy has two advantages. One, the maintenance of client relationships, and, two, the spread of product development costs across existing products and cost structures (Chapter 10). But it may have two long-term disadvantages for trustees. By the use of analogical reasoning, trustees may be 'captured' by particular investment companies whose expertise in cross-over products is actually quite limited, when compared against non-relationship specialty investment managers. Given the significance of underlying habits, funds may accumulate considerable losses (relatively speaking) before recognizing the situation. Thus, it may appear that innovation is a high-risk strategy.

There are other ways innovation can occur, principally through either meeting or encouraging the suspension of habits, rules, and norms. For example, let us imagine that a government (investor) puts together a proposal for a mixed income, medium-density housing project, combining ownership and rental properties with the goal of meeting existing needs for housing in a major city. How might pension funds treat this kind of investment opportunity? One way consistent with the previous discussion of REITs is for the investor to establish the investment option in a manner consistent with other investment projects included in successful REITs. The sponsor would then rely on the package being accepted by the REIT industry, and investment flowing through the trading process. There is no doubt about this being a viable option, although the investor may have to finance a large proportion of the project before there is any possibility of a REIT taking a share. Indeed, the investor may not be able to raise sufficient finance to begin the project or hold it long enough to attract investment (and thus pay off its initial investment), by virtue of its demonstrated revenue stream. Another development option may have to be found, one involving pension fund investment at the beginning of the project.

In Chapter 8, I discuss this type of problem in some detail, noting the institutional innovation side of the story. But it is also possible to imagine that certain pension funds may be able to meet or violate, in some manner, the shared habits, rules, and norms of the pension fund investment management industry. For example, if a fund has had considerable experience in housing investment, perhaps reflecting its sponsor's expertise and industry, what may appear to many funds to be an investment option which would violate trustees' preferences for certainty and loss aversion, may appear to a particular fund to be a 'safe' investment, easily justified by reference to the performance of similar kinds of investments in the past (local and national in origin). In terms of the rules of proprietary conduct, trustees could justify the project with reference to their beneficiaries' interests. Perhaps their beneficiaries are construction workers, employed by the plan sponsor or other industry firms recognizing the argument made by construction unions and contractors in Australia and the USA that pension funds can meet both the rules of conduct and beneficiary's general interests by ETIs. And in terms of the norms of relationships framing the trustees' decisions, perhaps they may be able to develop a joint partnership between the fund, the government, and specialty property investment managers.

Once we recognize that pension funds are different from one another with different underlying identities, benefits, and goals, then it becomes easier to see how and why funds may have different investment profiles. At the margin, pension funds may have very different asset allocation formulas, and quite varied investment products and managers. At the same time, I would also argue that pension fund trustees, regardless of fund characteristics, are very often dominated by shared habits, norms, and relationships. Their desired scope of independence is actually quite limited, given the formal and not-so-formal codes of practice framing the investment decision making process. When investment firms and developers of alternative kinds of investment options fail to recognize the significance of framing in relation to plan characteristics, pension fund trustees are pilloried as conservative, irrational, and unimaginative. To attack the habits of decision making as unjustifiably conservative seems to be a simple-minded understanding of the complex logic which actually frames decisions.

## Conclusions

Pension fund trustees are often accused of being unreasonably resistant to alternative investment opportunities and hostage to convention. And there can be little doubt that, on average, trustees make quite conventional asset allocation and investment product decisions, and unsurprising decisions regarding the management of pension fund assets. At the margin, however, pension funds do differ significantly in terms of their investment options. Whether this is sufficient, given the capital needs of so-called alternative investment (urban infrastructure and housing) opportunities, is a difficult issue to determine. It is clear, though, that trustees have not embraced ETIs, nor have they been enthusiastic supporters of community-based venture capital projects. Notwithstanding the rhetoric of community interest and community responsibility, pension fund trustees have resisted the siren songs of these types of investment advocates. The question is why.

There are a variety of ways of answering this question. It could be argued that unconventional investments are unjustified when their risk-adjusted returns are compared to conventional investment options. And there is no doubt that, when judged in relation to the standard rules of modern portfolio management, alternative investments may seem high-risk ventures. But this answer presumes that trustees have quite straight-forward tests of adequacy, and respect the standard rules of finance. Many finance analysts would dispute these two presumptions and argue that one reason trustees do not invest outside of the most conventional investment products is that they are irrational; on the available evidence, they do not invest in alternative investment opportunities when they should (based upon comparable risk-return profiles), and persist in investment strategies long after these strategies have outlived their usefulness. For many critics, trustees are either irrational or uneducated, or both. The presumption here is that if they could be taught the rudiments of finance theory, then they would make better (more rational) decisions. The idealism implied by this argument owes much of its force to the analytical claims of von Neumann and Morgenstern's (1944) recipes for optimal decision making.

In this chapter, I have been less concerned with idealism than realism, and less concerned with the evaluation of apparent (ir)rationality in decision making than I have been concerned with developing a comprehensive description of the logic of trustee decision making. At this point, two types of moves are commonly made. Either analysts invoke some kind of sub-optimal standard for decision making, like satisficing (Slote 1989), or invoke informational asymmetries to explain market imperfections, and hence, inadequate decision making (Grossman 1995). Here, I have actually gone down a rather different route. I have been most concerned with documenting three overlapping frames of reference in decision making, following the lead provided by Kahneman and Tversky, and their colleagues. I do not mean to suggest that trustees are irrational, unfortunately biased, or prisoners of convention. Rather, in proceeding this way I aimed to show that these frames of reference are very common, well-appreciated by decision makers, and valued for their virtues in coping with risk and uncertainty. It is insufficient to suppose that trustees are simply satisficers, and it is inadequate to suppose that they are the victims of asymmetrical information. Rather, these frames of reference play a very important role in managing an uncertain world.

As a consequence, the dominant ideas of rational choice and normative decision making are replaced here by a concern for the context and structure in which decisions are made. I argue that this perspective is a valuable part of any explanation of trustee decision making (an argument which should be readily acknowledged in the geographical literature; see Thrift and Olds 1996; and Sunley 1996). This is more than a summary of irrationality, to be replaced by rationality once trustees' decisions are corrected. Inspiration for this kind of analysis is, as suggested above, to be found in the recent behavioural economics literature. But it is also to be found in Keynes (1921). His study is a remarkable combination of the logic of probability applied to issues of risk, and a realization that risk and uncertainty require all kinds of strategies if they are to be managed in the world of limited resources and cognitive capacity to deal with the past and future. In so many respects, investment decision making is a gamble. But hopefully it is a structured gamble, framed by habits, rules, and norms that allow trustees both scope for decision making, and protection in case things go wrong. To think otherwise is to believe the perfectionist logic of investment managers.

One point of qualification should be noted. Whereas Kahneman and his colleagues tend to argue that identified biases or habits are ingrained, psychologically based patterns of behaviour, my own perspective is somewhat agnostic on this point. I argue that habits, rules, and norms are important for trustees in managing risk and uncertainty. I also identify similar and related habits like loss aversion and the preference for certainty. And it may be the case that these habits are psychologically ingrained as they suggest. However, I do not think these habits are innate. Rather, I argue that they have functional virtues. Furthermore, habits, rules, and norms may have moral claims as much as psychological claims for their persistence (Griffin 1993). It remains to be seen how far we can go with the behavioural psychology of habits, rules, and norms, as opposed to their moral foundations. In the next chapter, I extend the model towards the social psychology of decision making, paying attention (in part) to the significance of moral commitments in structuring decision making.

## Notes

1. While much of the discussion in this chapter reflects and responds to Kahneman and Tversky's path-breaking work on risk aversion, we should acknowledge that the issue they identified has had a long history in financial analysis. For example, A. D. Roy (1950) was very concerned about the potential impact disasters may have on individual behaviour. In his paper he referred to disasters which were in a broad sense entirely unexpected. Recognizing the fact that disasters could profoundly alter individual's circumstances, he developed the notion of 'safety first' as a behavioural response to that possibility (but unknown probability). In

summary terms he defined the principle of 'safety first' in the following terms: 'It is reasonable, and probable in practice, that an individual will seek to reduce as far as is possible the chance of such a catastrophe (disaster) occurring' (p. 432). He went on to discuss various strategies of deploying resources, such that if a disaster were to occur, then the consequences of such a catastrophe would be mitigated. In this context he introduced, perhaps for the first time, the notion of portfolio diversification. Of course, it might be reasonably noted that his analytical logic was focused around a big event, and its potential long-term effects on individual welfare. By contrast, Kahneman and Tversky were less concerned with catastrophic events and more concerned with customary behaviour in the context of repeated events or at least expectations of commonly known events.

2. The assumption that trustees have average competence and understanding of the principles of investment management is consistent with similar assumptions made in the finance literature. For example, A. D. Roy (1950) began his analysis with what he termed as 'the ordinary man'. While there is clearly a need for trustees to be better educated, with more experience in investment management and related issues, it would be misleading analytically to assume too much in terms of their competence. Indeed, recognition of this issue underlies the relationships between various agents in the financial services industry noted in chs. 4 and 5.

3. It might be suggested that trustees are captured by investment managers, the implication being that my approach is partial (compared to ch. 4). In part, the issue is entirely empirical, reflecting my own experience against that of other researchers in the field. I also believe that any claim that trustees are captured by investment managers would require considerable justification to be plausible. Clearly, the relationship between trustees and service providers is tense, contested, and subject to considerable patronage and influence. This point is expanded upon here and developed in more detail in previous chapters. I would also argue that the problematic nature of investment management, the impossibility of predicting returns as opposed to extrapolating the past, combined with the extraordinary turnover of people and products in the industry, conspire to make capture unusual in the short term and most unlikely over the long term (see ch. 5).

4. The data presented in Table 2.1 are obviously related to US pension funds. In the United Kingdom, many funds have a much larger allocation towards equities (national and international). In combination, 80% allocated to equities is not unusual. Although this appears to be a significant difference there are reasons to suppose that the gap is rapidly shrinking. On the US side, the growth in the value of equities relative to bonds has prompted many funds to move assets towards equities, although this is principally towards national equities rather than international equities. In the United Kingdom, new legislation regarding minimum funding requirements has forced pension funds to review their reliance on equities, prompting some reallocations towards bonds and related fixed-interest products.

5. Clearly, uncertainty is an essential and unavoidable part of trustee decision making. It cannot be denied by reference to certainty equivalents. In this respect, the analysis presented here is in considerable sympathy with Knight's (1921)

early work on uncertainty and with Shackle's (1972) more recent analysis of the significance of uncertainty for conventional economic theory. It must be recognized, however, that trustees also live in the world of decision making. Recognition of the existence of uncertainty is an inevitable ingredient in their decision making, and coping with uncertainty is part and parcel of justifiable behaviour. In this sense, reliance upon Shackle's critique is a luxury that few trustees can afford. Herein lies the significance of coping strategies.

# 7

# Corruption and
# Investment Decision Making

---

In Chapter 6, on pension fund trustee decision making, I sought to show how and why convention dominates trustee decision making. Trustees often reference protocols commonly accepted throughout the investment management industry: the dominance of convention is the product of a set of overlapping decision making 'frames', including habits of prudence, rules of proprietary conduct, and norms of relationships which structure decision making. My argument was that these frames are essential for coping with the ever-present reality of risk and uncertainty in the investment world. However, if convention is so important to trustee decision making, what would prompt trustees to deliberately violate those conventions in the interests of either members of the trustee board and/or others outside of the board? And how are we to characterize the decision making process in these cases? In part, these require a more general analysis of the social practice of decision making.

It might be argued that my concern for corruption is less of a concern for decision theorists and those interested in pension fund investment in urban infrastructure, and more properly the concern of political theorists or political philosophers (e.g. Shklar 1984). There are few related studies of corruption in the decision or urban studies literature.[1] If corruption were the concern of decision theorists, presumably it would be dealt with as a case of agents' (trustees) expected utility maximization, set against the collective interests of principals (beneficiaries). The principal–agent framework is relevant. But the application of expected utility maximizing models to the problem of trustee corruption would miss important aspects of the trustee institution. For many urban analysts, trustee corruption would confirm their prejudice against the market in favour of state intervention. But this prejudice runs the danger of being entirely empty, lacking even a rudimentary understanding of the logic of corrupt behaviour. Here, my analytical strategy is inspired by Kahneman and Tversky (1979), and their colleagues, if not their exclusive focus on individual psychology.

In the next section, I set out in some detail a definition of corruption, emphasizing intention and benefit, while distinguishing between negligence, recklessness, and corruption. These distinctions are important for narrowing the scope of analysis, and are illustrated with reference to a synthetic example. This is followed by an analysis of the logic of decision making, beginning with my previous argument, and drawing out the importance of the social psychology of trustee decision making; in particular, the collegiality of deliberation and the necessity of justification. Whereas Chapter 6 was focused upon individual decision making, in this chapter I extend that logic by arguing that corruption is a social practice with an identifiable social psychology. Furthermore, we must be aware of the various strategies of conspiracy and secrecy used to protect (from scrutiny) corrupt practices. The chapter then deals with the issue of regulation, and concludes by suggesting that the logic of corruption can be applied across a range of investment decisions, not just community development.

## Corruption Defined

Let us begin with an example, an instance of pension fund trustee corruption. This will allow us to both define the domain of corruption, and distinguish corruption from other related concepts in the context of trustee investment decision making. Note that the example is synthetic. It is designed to facilitate conceptual analysis rather than document the real world of pension fund investment. At this juncture, a real case may overwhelm the analysis with information unrelated to the issues at hand, and may also introduce an unfortunate element of caution when we come to speculate about the actions and intentions of trustees and their advisers. Stylizing the facts is a common strategy in the social sciences, and underpins the process of model building in economics, and, to some extent, geography (but see Thrift and Olds 1996). Nevertheless, anyone familiar with pension investment issues should recognize aspects of recent cases in the UK, Australia, and the USA.

*The first-cut* on the example goes as follows. Recently, a pension fund with assets of approximately £5 billion invested £25 million in a manufacturing plant which dominates a small, remote community. The original owner of the plant was a large, multinational corporation, with interests in many markets and production sites around the world. Having failed to sell the plant, the firm announced some time ago that it was planning to close it and make some 200 people redundant. At the last minute, a consortium of local interests, including union representatives of the plant's employees, announced their intention to save the plant. Led by local plant managers, the consortium established a new firm to buy the plant from the corporation. To do so required an initial investment of £25 million. Having failed to attract local investors and having failed to convince banks to underwrite the sale, the consortium approached the pension fund and secured the capital necessary to proceed with the venture. At the time, the case was identified in the business press as an instance of regional capital scarcity and myopia on the part of the existing venture capital institutions (a story also to be found in the academic literature; see R. L. Martin and Minns 1995).

Within two years, however, the venture had failed. The pension fund had lost its entire investment. In retrospect, it seems that the plant's capital stock was quite obsolete, requiring massive upgrading and rebuilding. To do so would have also required significant up-front investment in new environmental management technologies to deal with inherited environmental hazards and be consistent with new environmental regulations. Furthermore, it seems that the principal products of the new venture inherited from the original owner of the plant had quickly lost market shares; a new entrant to the market from a much lower cost of production location had drastically changed the structure of market prices to the detriment of the new venture. And finally, notwithstanding the impending collapse of the venture, the union's executive refused to agree to a new local labour contract which would have seen the loss of over 120 jobs, and massive wage and benefit discounting. The venture was doomed to failure. The reasons why no other company would buy the plant and the reasons why no other institution would finance the venture were, in retrospect at least, quite obvious. The pension fund seemed to be the only institution surprised by the turn of events.

*The second cut* on the story begins with a legal suit filed by a group of the pension fund's beneficiaries charging the trustees with having failed to discharge their fiduciary duty with respect to the fund's investment in the venture. Basically, the dissident beneficiaries believed that the trustees did more than make a poor investment. The suit charged the trustees with having failed to acknowledge the scope of the risks in the new venture, and with having failed to carry out an adequate assessment of the risks of the venture. The plan beneficiaries were suspicious of the motives behind decisions taken by the trustee board. Were they negligent or reckless? Did they engage in some form of corruption? How should we distinguish between these concepts? And what are their relevance to the case at hand? These questions prompt us to look behind the facts of the case, and make judgements of the virtues of decision making. These questions also ask us to distinguish between acceptable and unacceptable risk in the context of the accepted standards and conventions of trustee decision making.

There are common law and statute-based definitions of negligence, recklessness, and corruption. And there have been attempts to apply and distinguish between these concepts in the related trust case law concerning fiduciary duty. My approach here is more general than the application of concepts defined by the courts, and interpreted in specific ways in particular contexts. Take negligence—to be negligent is to ignore or fail to consider an issue or set of issues which may reasonably be thought to have been relevant in assessing the risks of an investment. In this respect, we are concerned with the manner in which trustees considered the apparent risks, their likely pay-offs (returns), and the opportunity costs of such an investment. Note, of course, that trustee decision making is assessed against standards common to the pension fund trustee community and the investment industry as a whole. Consequently, to be negligent may be to be incompetent, ignorant, or indifferent, given the competence, knowledge, and behaviour of others in the industry. Thus, while the trustees may be liable for their negligence, in many instances, there is no suggestion that they deliberately or intentionally disregarded their responsibilities. Negligence refers to the process of investment decision making believing, for the moment, that the trustees had the interests of plan beneficiaries in mind.

According to Duff (1990), to be reckless is to be aware of the risks of an action or set of actions, and act in a manner which would be thought to be irresponsible in the face of those risks. This does not mean that trustees should avoid all risks. On the contrary, there are few sure bets, and even fewer riskless investments. One of the lessons of modern portfolio theory is the need to balance rather than to avoid risks.[2] Duff's approach implies that risks should be evaluated against their likely returns, and decisions made taking into account the balance of probabilities, likely profits, and potential losses. Also implied are industry and institutional standards against which decisions are to be evaluated. Thus, recklessness is more than incompetence. It refers to an attitude, a set of actions, and a patent lack of responsibility which result in a knowing disregard of the risks of an investment. Whereas the trustees may be judged to have been negligent in making their decision to invest in the local buy-out venture, few observers would suggest that this single event would be sufficient grounds to dismiss the trustee board. However, if the trustees were judged to have been reckless in failing to properly take into account the known risks of the venture, their continued role as plan trustees would be open to dispute. Irresponsibility is more problematic than incompetence.

So what is it to be corrupt? What is distinctive about corruption, relative to negligence and recklessness? To be corrupt would be: (1) to knowingly place one's interests (or a third party's interests) ahead of those interests one is directly responsible for protecting; (2) to choose a course of action which one would not ordinarily countenance; and (3) to directly benefit from those actions. In many instances, this means that investment decisions made by trustees on behalf of plan beneficiaries are controlled or directly influenced by trustee's or trustees' pay-offs from such decisions, rather than the expected returns of the investment itself. Indeed it is likely that there is a much higher degree of certainty with respect to the nature and value of the pay-off to trustees, than there is knowledge at the time of the decision about the likely consequences for the investment performance of the pension fund. Of course, it is also possible that trustees may be bribed to make a decision, or set of decisions, regarding the allocation of the fund's assets which third parties know (or hope) will lead to a particular, desired outcome. Corruption could be confused with negligence, even recklessness. But corruption is more than negligence and recklessness. It involves a clear benefit to the trustee and a hierarchical order of actions and interests which denies beneficiaries their deserved priority.

It is also important to acknowledge that corruption often involves conspiracy. While it is possible for an individual trustee to affect the nature and course of decisions by the board of trustees so that only one trustee receives the benefits of a conspiracy, this is unlikely. For many boards jointly trusteed with appointees serving terms of five years or more, there is a degree of intimacy and collective appreciation of one another's interests that would make an unusual claim for a particular decision by an individual trustee incredible. There are instances of conspiracy between board members, and there is a subtle kind of conspiracy of silence: investment decisions may be led by particular coalitions of interests on the board, requiring the tacit consent of others on the unspoken understanding that their projects may be treated in a similar fashion by those who directly benefit from current decisions. In these circumstances, board members may have a collective interest in keeping secret the true bases of past decision making, the actual interests of those involved, and the relationships between the parties to investment decisions (both inside and outside of the fund).

Thus, in our example, the initial investment in the venture may have been driven by trustees' interests, rather than the virtues or otherwise of the investment itself. For instance, a local politician with close links to the chair of the board of trustees, and a group of consultants with interests in the fees generated by such a project and upon whom a section of the board relies for future employment, may have conspired to alter the criteria by which such projects are evaluated, so as to make the investment possible. The subsequent collapse of the venture may have been an embarrassment to the board, but a prospect fully appreciated at the time of investment. Hence, protestations of negligence or even recklessness on behalf of the board of trustees are likely strategies of concealment designed to shift the basis of plan beneficiaries' suspicions from corruption to lesser charges. Clearly, if we are to understand the practice of investment decision making and the logic of corruption, we need to look more closely at the social psychology of trustee decision making.

## Social Context of Decision Making

In this section, I look more closely at the context of decision making as a step towards understanding the logic of corruption. Here, I use the identity assumptions set out in Chapter 6 regarding the trustees of our plan: it is assumed that plan trustees come from the plan sponsor, be it the firm or a group of firms in an industry. Typically, trustees are neither particularly knowledgeable about pensions and investment management, nor especially endowed with great wealth in comparison to their investment decisions on behalf of the plan. As is the case in most jointly trusteed plans, our trustees are either appointed by the firm(s) or by plan beneficiaries; in the former case, they are likely to be middle-level executives, while in the latter case they are likely to be officials of the employees' union or similar organization. It is assumed they are appointed for an initial term of five years, with the prospect of reappointment for a further term.[3] At the end of their term, the presumption is that the trustees would return to their 'home' organization. As for the pension plan itself, it is a defined benefit plan with its assets of £5 billion allocated in a conventional manner between stocks (45%), bonds (35%), property (15%), and cash reserves (5%).[4]

From interviews with plan trustees, consultants, and investment managers (reported, in part, in Chapter 8), it is clear to me, at least, that the habits of prudence, the rules of proprietary conduct, and the norms of relationships play important roles in structuring trustees' investment decisions—these are essential tools for coping with risk and uncertainty. While shared amongst trustees and common to the investment decision making process across all kinds of pension funds and related investment institutions, these tools owe their status to the individual psychology of decision making. And yet, I would argue that corruption, as defined in the previous section, is essentially a social practice. We need to extend the previous model of decision making by incorporating some rudimentary ideas about the social psychology of decision making. Now this project could be an enormous undertaking, going far beyond the parameters of this particular issue. In order to contain the problem, let us consider just three issues which bear directly upon the context of trustee decision making.

Whereas much of the literature on individual decision making has little interest in the social identity of their subjects, the appointment of a trustee has considerable social significance. Obviously, trustees are appointed to represent the interests of plan beneficiaries. But their appointment also reflects relationships with others and, more often than not, their position in their 'home' organization. They depend upon patrons for their appointment, and it is inevitable that they reflect the interests of their patrons, even if those interests are ideally irrelevant to their fiduciary obligations.[5] Trustee boards inherit the social relationships of their members. Boards are not random collections of unrelated individuals, but systems of overlapping (even antagonistic) interests, represented by people who know one another prior to appointment or, at least, know of their status and significance in the related organizations. Furthermore, it should be apparent that social identity is more than organizational identity. Identity is deeply scored by all kinds of associations including community loyalties (Williams 1995). In this respect, there is considerable force in any argument that a full-fledged theory of decision making should be sensitive to the social identity of its subjects. To put this point plainly, it should not be surprising to learn that members of our trustee board had close, perhaps dependent relationships with their patron(s) outside of the board, and that these kinds of relationships played a part in decision making.

Another issue internal to the life of trustee boards, is also important. Investment decision making, and many other related decisions of the board, are collective decisions. As a consequence, collegiality is an important social custom, smoothing over tensions and disputes that erupt in particular decisions, and facilitating trustees' collaboration with one another over the long term (sequential and cumulative sets of investment decisions). Collegiality is a progressive, deepening custom, reinforced by the legal obligations on trustees to act in accordance with their beneficiaries' interests. By progressive, I mean that collegiality develops layer upon layer through close, intimate interaction with one another. Each layer of intimacy adds to past layers through the exchange of confidences, friendships, and even hostilities (Cave 1995). Collegiality can, of course, be superficial. But it can also have great depth, challenging a patron's influence or accommodating patrons' interests by reciprocal deals made between members of a board of trustees recognizing separate obligations to 'home' organizations. It is reinforced as a virtue, moreover, by fiduciary rules and requirements which, in effect, make each trustee responsible for their collective decisions. Trustees can hardly opt-out of decisions, even if they feel uncomfortable with the implications of them.

Collegiality is not simply a custom, to be arbitrarily rejected by any trustee fearful of the bonds of intimacy. It has a couple of instrumental virtues for trustee decision making. Collegiality is a means of enhancing trust between trustees, allowing the development, and then application, of templates of decision making in subsequent rounds of investment decisions. As Harré (1993: 45–6) notes, templates are 'structured synchronically' and 'endure through time', speeding the process of decision making, and reducing the potential for conflict between trustees as investment options are assessed, accepted, or rejected. Of course, templates rely on analogy which, as I suggested previously, is a very useful device for coping with new situations and new investment options (compare Keynes 1921). Collegiality also encourages the routinization of decision making by making possible informal, accepted codes of practice, rules, and responsibilities between trustees. Collegiality allows trustees to use the scope of one another's expertise, and allows them to set limits on their reliability.

Not only are investment decisions collective, they must be justifiable to one another (internal), and to the outside world (external). This is a remarkable and enduring feature of law (see Robinson 1996) and many modern institutions (see Habermas 1984). It requires trustees to be able to explain the logic of their decisions to 'outsiders' in terms that can be understood by specialists and regulators. Formally, trustees may be required to justify their decisions to beneficiaries, regulators, and the courts. In many jurisdictions, beneficiaries may challenge trustees on the 'reasonableness' of investment decisions, and have the right to bring suit in court if they believe decisions are not justifiable. At issue, more often than not, is the rationality of an investment decision: whether the process of decision making was reasonable, given the apparent risks and returns of different options, and whether the trustees were sufficiently knowledgeable about those risks and returns, given the available evidence and expert advice. Informally, trustees are commonly required to explain their decisions to the investment community, including investment consultants, investment managers, and the extended set of service providers that make up the industry. Being able to do so is essential to the formation and maintenance of trustees' reputations. At the end of their term(s) of appointment, their reputations will determine (in part) their future in the industry.

Consequently, at a formal level trustees use and mimic the language of the investment industry. While their own internal relationships (and their relationships with patrons) may be conducted in everyday parlance, reflecting the intimacy of emotional and reciprocal loyalties to one another, when investment decisions are taken, the language game is transfigured into the protocols of investment theory and practice. In this regard, it is not surprising that modern portfolio theory was so readily incorporated into trustee decision making. It has a formula (process), parameters (limits), and set of terms (language) that command external validity while being, internally, easily translated between the interests of trustees, consultants, and beneficiaries. In these terms, a 'failed' investment is not obviously evidence of wrong or irrational trustee decision making. Rather, if we take modern portfolio theory seriously, there will always be some investments that fail, given the theoretical value in constructing an investment portfolio with a diverse set of risks and returns. The issue here is not so much the outcome of a single investment decision so much as the rational process of investment decision making as a whole.

In these ways, pension fund trustees' decision making is enmeshed in a web of routine. As a matter of policy, many pension funds call for proposals to manage tranches of money according to pre-specified asset classes, performance targets, and time frames. Consulting companies pre-screen investment managers, paying particular attention to the persistence of advertised performance levels over various time horizons. And with respect to choices between asset classes and amongst investment managers, templates are used to structure those choices, relying upon experience inside and outside of the fund to define those templates. After the allocation of funds for investment, trustees rely upon performance protocols (or triggers) to routinely review and assess the performance of investment managers. Formality is part and parcel of routinization. It is difficult for an individual trustee to spontaneously suspend the routine processes of decision making to favour one manager, project, or patron. By virtue of routine, corruption must be systematic. It is hidden in routine, concealed by the process of decision making, and legitimized by the language of investment management. Conspiracy and secrecy are part and parcel of trustee corruption.

## Framing Corruption

In the previous chapter I showed how and why convention dominates trustee investment decisions by referring to the habits, rules, and norms that appear to structure or frame their decision making processes. The identified attributes of decision making are argued to be vital in coping with risk and uncertainty. Notice these attributes are presumed shared by trustees, supposing that their utility and value in the investment management industry are such that they are widely accepted, if not universally deployed by each and every trustee. But we must not presume too much: Tversky and Kahneman (1986: S256) observe that 'people do not spontaneously aggregate concurrent prospects or transform all outcomes into a common frame'. In this respect, the previous section of this chapter sketched out some of the important social and social psychological imperatives that encourage accepted (even standardized) decision frameworks and common decision making practices amongst trustees.

At one level, habits of prudence, rules of proprietary conduct, and the norms of relationships structure decision making with respect to risk and uncertainty, while, at another level, shared social identity, customs of collegiality, and the necessity of justification structure collective decision making by plan trustees with respect to industry standards and conventions. Both aspects of decision making are important; one is inadequate without the other. However, care must be taken not to idealize decision making in any moral or normative sense. While decision theorists hardly ever focus on criminal behaviour, it is more common than we might suppose. From this logic then, I have argued that corruption in trustee decision making, referencing the synthetic example introduced in a previous section, is a systematic kind of activity, often hidden in the routine and order of investment decision making, and involving secrecy and conspiracy between trustees and their partners in crime. Corruption in this context is hardly ever spontaneous, arbitrary, or easily discovered by the diligent investor (or, for that matter, plan beneficiary).

The next step, then, is to analyse the decision making logic which frames trustee corruption. The logic which underpins this analysis is loosely based on Kahneman and Tversky's (1979) 'prospect theory' which models the decision making process, paying particular attention to the phase of framing and editing, and the phase of evaluation. Here, I am most concerned with the framing process which structures 'the effective acts, contingencies, and outcomes' of trustee behaviour and is controlled by 'the manner in which the choice problem is presented, as well as by the norms, habits, and expectancies of the decision maker' (Tversky and Kahneman 1986: S257). In my case, I focus on what I term the weapons, strategies, and emotions that structure corruption. In effect, it is suggested that corruption should be understood as a knowing departure from established decision making practice, where means and ends are set against the interests of beneficiaries (Simester 1996). It seems obvious to me, at least, that trustee corruption is profoundly structured by the institutional content of decision making, as well as the behaviour imperatives of risk and uncertainty (compare with Sunley 1996).

Figure 7.1 summarizes the logic of corruption. The reader will notice that there are actually three, interrelated 'frames' which structure corrupt behaviour. Each frame has its own place in the set of frames.

FIG. 7.1. Structure of corruption

And it should be understood as a hierarchical set of frames, moving from the core of the decision making process, out to the world at large. The first frame, 'weapons', is closest to the decision making process and represents the driving forces that influence each trustee and the board in general. The next frame, 'strategies', is also about trustee decision making and concerns the common strategies of legitimization; how investment decisions are justified to outsiders, including plan beneficiaries, regulators, and the industry at large. And the third frame, 'emotions', refers to the relationships of trustees to plan beneficiaries and the community at large. As described, there is a certain order or path to this set of frames, moving from the particular (the trustee board), to the general (society). This order may appear somewhat arbitrary in that, theoretically speaking, the moral world may exist prior to the world of particular interests and behaviours. However, I would suggest that this order reflects the exigencies of trustee decision making.

*The weapons frame* refers to those forces that would influence trustees to suspend their normal or customary rules of decision making in favour of another set of rules or a revised set of rules that would accommodate the chairperson's goals. The simplest and most obvious action would be to bribe a group of trustees to act in accordance with the interests of the conspirators. Very simply, this means to alter a trustee's rewards or pay-off matrix so that they willingly set aside the normal routine of decision making in order to benefit themselves and others. The precise level of bribery required to force a change in behaviour is difficult to a priori specify. It would depend, in part, on the benefits of such an action to trustees, in relation to the benefits of the action for the conspirators, as well as the risk of discovery: (1) whether the offer of a bribe was for a single decision, as opposed to a set of related decisions in the future, and (2) whether the acceptance of the bribe implied an ongoing relationship with the conspirators from which there may be no retreat. Here the promise of reciprocity may play a significant role in equalizing trustees' long-term benefits from corruption, and ensuring the long-term commitment of both sides of the deal to protect one another from discovery (Scheppele 1988).

Reciprocity has a variety of dimensions. It could be thought to refer to 'fair dealing' in a relationship, rather than the calculation (and recalculation) of the costs and benefits of separate actions by independent agents (Gibbard 1990: 261). It also may refer to gratitude (the exchange of favours), and the threat of retaliation (if promises are not honoured). Of course, many owe their positions to patronage; they rely upon one another for good will when their own projects come before the board for assessment, and they rely upon particular influential individuals in investment management for their long-term careers in the industry. For reciprocity to work, favours to be exchanged, and relationships maintained and regulated over time, trustees and those who would influence trustee decision making, require a currency of exchange: what Gibbard refers to as the 'terms of trade'. Here, the chairperson may offer his/her cooperation in the future for another trustee's 'pet' project. But that offer of cooperation has to be credible, just as the chairperson has to be sure that the bribed trustee will live up to his/her side of the bargain. Not surprisingly, in these situations commitment requires, more often than not, a set of commitments: one conspiracy begets other conspiracies.[6]

The preceding discussion focused upon trustees' interests. Subversion of the customary rules of decision making was accomplished by trading off interests. But the chairperson could use a different weapon: he/she could invoke his/her authority as chair of the board of trustees and, hence, dominate the decision making process when his/her particular project came up on the agenda for decision (investment). Authority seems a vague and somewhat irrelevant factor in the analysis. It hardly figures at all in models of decision making, which assume relationships are, more often than not, entirely cooperative (and pareto optimal). Raz (1986: 28) defines authority in the following manner. If an agent (Y) has authority (a legitimate place and power in the organization), he may decree that another agent (X) (who is directly accountable to Y for his actions) ought to do A (vote for an investment he knows to be unjustified). For Raz, the exercise of authority is an instance of demanding action where 'there is no direct connection between the reason and the action' (p. 35). In this respect, the reason is 'extraneous' to the action. While this may seem to go against the previous discussion about collegial decision making, it does reflect the formal structure of some trustee boards and the formality of decision making when collegiality is bound by rules of procedure, rather than the long-term relationships which underpin collegial decision making.

Formality is one weapon of influence (Cialdini 1993). Sennett (1980: 17–18) also notes, however, that '[a]ssurance, superior judgment, the ability to impose discipline, the capacity to inspire fear: these are [also] the qualities of an authority.' He illustrates this argument with reference to the behaviour of an orchestral conductor, noting the subtlety and nuanced manner in which authority can be deployed (in his case, at least). But it is a fine line between authority as the legitimate exercise of power and coercion. Indeed, our chairperson may well back his/her demands on other trustees to vote for his/her project by reference to his/her authority while, at the same time, threatening them with the withdrawal of all favours should they go against his/her wishes. What can a chairperson withdraw? He/she might 'black-ball' their reappointment, attack their reputations in the industry, accuse them of negligence, even wilfulness, by threatening to bring to light previous decisions that might be interpreted to have favoured the target trustees' interests. He/she might also threaten to cut their relations with outside patrons by going directly to those patrons to complain about trustee behaviour. Coercion has many various dimensions (see Lamond 1996). Here, two are crucial: the dominance of one's will by another's, and the use of credible threats to ensure the desired result. (For instance, A voting for the chairperson's investment project knowing that his/her own opinion has been wrongfully silenced and taken over by another's.) See also Raz (1986: 149) and compare with Nozick (1981: 49).

*The strategies frame* refers to the mechanisms whereby corrupt decision making is protected from scrutiny. As assumed above, corruption, more often than not, involves conspiracy and secrecy; interests are hidden, relationships obfuscated, and the true basis of decision making protected by a web of formal justification. In this respect, it is important to recognize that authoritative claims of 'corrections' made by the board of trustees are an important weapon in protecting corrupt decision making. Trustees can invoke the historical record of their fiduciary duty, information to which they alone have access, and their (and their advisers') expertise. More specifically, although the reasonableness (risk-and-return) of an investment decision is open to competing interpretations because its authoritative meaning is rightly claimed, in the first instance, to be the prerogative of the board, strategies like claiming expertise have immediate plausibility. As is the case in so many spheres of social life, the social 'facts' we deal with 'have a peculiar kind of self-referentiality' (Searle 1995: 32). Their proper definition is owed to a combination of institutional authority and accepted functional use. Thus, the strategies frame relies upon a realization that the terms of investment discourse are neither neutral nor transparent. Rhetorical devices, including media communication control techniques, may be important in sustaining one definition of reasonableness over others (see generally Bender and Wellbery 1990*a*).

So imagine that the group of dissident plan beneficiaries pursue the trustees, suspecting, as I have suggested, corruption. In court, the ultimate institution responsible for defining reasonableness, the trustees could invoke risk and uncertainty to explain the outcome of their investment, even the procedures they used to make the investment decision. In the next chapter, I show that given limited resources, the need to

make investments across a range of asset classes and varying proportions of investment options amongst asset classes (a variation on
Ellsberg's 1961 'two colour problem'), the existence of risk can lead to
less than perfect (desired) consequences. While risk-and-return should
be proportionally related, there is no guarantee that a single investment
will achieve a return consistent with average returns for that asset class.
When uncertainty is factored into the equation, trustees could reasonably claim that they did not know that the plant was a poor bet, given
the subsequent 'sudden and unexpected shift' in industry competition.
It might be argued that they ought to have known, or they should have
had expert advice to make up for their lack of knowledge. But if it tran-
spires that the trustees did, in fact, obtain expert advice (keeping secret
the prior relationship between the expert and the chairman of the board
of trustees), the dissident beneficiaries may be left with the difficult task
of disputing the plausibility of the expert's theory of industry competition, entry, and exit.

Expert advice and the existence of risk and uncertainty may be
invoked by trustees to explain the failure of an investment. As trustees
may invoke risk and uncertainty to 'cover' themselves on a single investment decision, so too may experts, especially when, after the fact, the
structure of an industry changes. It is very difficult to make a definitive
causal connection proving corruption when the evidence is an investment decision, and the outcome of that decision in a specific case. To
prove culpability requires a set of investment decisions characterized by
similar decision making protocols, networks of interests and expertise,
and outcomes. In this respect, to claim that the investment was important to the region and community is of minor significance as a
legitimization strategy, compared to the risk and uncertainty strategy. It
may carry weight in the media, and it may reference important political sentiments about the need for the greater responsiveness of finance
capital to local concerns. But trustees can hardly claim that they over-
ruled customary decision making criteria to make an investment in the
interests of community solidarity; to do so would go against legal
requirements concerning their fiduciary duty to plan beneficiaries.

The utility of these three strategies depends upon keeping concealed
the true circumstances of the investment decision. Whereas trustees
might have joined the conspiracy believing that their only obligation
was to remain silent about the decision, as the decision is scrutinized by
plan beneficiaries, and then by the courts, trustees may face a more
demanding situation. They must remain silent about their and others'
interests, and they must also closely monitor the commitment of other
conspirators. We could expand this issue by referencing the tools and

methods of game theory (Axelrod 1984 provides a useful exposition). It is sufficient to note that corrupt trustees would be wary of defections from the conspiracy, and may be mindful of the possibility of a prisoners' dilemma game to be played willingly or unwillingly between the conspirators if the conspiracy were to collapse. For the leaders of the conspiracy, it is important to maintain the commitment of the partners to the investment decisions. This can be achieved using the weapons of influence, and it can be done by escalating commitment: requiring trustee conspirators to shift from silence, to active concealment, even public denials of wrong-doing and the justification of the logic of the original investment decision. The chairperson's strategy would be to increase the costs of trustee defection to the point where trustees' commitment is irrevocable (see Staw and Ross 1989 on the social psychology of escalation situations).

*The emotions frame* refers to the trustees' costs of corruption; the emotional costs of violating the trust relationship between trustees and plan beneficiaries. It may seem odd to even acknowledge these costs, given the initial focus of this chapter on the social psychology of decision making, and the argument made in the next chapter about the centrality of individual habits of prudence. However, it is important to acknowledge that the trustee institution is both a legal regime codified by common law and statute, and a moral order which reflects societal expectations that trustees honour and protect the trust relationship. In this sense, to honour the trust relationship is to respect the external obligations of the trust institution, set against the internal relationships which dominate a conspiracy. Empirically, I would locate these external obligations at some distance from the core of the decision making process. The implications of this location are, at once, obvious and disturbing. The core of the decision making process is driven by two imperatives: the logic of risk and uncertainty, and the logic of collective decision making. In this context, I agree with Baier (1994: 13) who observed that, '[i]t is not difficult to become a sensible knave, and to harden one's heart so that one is insensitive to the moral condemnation of one's victims and those who sympathize with them.'

Nevertheless, the emotional costs of corruption can be significant for some trustees, and may affect the stability of a conspiracy (see generally Braithwaite 1989). Most obviously, trustees may suffer from a guilty conscience affected by the plight of those impacted by their investment decisions—both the plan beneficiaries, if the investment puts at risk the pension plan, and especially the community, whose welfare may have been directly dependent upon the quality of the original investment decision. From experience, it would seem that the closer trustees are to the community, and the closer they are to their 'home' institutions, the more apparent are the emotional costs of breaking the trust relationship. Guilt may prompt defection from the conspiracy, and it may even prompt whistleblowing to the authorities. Regulating defection are two other emotions: fear and shame. The former refers to the consequences of defection, where trustees may have to suffer retribution from their co-conspirators and the breakdown of the relationship with their patrons. Whistleblowing has even higher consequences, both for defectors and for conspirators. The fact that whistleblowing is a public act, directly and immediately affecting relationships with colleagues and friends, makes it a high-cost defection strategy. The public shame which would result from such a strategy could be such that the defector is ostracized by friend and foe alike.

In these ways, it should be apparent that trust relationships are quite fragile. While a great deal has been written in recent years about the centrality of trust to market institutions, the logic of corruption is the subversion of trust. Abstractly, corruption is a process whereby internal (or local) interests overtake and dominate external (or social) obligations. Less abstractly, it is a process of influence peddling, even coercion legitimated by strategies of justification, and bound together by escalating commitments. Whereas I argued above that the closeness of trustees to their communities may affect their recognition of the emotional costs of corruption, it is also likely that the closer trustees are to their patrons and related community interests, the more effective are the weapons of influence. Thus, one reason why pension fund investments in community-based development projects have a bad reputation is the presumption of guilt: that local interests are antithetical to social interests, and that when local interests dominate investment decisions, the trust obligations of trustees to plan beneficiaries are more easily subverted.

## Regulation of Corruption

This discussion, then, brings us to the implications of my argument for the theory and practice of regulation. In Anglo-American countries where trust law is dominated by the heritage of English common law and reliance upon private, employer-based pension systems, regulatory regimes are commonly an amalgam of statutes and case law focused, in part, upon the fiduciary duties and obligations of trustees. While some countries have pension regulators, others pension ombudsmen, and still others have third-party grievance and arbitration procedures, the courts play a major role in defining and sanctioning trustee behaviour (as they have done so for centuries; Getzler 1996). This is a highly decentralized system designed to monitor and appeal against trustee behaviour. It is also a system of regulation which is backwards-looking. It relies upon the flow of cases to set rules and procedures, adjust the system of penalties and sanctions, and provide (or not, as the case may be) remedies for wrongs done to plan beneficiaries (see generally J. L. Coleman 1992).

In the light of my analysis of trustee decision making, two questions appear relevant. (1) How does my argument relate to recent debates about regulation? (2) If regulation of trustee decision making were to be 'reformed', what should be the focus of regulation, given the three frames which structure decision making? The first question is obviously very difficult to answer in any profound way. Any test of 'fit' would, presumably, have to be more detailed than this project has been, certainly more comprehensive in terms of instances and cases. Nevertheless, it is important to place my analysis in the broader debate about pension and trustee regulation. As we shall see, there are a number of points of intersection with common arguments about regulation which may be of value in evaluating the virtues or otherwise of different points of view.

One argument made in the law and economics literature, and echoed (or is it the other way around?) in politics suggests that regulation is, in general, inefficient, compared to the efficiency of the market. If redress is to be a part of regulation, it ought to be benign with respect to market efficiency, and, in any event, if we allow the market to function efficiently, instances of corruption will be weeded out systematically by market arbitrage and the reputation maintenance processes. The strong-efficiency market hypothesis supposes corruption is either vulnerable to long-term market pressures and/or individually self-defeating. Notwithstanding the theory of efficient markets, there has been a great deal of research questioning the plausibility of strong-efficiency. Doubts have been raised by its early advocates (Fama 1991), and evidence introduced which attacks the robustness of arbitrage processes in financial markets (Shleifer 1998). My argument, in effect, is that plan beneficiaries face significant interpretive hurdles in discriminating between poor investment performance due to market risk, and uncertainty and poor performance due to corruption. The 'signal' is open to interpretation. Likewise, while I do think reputation is very important to trustees, it is not a profound impediment to subversion. Indeed, as I have argued, trustees mindful of their reputations may engage in all kinds of strategies of justification and concealment.

Another argument found in the law and economics literature, which seems to be owed to sociologists and, perhaps, geographers and anthropologists, is that regulation is ineffectual in 'close-knit' relationships bound together by shared values, commitments, and community loyalties (E. Posner 1996).[7] Like Braithwaite (1989), Posner supposes that non-legal local sanctions may be more effective than remote legal sanctions in deterring wrongdoing. Extending this point, as these relationships are self-regulating, care must be taken not to disturb the efficiency of their codes of conduct with blunt instruments of law. Unfortunately, this is only half the story. Relationships may be self-regulating, and they may have established internal mechanisms for monitoring and sanctioning behaviour (relative to the collective interests of the group). But enduring relationships may be 'subcultures' of corruption. This is a version of the argument referred to in the previous section, the argument that local trustee–patron relationships may promote corruption, as opposed to ideal trustee–plan beneficiary relationships which are based simply (and only) on social or moral obligations embodied in trust law. There is a real danger that regulation is ineffectual in the face of enduring relationships. But the answer is not to deny the need for regulation.

Less theoretical and more practical has been the debate about pension regulation in the UK in the aftermath of the Maxwell debacle. Maxwell, it might be recalled, switched assets at will between his corporations' pensions as needed (Clark 1997*b*). The trustees of the funds acquiesced to his decisions, and have claimed ignorance as their defence. For some commentators, this case and the corporate world it represents suggest the need for a more comprehensive (pro-active) regulatory system, focused upon strengthening trustee accountability and responsibilities. It is argued that such cases question the desirability of regulating trustee conduct through trust law adjudicated on a case-by-case basis. Given the public and private institutions involved, the systematic nature of discovered corruption, and the potential for harm to large numbers of plan beneficiaries, one could query whether case law adjudication is adequate in the face of the burgeoning growth of finance capitalism? The UK Pension Ombudsman thinks so (Farrand 1996). Still some doubt that the nineteenth-century model of trustee responsibility, developed, as it was, for the management of family trusts, can cope with the modern finance industry (Getzler 1996). For many, Farrand's reassurances are superficial, reflecting a quaint sense of history, rather than the reality of pension fund decision making.

If we are to regulate trustee behaviour, and if we are to protect plan beneficiaries from the costs of corruption, what should be the focus of a pro-active regulatory regime (as opposed to a regime which simply provides an opportunity for remedy)? In asking this question, we must be careful not to overstep the logic of my analysis. In the preceding sections I have sought to sketch the structure of corruption, not comprehensively describe all its elements. Thus, one implication of my analysis is that a pro-active regulatory regime will not be able to capture all possibilities, and that redress will always have to be an option. Inevitably, regulatory regimes lag behind the leading edge of innovation whether it be criminal or not. The next question is: what form is the most relevant frame for regulation to focus upon?

Braithwaite's (1989) theory of deterrence (and regulation) focuses on an element of the third and most general frame. His theory is termed 'reintegrative shaming' and goes as follows. Most people act in accordance with social expectations, rarely, if ever, transgressing the boundary between acceptable and unacceptable behaviour. Those that contemplate transgressing the boundary are rarely deterred by formal sanctions; they are deterred by the likely shame and guilt (emotions) that such actions would bring to the surface. Whatever the rewards of belonging to a conspiracy, Braithwaite argues that we are psychologically conditioned to act in a responsible manner. Thus, subcultures of crime only exist and prosper because of the isolation of members of those groups from mainstream society, and because of the weakness of social claims on the behaviour of those groups. While these subcultures operate in the shadow of the law, they offer the disaffected 'symbolic resources' through which they rationalize their behaviour. Put most directly, he argues that '[s]ocieties that shame effectively will be more successful in controlling predatory crime because there will be more shaming directed at noncompliance with the law than shaming (within subcultures) for complying with the law' (pp. 13–14).

For Braithwaite, the core of the matter is our emotional commitment to social customs and norms. To the extent that those customs and norms are ambiguous, fraught with dispute, and arbitrarily applied, any claim we may have on potential conspirators to respect the boundary between acceptable and unacceptable behaviour will be attenuated and diluted. I have considerable sympathy for his argument, and believe it has merit when applied to corporate wrongdoing (Clark 1993*b*). At the same time, how would shaming work to regulate trustee behaviour? What are its instrumental mechanisms? Embedded in his argument are two functional levers. One is the effect that shaming can have on close relationships valued by conspirators. The other is the effect that shaming may have on conspirators' reputations in the wider community. For instance, public shaming, combined with the likely harm done to trustees' reputations (hence remuneration and employability), may be such that their 'home' organizations would be wary of re-employing them once their terms have been completed, just as others in the industry would be wary of the negative publicity attached to hiring such tainted individuals.

But this type of argument is not entirely convincing. At one level, the shaming argument allocates pride of place to emotional commitments (frame 3), while at another level, it invokes functional disciplinary mechanisms that owe their 'powers' to their place in the weapons and strategies frames (1 and 2). That is, if we take seriously reputation as the functional lever, converting shame into a regulator of the trustee–plan beneficiary relationship (as others appear to do in the literature on corporate governance; see Rose-Ackerman 1991), we must also acknowledge the significance of other levers such as bribery, coercion, authority, and reciprocity (frame 1) which drive the trustee–patron relationship. Likewise, we must also show how and why the elements of frame 2 are neutralized or are made irrelevant, so as to allow the effects of shaming to work their magic. Braithwaite argues that 'sanctions imposed by relatives, friends . . . have more effect on criminal behaviour than sanctions imposed by a remote legal authority' (p. 69). But it may also be true that shaming sanctions are remote, relative to the imperatives outlined in frames 1 and 2. In summary terms, Braithwaite's model presupposes that criminal actions are definitively identifiable and unjustifiable in the common language of society. By contrast, I have argued that trustee corruption is difficult to identify, and often represented by conspirators as justifiable (if not desirable) in terms accepted by the investment industry.

How should we regulate trustee corruption? Shaming may be important, but it is likely to be episodic and event-specific. Like legal remedies for past wrongdoings, it is backwards-looking, and subject to the power of all kinds of strategies of subversion. At the very least, we should look closely at formal mechanisms of regulating the weapons of influence and the strategies of concealment. One way would be to sever or attenuate the trustee–patron relationship, encouraging greater independence of trustee board members from one another and from their 'home' organizations. This could mean changing appointment terms, introducing independent board members, and requiring public disclosure to plan beneficiaries and regulators on a routine basis of trustees' interests and relationships. Another way would be to alter trustees' pay-offs so that the potential power of bribery is mitigated. At this point, it is difficult to be precise. My argument is simply that if a pro-active regulatory strategy is desirable, it would have to be focused on the elements of the first two frames which structure corruption. And it would have to neutralize those imperatives if the third frame was to be effective.

## Conclusions

Pension fund investments in community development projects are not significant when compared to pension funds' investments in conventional products (see Chapters 6 and 8). There are many reasons why this is the case, some of which relate to problems of characterizing the risks of such supposedly idiosyncratic investments. But there are other reasons, including claims made in the media and elsewhere that pension funds have no business investing in these kinds of projects, given the opportunities for corruption and subversion of customary rules of investment decision making. These claims are given credence by spectacular instances of failure, as well as cases of known political interference in trustee decision making. As I have suggested in this chapter, pension fund investments in community development projects are presumed guilty by association; the existence of close-knit relationships which often support and promote pension fund investments in community development are presumed to be subcultures of corruption.

In this chapter, I have sketched out the logic of corruption, emphasizing the three frames structuring decision making. This analytical approach is owed in the first instance to Kahneman and Tversky, and their colleagues. By emphasizing the framing process, I have tried to be systematic in identifying the important determinants of trustee corruption, referencing both the trustee institution and the social psychological foundations of investment decision making. In the previous chapter, the focus was reserved for individual decision making, coping with the world of risk and uncertainty (Chapter 6). That chapter contains vital clues about the basic psychological imperatives that drive investment decision making. This current chapter is not a rejection of that framework, but rather, an extension of its logic by emphasizing the social logic of trustee decision making. Whereas the focus of this chapter has been on corruption, it should be apparent that the social psychology of decision making is crucial for understanding trustee decision making in general. In this sense, this particular chapter provides a set of concepts (like collegiality and justification) which would be vital in any analysis of trustee investment decision making.

The generality of my argument should not be underestimated. While I have used a synthetic example to focus the analysis, it is not the case that the logic of corruption, as outlined above, is only relevant to community development projects. In fact, I would suggest that the frames, the elements within those frames, and the order of the frames can be usefully applied to other kinds of corruption. For example, it may be very useful in understanding the process whereby equity portfolio managers obtain investment mandates. It may be useful in understanding pension funds' purchases of investment services of all kinds. The weapons of influence can be applied across a broad range of issues, just as the strategies of justification may be deployed to explain all kinds of poor investment decisions. Whether community development projects are especially prone to corruption, compared, for example, to specialized investments, in general, is hard to judge. These kinds of investments are invariably more risky and more uncertain than conventional investments. As a consequence, new kinds of financial intermediaries have been developed to handle the risks inherent in these projects (Chapter 8). On the basis of the analysis in this chapter, I would argue that the nature of corruption in the investment industry is a general process, not one limited to a special kind of investment class.

At the heart of the trustee decision making process is the fact that trustees have more information than plan beneficiaries. At a theoretical level, the trustee–beneficiary relationship is assumed to be one of delegated responsibility where the trustee represents beneficiaries' interests. In theory, trustees are the servants of beneficiaries. However, the presumption in favour of the beneficiary is fundamentally threatened by the asymmetrical distribution of information. Beneficiaries can neither afford to collect, nor reasonably expect to be able to expertly analyse the information necessary to independently assess the veracity of trustees' decision making. In any event, the appropriate investment information is neither ubiquitous nor reliable. Like so many others in the finance industry, trustees rely upon networks of relationships to judge the efficaciousness of information. Plan beneficiaries hardly ever glimpse this part of the investment process. Even if they could, the existence of risk and uncertainty is such that even well-meaning professionals in the industry may reasonably disagree over the meaning and significance of certain pieces of information.

In this context, trustees have an obligation to disclose their interests, and disclose information about the bases of their investment decisions, in general. They also have an obligation to meet standards of behaviour not normally expected of individuals whose relationships with others can be more easily monitored. In this sense, the trustee relationship with beneficiaries is more than a simple contractual relationship. Because of the asymmetry of information, the presumption in favour of expertise in explaining investment decisions, and the potential for collusion (if not corruption), beneficiaries rely upon the honesty of trustees. This is not a relationship between equals; it is a relationship of dependence. It is for these reasons that plan beneficiaries deserve a more pro-active regulatory regime. If corruption is widespread, it is because there is little opportunity to scrutinize, let alone understand, trustee decision making.

## Notes

1. Graft and corruption in urban politics are recurrent themes in urban studies. A recent example is Logan and Molotch's (1987) book on city growth machines, in which they explain the link between property development and local office-holders. With respect to the United States, they note the long history of real-estate interests in community politics, arguing that while 'a little grease always helps a wheel turn' (p. 67), the intimate connection between real-estate interests and local political interests is often as much functional as it may be corrupt for both sides of the equation. Those writing in this tradition tend to use historical narratives and, sometimes, network analyses to illustrate their arguments.

2. The classic papers behind the development of modern portfolio theory include Markowitz (1952) and Sharpe (1964). Note that both authors developed their theories of portfolio structure by means of a utility maximization framework owed to Von Neumann and Morgenstern (1944). Not surprisingly, modern port-folio theory is vulnerable to criticisms of this framework, esp. those which focus on the process of decision making (on related issues in economics, see Simon 1986).

3. Notice that I retain the assumption that the pension plan is sponsored by a private employer. I do so simply to illustrate that corruption (and the logic of decision making in general) can be located in common types of pension fund. However, it has been observed by some analysts that pension fund trustees in public sector funds may be more vulnerable to the types of pressures I identify than trustees of privately sponsored pension plans. For example, Romano (1993: 796), writing about corporate governance, notes 'Public fund managers must navigate carefully around the shoals of considerable political pressure to temper investment policies with local considerations, such as fostering in-state employ-ment.' She also notes that these kinds of pressures are not unique to the public sector but that 'It is an empirical question whether the geographically-based conflicts confronting public funds impose greater constraints on their managers' decision making than conflicts involving other business relations that confront private fund managers' (p. 797).

4. In this context, it does not really matter for my analysis what the precise distri-bution of assets are (or were) between asset classes. In the previous chapter, I focus on the distribution of assets as part of my argument about convention. Here I am simply assuming that the allocation of assets is conventional, and probably much like similar funds in the United States or Australia.

5. See Mitchell and Hsin (1994) on the appointment process of trustees to public sector pension plans in the United States. They note that this process is legit-imately political, often reflecting the party affiliation of the incumbent governor. At the same time, of course, once appointed it is expected that trustees act on behalf of plan beneficiaries' interests rather than their patron's interests, as dis-cussed in the next section of text (see also Ch. 11).

6. In this respect D. Hirshleifer's (1995) paper on informational cascades is a nice reference point. He argues that small events can generate long-term and significant effects by virtue of the partial data of many market agents and the matching behaviour of those agents with others who are acknowledged as market leaders or indicators of market processes.
7. For example, see D. Hirshleifer (1995) on what he terms 'localised conformity', and Romano (1993) on the distinctive geographical loyalties of public officials. For many writing in the law and economics field, these loyalties are at once an aberration compared with the more abstract imperatives of the market (assumed to exist beyond geography) and a real threat to the independence of public officials who owe their positions to geographically based politics.

# 8

# Four Models of Financial Intermediation

COMPARED to most governments' social security programmes, pension schemes are normally funded as an individual's benefit entitlement grows with their paid income and length of service. Thus, as the baby boom generation has moved through the workforce, as more workers have become entitled to participate in pension schemes, and as benefit levels have increased in proportion to paid wages, pension funds have grown astronomically, in terms of their total funds and their significance with respect to other sources of savings and investments.

The growth of pension fund assets has been noted by many commentators. Not surprisingly, arguments have been made in favour of mobilizing pension funds for social purposes like the investment in housing and urban infrastructure, assuming the interests of plan beneficiaries can be thought consistent with such purposes. There is, of course, considerable debate about the virtues or otherwise of this kind of pension fund investing. Recent Republican-led actions in Congress against the US DoL's encouragement of ETIs are evidence of the political contentiousness of the issue and the narrow scope of conventional interpretations of pension fund trustees' fiduciary responsibilities (Chapter 10). It would appear that the 1980s debate concerning pension fund disinvestment from South Africa has been transposed onto so-called alternative investment products (AIPs).

Even so, there is growing interest in AIPs. As pension funds come to grips with lower-than-expected returns from their conventional asset classes, and as pension fund assets have grown in size, AIPs have been touted as a way of regaining higher returns. The parcelling together by mutual funds of traded equities into distinctive products with distinctive investment styles, and the increasing significance of member choice in determining investment options have all combined to encourage pension funds to broaden their investments to include new traded products, perhaps even private placements, in their portfolios. On the supply side of the equation, the rapid rate of product innovation by leading firms in the financial services industry has added some credibility to exotic and unconventional products, notwithstanding the inherent conservatism of investment managers. In theory, then, there is demand for AIPs: pension funds are actively exploring ways of making investments in urban housing, infrastructure, and small to medium firms. At issue, however, is the likely rate of adoption by pension funds of AIPs, the long-term potential in terms of pension funds' total investments of AIPs, and the role the public sector should play in promoting the growth and development of AIPs. These interrelated issues are the focus of this chapter.

In brief, the chapter has five sections. In the next section, I summarize the current structure of the pension fund investment management industry. It is noted that just two asset classes (equities and bonds) dominate pension fund portfolios and investment management companies. Even though AIPs have been the subject of considerable interest, the low rate of adoption of AIPs is a significant issue to be explained. It is argued in the subsequent section that low rates of adoption can be attributed to trustees' conservatism. But this is not the complete story. In fact, more important 'problems' limiting adoption are the costs of imperfect information and the relationship between pension plans and investment managers, given the potential for conflicts of interest between these agents. The chapter then identifies a set of institutional solutions to these problems, noting the increasing importance of what Robert Clark (1975) termed as 'second-order financial intermediaries'. The penultimate section of the chapter analyses the role of the public sector with respect to these intermediaries, and the chapter concludes with a sketch of a possible pension fund investment portfolio five years hence.

## Pension Investment Fund Management

Some accounts of the possible role of pension funds in public investment seem to imply that the process of pension fund investment decision making is unfettered. It is presumed that the choice of investments is entirely in the hands of pension fund trustees (see Rifkin and Barber 1978). Of course, it is the case that pension fund trustees are ultimately responsible (in law) for the management of funds in relation to promised pension benefits. Nevertheless, there are a set of formal and not-so-formal organizing principles which dominate the Anglo-American pension fund investment process. These principles are, as we shall see, derived from common law as well as industry expectations (since modern portfolio theory) about the putative efficiency of markets, and the cost-effectiveness of various kinds of investment products. It is useful to divide these principles into three types relating to responsibility, market structure, and investment focus.

*Responsibility.* According to English common law, pension fund trustees are ultimately responsible for pension plan investment. It is also the case that plan trustees act on behalf of plan beneficiaries, managing funds contributed by employers, employees, or both. For many US corporations that offer defined benefit programmes, this means that while they are ultimately responsible for the funding of pension plans (plan benefits against the flow of contributions in relation to liabilities), the management of plan funds is the responsibility of others, either inside the corporation but otherwise separated from the operation of the company, or outside of the corporation acting on behalf of the corporation. Unlike Germany or Japan, Anglo-American companies are significantly limited in the extent to which they can self-invest. Moreover, in many Anglo-American countries there are strict rules regarding the rate at which pension liabilities must be funded. Most countries require at least 90 per cent or better funding of expected liabilities at any point in time. For those employers that offer *defined contribution* plans, the separation between corporations and their employees' pension entitlements is practically total. *Defined contribution* schemes are normally maintained and managed by external investment companies.

One important difference, however, between private and public pension plans is that governments are normally not bound by the same funding rules as corporations. It is often the case that public plans are drastically underfunded in relation to expected liabilities, there may be no separation between the funding and management of funds, and there may appear to be little in the way of constraints on self-investment. Indeed, many of the most egregious instances of pension fund corruption and mismanagement come from the public sector rather than the private sector, notwithstanding highly publicized instances like the Robert Maxwell case and the cases of corporate restructuring documented by Clark (1993b) in the USA. This is changing, however, as public pension plans are, in effect, privatized by Western governments as part of a strategy of shifting the tax burden of financing retirement in the twenty-first century back onto their citizens—employees or their representatives (something clearly apparent in Australia). In some cases, attempts by some US state governments to use claimed excess funds in public pension plans to finance budget deficits have been met with legal and legislative initiatives by pension fund trustees.

*Market structure.* The formal separation between the funding of pension obligations and the management of pension fund investment has spawned a large (and growing) investment industry. As a consequence, there are now marked differences, in terms of the scope and sophistication of financial products, between the financial services industries of the Anglo-American world and European countries which remain dependent either upon state pensions or industry pensions. For many public and private funds, external investment consultants (like Frank Russell) provide a bridge between fund trustees and the investment services industry, linking investment managers to pension funds on a contractual services basis. Many of the largest investment companies (like Rothschilds, Bankers Trust, etc.) provide a comprehensive set of well-understood financial products with well-established performance profiles. These companies, and the so-called custodial companies, like State Street Bank of Boston, can also provide a range of services to pension plan administrators, including the collection and disbursement of pension contributions from plan contributors to plan beneficiaries.

This decentralized market-dependent process of investment management dominates the structure of the pension fund industry. While not all services are bought by pension funds from the market, it is now very unusual for private funds to completely manage the flow of funds and the investment process internally. As well, it is increasingly common for Anglo-American public plans, concerned to match the range and sophistication of private pension plans' services and products, to outsource many of their functions. If plan beneficiaries are the ultimate 'principals' of the pension fund and plan trustees their 'agents', in this complex chain of market relationships there are actually many agents providing a myriad of investment services normally evaluated against diverse (even conflicting) performance and cost-effectiveness standards (B. Black 1992).

*Investment focus.* It is also true that the vast majority of pension funds managed in this manner also rely upon the market for funds' accumulation. In general, in the Anglo-American world pension fund investments are split between three or four asset classes (see below). In order of importance these are: equities (domestic and international stocks), fixed income bonds (government and corporate), property (pooled trusts and private placements), and others (including cash). Characteristically, investment products that represent these asset classes are traded products; investment managers buy into and sell out of investment products on the open market, in accordance with the current and expected values of those products and the liability stream of their clients (pension obligations). Normally the accrued value of an investment in a stock or related composite product is its net value: its purchase price set against its sales price, discounted by the costs of trading and administration. Here, then, are a couple of essential elements in the pension fund investment process. By convention, funds invest in market products, rarely idiosyncratic (non-traded) products. And funds have an active interest in minimizing the costs of investing. To summarize, funds value liquidity subject to the costs of switching investments.

As I noted above, the vast majority of Anglo-American pension funds rely upon market-traded securities and investment products to earn returns on accumulated funds. In some cases, notably defined benefit programmes, market returns on funds invested are set against expected liabilities and a profile of investments designed and managed accordingly. In other cases, notably defined contribution schemes, there is no long-term pension benefit value target, just the accumulated value of funds invested, given the performance of selected investments and related products. Guiding the investment process, however, are two commonly accepted rules regarding the nature and behaviour of security markets: one, given the pattern of systematic risk in individual securities, it is desirable to diversify holdings to the point where the marginal returns of diversification are fully offset by the extra costs of managing such a diverse portfolio; and, two, the expected value of a bundle of securities is a function of current market prices (ubiquitous information) and the judgement of market analysts (proprietary information). Put slightly differently, the value of a pension fund's investments is a function of the market and the expertise of its investment managers (Grossman 1995).

## Asset Allocation

As I have emphasized, most pension funds depend upon the market for investment products and investment services. To illustrate, let us briefly review the asset allocations of three typical US pension funds: Dow Chemical (corporate), the Arizona State Retirement System (ASRS) (public), and the Western Conference of Teamsters Pension Fund (WCTPF) (union). Note that in 1994 the proportionate share of assets of the 200 largest US pension funds attributed to these three different types of funds by the trade journal *Pensions & Investments* was (respectively) 36.9 per cent, 49.5 per cent, and 10.9 per cent (the balance being universities and private foundations). Also, it is important to recognize that the vast bulk of assets in these funds were in defined benefit (DB) programmes (77.9 per cent) notwithstanding the rapid growth of defined contribution assets over the past few years. Each of the three funds was dominated by defined benefit entitlements.

According to *Pensions & Investments*, in 1994 the Dow pension fund was valued at US $5 billion, most of which was concentrated in defined benefit programmes. In terms of investment, the asset mix was as follows: stocks were allocated 65 per cent, fixed income 25 per cent, cash equivalents 5 per cent, and real estate equity 5 per cent. The ASRS was more than twice the size of the Dow pension fund ($10.9 billion in assets), but had a similar asset mix profile: stocks 56.4 per cent, fixed income 39.5 per cent, cash equivalents 2.3 per cent, and real estate and mortgages 1.8 per cent. By comparison, the similarly-sized Teamsters' fund was more diverse but dominated by fixed income products: stocks 28.1 per cent, fixed income 56.4 per cent, real estate and mortgages 6.7 per cent, annuities 7.7 per cent, investment certificates 0.6 per cent, and cash equivalents 0.5 per cent. Compared to the average asset mix of the largest 200 funds (specifically defined benefit funds), the Dow fund was slightly over-concentrated on stocks, the ASRS significantly over-concentrated on stocks and relatively light on fixed income, and the Teamsters' fund was relatively light on stocks and over-invested in fixed income. Very few funds listed in *Pensions & Investments* had asset mixes significantly different than their fund type average. And very few had an asset mix skewed towards AIPs. Likewise, the average defined contribution plan has no AIPs, but an average asset mix spread more evenly between stocks, bonds, annuities, and investment certificates.

Why are plan trustees so cautious with respect to asset allocation? Why is the demand for AIPs, in practice, so limited, given the apparent interest of public and private commentators in diversifying pension plan asset allocations? Below I identify a set of reasons for the conservatism of plan trustees with respect to asset allocation. Elsewhere, I have analysed in detail the reasons why investment product providers may also be reluctant to offer new and innovative products outside of the two dominate asset types (stocks and bonds) (Chapter 5). Notice, however, these reasons for trustee conservatism are proximate reasons: that is, they are important reasons reflecting significant issues in the investment management industry, but reasons, nevertheless, that reflect upon more fundamental problems inherent in the investment process. I deal with these proximate reasons showing how they relate to these other, more profound problems.

Whatever the language of investment management, often described in presentations to potential clients (fund trustees) as a deliberate process of risk control and selected investment within a set of well-defined protocols, lower-than-expected returns is an ever-present threat. Trading in markets involves risk and uncertainty; witness the recurrent but unpredictable crashes over the past two decades and the erratic bond markets of recent years. More important, perhaps, for individual trustees there are significant risks in making asset allocation decisions, and selecting fund managers and investment products. Trustees risk making the wrong decision, and finding, after the fact, that past performance profiles are unreliable predictors of future performance. Recognizing this reality, plan trustees have all kinds of strategies designed to limit their risk exposure to embarrassment: one kind of strategy is to choose investment managers and investment products that other fund trustees choose. Subsequent poor performance can then be 'explained' by reference to similar decisions made by well-accepted market institutions, not the particular choices of individual trustees. Not surprisingly, this kind of behaviour limits innovation and reinforces the dominance of conventional products and managers (see Zeckhauser, Patel, and Hendricks 1991).

It is also the case that plan trustees are often chosen because of their 'reliability'. For example, industry consultants report that union-appointed pension plan trustees are, more often than not, peripheral to the union executive. As a consequence, they are reluctant to make decisions which would expose them to the critical scrutiny of union officials or their members. The fact that many such trustees reasonably believe their own (limited) wealth is at risk if they make a decision which is then found to have been not in accordance with their fiduciary responsibilities further encourages conservatism (Jobling 1994). Indeed, many US union-controlled pension funds appear to be wary of even investing in stock markets, let alone AIPs; these funds typically rely upon a small, accepted network of pension fund consultants and advisers whose reputations are built around risk minimization in the bond market. Similar kinds of arguments can be made about public and corporate pension fund trustees, although it is harder to generalize. For many corporate funds, the basic goal is predictability: the minimization of unexpected claims for increased funding of corporate pension liabilities in the context of the continuing needs of operating units of the corporation for investment resources.

Given the significance of DB programmes, the issue of predictability may have another effect on the rate of adoption of new types of investment products. Well-defined (over time) liability profiles tend to encourage fund trustees to make asset allocation decisions that promise an overall return consistent with the predicted liability profile and the current rate of contributions, instead of the likely highest rates of return. For many DB plans, the crucial decision is the asset allocation decision, rather than the investment product decision. And given the often untried nature of AIPs, as well as the common lack of plausible temporal profiles of likely returns matching the temporal profile of plan liabilities, to make an investment in AIPs would be, in effect, to make an investment outside of the liability profile. In theory, defined contribution plans are more likely to accept AIPs because the value of an individual's pension is the accumulated value of particular investments made over the course of that individual's working career. Here, asset allocation is thought by many to be less important than the performance of investment products over quite short periods of time. This may mean, however, that for AIPs to be adopted at a significant level, they would need a liquidity (exit) potential much like mutual fund traded equity products.

It might be supposed that trustee conservatism is an insurmountable barrier to the adoption of AIPs. However, recognizing the need for greater scrutiny of investment options in the face of recent events in the markets, pension funds have widened their use of investment consultants. In part, this has involved more detailed and systematic analyses of the performance of competing investment managers, as well as the comparative analysis of a wider range of investment options. There has been a growing realization, of course, that pension fund trusteeships are more important than many institutions heretofore acknowledged. Thus, the average trustee is increasingly younger, better educated, and more closely related to the financial interests of pension fund sponsors. Indeed, in some companies and, most significantly, in many public pension plans there has been a realization that an active, professional, and closely managed investment programme could reduce the funding (liability) burden of plan sponsors over the long term. And perhaps most significantly, the apparent range of investment products available to participants in defined contribution plans has prompted many DB plans to reconsider their investments in light of plan participants' possible investment preferences.

Trustee conservatism can be mollified or assuaged. We must be careful not to exaggerate its significance. As a consequence, AIPs may become more widely adopted as legitimate investment products. Even so, as mentioned in the introduction, there are two interrelated problems, more profound in the sense of reflecting basic elements of the Anglo-American investment management industry, that may limit the significance of AIPs with respect to funds' total investments. These are (1) the costs of imperfect information; and (2) the management of the agent (plan trustees)–agent (investment managers) relationship, given the potential for misrepresentation (at best) and corruption (at worst).

Recognizing that plan trustees (representing plan sponsor and plan participants) have a legitimate interest in making informed decisions about investments, products, and managers, it should also be acknowledged that collecting the relevant information can be quite costly. Just assembling the basic data on investment performance is a significant task. Making sense of that information, and distinguishing between noise, misinformation, and true information is a very sophisticated task, one which involves problematic questions of financial and economic theory, as well as judgements about the veracity of investment managers. Whereas it might be imagined that investment managers would willingly offer 'objective' information to plan trustees in the hope of attracting funds to manage, in fact, investment managers are incredibly selective in the information they provide and cannot be trusted to provide information that would reliably discriminate between systematic and non-systematic trends in their investment performance. Investment managers have an undeniable interest in representing their performance in the best possible light. Plan trustees face real problems in discriminating between investment managers who 'fudge' the data, and those who systematically misrepresent the true situation for short-term reward. Whereas it might be thought that investment consultants may easily solve these problems of information and veracity, plan trustees must also be careful to select independent consultants whose motives are known and reliable.

These are important problems for the investment management industry as a whole. In the case of AIPs, however, it would appear that the costs of information and the potential for corruption are far higher than is commonly the case in the investment management industry. Because AIPs are, by definition, new and innovative, few investment consultants and even fewer pension plan trustees have developed routines by which to evaluate claims about the potential performance of these types of products. And because many AIPs typically come from vendors outside of the core of the industry, it is also difficult to evaluate the veracity of those who claim to manage these investment products. Reputations are fragile, often unproven, and subject to dispute given the complexity of many of these types of products. Another way of representing the issue is to say that, in general, AIPs are *opaque* investment products; how they are managed, how they are structured, and how they perform relative to third-party defined benchmarks are all issues which cannot be determined directly from the market (Clark and O'Connor 1997). Unlike many conventional investment products derived from the two dominant asset classes, investors (plan trustees) can only obtain this kind of crucial information from the vendor. Not surprisingly, pension fund trustees are preoccupied with vendor veracity.

## Second-Order Financial Intermediaries

If the rate of adoption of AIPs is to increase, and if pension funds are to allocate a significant and increasing portion of their total assets to AIPs, it is my contention that, relative to conventional investment products, the costs of information have to be reduced, and reliable tests of the veracity of product providers introduced. In a sense, this means that the risks of investing in AIPs should be demonstrably consistent with their likely returns. For many pension funds, however, the risks of AIPs are either too large relative to expected returns, or, worse, undefined (subject to uncertainty) given the lack of adequate a priori defined measures of performance and tests of veracity.

It is also my contention that single, stand-alone projects designed and managed for individual clients are rarely the most efficient way of providing AIPs, nor the likely long-term 'best' practice of the industry. While there are instances of stand-alone AIPs, more often than not, public pension fund investment, in particular, infrastructure projects and community-based industrial developments, are less attractive to outside investors. This is for three reasons. First, given the risks inherent in AIPs, to invest in a single, stand-alone project is to amplify those risks. Risk-sharing or pooling is a desirable ingredient in any investment. To the extent that the risks of investing in AIPs can be offset by risk-sharing, both the rate of adoption and the level of investment in AIPs will increase. Second, given the risks of investing in AIPs (and the need to match the flow of revenue to expected liabilities), trustees prefer an exit option (an option to liquidate their investment). Absent an exit option, single, stand-alone AIPs may easily capture pension funds holding them hostage to the (unrevealed) interests and ambitions of project developers. Third, stand-alone investment projects typically have higher-than-average administration costs. They lack the scale economies of more conventional products.

My argument that AIPs must solve information and veracity problems if they are to be successful, in terms of the rate of adoption and volume of investment, is implicitly an argument for a solution. Given the lack of robust markets for AIPs and apparent need for ways of risk-sharing, guaranteeing liquidity, and ensuring a reasonable match between risk and net return, financial intermediaries are essential for designing and managing what Merton and Bodie (1995) termed 'customised products'. For Robert Clark (1975: 1608 and 1610), 'second order financial intermediaries' are institutional mechanisms for parcelling or pooling together diverse sources of funds, so as to take advantage of diversification ('the law of large numbers') on a cost-effective basis (the virtues of 'larger scale'). These intermediaries are functionally located between pension funds and financial services markets offering expertise in project-based investment management and management of the flow of funds.

Some major investment companies like J. P. Morgan and Rothschilds do offer AIPs to their clients. But these are unusual investment management companies; it is clear that the expertise and knowledge necessary to design successful AIPs are such that speciality institutions are the most common sources of AIPs. The obvious questions that derive from this kind of analysis are, then, fourfold. First, what are the common forms of AIP intermediaries? Second, how are they designed? Third, what is the relationship between AIPs and the financial markets? And fourth, is there any evidence that AIPs, once designed and implemented, migrate to the financial markets to become 'standardized products' by virtue of their established track records? For the balance of the chapter, I analyse and discuss four AIP intermediaries in relation to these questions.

*Type 1 AIP: Modified Mutual Fund.* One way of designing an AIP is to modify an existing, standardized product. Modification is a common strategy of product innovation in the investment management industry; it is a strategy which draws upon the established expertise and management capacities of the firm. In the main, the costs of such a strategy are marginal to the existing cost structure of the firm, when compared to the high costs of setting up a completely new venture (Clark 1994). Given the already diverse product mix of many large, established mutual fund companies (such as Fidelity, MFS, Mercury, etc.), it is not surprising that these companies have sought ways to extend their reach from the retail side, to the funds management side of the market, by tailoring existing products to meet pension fund trustees' investment goals. Since so many of their products are portfolios of traded stocks, bonds, or both, mutual companies tend to offer tailored products that are based upon selected securities, as opposed to the whole universe of a market's stocks and bonds. This is a very common strategy on the ethical investing side of the retail market (see Kinder, Lydenberg, and Domini 1992 for details).

The value of bundling together selected securities into a product for pension fund trustees depends upon a number of factors. First, security selection must be done in such a way that achieves trustees' interests at a cost which is acceptable compared to either a standardized product or a traded index product. Second, since stock selection is an information-intensive process combining both quantitative and qualitative assessment, firm-specific expertise is an essential aspect of the development of any tailored product (F. Black 1985). Otherwise, if the product simply mimics or matches a standardized product already available in the market, net returns may be much lower than the accepted benchmark. Delegation of the design of investment products is common; some analysts would suggest it is an essential step in the investment process, given the relative isolation of fund trustees from the market, in general, and the leading edge of product innovation, in particular (D. W. Diamond 1984).

Now, it might be argued that this type of AIP is trivial or rather prosaic, compared to those AIPs that attract the political limelight. Even so, it is a type of product which has attracted considerable interest amongst US union pension fund trustees. To illustrate, the Massachusetts Financial Services (MFS) Union Standard Trust ('Trust') was designed to take advantage of the company's securities selection and bundling expertise associated with its mutual fund business. It is a product which allows union pension fund trustees (and, by extension, their members) to invest in companies and institutions that are identified as 'sensitive' to organized labour's interests. It is comprised of the following components: stocks, bonds, and ETIs (private placements). The last component may be as much as 10 per cent of the total assets of the Trust. So as to ensure the credibility of their product, MFS contracts with another financial services company for the management of an index against which to evaluate the performance of the Trust, and relies upon an Advisory Board of union officials and academics to ensure security selection and direct investment are consistent with the goals of pension fund trustees.

Although apparently a well-understood product (referencing the mutual fund industry), it is quite sophisticated. At one level, it draws upon the expertise of the company in collecting, sorting, and valuing information. At another level, there are third-party tests of the performance of the product, providing institutional-independent tests of competence. In this respect, the Trust offers a formal and institutional solution to the twin problems of costly information and veracity. It also offers a chance for pension fund trustees to share risk and pool resources, as well as promising liquidity (shares in the Trust can be offered for sale) and low administrative costs compared to other AIPs. Of course, in the end, the value of the Trust may well be determined by the performance of the ETI component. Compared to the other two components, the ETI component should be thought of as a long-term investment; there is a risk that trustees may be locked in if it performs poorly. Nevertheless, it is an AIP that may be significant in the asset allocation decisions of union pension fund trustees.

*Type 2 AIP: Secured Investment Trust.* In general, Type 1 AIPs are valued for their underlying diversity, discounted by their degree of specialization (as implied by modern portfolio theory; see Sharpe and Alexander 1990). In recent years, many specialized mutual funds have been developed and offered in the market, some of which specialize in urban infrastructure, construction, and development securities. To the extent to which there is a relationship between firms' capital costs and the market value of their securities, recognizing that this relationship is open to dispute, just as the more general hypothesis of market efficiency is open to debate (compare Cragg and Malkiel 1982 with Grossman 1989), then it may be argued that Type 1 AIPs may play a significant (if indirect) role in promoting pension fund investment in urban areas. Alternatively, funds could invest in trusts which directly invest in urban development and urban housing, eschewing the virtues of diversification for the benefits of commitment.

Type 2 AIPs generally have three characteristics (based upon the AFL-CIO Housing and Building Investment Trusts). First, they are typically highly specialized: in a segment of the market, perhaps low- and medium-income housing, a geographical region, or a sector like construction. Second, trust investments are not normally traded on the open market, although there are some listed property trusts and the like. It is possible to sell out of a trust, perhaps to the trust manager or holding company, but more likely to another potential investor willing to assume the obligations of the existing trust investor. Third, in many cases trust investments are either guaranteed in the sense that investors' commitments are backed by mortgages on the properties held by the trust, or they are insured in the sense that the government provides insurance in case of default on loans. This does not mean, however, if the trust were to fail, investors would be able to redeem their expected returns, nor does it necessarily mean they would be able to redeem the full value of their initial investment. Trust investors would have, nevertheless, preferential status in terms of the distribution of residual assets.

For pension fund trustees seeking to diversify their asset allocation profiles, Type 2 AIPs are attractive for a variety of reasons. Over the past couple of decades, property and related investments have performed well in many markets when compared to bonds and other similar securities. While the variance of returns (risk) has been larger than standard securities, many pension funds have looked to investment trusts for higher-than-average returns. In choosing between trusts, however, the twin problems of costly imperfect information and the veracity of trust managers are especially significant. While it is generally understood how investment trusts function, it is very difficult to obtain reliable third-party information on the internal operation of particular trusts. Consequently the stability, expertise, and performance record of trusts are very important information for pension fund trustees: all three types of information can be verified by consultants and can be used as indicators of the quality of trust management. Likewise, on the veracity side of the equation, the participation of other pension funds and the reputations of trust investment managers can be verified outside of the information provided by trust managers.

In terms of risk-sharing, investment trusts can spread risks in a variety of ways. By limiting investors' shares of particular projects, as well as by providing a variety of projects with different risk profiles (housing versus office development etc.), the risk of poor performance can be spread between different projects. Equally, pension funds can spread risks by investing in a variety of trusts, as opposed to just one trust. Even if the potential liquidity of individual trusts is problematic, investing in a set of trusts, each with a different time horizon over which returns will flow and reach maturity, can provide pension funds a portfolio of related investments whose risk-and-return characteristics can be traded off against one another and the performance of other assets. The limits to this kind of strategy are twofold: the higher costs of administrating a bundle of investment trusts, each of which is a lower investment than that which would flow to a single investment; and, the competence of investment trusts offering diverse opportunities within the trust or the competence of investment advisers in choosing between trusts offering different types of projects.

Why do pension funds prefer secured investment trusts over other kinds of property and investment trusts that are not so guaranteed or insured? We could argue that because pension fund trustees are conservative, any risk that can be covered will enhance the value of a potential trust investment. This is important. But more important, I believe, are a couple of issues which derive from the discussion about the costs of diversification: the costs of diversifying trust investments, given the expected returns may be too high relative to the costs of investing in conventional asset classes' products. Furthermore, the costs of discriminating between competing information about trusts' managers and their potential performance may be such that fund trustees prefer to hold a smaller set of investments with a larger investment per trust. Fund trustees may be more willing to make 'big bets' on selected trust managers than spread their investments amongst a larger set of trusts and incur higher administration costs for lower individual returns. Underlying this logic, is the presumption that commitment backed by securitization is a better long-term investment strategy compared to a simple strategy of risk management.

*Type 3 AIPs: Pension Fund Investment Innovation.* The two previous types of AIPs draw heavily upon existing market-based investment firms, and analogous products that are either traded, or bought and sold through financial intermediaries. These are important products. In terms of the total volume of investments, specialty mutual fund products are a huge and growing part of the industry; pension funds are increasingly using these products or modified like-products to meet fund participants' interests in self-managed active investment strategies. Modified products along the lines suggested by the MFS example are also increasingly popular in areas like infrastructure, property, and technology. Not surprisingly, given the conservatism of so many trustees, these products and secured investment products linked to mortgage guarantees and the like, are the limit for many pension fund trustees.

However, there are other kinds of financial intermediaries which are based less upon existing market products, and are more deliberately innovative in design and intention. Type 3 intermediaries have three characteristics. First, like MFS, they are multi-purpose financial managers; they may be fund custodians, administrators, and advisers. Like MFS, they tend to use the administrative and technical infrastructure of the organization to develop investment products at the margin of their core activities. In a sense, these intermediaries use the sunk costs associated with their other activities to reduce the set-up and accumulated costs of developing new products. A second important characteristic of these organizations is that they are the beneficiaries of scale economics; funds managed or administered are large by industry standards. Thus, the overhead costs of new, innovative AIPs can be easily spread across the other activities of the organization. Third, these organizations, unlike MFS and even Type 2 intermediaries, aim to hold their AIP investments over the long term, matching the temporal profile of their pension funds' defined benefit programmes.

In some instances, these organizations are individual pension plans. The largest US pension funds have enormous internal expertise and, by virtue of the size of their funds, low per-unit administrative costs. These may be public, non-profit, and private funds. In other instances, these organizations are the fund managers for sets of public funds. For instance, the New York City Bureau of Asset Management (BAM) acts as an investment services 'firm' to five of the largest New York City pension plans, providing the conventional asset management services of Wall Street investment houses, as well as specialized expertise in urban investment. In other cases, these organizations have been established by large private funds concerned to reap the benefits of scale in terms of promoting new kind of products not provided by the market or market-based financial intermediaries. An example of this kind of organization is the IFS company, a financial services firm established by a number of large, private industry (occupational) pension plans in Australia.

With respect to the New York BAM, there are a number of advantages to such an arrangement. Because of their scale and independence from private investment management firms, their knowledge base is more extensive about the margins of, and intersection between, markets. This means they are able to draw upon expertise throughout the industry, rather than having to rely upon particular, firm-specific expertise. Unlike private financial companies, they also have the luxury of patience: they can take the time to design and structure a deal, involving both public and private agencies, in investment projects normally considered too complex for a single firm to package together. Over time, then, the BAM has become skilled in deal-making. They have become brokers for public and private agencies seeking new and innovative ways of developing large-scale urban investment projects. The fact that they have close, intimate, and long-term relationships with their trustees adds to the confidence that outside organizations place in their developments. The fact that they (Bureau employees) are paid by salary, rather than by a proportion of the value of the brokered deal, also adds to a perception of independence when compared to private investment companies.

Notice also that the BAM has a peculiar relationship to other financial intermediaries. If they are able to develop financial products or standardize financial arrangements in ways that may be replicated, then, not surprisingly, commercial companies often take up those 'products' for the market at large. Notice also that the BAM is willing to make project-specific commitments; thus the conventional presumptions in favour of risk-sharing and liquidity are deliberately flouted in the interests of making a long-term difference to the quality of urban life. This is only possible, of course, because of the enormous volume of assets in the five funds, and the fact that they allocate and manage assets in the standard classes. Risk-sharing is not done with specific projects but between asset classes. The degree of project specificity is such, however, that few other organizations are willing to assume a significant burden of risk. While the BAM does accept partnerships, partnerships are not essential for its investment strategies. They are willing to assume all risks.

In summary, the costs of imperfect information are minimized by the BAM by internalizing market relationships. The potential costs of agent-to-agent relationships are eschewed by virtue of the close relationships between the Bureau and its pension plan trustees. The issue of veracity is dealt with by making the relationship personal and political, instead of commercial and purely financial. This does not mean that corruption is impossible, nor does it mean that the interests of the BAM, and pension plan trustees and beneficiaries are always closely aligned. Corruption is clearly a real threat to the integrity of the whole institutional structure. Indeed, there is a real risk that just one instance of corruption would threaten the viability of the public management of pension funds. In a world in which there is great suspicion of the motives of public officials, an instance of corruption could be the switch-point for privatization. Furthermore, the assumption of risk and the lack of liquidity could easily make the BAM vulnerable to political intrigue, should a project fail even if for no fault of the BAM. Political risks are high, even if the potential for AIP innovation is also significant.

*Type 4 AIPs: Venture Capital Investments.* At the margin, the BAM is involved in venture capital development. It is not, however, a necessarily desired arena for the BAM. Given the costs in monitoring the performance of venture capital projects, they would prefer to leave the field to others more skilled and experienced in the area. At one level, it might be imagined that venture capital projects are an obvious and important arena for pension fund investment. These types of projects can have significant and long-term effects on local employment and income. The fact that most venture capital projects are in small and medium businesses also means that there is considerable potential for development of new businesses and industries in areas dominated, for example, by traditional industry. However, it is clear, in the USA at least, that despite the obvious appeal of such investments, pension funds have become increasingly concerned about the advisability of playing a significant role in this area.[1] Some industry commentators believe, in fact, that venture capital is scarcer now than ten years ago.

Why? According to Economic Innovation International, a Boston-based development finance company, pension fund investment in venture capital projects face three significant barriers to success. First, many pension funds lack the internal expertise to adequately assess firms' capital needs. Characteristically, start-up firms have practically endless capital needs. The challenge for pension funds is to assess those claimed needs in the context of the firms' markets and growth potential. Second, many pension funds do not realize that the single most important determinant of venture capital success is the managerial competence of the start-up firm. Even if pension funds do acknowledge the significance of this issue, they typically lack the internal expertise and the resources to assess managerial competence. Third, many pension funds treat venture capital as an investment outside of their liability commitments. That is, they treat these kinds of investments as high-risk ventures which have to be insured against by higher returns from other asset classes. Again, the problem is the lack of expertise on the side of the pension funds, and the inability of trustees to be able to discriminate between good risks and bad risks.

Not surprisingly, pension funds have tended to withdraw from venture capital financing. The risks of making a bad investment are significant, and the basis for making investment decisions seems, to many trustees, to be arbitrary and subject to political pressure. Highly publicized failures, and the involvement of public pension funds in many of those ventures, have raised serious questions about the integrity of the process of direct pension fund investment in new ventures. In this respect, the twin problems of costly imperfect information, and the lack of reliable mechanisms for a priori judgements of the veracity of venture firms, combine in a most savage way: in the absence of trust, pension funds necessarily have to withdraw from the venture capital market.

However, while these are significant barriers to pension fund investment in venture capital projects, a number of consulting companies have

developed tests of performance and measures of veracity to help inform
trustees in making investment decisions. There are three kinds of tests:
tests of commitment, tests of reputation, and tests of responsibility. Since
the motives and intentions of venture company principals cannot be
directly assessed, tests of commitment are one way of judging their long-
term involvement in the project. For instance, one important test of
commitment is whether the firm's principals would invest their own
resources in the venture, and the scale of that investment relative to
their total wealth. Since it is difficult to assess new ventures in relation
to market opportunities, one test of reputation is whether the firm can
attract other stakeholders who have made independent assessments of
the viability of the project. And since management is so essential to the
success of a new venture, a test of responsibility is whether the principals have management routines and structures consistent with the
goals and objectives of the firm. None of these tests guarantee success;
new ventures are notoriously vulnerable to shifts and changes in market
conditions, including the actions of other competing firms.

Another set of issues, of course, relate to risk-sharing, liquidity, and the
costs of administration (relative to returns). Inevitably, liquidity is problematic; the success of these kinds of ventures requires long-term commitment. Liquidity options may actually serve to undercut the potential
of these kinds of projects by allowing investors an exit option in circumstances where they ought to be highly committed to the principals of the
firm. Risk-sharing is also problematic. Discounting the importance of a
project, by insuring the risk of poor performance with other competing
projects or other asset allocation decisions, may also undercut the importance of commitment. In this sense, the conventional logic of diversifying risk owed to modern portfolio theory is a threat to the coherence of
long-term investment. For many trustees schooled in modern portfolio
theory, convinced by investment consultants of the advantages of asset
diversification in conventional investment products that rely on the stock
and bond markets, to go against modern portfolio theory is to enter a
world which has been heretofore conveniently closed: the world of
imperfect markets, inefficient markets, and capital scarcity.

But to enter this world is to also realize there may be significant costs
in administering these types of projects. Compared to the costs of
managing stock portfolios, the costs of venture capital investment may
be thought very high indeed. Thus, the development of new kinds of
financial intermediaries, specializing in the management and provision
of expertise relevant to these kinds of ventures, is a vital ingredient in
any pension fund investment system. Just at the moment, however, there
are few such intermediaries that can claim to have been so successful

as to be able to make a significant difference to pension funds asset allocations and rates of adoption of AIPs.

## Role of Regulation

What, then, is the proper role of government policy with respect to pension fund investment in AIPs? Does public regulation have a role in fostering AIPs? If so, what kind of role? These are difficult questions. As I indicated at the beginning of this chapter, the pension fund industry operates in a quite decentralized manner within a framework of customs and rules that owe their origins to English common law. For regulation to make a difference to the rate of adoption of AIPs and the share of assets allocated to AIPs, we have to suppose that a set of incentives and sanctions could be designed and implemented by governments in ways that would change (for the better) existing behaviour. It is true that there have been significant changes in the pension fund investment management industry, partly the result of government policy. For example, the adoption of modern portfolio theory by fund trustees required a reassessment of common law rules regarding fiduciary duty. Recently, the US DoL had a significant impact on pension fund decision making when it introduced the Avon letter regarding the obligations of fund trustees to vote proxies. The impact of their ETI determination, allowing trustees to take into account other factors when making investment decisions, has been less clear.

It should also be recognized that, notwithstanding the English common law heritage which marks off Anglo-American countries from others (e.g. Germany and Japan) with very different investment principles, the advanced English-speaking countries have quite different financial systems and regulatory cultures (as should be expected; Clark 1992). The collapse of Barings is a reflection on the institution and its management, but also a reflection on the British regulatory system. Thus, it is very difficult to be precise about the best kinds of regulation with respect to promoting the adoption of AIPs. At the same time, it should be also recognized that country-specific regulations which go against the grain of the international finance industry may have significant negative consequences for those countries' investment communities; local regulation of finance is inevitably implicated with the international arena (Kane 1993). It would be naive to believe otherwise and, worse, counter-productive to imagine that a set of regulations which went against the grain would survive the arbitrage potential of international financial flows. So, in this context, the points made below about regulation and AIPs relate most specifically to the underlying theoretical framework of the chapter.

Throughout the chapter, I have emphasized the significance of the twin problems of information acquisition and veracity as barriers affecting the rate of adoption and volume of AIP investments. To the extent that Anglo-American countries have policies aimed at stimulating AIPs, there are two commonly advocated types of policies: preferential tax treatment and mortgage guarantees. In effect, preferential tax treatment of AIPs increases the net return to investors of such investments. This makes them more attractive, compared to the established risk profiles attributed to such investments and compared to other asset classes. At the same time, they make no difference to either the costs of information acquisition, nor do they make any difference to the issue of veracity. In fact, given the likely short-term nature of such policies, normally being contentious in the political arena and subject to change as political parties come and go, it could be reasonably argued that they make no difference to the long-term investment strategies of pension funds. In any event, in most countries individuals do not pay taxes on their year-end accumulated pension investments (except Australia), unless they cash-out their benefits. Preferential tax treatments of AIPs are most likely irrelevant, possibly a windfall for the individuals involved, and most obviously an unwarranted distortion of the comparative risk-return profile of investment products.

The other commonly proposed policy is for government to provide mortgage guarantees and the like, so as to encourage investment in AIPs. This kind of policy has been an important element in the success of the AFL-CIO's Housing Investment Trust/Building Investment Trust (HIT/BIT) (Type 2) housing and construction funds, and, more generally, the provision of low- and moderate-income housing by banks and other related financial intermediaries in the USA over the past couple of decades. And yet, there are increasing doubts about the advisability of continuing these kinds of insurance programmes. The savings and loan crisis, recurrent funding problems faced by the Pension Benefit Guaranty Corporation, and the threats posed to the banking system of mounting debts in that sector's deposit insurance programme, have all been taken as evidence for rethinking the costs and benefits of investment insurance programmes (see Bodie and Merton 1993). In general, it is argued that these kinds of policies encourage moral hazard and promote adverse selection. That is, because the downside risks of a decision are borne by others, it is supposed that investors will take advantage of that fact by undertaking investments that, absent the insurance programme, would be assessed as too risky, given expected returns.

If an insurance programme were to promote AIPs, there is a risk that AIPs designed and developed in the investment community would have significant moral hazard components. The question is, of course, as follows: how significant would the moral hazard component be, given the benefits of AIPs for the community? Put slightly differently: what level of costs would the community be willing to bear in exchange for the development of an AIP industry? Answers to these questions are obviously, and legitimately, political. Answers would vary by country and by virtue of their particular political cultures. And while the evidence for moral hazard is considerable in those instances noted above, there is little systematic evidence available which could help define the potential for moral hazard in the pension fund investment management industry. So, the potential for moral hazard seems to be an open question.

Still, it could be argued that the threat of moral hazard might be best managed at the industry level rather than the community level. It seems obvious that the public at large, and even government regulatory agencies charged with representing the public, are not well located to monitor investment decision making. Moreover, it is also obvious that individuals have very little at stake in monitoring decision making. On the other hand, those pension funds and investment companies that have sought to develop the AIP industry do have a large stake in the practice of investment decision making. In this respect, it may be more appropriate for government to foster the development of industry-based co-insurance programmes, rather than society-wide insurance programmes. Jackson (1994) makes a similar argument with respect to the problems of managing the threat of moral hazard in US banking holding companies. He cites nineteenth-century examples of industry-based co-insurance programmes, arguing that the incentive structure was more attuned to the level of decision making, monitoring was more effective, and the market recognized the relative efficiency of such arrangements, by virtue of the lower interest rates borne by participating firms.

In effect, the cooperation of pension funds in the development of their own investment firms and products (Type 3 intermediaries) is a step in this direction. While it was argued that this type of institutional structure is very effective in distributing the costs of product innovation, it is also an institutional structure which could be conceived as a means of co-insurance (minimizing the threat of moral hazard). If Type 3 intermediaries were designed along these lines, and if there were clearly defined, formal mechanisms of oversight and reporting, internal to the organization, then it seems likely that these types of intermediaries may be able to attract more funds under management and, hence, spur the development of AIPs. Formal mechanisms of risk-sharing and insurance might then decrease the overall risk profile of the organization relative to expected returns, thereby enhancing the competitiveness of the participating firms. This is a model which deserves more analysis and investigation; it seems preferable to government-based investment insurance programmes.

There are two other ways in which governments could contribute to the adoption and increased volume of investment in AIPs. Given the significance attached here, at least, to solutions to the twin problems of costly imperfect information and veracity, I would argue that this is an important arena for government policy. These are, of course, problems common to the finance industry as a whole. Thus, the policies I suggest below should be understood as policies which would improve the performance of finance markets in general. As well, it should be recognized that these twin problems can never be solved in any complete manner. By its very nature, information is valuable. And information is proprietary. There will always be gaps in the available information on investment performance. At issue, though, is the reliability of the available information.

In particular, I would argue that public disclosure of investment performance by product and firm, according to generic standards of disclosure, is a vital requirement for reducing the high costs of acquiring imperfect information. There are many companies that specialize in collecting such information. This information is, however, often 'selected' information provided by companies concerned to enhance their relative position against competitors. There is extraordinary manipulation of investment performance information at the source (the investment firms), and at the point of publication (the firms which specialize in the sale of information). Each firm has its own framework, and each firm protects the information as it should, recognizing the value of information in the market. However, this information is hardly ever neutral. The selectivity of information is such that many pension fund trustees are unable to competently assess the value of this type of information. They rely increasingly upon consulting firms to make sense out of this information. Disclosure standards should also carry enhanced legal obligations regarding its veracity. This is the case with many stock exchange disclosure standards; these legal obligations should be extended to investment companies' performance.

Should governments regulate risk pooling, liquidity, and the costs of managing investment products? These are other elements identified in this chapter related to the success or otherwise of AIPs. In general, the answer to this question is no. It is clear that just as trustees have different and often non-comparable risk and liquidity preferences, the role of AIPs in fund portfolios vary in terms of their contribution to overall risk-and-return objectives. To legislate risk-sharing and liquidity standards would be to cut against the decentralized nature of the investment process, and unnecessarily impose arbitrary standards on funds with particular liability profiles. At the same time, just as it is very important that pension fund trustees have reliable data on investment performance, it is also essential that they have reliable data on the costs of managing investment products. Thus, I would argue that investment managers should be required, as part of their disclosure requirements, to publish information on management costs according to a generic comparable framework consistent with industry practice.

Should governments sponsor, or in some way promote one type of AIP financial intermediary over others? Again, the answer is no. Actually, Type 1 intermediaries hardly need promotion. They are more common than generally recognized, being part of the core of the investment management industry. Type 2 intermediaries are also well known, if not as important to the core of the industry. The existence in many countries of mortgage securities, and the availability of various risk insurance programmes means that there are mechanisms of developing this part of the AIP market without necessarily relying upon government policy. There is a temptation, of course, to mimic the US with its various mortgage guarantee programmes. But, as I have suggested, this may not be necessary or thought advisable over the long term. It is important to promote Type 3 models of inter-firm and inter-pension fund cooperation. Industry co-insurance may be one important result of such arrangements, as may be new innovations in the organization of product innovation in the AIP market. This type of intermediary, and Type 4 intermediaries are, ultimately, the most likely sources of new products related to AIPs. Tax incentives might be devised for enhancing the design process, or the research and development process with respect to AIPs.

Perhaps most importantly, it might be necessary for regulators to consider relaxing antitrust and related competition policies in the area of AIPs. One wonders how firms would be treated by regulators if they were to group together for co-insurance purposes. It could be argued that such 'collusion' would disadvantage non-participating firms, especially if non-participating firms came from outside of the domestic industry. Indeed, given the World Trade Organization's brief to foster free trade, exclusive co-insurance programmes may be thought to be a restraint on trade if the effect of such programmes was to balkanize a segment of the global finance industry. Whatever the status of these programmes in law, it seems that Type 3 and 4 intermediaries are very important for the future of AIPs in terms of the rate of product innovation, even if Type 1 and 2 intermediaries are the most common forms, in terms of the sheer volume of AIP investment.

## Conclusions

There is a significant gap between the real world of pension fund investment management, and the claimed potential role of pension funds in adopting and funding alternative investment products. In this chapter, it was shown that the rate of adoption and the level of funding of AIPs is very low amongst the major 1,000 US pension plans. Just two kinds of products dominate asset allocation: traded equity and traded bond products. There are slight differences between pension funds, and between the countries generally considered part of the Anglo-American world of finance. Given the cost-efficiency of administering these kinds of products, compared to more complex and costly AIPs, and given the above-average performance of some of these products over the past decade or so, for the next five to ten years, Anglo-American pension funds will continue to allocate the vast bulk of their assets to equity and bond products which promise superior performance. This does not mean that pension fund trustees are disinterested in, or ignorant of, AIPs. Quite the contrary. The issue is how to design and manage AIPs so that the twin problems of costly imperfect information and veracity are reasonably contained within acceptable bounds.

In the main, equity and bond investment products are transparent in structure, and routine in their operation. This does not mean that they all perform much the same. There remain crucial and significant differences between these products in terms of their performance, reflecting, many suppose, the technical sophistication of companies' trading systems, as well as their underlying ability to collect, sort, and value market information. If the structure and management of such products are well known in the investment industry, this is not true of AIPs. It has been argued in this chapter that there are many competing and different ways of managing AIPs; essential to the development of AIPs is the design of financial intermediaries which are to be responsible for their design and management. Here, four types of financial intermediaries were identified, matched with and reflecting different kinds of AIPs. Each of these intermediaries offers a particular way of managing the twin problems of costly imperfect information and the potential for corruption. Each has implications for risk-sharing, liquidity, and the costs of administration.

What is also apparent from this analysis, however, is that those intermediaries offering AIPs which are close to, or mimic, existing traded products in the equity and bond markets, will garner the most resources from pension funds seeking ways to diversify their asset allocations. In part, the apparent significance of these types of AIPs can be attributed to the conservatism of pension fund trustees. They are rightly wary of products which are so opaque that they must trust investment managers to provide them the data and performance standards by which to judge such products' relative value. Those intermediaries which are able to match or mimic the operation of more transparent products should be able to attract even the most risk-averse pension fund trustees. Moreover, those intermediaries able to differentiate and spread the risks of particular investments, while providing the option for liquidity, are also likely to garner a large share of the market for AIPs. The implication of my analysis is that to the extent to which financial intermediaries can design AIPs which have some or all of the known characteristics of existing equity and bond products, then they have a chance of increasing the rate of adoption of AIPs and increasing the level of funding of AIPs. There is a certain irony in this implication, however.

It might be argued that pension funds ought to be less interested in risk-sharing, liquidity, and investment flexibility, given their long-term liability profiles. And it is true that some of the most innovative financial intermediaries and AIPs rely upon the long-term commitment, as opposed to short-term flexibility. For pension funds dominated by defined benefit programmes, it would seem obvious that their interests would be best served by taking a long-term view. But the twin problems of costly imperfect information and veracity have a vicious side-effect: commitment to long-term investment through Type 3 or 4 intermediaries requires a degree of trust and reliance on external investment managers that few pension fund trustees are now comfortable with; it is all too obvious that trust must be earned over the long term, and must be located in institutional frameworks designed around incentives and sanctions that have a clear relationship to the real interests (as opposed to the expressed interests) of trustees and investment managers. There are few such institutional frameworks, and even fewer that have a long-term performance profile which would encourage emulation.

It has been suggested, however, that there are a few examples of Type 3 and 4 financial intermediaries which may be worth developing. Clearly, this is a process of institutional building, perhaps more so than simply a process of product design. It is also a process of coalition formation, coupled with a commitment to collective interests for long-term product innovation. For many theorists, however, this idea would seem to be at odds with the common presumption that the market will provide such institutions if there is sufficient demand. Implicitly, this presumption is derived from the efficient markets thesis, attributed to the originators of modern portfolio theory and associated developments in modern finance. Allen and Gale's (1994*a*) study of product innovation in the finance industry is silent on the issue of institutional structure; they presume a world of complete markets and, implicitly, of institutional supply consistent with market demand. It is also a view associated with the work of theorists like Ronald Coase who have argued that institutional innovation is a market process. His analysis of the private provision of public goods (like lighthouses; see Coase 1974) seems to suggest a process of spontaneous innovation which is hard to credit, given the barriers to commitment and cooperation.

Of course, the real world of market inefficiency and incompleteness has been reluctantly acknowledged by economic theorists (Hahn 1989*b*). It remains to be seen if governments are able to come to a similar realization and understand that they can play an important role in promoting institutional innovation in the pension fund investment management industry. There is a real danger that ideological squabbles over the proper role of government, in general, will swamp the issue of financial innovation. The recent attacks by the Republican majority in the US Congress on the DoL encouragement of information sharing amongst pension funds, with respect to ETIs, seem to be misplaced. If the market for investment products is taken seriously, it should be recognized that we cannot rely on market spontaneity for institutional innovation. At the same time, I doubt that the DoL's ETI policy would make a significant difference to the rate of AIP adoption and the volume of AIP investments. As I have tried to show, the issue is more complex than the ETI policy would seem to suggest.

## Notes

1. Of course, the relationship between the venture capital industry and institutional investors is often difficult and contested. In part, there are profound asymmetries of knowledge and expertise that make it difficult for pension funds to embrace what appear to be high risk, open-ended projects. As well, the elaborate nature of past links and co-dependencies between venture capitalists means

that partnerships between institutional investors and venture capitalists are mediated by third-parties not formally integrated into these agreements. As a consequence, the venture capital industry is both very uneven in terms of its geographical scope and limited in terms of its funding partners. Many states and communities are isolated from the venture capital industry, and will remain so. See the Joint Economic Committee (1985) report on the US venture capital industry which remains as relevant today as it was when first introduced to Congress.

# 9

# Provision of Urban Infrastructure

UNDERSTANDING the role that private financial institutions may play in mobilizing pension fund investment in urban infrastructure is an essential theoretical and practical task. In doing so, this chapter is part of a growing interest in urban studies in the structure and performance of financial institutions (see Pryke 1994, and Pryke and Lee 1995), and has relevance for those studying the connection between money and the built environment (Harvey 1989). Here we are particularly interested in the design and management of financial intermediaries, an aspect of the investment process which has received less attention in the urban literature (but see Baxter 1994).

There are, of course, all kinds of urban-related investment products, some of which are traded in the market. But here we focus upon the process whereby pension funds invest in urban projects or products which have long gestation periods, few opportunities for liquidation (exit), and few opportunities for risk-discounting through risk-sharing. To be more specific, our concern is with AIPs, and is consistent with the UK's private finance initiative (re-focused as public–private partnerships), and may be related to the privatization of government investment in urban infrastructure in Australia and the USA.[1] One contribution of the chapter is an analysis of infrastructure investments comparing and contrasting the characteristics of pension fund investment in roads and bridges (at one end of the spectrum), with investments in hospitals and housing (at the other end of the spectrum). Another contribution of the chapter is an assessment of the risk-and-return profiles of infrastructure projects, compared to other, more conventional asset classes. Most significantly, the chapter focuses upon the logic behind contractual solutions to problems of financial intermediation involving urban and public infrastructure.[2] The chapter concentrates on infrastructure investment projects that involve long-term contracts, binding parties together for the provision of urban infrastructure, in exchange for an agreed allocation of risks and returns.

In the next section, the demand for infrastructure investments is discussed, focusing attention on their risk-and-return profiles. The goal of this section is to identify and characterize the nature of infrastructure projects according to the formal language of the investment industry. I then identify and analyse three steps taken by pension funds in their evaluation of the risks and returns that flow from different types of infrastructure investment projects. The following two sections consider the advantages and disadvantages of managing risk and uncertainty through formal long-term contracts, before dealing, in the conclusion, with the political context of infrastructure investment. The chapter reports on new initiatives in the pension fund investment management industry, drawing upon interviews in the USA, the UK, and Australia. While there exists a close involvement with a number of pensions funds and related consulting firms, unfortunately, I have not been able to directly attribute sources for arguments and opinions, for reasons of confidentiality.

## Infrastructure as an Investment Product

Convention dominates pension fund investment strategies: in Australia and the USA, this means, more often than not, that funds are allocated to a mix (in order of importance) of equity products, fixed income products, property, and 'other' investments (including cash). Whereas equities and bonds, together, dominate US and Australian pension fund investments, in the UK equities tend to dominate all other asset classes (for details, see EFRP 1996). These differences are significant. But reasons for these differences between countries need not detain us here. It is sufficient to observe that in Anglo-American countries, industry practice is dominated by the largest pension funds and the service providers. The industry is remarkably concentrated on both sides of the equation (pension funds and investment managers), even if there are many thousands of funds and many, many service providers (see Clark et al. 1996 for Australian data).

The mix of pension fund investments also varies according to the type of pension fund, its relative maturity, and (sometimes) its membership base. To illustrate, defined contribution plans (or accumulation plans) do not promise a final benefit or retirement value. Rather, they rely on the flow of contributions and the accumulated short-term performance of investments to generate an individual retirement annuity for plan beneficiaries. Contribution plans are particularly sensitive to the relative short-term performance of different asset classes. By contrast, defined benefit plans typically take account of the expected in-flow of contributions and the expected out-flow of benefits, matching both through the use of investments that seek to maximize returns consistent with the temporal profile of expected benefits. Not surprisingly, given the relative immaturity of many Anglo-American pension plans (more active members than retired beneficiaries), this matching process places a premium on long-term relative performance and predictability.

Performance data for traded products like equities and bonds can be obtained from specialist industry consultants. But there are few databases on infrastructure investment performance that can match the scope of standard databases. This is for a variety of reasons. Because few pension funds have had experience with infrastructure investment, data collection exercises across the industry are expensive relative to the size of the market for the collected data. Because much of the data is proprietary, reflecting the interests of particular investors and vendors of infrastructure projects in maintaining confidentiality regarding the design of such products, there has been reluctance to report performance results. And because it has been difficult to come to common agreement on the appropriate benchmark against which to evaluate infrastructure performance, it has also been difficult to assess the significance of the available performance data. In this context, a research project on infrastructure performance, sponsored by Nippon Credit (Australia), and a group of major financial institutions have provided valuable insights into the performance of infrastructure as an asset class.

The results of the project are summarized in Figure 9.1.[3] Infrastructure performance is located in relation to the risk–return relationship for conventional asset classes, consistent with the theoretical expectations of the capital asset pricing model (see Sharpe and Alexander 1990). This is to facilitate comparison with the performance of other common asset classes over the period 1984–94. Notice that the intercept at zero risk may be higher in Australia than in the USA or in the UK, because interest rates, and, hence, the long-term rate of return on government bonds, are typically higher and have been so for more than one hundred years. Notice also that the relatively poor performance of property compared to the other asset classes, including infrastructure, reflects the remarkable boom–bust cycles of this asset class in Australia over the past few decades.[4] The asset class A Fixed refers to Australian government securities, while the class A Equity refers to the main listed Australian equities, and I Equity refers to international equities (measured by reference to the Morgan Stanley Capital International index). The results for the infrastructure assets were determined by taking the

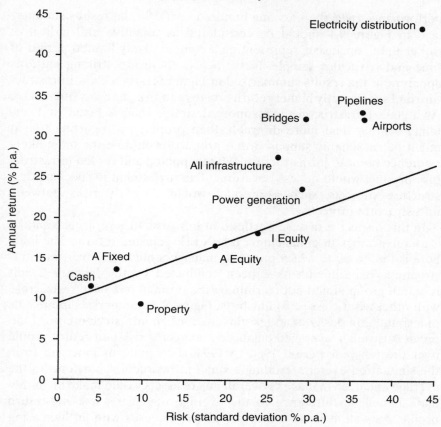

FIG. 9.1. Risk-and-return

yearly returns for each group, and then adjusting for commercial considerations, such as debt/equity ratios and dividend payouts.[5] Naturally, the results also reflect the past national and international environment, and great care would be needed if extrapolating these results into the future.[6]

Recognizing there may be considerable value in individual infrastructure projects, the research programme sought to distinguish between different kinds of infrastructure investments—hence, the identification in Figure 9.1 of bridges and other kinds of infrastructure such as power generation stations, where the evidence can be generalized beyond identifiable individual projects. No infrastructure study, however well conceived and implemented, can hope to be as comprehensive as the available databases on national and global securities' performance over the past one hundred years. So the results summarized in Figure 9.1 should be considered as tentative and indicative rather than conclusive, representing a comparatively limited period of time and particular sample. Nevertheless, there are striking patterns apparent in the results summarized in Figure 9.1. As a class, infrastructure had significantly higher returns, relative to risk, than any other class. As a class, infrastructure is far more desirable than A Fixed, and certainly a great deal more desirable than property, recognizing that it might be reasonably supposed that property would be the most likely reference point to infrastructure. While a pooled and traded infrastructure product would be less rewarding than investment in specific infrastructure projects, such a product would diversify risks between infrastructure projects.

In this respect, a diverse portfolio of infrastructure projects could be a useful strategy in enhancing a fund's risk-adjusted returns. The issue here is the *extent to which* portfolio managers ought to invest in infrastructure. Experiments have been conducted by the Nippon Credit research group aimed at determining the optimal mix of infrastructure with other asset classes. To illustrate, Figure 9.2 summarizes the results of a simulation designed to test the effect of an infrastructure portfolio on an Australian 'averaged balanced manager's' risk-and-return profile over the ten-year period 1984 to 1994.[7] Two patterns emerged from the simulation exercise. Adding a small infrastructure portfolio to the average balanced manager's overall mix of assets would make an immediate beneficial difference to the average manager's risk-and-return profile. As well, it is clear that the effect increases with an increasing proportion of assets (more than 30 per cent) allocated to infrastructure. Thus, an average balanced manager could justify a significant investment in infrastructure, and by implication, most pension funds should hold some exposure to this asset class. This analysis ignores, of course, issues such as the supply of infrastructure investment opportunities and the particular liquidity needs of pension funds. It also assumes that a diversified investment portfolio could be established within the parameters set by investing pension funds.

With respect to the correlation of infrastructure with other asset classes, it was found that infrastructure returns were positively correlated with A Fixed (0.53), but otherwise negatively correlated with A Equity (−0.47), I Equity (−0.38), Cash (−0.55), and, most significantly, Property (−0.86). These results reinforce the point made above about the value of infrastructure to a balanced portfolio and the assumption that infrastructure is a form of higher-value fixed income. Notice, however, that the range of returns within the infrastructure class is quite

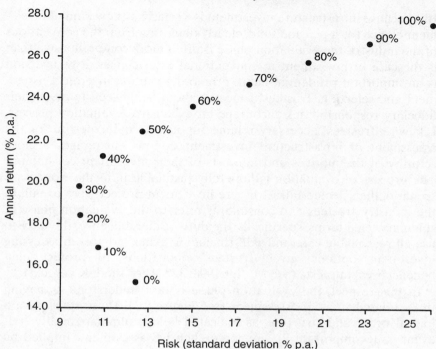

FIG. 9.2. The effect of infrastructure on an average balanced manager's risk-and-return profile

large compared to other conventional classes, raising questions about the internal logic of a pooled infrastructure investment trust. More problematical, the number of observations which is the basis of these results is very small when compared to conventional asset classes such as equities and bonds. We must take care not to underestimate the risks inherent in infrastructure.

## Evaluation Phase of Investment Decision Making

Chapters 6 and 7 sketched out the framing process behind pension fund investment decision making. Here, I deal with what Kahneman and Tversky (1979) have identified as the evaluation phase of decision making. As in the framing phase, habits of prudence, rules of proprietary conduct, and norms of relationships play a role in the evaluation phase.

But because infrastructure investment is a relatively new kind of invest-ment choice for a pension fund, clearly departing from the conventions of the industry, the evaluation phase is often more comprehensive than is the case of investment in conventional asset classes. Risk aversion is an important prudential habit, promoting caution in project assess-ment and selection. Trustees' concerns about being seen to meet their fiduciary responsibilities encourage an exhaustive evaluation process. Likewise, trustees' necessary reliance upon external expertise for the assessment of infrastructure investment options encourages a close scrutiny of the motives and interests of their investment consultants. The process of evaluation is hopefully justifiable if, in the worst case scenario, the selected infrastructure investment project were to fail. In the industry, trustees and consultants refer to the evaluation phase in summary legal terms, specifically the duty of due diligence: the duty to use all reasonable care and skill (including expert advice) in assessing investment options, given trustees' obligations to protect plan beneficiaries' interests (see Moffat 1994: 322–4 for the UK context).

In this respect, the evaluation phase is best understood as having three related steps of assessment (see Figure 9.3). These steps have a logical order and structure, as indicated below, summarizing the rel-evant issues important in any comprehensive assessment. Implied by Figure 9.3 is a hierarchy of steps, suggesting that the third step presup-poses affirmative decisions in the first two steps. But it is likely, more often than not, that the three steps are executed simultaneously, one with the others. Also implied is a certain symmetry or logical coherence, the product (we suspect) of the design of the figure itself. It should be recognized that trustee behaviour need not be as ordered as implied, and that decision trees like Figure 9.3 are more valuable as 'maps' of decisions than normative claims about the proper structure of invest-ment decision making (compare Chapters 6 and 7, with Machina 1991). The first step of evaluation is identified as *functional risk assessment*, and involves a close analysis of the internal structure of the project. The second step of evaluation is *environmental uncertainty assessment* which involves analysis of the place of the project in the wider 'environment' not directly part of (or controlled by) the project. And the third step is *commitment assessment*, referring to the desired level of investment by the fund, given the investment of other partners or parties involved in the project.

Risk assessment refers to the likely consequences of an investment decision given the distribution of possible outcomes (paraphrasing Knight 1921: 233). But risk assessment does not guarantee a particular outcome. Rather, it allows investors to predict the flow of revenue

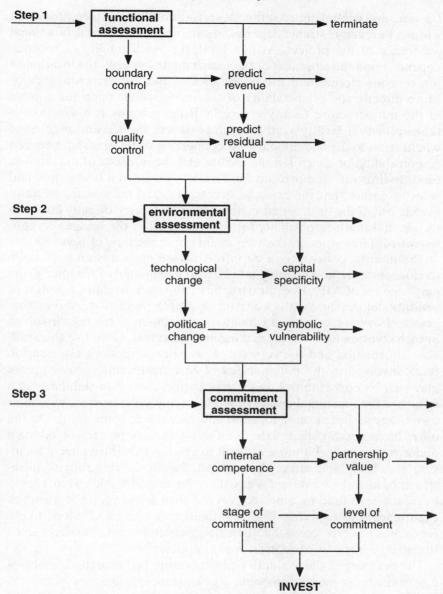

FIG. 9.3. The evaluation phase of investment in infrastructure

(income and capital appreciation/depreciation). For trustees, predicting a project's revenue stream depends, in part, upon the internal, functional coherence of the project. At one level, the predictability of revenue depends upon the closeness of the match made between the location of the revenue stream and the boundaries of the infrastructure facility. More directly, the predictability of revenue depends upon the control of the infrastructure facility especially if *net* revenue is a function of the use of that facility. And most importantly, the stream of revenue would seem to depend upon a clear connection or relationship between responsibility for control of the facility, and the interests of the pension fund. To illustrate, if a pension fund were to invest in a bridge, it would want to ensure that the revenue stream matched the volume of automobile use of the bridge, that maintenance costs were directly linked to its use, and that responsibility for the operation of the bridge was consistent with investors' interests in maintaining the flow of revenue.

The internal coherence of an infrastructure project is an issue open to close scrutiny, and possibly influence. As suggested in Chapter 8, the performance of AIPs, like infrastructure projects, is as much a matter of institutional design, as it is a matter of simple prediction. And as suggested elsewhere, to make an adequate assessment of the risks involved in such investments requires making an assessment, as well, of the available information and the veracity of investment vendors. For pension funds involved in the initial stages of an infrastructure project, there may well be opportunities to set information disclosure standards, and influence the functional design of a project in ways consistent with their own interests in risk minimization and revenue maximization. On the other hand, funds coming late to an infrastructure project, or taking a minor role, may find it more difficult to establish their preferred disclosure standards, and affect the internal, functional structure of infrastructure facility investment. Thus, there are considerable advantages in being the lead fund on a project, even if such a role requires a level of experience and expertise that few funds can command. More likely, funds may have to accept that their risk assessments are imperfect given the offered infrastructure investment opportunities.

The next step in the evaluation phase is more problematic. It involves assessing the scope and possible consequences of changes in the external environment with respect to the functional performance of the project. Whereas internal risk assessment may prompt the introduction of risk control measures by pension fund investors, the external environment is not so amenable to control. Trustees may not be able to determine the scope of possible changes in the external environment, nor may they be able to use past experience to estimate the likely consequences of possible changes in the environment: uncertainty is a real threat to trustees' long-term residual value of their investment. To illustrate, the long-term value of a bridge may depend upon the relative accessibility of that site, given the evolving pattern of urban development (most generally), and the ancillary development of competing facilities (more specifically). While it may be possible to limit direct competition, no government could guarantee the shape or pattern of urban structure. Likewise, it would be difficult for a government to stop the introduction of private communications technologies that would indirectly affect the profitability of an investment.

It is impossible to be precise about the scope and nature of the uncertain environment. Nevertheless, in recent years pension funds have been concerned about two categories of uncertainty, both of which have implications for the residual value of an infrastructure project, if not the predictability of its income stream. Technological change might be thought as an especially important category of uncertainty for investments in facilities that have fixed capital structures (like bridges). But it is also important for investments in facilities (like hospitals and airports), where technological change is rapid, and the inherited capital stock is subject to obsolescence. Either way, a fund may become trapped in an obsolete facility or a facility that requires recurrent rounds of reinvestment simply to maintain its revenue base, let alone its long-term residual value. The fact that many infrastructure facilities have political significance, being the symbolic objects in debates about governments' fiscal and social responsibilities, and because such facilities are a crucial part of people's everyday lives, suggests that another category of uncertainty is the long-term public commitment to the private financing of urban infrastructure projects.[8]

Both categories of uncertainty loom large in pension funds' assessments of infrastructure investment projects, and may intersect with, and amplify, one another. For example, imagine that a pension fund invests through the UK PFI in a hospital facility which will require at least two phases of reinvestment over the life of the investment (say twenty years). Also assume the costs of these two phases of reinvestment are to be met through higher user charges. If government funding of the health sector was to fall behind the escalating costs of medical technology, the public may have to pay a higher and higher proportion of the costs of health care. Alternatively the hospital itself may have to divert scarce resources into the PFI facility. The danger is that the priority assigned to maintaining the revenue flow and residual value of PFI facilities may bankrupt community health programmes. Recognizing this possibility, the UK government passed the National Heath Service

(Residual Liabilities) Act of 1996. In doing so, the government effectively politicized the question of who (investors, users, or governments) should pay for technological change in privately financed infrastructure projects. Pension funds are wary of their exposure to substantial shifts in political opinion with respect to the responsibility for providing urban infrastructure, reinforcing their concern to diversify project-based investments through either risk-sharing or pooling.[9]

The third step in the evaluation phase concerns commitment assessment: the level of investment in an infrastructure project, given the interests of other partners in the project. We must recognize that pension funds rarely take the lead on a project. More often than not, pension funds are investing (limited) partners, rather than project developers (general partners). There are exceptions to this rule. Some of the largest funds, with assets of more than $10 billion, have such a wide scope of activities that they are able to build up and maintain in-house expertise in the area of project initiation and design. And as discussed in Chapter 8, groups of pension funds may join together to share expertise and knowledge if projects are large enough, and in sufficient numbers to sustain the added costs of being project entrepreneurs. Of course, the initial stages of project development can carry significant profit opportunities. For pension funds, commitment assessment involves two separate but related issues: the stage at which investment ought to be placed, and the level of investment in each stage of development given partners' commitments.

Characteristically, in the earlier the stage of development the more committed is the investment, and the greater the risks of total loss. In the early stages of project development, there are many development costs which cannot be recovered until the project is either passed on to other investors once the project has been successfully launched, or the project has been totally completed. While these costs may appear, at one level, to be an investment, there are substantial risks that these 'investments' may become sunk costs in the sense that they cannot be recovered in later stages of development. The discounting of initial stakes in development is a common enough experience in the property development industry. Furthermore, in the early stages of development, investors typically have no opportunities to liquidate their investments: they are, more often than not, locked in by prior agreement with other partners who have much less in the way of financial resources. Not surprisingly, given the risk-averse nature of trustee decision making, pension fund investment in the early stages of a project may only occur if: (1) other decision criteria, like commitment to ongoing relationships with other partners, overwhelm prudential caution; (2) if pension funds have prior experience of such complex and intricate projects; or less likely (3) if pension funds are able to convince themselves that the potential returns are such that they are able to justify the risks.

The stage and level of investment also depend, profoundly, upon trustees' assessment of the integrity of their general partners. In many cases, however, partners do not have deep pockets. They are general partners by virtue of their special knowledge, expertise, or skill. They are partners because pension funds are unwilling or unable to internalize project development expertise. The relationship between limited and general partners is complex and the subject of considerable dispute in the industry (see the report by William M. Mercer 1996 on behalf of a group of nine large US pension funds). The very small financial stake of general partners in most projects, and the rather different interests and time horizons of those interests (short-term versus long-term), are all contentious issues reflecting the particular nature of infrastructure investments. The institutional organization of these relationships is at the heart of the infrastructure investment management process.

## Demand for Contract

Pension fund investment in urban infrastructure relies upon the financial intermediation process—an institutional process of mobilizing and managing pension fund assets for placement in unconventional sectors and products (compare with Merton 1994). Whereas so much of financial activity takes for granted the existence of markets and networks of exchange and information, one of the most important functions of intermediation is to organize disparate sources of funds and relevant investment opportunities in circumstances where markets are either missing, or transaction costs are so significant that existing market institutions have few incentives to spontaneously price risk and allocate funds (compare Hahn 1989a, with Houthakker and Williamson 1996). In this context, institutional intermediation is a vital ingredient in infrastructure investment, given the *ex-ante* significance of project data in estimating the virtues of investment (compare with Boot and Thakor 1997).

I would also suggest that contracts are a necessary ingredient in pension fund investment in urban infrastructure, and that the language of contract is pervasive throughout the finance industry. And yet, there are a number of social scientists and analysts who would contend that contracts are either superficial (being a reflection of deeper moral sentiments), or only a formal device to be invoked when all else fails. One

way or another contracts are thought less important than the social relationships which structure and focus the finance industry. Casson (1991)
and Baier (1994), for example, might argue that trust relations are more
important than formal contracts, trust being the 'real' basis for long-
term relationships, in general, and in the investment industry, in particular. They might also reference Luhmann (1979), who suggested some
time ago that trust is a most important social institution for coping with
complexity, and risk and uncertainty. Luhmann's argument was that, in
either case, formal institutions like contracts are inadequate: trust means
relying upon others to bridge the 'gap' when complexity, or risk and
uncertainty overwhelm customary practice. Luhmann's argument and
Gambetta's (1988) edited volume are crucial references for recent
research on economic relationships. But I am not convinced of the
resilience of trust in the finance industry.

In Chapters 6 and 7 it was suggested that decision making is framed
by three sets of imperatives—at the core, habits of prudence, then the
rules of proprietary conduct, and then, the norms of relationships. The
implication of this framing process for trust is clear: risk aversion and
fiduciary responsibility would normally dominate trust, unless trust was
consistent with, or a means of enhancing, risk aversion and fiduciary
care. A more empirical, less theoretical argument would be to observe
that distrust is endemic to the investment management industry, and to
finance in general. Distrust is particularly threatening in project-specific
investments where information is unreliable and often unavailable,
and the motives and interests of potential partners are hard to discern
before making investment commitments. It is difficult to assess a priori
whether potential investment partners are committed to a long-term
relationship, or are seeking a one-time cash-out opportunity at the
expense of the pension fund. In any event, it is very likely that any relationships important in promoting an investment project would give way
over time as individuals move on to other projects, employers, and institutions, and as the institutions themselves reassess the virtues of remaining in the project. Distrust is significant because investors do not know
future partners and can only lock in the current institutional investors
through contracts (compare with Misztal 1996).[10]

Most importantly, it could be argued that trust is itself the product of
contractual relationships. In an analysis of Luhmann's trust model,
Hardin (1996) argues that trust presupposes the existence of past
commitments or relationships that encourage trust in others. In this
analysis, trust derives from relationships rather than creating them,
unless trust is to be understood as an emotional (non-cognitive) disposition about the world in general. This non-cognitive approach is

common enough (see Becker 1996), but seems somewhat irrelevant for strategic and defensive thinking about financial relationships with others. Hardin believes that trust is the result of a variety of social processes, including the structure of incentives in exchange relations, institutional patterns of decision making, and social conventions of all kinds. And it is clear from previous research on trustee decision making that the structure of incentives in the investment management industry are such that distrust is the more likely disposition than trust. In this context, contracts can provide a formal mechanism through which informality can flourish, bounded by a set of sanctions and a process of recovery if trust is misplaced. It may be, of course, that the investment industry is unusual.[11]

For pension funds concerned about the reliability of information and the veracity of investment partners, contracts could be thought to function like other financial intermediaries. And there is no doubt that contracts offer a kind of institutional formality different from, but none the less consistent with, the types of intermediaries identified in Chapter 8. But it is also the case that contracts have other virtues— virtues that may have contributed to the re-emerging significance of private contracts in Anglo-American economies (compared to twenty years or so ago, see Atiyah 1995). In recent years, the institution of contract has been rediscovered, practically and theoretically. Neoclassical economic theory now dominates the theory of contract, emphasizing concepts such as voluntary commitment, informed decision making, and (at the limit) pareto optimal exchange relations (Easterbrook and Fischel 1991). In place of paternalism, the ruling ethos justifying past regulation of contract, the neoclassical contract assumes economic agents are autonomous and fully responsible for their actions. In this context, pension funds are increasingly seen as just another kind of investor, rather than being our agents with general responsibility for social welfare. The formal language of contract matches, in substance, the presumed separation of pension funds from the public arena, and the increasing importance of pension funds as institutions at the heart of economic decision making.

In particular, contracts provide pension funds a formal mechanism for (1) allocating risk and uncertainty between investment partners, (2) for setting partners' performance standards in relation to accepted benchmarks, (3) for defining the rewards and penalties of performance, and (4) for setting the time horizons of investment projects. Formality is essential to the contractual process, either deliberately or indirectly using the language of contract law to set out (in an impersonal manner) the terms of agreement between investment partners. In doing so, a contract is an essential mechanism for clearly establishing parties' obligations and responsibilities prior to entering a long-term investment relationship. And by implication, having signed a contract, the invest-ment partners are presumed to accept the terms and conditions of the contract. In theory, at least, the contract is also a means of establishing pension funds' rights to abrogate an investment contract when a partner cannot perform according to previously agreed conditions.

Given the advantages of contracts, pension funds have come to demand extensive negotiations over the structure of infrastructure investments contracts. The negotiation process is highly involved and must deal with, at least, three issues: the identification of pension fund investment partners' initial costs and benefits, the allocation of risks and rewards over time, and the terms and conditions of compliance (see J. L. Coleman 1992 for a theoretical treatment of these issues). There is a temptation to negotiate contracts that are at once extraordinarily detailed (about the terms and conditions of performance, for example) and comprehensive (about partners, obligations, and responsibilities with respect to anticipated contingencies, for example). In part, this is because detailed and comprehensive contracts allow pension funds to assess, independently of their advisers, the interests of their partners. And just as importantly, complex contractual specifications are con-sistent with trustees' habits of prudence and rules of proprietary conduct.

Nevertheless, complexity can involve very high transactions costs, often sunk costs. In this environment, pension funds and other related financial institutions normally require potential investment projects to meet certain size and structural thresholds so as to spread the costs of due diligence and contractual negotiation. And absent third parties, like governments, that are willing to bear the costs of contractual complex-ity, pension funds and their partners have strong incentives to develop decision making templates which can reduce the costs of contractual complexity in particular projects. Not surprisingly, the search for tem-plates may also be a search for common types of infrastructure invest-ment projects.

## Long-Term Contracts as Managerial Institutions

In theory, '[c]ontracts allocate risks; they specify who bears what costs in the event such-and-such occurs' (J. L. Coleman 1992: 80). So far I have argued that contracts are essential instruments in pension funds' relationships with project partners. And I have suggested that contracts fulfil certain, crucial functions—functions that enable pension fund investment in projects otherwise deemed too illiquid, risky and costly, compared to conventional investment products. Underlying trustees' reliance upon contracts is a combination of formalism and idealism. As we have seen, formalism has many advantages, including the systematic evaluation and deliberate allocation of risks between partners. But notwithstanding the perceived advantages of formalism, many pension funds seem to ima·ine that contracts have a desirable ideal form: the promise of perforᵤᵢ. ·e according to a priori defined terms and conditions, and, if necessary, termination and the assessment of damages for non-performance. Rakoff (1994: 204–5) refers to this ideal as the 'perfect tender' model of contract, analogous to neoclassical discrete exchange models of contractual relationships.

There are reasons to be sceptical of the idealism embedded in the perfect tender model of contract. For a start, it presumes the existence of complete (and comprehensive) contracts covering all possible contingencies. No doubt such contracts are designed and executed; UK industry analysts report contracts for privately financed infrastructure projects, such as hospitals, running for more than 15,000 pages of legal script. But mistakes can be made, a party's interests hidden in obscure detail, and gaps left unfilled, simply because of the incoherence of such large documents. Not surprisingly, there are financial limits to scrutinizing contracts, just as there are cognitive limits to conceptualizing the overall structure of such complex documents. In any event, it is impossible to foresee all possible contingencies, and it is not always possible to incorporate unlikely, but recognized, possibilities into them. Hence, the prospects of injustices, misallocations of risks and returns, and mutually undesirable outcomes loom large. Inevitably, the contracting parties may have to establish their own arbitration procedures to provide advice on a wide range of issues, short of the dissolution of an investment contract (William M. Mercer 1996). Alternatively, they may have to rely upon the courts to settle *ex-post* disputes over the implementation of such contracts.[12] There are real, unresolved issues about the relative costs and benefits of these types of dispute resolution procedures (see generally Cooter and Rubinfeld 1989).

This argument (the inefficiency of complete contracts) is not universally accepted. Nevertheless, it is apparent in the common law and some areas of economics.[13] Rakoff (1994: 204) identifies an alternative notion: the 'substantial performance contract'. Here, the execution of a contract should be evaluated against its substantive design: a contract should not be terminated, nor punitive damages awarded for non-negotiated variations from its terms and conditions, if the substantive performance of the contract is unaffected. Rakoff (1994: 205) makes a crucial observation about the relevance of this notion, and cites an important majority opinion of Cardozo in *Jacob & Youngs* v. *Kent* (1921) to illustrate his point.[14] By his assessment, 'the archetypical case . . . of substantial performance is the building contract' (footnote omitted). In the *Jacob* case, a building contractor had substituted one brand of pipe for another (specified in the contract), leading to a claim for damages from the injured party. The court argued that since the terms of the contract had been substantially met, and since the costs of reparation were disproportionate with respect to the harm inflicted, on balance, it was better to honour the performance of the contract than its literal terms and conditions.[15]

In coming to his decision, Cardozo (p. 890) observed that the nature of an object (service or commodity) subject to contract can have an important bearing upon the courts' determination of non-performance. Referring to the construction of large buildings, he noted '[t]here will be harshness sometimes and oppression in the implication of a condition when the thing upon which labor has been expended is incapable of surrender because united to land, equity and reason in the implication of a like condition when the subject matter, if defective, is in shape to be returned.' Many urban infrastructure projects are 'united to land'. Likewise, they cannot be 'returned'. Indeed, part of their value (risk-adjusted returns) may be directly attributed to their spatial and functional fixity. Two implications follow from the fixity of infrastructure investments for the contractual relationships between pension funds and their partners. One is entirely obvious. Once construction has begun, pension funds may not be able to simply terminate a contract with an investment partner for unacceptable variations on the agreed terms and conditions. The second is less obvious, but no less important. The courts may allow considerable latitude in meeting the terms and conditions of contractual performance, given the economic consequences of an excessively narrow reading of a contract: the courts have an interest in the overall efficiency of the contractual institution (see J. L. Coleman 1992).

There is another reason why the idealism of the perfect tender model is misplaced with respect to pension fund investment in urban infrastructure—it ignores or trivializes the process whereby value (risk-adjusted returns) is generated and the long-term residual value of investment protected (even enhanced). The conventional discrete choice model of contract assumes 'performance is more or less instantaneous' (Bell 1989). In fact, in some long-term contracts there may never be a point in time when the contract is deemed to have been executed and concluded. In these cases, contracts are an umbrella for long-term, committed relationships of one kind or another. For many infrastructure projects, 'performance' occurs incrementally over many years, and depends upon the actions and behaviour of pension funds' agents and their consortium partners. To illustrate, while pension funds may be the ultimate 'owners' of a bridge, they either rely upon a partner to manage the facility, or contract out the management task to third parties that specialize in the management of bridges. Different kinds of infrastructure investments demand more or less management expertise. Notwithstanding the inherent risks of construction, bridges appear to be a relatively simple kind of infrastructure investment, often involving known technology and well-defined performance protocols.

This point is illustrated by Table 9.1. The table summarizes the intersection between two essential components in the management of value (performance) in long-term infrastructure investment projects. These components are management intensity (compared to capital investment), and management autonomy (compared to automated revenue collection). To illustrate, let us return to the bridge example. Assuming the investing pension funds and consortium partners manage the facility, the management task appears trivial compared to other types of facilities. The management resources necessary to operate the facility are small, and management autonomy practically non-existent. Automated toll booths could easily replace those employed to collect tolls if toll agents proved unreliable. But hospitals seem to be an entirely different matter. Management resources are a significant component of the operation of such a facility and are essential to the delivery of quality care and, hence, the flow of patients to the facility. While it is possible to squeeze management resources in the short run, thereby either producing higher levels of performance and/or greater resources for capital investment, the quality of care could suffer (thereby affecting the longer term flow of revenue), and facility managers could face resistance from

TABLE 9.1. *Value and the management of infrastructure projects*

| Management intensity | Management autonomy | | |
| --- | --- | --- | --- |
| | Low | Medium | High |
| Low | Bridge | XX | Utility grid |
| Medium | XX | Airport | XX |
| High | Railway station | XX | Hospital |

the relatively autonomous professionals they rely upon to deliver quality services.

These are two extreme examples, separated by management complexity (low and high), as well as management expertise (low and high). There are clearly other kinds of facilities with very different combinations of management intensity and management autonomy. For example, owning and operating a railway station or airport may require significant management resources, but, nevertheless, rely less on the expertise of specialist professionals than the willing cooperation of employees to meet performance targets. I do not mean to suggest, of course, that this is necessarily an easier task; there are many other variables to be considered and cases to be studied before making a categorical determination of the 'best' type of facility with regard to management ease and performance predictability. But is clear from the UK, at least, that hospital professionals have been better able to claim the sympathy and support of the general public than unionized railway workers, whose skill and competence are believed (rightly or wrongly) to be less significant in the provision of essential services. Some pension funds and their partners, having become aware of these issues, have come to recognize that the outsourcing of management through long-term performance contracts may be a desirable option in mitigating any direct responsibility for what are, after all, contentious political issues.

Pension funds are the agents of plan beneficiaries, fund administrators are the agents of trustees, and investment managers are agents of pension funds (B. Black 1992). Many funds delegate the investment decision making process to investment managers who are expert in particular products and conventional asset classes. Delegation is desired for all kinds of reasons, including the relative costs associated with different scales of investment management (see Demski and Sappington 1987). What remains unclear, however, is the proper design of agency relationships and the allocation of delegated powers in the context of long-term investment contracts. Most delegated, agency relationships are designed for the short term; they mimic the logic of discrete exchange contracts. And like discrete contracts, there is an implied threat of termination if performance is less than acceptable. But to run a hospital (for example) by this kind of institutional arrangement would seem problematic. The management resources and expertise necessary to sustain performance are such that neither pension funds nor their agents would benefit from such short-term arrangements. At the same time, pension funds are wary of long-term reliance upon particular managers; the costs of status quo bias are apparent to many in the industry (see Samuelson and Zeckhauser 1988).[16] Thus, there is a real dilemma embedded in infrastructure management.

## Conclusions

In this chapter I have argued that private investment in urban infrastructure requires the creation of financial intermediaries capable of governing the long-term relationships between investors, and those who manage and operate the relevant facilities. I have also argued that pension fund evaluation of the virtues (and otherwise) of urban infrastructure investments is a three-stage process, involving assessment of the integrity of investment partners, and the spatial and functional specificity of particular projects. Evaluation is costly, information-intensive, and rarely amenable to third-party market intermediation. In this respect, it is inevitable that pension funds will require higher rates of return to cover these kinds of costs, or will demand from government all kinds of risk guarantees. Neither may be politically palatable.

It was also argued that desired contractual instruments for long-term investment may never quite realize the idealism of investors. In summary terms, I agree with Oliver Williamson (1985: 29) who noted: 'it is impossible to concentrate all the relevant bargaining action at the *ex ante* contracting stage. Instead, *bargaining is pervasive.*' In effect, I believe that the governance of infrastructure investment projects over the long term will turn out to be more important than the initial agreement which binds the contracting parties. And yet, for all the current emphasis placed on the contractual process, few in government or in the finance industry recognize the long-term significance of the governance process for delivering promised rates of return.

Contracts are desired for a number of reasons, including pension fund trustees' concerns that their actions and commitments be externally justifiable. But long-term investment contracts are not so easily terminated or altered, as theory would imply, and the necessary reliance of pension funds upon facility managers for the flow of revenue may combine to lock in pension funds to urban infrastructure projects. This does not mean that being locked into an investment is necessarily bad. The inability of markets to completely accommodate risk is an important source of institutional innovation and, at times, significant reward. Those funds willing to risk the dangers of irrevocable commitment are also the institutions that may benefit from such commitments. One problem with contracts as a form of financial intermediation is political.

For instance, in response to questions from the, then, Labour Opposition, Major's Conservative government argued that infrastructure investment contracts would absolve the government from fiscal responsibility and the risks of technological change in the hospital sector (for one).[17] The model of financial intermediation implied by this argument seems implausible, even if experience of this form of intermediation is limited. The notion that such contracts are just like discrete exchange contracts is not credible for infrastructure projects that have a significant management component.[18]

If urban infrastructure needs are to be met through pension funds, new institutions may have to be established to cope with recurrent and evolving conflicts of interest between investment partners, investors, and facility managers. Since long-term investment contracts are desired for their formality, the courts may nevertheless have to appreciate the limits of the perfect tender model of contract compliance—if widely applied, it would be a real threat to pension fund infrastructure investment. In effect, the application of such a doctrine would deny the spatial fixity of returns, and their dependence upon the continuity of investment relationships, by emphasizing investors' short-term interests. In this respect, it may also be desirable for pension fund investors and governments to encourage the formation of arbitration procedures which operate in the shadow of contract law, relying upon third-party arbitrators familiar with the imperatives of such investments. This kind of arbitration model exists in other industries, notably insurance. Should governments promote such arbitration procedures? Here is the most problematic aspect of pension fund investment in public infrastructure: the extent to which individuals' interests in their retirement benefits are consistent with their agents' interests in institutionalized intermediation.

## Notes

1. There is considerable interest in pension fund investment in urban infrastructure, in part allied to moves towards the privatization of infrastructure facilities in the UK, USA, and Australia. See e.g. the General Accounting Office (1996*a*) review of the opportunities and consequences of the privatization of US airports including reference to new investment, revenue effects, and shareholder value. In Australia, the previous Labor government instituted an inquiry into the potential of pension funds contribution to infrastructure provision including recommendations for encouraging the process (see the report of the Economic Planning Advisory Commission 1995 and the December 1996 report of the Senate inquiry). And in the UK, the previous Conservative government

sought to speed the private role in infrastructure financing through the PFI process (see HM Treasury 1995). The recently elected Labour government has indicated that it too will use a PFI type of process. See Terry (1996) for a general overview.

2. Inevitably, this focus requires broader literature and analytical perspectives than that apparent in the urban studies and economic geography literature. Useful methodological perspectives are provided by Thrift and Olds (1996), Hahn (1989*a*), and Williamson (1985) although it will become apparent that we diverge from all on crucial issues.

3. Subsequent to the report upon which we based this chapter, further data (to the end of 1998) has been collected on the risk-and-return profiles of infrastructure investments. This new data confirms the trends apparent in Figure 9.1. In particular, rates of return of listed infrastructure projects exceed traded market products but with higher rates of volatility while unlisted infrastructure products do better than equity markets with lower volatility. In terms of the design of pension funds' investment strategies, these results confirm the value of such projects for portfolio diversification. John Evans brought my attention to the new data.

4. Over the past two years, the S & P 500 index has increased by 65%. Although other Anglo-American markets have benefited from this rise, both the Australian and UK stock markets have been more volatile and have not risen near as much. The buoyant performance of Anglo-American stock markets have had significant consequences for pension funds and individual portfolio managers. The temptation to delay or switch fixed income investments into equities is clear and has been rewarded in some cases. By contrast, the virtues of alternative investments in areas like housing while apparent in 'normal' conditions are less obvious at present.

5. In this case, risk and returns were calculated using actual, historical data. However, estimating returns on project-based investments would be a more complex task. Any comprehensive treatment should presumably involve assessing the expected values of net cash flows discounted by the cost of capital to arrive at the net present value of an investment. Inevitably, this would also involve choosing an appropriate discount rate in the context of expected market values. Fama (1996) provides an intriguing insight into these issues.

6. By convention, reflecting the apparent reality of investment management and regulatory requirements, fund managers are properly very circumspect about forecasting past performance into the future. Fidelity Investments (*The Times*, 18 Jan. 1997, 31) in advertising their funds note (in part) '[p]ast performance is no guarantee of future returns. The value of investments and the income from them can go down as well as up and an investor may not get back the amount invested.' These cautions apply here as with any investment product.

7. A balanced manager provides a well-diversified pooled product for pension fund trustees to use for investment and the returns are publicly available. Data on the average balanced manager was obtained through industry sources and compiled using PGE's software programme SuperCMS.

8. A great deal has been written about the political and symbolic significance of the urban landscape, including reference to the power of major infrastructure projects and their representation of citizenship in the city. Gregory (1996) has

a wide-ranging survey and Harvey (1985) develops a close reading of this issue with respect to the historical urban landscape.

9. There has been debate in the industry about the probable legal liability of future governments for past and current investment contracts written with private investment institutions to provide urban infrastructure. The issue debated is whether future governments could arbitrarily abrogate such contracts given a change in political philosophy with respect to the proper responsibilities of government. Clearly, if a government was to do so they would face a lawsuit for damages consistent with the expectations and entitlements of the aggrieved financial institution. Could a future government argue, however, that its sovereignty should not be fettered by a previous commercial contract? Could a future government simply walk away from past commitments without compensation? Conclusive answers to these questions are difficult to find (see Rudden 1989). In conversation Maurice Byers (a previous Commonwealth Solicitor General of Australia) and Patrick Atiyah (the most eminent authority on contract law) have observed that there are few (if any) relevant cases where governments were excused from their contractual obligations for reasons of a change in political philosophy. They also observe that even in circumstances where nationalization effectively abrogated private contracts, compensation was deemed necessary even if inadequate.

10. The Mercer report was commissioned by a group of nine large US public sector pension funds (including CALPERS and the Pension Reserves Investment Management Board of Massachusetts) with a strong interest in private equity deals and the emerging alternative investment market. Mercers emphasized the need to design 'proper incentives', the need to 'minimise distractions' on general partners and the need to recognize 'the long-term nature of private equity investing' (p. 71). They also argued for industry-wide benchmarks against which general partners would have to justify their fees and transaction costs. These recommendations have not been universally accepted by project developers concerned to maintain their discretion in the face of concerted pressure from the pension funds.

11. People move between institutions, and past commitments established between individuals which require the commitment of their employing institutions are difficult to maintain when people move. This is apparent in the short term, witness the mobility of some of the most prominent investment managers, and is highly likely over the long term as the institutions are themselves subject to considerable restructuring through mergers and acquisitions. Amin and Thrift (1992: 582) discuss the transformation of the City financial industry since the 1960s arguing that 'there has been a sea change in the way the City of London has been able to go about its business'. They would be more circumspect about the implications of these changes for the significance and continuity of relationships and institutions than us, although it is clear that the old model of trust relationships amongst peers has had to give way in the face of profound changes in the gender, age, and ethnic composition of the City (and global) financial workforce.

12. The courts do allow for the rectification of mistakes in written contracts, especially if there are commitments in the contract which one or more parties did not intend. More importantly, the courts have been willing to review contracts

which one party contends was agreed to under duress or undue influence as long as unequal bargaining power can be shown to have affected the bargain to the detriment of the aggrieved party (Cartwright 1991). For a more critical perspective, see Dalton (1986) who argues that the courts have also been willing to look at the substantive fairness of contracts referencing social standards of performance not just the terms and conditions of private bargains. Compare with Klein and Leffler (1981) who contend that the market is a common mechanism by which such disputes may be resolved.

13. Recent research on firms' optimal investment has come to suggest that, given the existence of asymmetrically distributed information between owners and managers and the scale of investment, there may be instances where contracts are unstable and vulnerable to renegotiation (and renegotiation). Chen and Huang (1995) show that in these circumstances under- and over-investment can occur, creating the possibility of investment traps which are not resolved by internal negotiation. Their argument is analogous to our argument in that we contend that given unrevealed different interests between the investing parties (pension funds, general partners, etc) and given the level of commitment implied by many infrastructure projects, it is unlikely that an initial contract will survive over the long term.

14. Cited as 129 NE 889, rehearing denied, 130 NE 933 (NY, 1921).

15. Note that the minority opinion argued for a perfect tender model of contractual obligation. Judge McLauglin (p. 892) began his opinion by noting '[t]he plaintiff did not perform its contract. Its failure to do so was either intentional or due to gross neglect which, under the uncontradicted facts, amounted to the same thing. . . .' Also, later, in the dissenting opinion, the Judge observed that even if a person's preference is 'mere whim' if he contracts for performance of that whim he would be entitled to that contracted performance.

16. Thaler (1980) coined the phrase 'endowment effect' to recognize circumstances where people hold on to something or some commitment beyond that justified by standard rational assessment. He suggested that such behaviour is closely related to risk aversion in that losses are valued more highly (in a sense) than equivalent gains in the market. Given the significance of risk aversion for pension fund trustees, it would seem that Thaler's observation is of considerable significance for the issue of long-term investment contracts.

17. In debate over the passage of the National Health Service (Residual Liabilities) Act of 1996, the Government argued that the PFI process is a process of risk transfer, shifting to the private sector all kinds of risks that the public sector can now no longer afford to carry. See the parliamentary debate in the Second Reading, 12 Mar. 1996, Vol. 273, No. 68, col. 851. Arguments against the PFI, and its relationship to the hospital sector dominated the Opposition's commentary. They argued that the PFI process is actually a process of 'privatization by stealth' (col. 821), implying the 'cherry picking' of investment opportunities (cols. 825–6), and worse (the loss of flexibility in resource decisions in NHS Trusts) (col. 858), This last point has been also suggested by analysts more sympathetic to the PFI process. See e.g. Tyrie (1996).

18. Oddly, the Secretary of State for Health argued in debate over the passage of the National Health Service (Residual Liabilities) Act of 1996 that PFI investment contracts in the health service (like related PFI investments in urban

infrastructure in general) are no different than contracts to buy potatoes (see generally the introduction to the Second Reading, 12 Mar. 1996). These sentiments were then repeated in discussion about the virtues of contracts in hearings of the Standing Committee E, Second Sitting, 21 Mar. 1996 (cols. 49–50). Not surprisingly, the Opposition was uncomfortable with the analogy, although none thought to tackle the plausibility of the analogy.

# 10

# Contested Terrain

COMMUNITY development advocates often look to pension funds as significant, albeit untapped, sources of finance. More than twenty years ago, Rifkin and Barber (1978) claimed that community control of workers' pension fund assets could promote alternative forms of corporate ownership, and reverse the decline of the US industrial heartland. Notwithstanding the enormous loss of unionized jobs and community dislocation occasioned by corporate restructuring, the Northeast and Midwest have seen a renaissance in terms of labour productivity and investment in value-added production. Even so, labour leaders continue to lament the fact that 'workers' own pension funds' have fuelled 'the continuing spiral of corporate mergers and downsizing', and have called for strategies to take control of 'our money in support of long-term, quality jobs' in local communities.[1] Such clarion calls for pension fund socialism have been ignored. Likewise, the DoL ETI initiative, designed to encourage pension fund trustees to take account of the community effects of investment strategies, was blocked by Congress.

Arguably more important have been state and local government pension plans' venture capital investments and economic development projects. But analysts like Romano (1993) are critical of such initiatives, accusing local political interests of subverting the proper goals of public sector funds. In a similar vein, congressional critics of the Clinton administration accused the DoL of 'mischief', representing ETIs as a 'radical' scheme designed to divert private pension assets into 'social investments' such as 'public housing, infrastructure, and pork-barrel projects'.[2] Rhetoric is, of course, a basic tool of politics. Even so, we should not underestimate the deep disagreements over basic principles embedded in these disputes. And we should not ignore the expanding market among institutional investors for alternative investment products (AIPs). Private equity placements, junk bonds, and venture capital investments are AIPs; public–private partnerships in housing, infrastructure, and economic development also may fit the category. While the volume of pension fund assets allocated to this asset class is small, there is an investment market for urban development in all its many dimensions.

One goal of this chapter is to promote a better understanding of the issues involved in pension fund investment in urban development, referencing the partisan political rhetoric of debate over the ETI programme and public sector economic development investments. More often than not, these kinds of debates have ignored the actual practice of pension fund investment. A more substantive goal is to prompt a reassessment of the obligations of pension funds, referencing the nineteenth-century ideal model of fiduciary duty which underpins arguments set against broader conceptions of the relationships between plan sponsors, trustees, and plan beneficiaries. These threads of analysis are the basis for a reassessment of pension fund investment in community economic development. It seeks to chart a course between the siren songs of pension fund socialism (Ghilarducci 1992), and the idealized principal–agent (beneficiary–trustee) relationship inherited from the past (Langbein 1995). In this respect, I make the case for a more systematic analysis of pension fund investment, consistent with the new-found status of pension funds in the twenty-first century (Chapter 3).

Notice that I do not dispute the need to protect plan beneficiaries from those who would be reckless (or worse) with their interests and rights. At the same time, I am not convinced that this is an issue particular to pension fund investment in urban development. The potential for corruption is inherent in any system of delegated investment decision making; it is an integral aspect of the current structure of pension fund administration, and is not an obscure parochial phenomenon (Chapter 7). While Langbein and others are right to emphasize the fiduciary duties of trustees, this particular institution is not now an adequate or realistic depiction of the scope of relationships normally encompassing investment decision making. It is *inevitable* that pension funds take into account the social and economic consequences of their investments. The real issue is how to regulate such accounting practices given the interests of plan beneficiaries, the overarching social importance of protecting the integrity of private pension systems, and the threat of recklessness and corruption which pervades the investment management industry in general.

## Rhetoric and Political Practice

On 7 October 1994, Rep. Jim Saxton (Republican, NJ) read into the *Congressional Record* an article he had written which had appeared the previous week in *The Wall Street Journal*. A leading Republican, he attacked President Clinton and the Secretary of the DoL, Robert Reich, over the ETI initiative, suggesting that ETIs were 'social investments' with 'dismal' track records. He also claimed that 'ETIs are really PTIs—Politically Targeted Investments—and use the participants' money in ways that would not occur except for political pressure' (1994 WL 554092). On 9 May 1995, he again attacked the ETI initiative, this time introducing a new bill (the Pension Protection Act of 1995) on behalf of the Republican congressional leadership (1995 WL 270324). His rhetoric was bold: 'targeting private pension fund investments is a radical and dangerous idea'. He referred to 'President Clinton's pension fund grab', and threatened that 'Secretary Reich' would make ETIs 'compulsory'. This was followed up with an argument that 'Clinton's pension grab' was part of a furtive strategy designed to divert pension assets into the administration's 'liberal social spending agenda' (1995 WL 270412). In conclusion, he claimed that the 'ultimate objective' of the administration was to impose on pension funds community lending requirements like those regulating banks' community lending practices.

Saxton believed the administration had a five-stage strategy. In the first instance, 'faced with an angry revolt of voters' (the congressional elections of November 1994), a secret plan had been hatched to fund 'social investments'. Stage 2 came with the ETI Interpretive Bulletin (94-1) which 'undermined' the law in this area. Stage 3 was the ETI clearinghouse which had been implemented 'without congressional authorisation'. Stage 4 was the 'likely' appointment of Alicia Munnell as Governor of the Federal Reserve Bank. She was identified as having previously supported a tax on private pensions to 'help finance' the government's 'liberal spending habits'. Saxton suggested that once appointed, she would be beyond congressional control and would use the Fed to introduce the policy. Having again argued that the evidence against ETIs was clear, invoking a previous report by Munnell critical of ETIs, Saxton said that Stage 5 would then be the introduction of mechanisms designed to 'shield pension fund trustees from blame when ETIs . . . get into trouble'. Possible government guarantees were mentioned, as were other forms of risk-sharing and pooling, options which, it appears, he derived from material provided by Washington-based lobby groups (Ferlauto 1993; Ferlauto and Clabourn 1993). Having established the threat to 'every American', he concluded that his bill would allow 'everyone working' to 'rest easier'.

How seriously should we take Saxton's rhetoric? Why did he believe that referring to ETIs as 'PTIs' had such significance? There are many who believe that rhetoric is a barrier to good public policy decision making. Either rhetoric is used to improperly encode information with pre-existing biases and prejudices, and/or it is used to screen public access to the full range of possible and proper solutions.[3] Those concerned with the 'public good' often decry partisan party politics in a similar manner, suggesting that the facts stand independently of partisan interpretation and that partisan claims should be judged against those facts. Perhaps we should be less concerned with Saxton's rhetoric signalling a conspiracy, and more concerned with his attempts to subvert reasoned public debate about important issues (like funding infrastructure). The implication is that any attention paid to Saxton's rhetoric would be antithetical to informed public debate, lending credence to appeals to the prejudices of the electorate, rather than debating, in an informed manner, the possible options to an issue that is both complex and subject to reasonable dispute.

Some analysts of civic discourse also contend that rhetoric is superficial and largely irrelevant in the face of reality. By this logic, rhetoric could not coerce belief or even subvert reason. To the extent that the state or some other institution was to assert a claim about the world on the basis of its control of the rhetoric of civic virtue, people would not be fooled by such superficial gestures. Still, claims on behalf of an unencumbered truth seem misplaced. Most obviously, there seem to be many 'worlds' in the sense that there is a plurality of experience. It is easy enough to construct coherent and principled worlds that are *rival* worlds: there is basic disagreement about how our lives ought to be arranged. Resolving such disagreement is notoriously difficult, rarely made any simpler by appeals to an independent world. Not surprisingly, advocates of competing visions of the world seek our support, hoping to change our minds and support them in specific cases. How arguments are 'framed' in such circumstances is an essential ingredient in a winning strategy. Inevitably, rhetoric plays a crucial role in the framing process, affecting both how claims and counter-claims are displayed, as well as affecting the reception of those claims, given what we know about the attitudes of the intended audience.[4]

Claims for a given world also presume a static world of fixed roles and relationships—a fixed set of parameters that describe the world in its entirety. But so much of political argument is about what the world ought to be, going beyond the world inherited to another better world (or worlds). Idealism is part and parcel of partisan debate. And being able to articulate a desired ideal, deliberately including those who may or may not be the immediate beneficiaries of such an ideal, while politically debilitating those who would oppose such an ideal, is an essential part of any strategy of change. Inevitably, looking to the future involves connecting the (undesired) present to the (desired) future, invoking all kinds of commitments, including emotional loyalties. Whereas I argue that rhetoric plays a crucial role in framing debate, it is also the case that rhetoric plays a crucial role in constructing futures. At the same time, rhetoric plays a vital role in closing off options, denying the relevance, and even legitimacy, of canvassed options. To think otherwise is to imagine that the world is entirely known now and in the future.[5]

It is possible, of course, that all modes of persuasion are rhetorical. This is a tempting conclusion.[6] It would obviate the need to classify and clarify tropes, whether by reference to Socrates or more modern theorists of rhetoric. Like R. A. Posner (1997), I suspect such a conclusion would reach far beyond this chapter into the theory of communication in general. So as to impose limits, I contend that rhetoric is not just argument. It is a mode of public performance which is designed to convince others of a particular claim, while denying the virtues of counter-claims. Implied here are three particular characteristics of rhetoric relevant for my analysis of congressional debate over ETIs. First, being part of a public performance, rhetoric is used to convince a target audience. Second, rhetoric is deliberately deployed and can be analysed for its structure and logic. Rhetoric is more than spontaneous argument made for immediate good effect, but largely uncalculated in terms of its place in an overall strategy of deliberation. Third, more often than not, rhetoric exaggerates virtues and vices. It is not 'balanced' in the sense we expect everyday communication to be balanced.[7]

Since I have suggested that rhetoric is an act of persuasion, we need not identify a definitive list of separate and distinct rhetorical tropes compared to other forms of communication. In the following analysis of congressional debate over ETIs, traditional tropes like allegory, the invocation of the commonplace, emotion, and the trumpeting of vice and virtue are clearly important (as they have been in the past; see Skinner 1996). In large part, I identify these (and other related) tropes so as to understand how arguments against ETIs were framed. In doing so, however, I am also concerned to indicate when and where rhetoric refers to other, oftentimes unstated principles. Uncovering these reference points is an essential goal of analysis. Once we accept this strategy of analysis, it is hard to credit Neil Peirce's (1995: 1671) outrage at the Republican's use of 'ideology' in attacking the DoL's ETI strategy.

## Economically Targeted Investments

The ETI initiative can be understood as an attempt to mobilize the power of pension funds in financial markets for urban and regional economic development and infrastructure investment. Olena Berg, until recently an Assistant Secretary in the Pension and Welfare Benefits Administration of the DoL, and previously an official of CalPERS (the California public employees retirement system), observed as much in a September 1993 speech to the AFL-CIO. There she said '[p]ension funds can serve as an important source of long-term capital for investments which also serve to stimulate economic development, growth, or job creation for a specific region' (p. 6). While clearly a vital connection, there were other forces in play at about the same time. In particular, I identify below four more-or-less related initiatives that, together, provided much of the political impetus in the early 1990s for the promulgation of the DoL Interpretive Bulletin (1994) and the introduction of its ETI Clearinghouse.

In brief, the DoL defined ETIs by reference to a set of inclusive, rather than exclusive, criteria. That is, a pension fund community investment was to be deemed an ETI if it met three conditions. First, investments were to be judged against independent benchmarks of risk-and-return. In this regard, the first test was entirely conventional, matching industry standards and notions of fiduciary responsibility. Second, ETI investments should have an 'identifiable collateral economic benefit' for the community or relevant target group. Third, the investment must fill an apparent need in existing capital markets. In this respect, the DoL referenced possible market inefficiencies as well as 'gaps' or sectors under-served by existing markets. Consideration was given to a further restrictive criterion, namely that collateral benefit must be linked to the beneficiaries and participants of the particular investing pension fund. While commonly discussed and examples noted, this criterion was not, in the end, thought to be one of the essential criteria (US DoL 1993). The actual Interpretive Bulletin (94-1), published in June 1994, simply stated that trustees could take into account an investment's collateral benefits so long as all prudential fiduciary standards were first met. The ETI clearinghouse was established by the DoL by an administrative action. Its implementation was then contracted out to a consulting firm.

Many states have public sector pension fund economic development investment strategies. While hardly ever referred to as ETI programmes, there is a vibrant consulting market for state pension fund local development services (see Economic Innovation International 1995, 1997*a*, *b*). Some projects have been handled by fund trustees, others have been managed by specialized investment managers, and yet others have been established by states as independent investment partnerships. A survey of over 100 large public sector pension funds conducted by Boice Dunham Group Inc. (1993) for Goldman Sachs concluded that ETI invested funds were spread between three basic asset classes: fixed income, real estate, and venture (and mezzanine) capital.[8] Many investments have been private equity placements, reflecting the long-term nature of ETI-like investments (see Chapter 8 for a survey and analysis). Following the apparent success of CalPERS and other large funds in private placements, as well as a study on ETIs funded by the Ford Foundation, many states reassessed their investment strategies during the late 1980s. For instance, Pennsylvania established an independent commission to review the costs of managing their funds, the proper role of state funds with respect to corporate governance, and their options with respect to ETIs. Reporting in early 1993, the commission noted that as long as investments were managed according to prudential standards, ETIs could help bridge apparent gaps in financial markets for housing, infrastructure, and venture capital (job creation in general) (Knoll-Shaffer 1993).[9]

As states were actively reconsidering their investment strategies, a number of panels had been convened to study the consequences of financial markets' focus on short-term returns. One panel headed by Michael Porter (1992*a*) reported that US capital markets were not as effective as other countries' systems of mobilizing and sustaining investment. Porter's report suggested that US corporations were investing in R & D and human resources at a lower rate than their immediate foreign competitors. One explanation for these patterns was believed to be the short-term stock-churning strategies of institutional investors (pension funds and their advisers). While he stopped short of suggesting that US capital markets were inefficient, he did argue that their myopic, short-term focus had long-term negative consequences for US international competitiveness. These themes were then developed in a GAO (1993) report on the comparative business environments of the USA, Japan, and Germany, which focused upon institutional structure of US capital markets, as opposed to the close ties linking other countries' banks and firms. A later report, coordinated, in part, by Porter, suggested ways in which markets could be encouraged to take a longer term perspective on investment, and improve the access of smaller firms to patient capital (Denham and Porter 1995).[10]

Coincident with Porter's and the related GAO studies, Congress initiated a bipartisan study of the apparent problems in financing national infrastructure. While sponsored by the Democratic majority, it had the support of the Bush administration and the minority Republican leader in the House (Robert Michels). The Commission held hearings on the scope of infrastructure shortfalls (including transportation and environment), drawing upon previous studies of federal agencies (see also Munnell 1990). In early 1993, the Commission issued a draft report organized around five sets of conclusions:

(1) there was a 'wide gap' between infrastructure needs and current financing;
(2) government grant programmes could be 'strengthened and made more effective';
(3) private and public pension plans were a 'new source of capital for infrastructure', although any pension fund investment in infrastructure would have to be voluntary and consistent with trustees' fiduciary duties;
(4) new financial 'structures' could make a difference; and
(5) there were barriers, including regulation, to be overcome before private capital could be channelled into infrastructure financing.

Referenced in the report were other studies on ETIs. The report also made available summary statements from witnesses favourable to ETIs, and quoted the Secretary-Treasurer of the AFL-CIO to that effect.

In this context, the AFL-CIO played an important role in setting the policy agenda. Although the union organization was to become preoccupied with the Clinton administration's campaign for a national health care policy, its report *Pensions in Changing Capital Markets*, as well as a series of conferences held on the topic through 1993, promoted an active debate about pension investment policy. A variety of themes ran through the AFL-CIO report. One was the globalization of US industry. Echoing arguments made at much the same time by Porter and others, the AFL-CIO suggested that US corporations and pension funds were under-investing in domestic industry and infrastructure, and were investing in foreign jurisdictions that had much lower regulatory standards. In part, the union organization sought to encourage greater a wareness of the 'control and ownership of pension assets', while promoting greater accountability of trustees, especially with respect to their increasing responsibilities for voting proxies. At the same time, the report also emphasized ETIs, suggesting that these types of investments were an attractive way of linking workers' pension contributions to community welfare. Examples were cited, including the AFL-CIO's construction industry investment trusts. The agenda was clear. Pension fund assets could be and should be mobilized for community economic development. The DoL was singled out as the federal agency that could 'do more to actively promote ETIs' (p. 68).

Parallel to these developments, the DoL had begun working on an ETI policy agenda. A working group on pension investments had been formed as part of the DoL's ERISA Advisory Council. In late 1992 it reported on the arguments for and against ETIs, concluding that ETIs were a viable investment option for pension funds (US DoL 1992). In doing so, the working group made four sets of recommendations. The first set began with the observation that '[t]he primary purpose of pensions is providing retirement income' (p. 30). It then went on to suggest that the DoL should encourage funds to consider 'non-traditional' investments. The second set of recommendations dealt with the proper role of the DoL in facilitating the collection of information on ETIs so as to 'aid' investment decision making. While not explicitly mentioned, the DoL was thought to be the institution best placed to create a clearinghouse of information about ETIs, and their risk-and-return profiles set against relevant benchmarks. The third set of recommendations observed that ERISA allowed ETIs, 'once such assets meet a prevailing rate test based strictly upon their financial characteristics' (p. 31). In cases where ETIs did not meet such financial standards, the fourth set of recommendations set out mechanisms for monitoring and evaluating related investments.

A year later, the same working group issued a draft report detailing the logic and structure of an ETI clearinghouse (US DoL 1993). The report suggested that a clearinghouse would accomplish a number of related goals. It would help funds assess related investment options in circumstances where the available information on the design and performance of ETIs are limited. Importantly, the clearinghouse would address the widespread perception that ETIs were incompatible with fiduciary duty. And it was suggested that an ETI clearinghouse would encourage investment management firms to develop new, innovative investment products relevant to community investing. But there was considerable unease about the proper role of the DoL. Some members of the working group believed that the DoL's involvement would be a conflict of interest with its other statutory responsibilities. Other members argued that the DoL would not be best placed to collect or analyse the data which would, in any event, come from many different sources. At the same time, there were questions raised about the funding of the clearinghouse. Who would pay for information? Would such a 'service' compete with investment firms already active in the ETI field? Would the market take an ETI listing in the clearinghouse as an 'endorsement' of the investment product and its manager? Should the clearinghouse assess listed ETIs for their performance? In the end, the report concluded that the DoL ought to sponsor the clearinghouse, but use external expertise to implement it.

In June 1994, the DoL issued Interpretive Bulletin 94-1. In part, it noted that the objective of the Bulletin was to clarify the status of ETIs. It stated 'a plan fiduciary may invest plan assets in an . . . ETI provided the fiduciary determines that such investment is appropriate for the plan in terms of the same factors that a prudent fiduciary would use in determining whether any other type of investment is appropriate' (p. 1). Later in the year, the Department let the contract to a consultant to establish the ETI clearinghouse.

## Rhetoric and the Commonplace

Rep. Saxton's attack on the ETI initiative was empowered by the results of the November 1994 congressional elections, which saw the election of a Republican House majority. Personified by Newt Gingrich and given form through the Republican 'Contract with America', there is little doubt that Republican success was owed, in part, to their political offensive against the Clinton administration's health care reform agenda, as well as the disaffection of traditional Democrat voters in the aftermath of the ratification of NAFTA. Immediately after the election, Robert Reich (1997: 209–11) argued with Clinton that the lesson to be drawn from the results was that those who had 'abandoned' the party, were those who had lost the most through corporate restructuring over the past decade. Reich believed that the best response was to emphasize 'bread and butter issues' like pension security, the minimum wage, and job training, while attacking Republican plans for middle-class and corporate tax cuts. While not successful in setting Clinton's subsequent political agenda, Reich set about implementing a counter-response.

Earlier in 1994, Reich had a meeting with Robert Michels, then the Republican minority leader in the House. They enjoyed a good working relationship, though Michels had recently announced his intention to retire in November. During their meeting about DoL retraining initiatives, Reich was warned by Michels that Gingrich and 'his friends' were out to destroy the civility of the House and anything that stood in their way 'using whatever tactics are available' (p. 167). Less than a year later, the Republicans controlled Congress. For Reich, early 1995 was dominated by debate over raising the minimum wage. Whereas one side of the public debate involved the Republican House leadership, another side of the debate was internal to the Clinton administration and the House Democrats. By Reich's account, he sought to draw Clinton into supporting the issue against the advice of Clinton's political advisers. He also sought to shore up support from House Democrats who were divided and suffering from low morale after the November elections. The last piece of the puzzle was to win the media contest for 'framing' the issue. His ambition was to 'crystallise a much larger debate about whether Americans are mere participants in an impersonal market or are members of a common culture and society' (p. 237).

To the alarm of his DoL advisers, a series of events then propelled Reich into the spotlight. In late February, Reich appeared before the Joint Economic Committee (chaired by Jim Saxton), and found his economic competence questioned. Saxton charged that an increased minimum wage would result in higher unemployment, citing academic studies to support his position. Playing to the TV cameras, Saxton called him a quack economist and exaggerated the significance of conventional economic theory, but gave him few chances to respond.[11] In early March, Reich gave a speech at the National Press Club attacking Gingrich, accusing the Republicans of 'rewarding their wealthy and corporate benefactors' (p. 251). Almost immediately after, he appeared before the Senate appropriations committee to defend the DoL budget. Reich was accused by the ranking Republican (Specter, Penn.) of engaging in partisan politics, and of undermining the bases for cooperation between Republicans and the Clinton administration. By June 1995 Reich had managed a series of high profile events, including the Executive Order limiting 'striker replacements', attacks on the DoL by House Republicans charging internal problems with the DoL, as well as the introduction of training programmes for the welfare poor. Also in June, Clinton announced his intention to propose a balanced budget. Reich's internal and external campaign ground to a halt.[12]

In this context, the House debated and passed Saxton's Pension Protection Act on 12 September 1995.[13] Given the Republican majority, the alliance between Saxton and Gingrich against the Democrats, and the divisions between the DoL and the House Republicans, and between Reich and Clinton's policy advisers, the bill could hardly have failed. In Table 10.1 the votes cast during the debate are summarized according to the sequence of three amendments (Roll Nos. 649–651), sponsored by the Democrat minority, and the final vote (Roll No. 652) on the bill itself. Apart from slight variations in yes/no/abstentions between amendments, the final vote was never in doubt. Nevertheless, over the course of the afternoon, Saxton deployed a highly orchestrated

TABLE 10.1. *Votes cast in the debate over the Pension Protection Act, 12 September 1995, US House of Representatives*

| Issue (roll number) | Distribution of votes | | |
|---|---|---|---|
| | Ayes | Noes | Not Voting |
| Amendment (No. 649) *Protection of domestic investments* | 192 | 217 | 25 |
| Amendment (No. 650) *Protection of domestic investments* | 179 | 234 | 21 |
| Amendment (No. 651) *Powers of the Secretary of Labor* | 178 | 232 | 24 |
| Final Vote (No. 652) | 238 | 180 | 16 |

*Source*: 1995 WL 544597 (Cong. Rec.).

rhetorical debate to de-legitimize the DoL's ETI initiative. We now look in detail at the management of the debate, the rhetoric used to sustain the Republican position, and the counter-moves of the Democrats. In the next section, I assess the significance of the debate in the light of basic differences of principle regarding the proper roles and responsibilities of pension funds and their trustees.

Because the Republicans controlled the House, they controlled the introduction of the bill and the pace and timing of the debate. They held the initiative, setting the rhetorical tone from the outset, while damping counter-moves designed to either redirect the focus of the debate or change the terms in which ETIs were to be 'properly' understood by the electorate. Throughout, a set of rhetorical tropes dominated proceedings. The *description and re-description* of ETIs preoccupied the House. Republicans re-described ETIs as 'social investments' and 'politically targeted investments'. On the other side, Democrats accused the Republicans of 'unadulterated demagoguery', returning time and time again to the formal language of the ETI initiative as set out in the Interpretive Bulletin (1995 WL 544597, 1:16 p.m.). Both sides claimed *legitimacy* for their positions, using expertise, empirical evidence, and past and present associations to squeeze the other side. Claims of *virtue and vice* saturated Republican rhetoric, on one hand, claiming to be 'protecting' the ordinary American worker, while, on the other hand, vilifying Reich, Clinton, and the DoL. On the Republican side, vilification was accompanied by *highly emotive language*. And most importantly, the *commonplace* was invoked time and again to establish the significance of claims and counter-claims.

These rhetorical tropes are readily identifiable in the proceedings. They are particular neither to the US Congress, nor to contemporary politics. Indeed, Skinner (1996) identifies many of the same or similar tropes that caused Hobbes so much concern, tracing their origin as far back as Aristotle. To illustrate, consider the use of emotive language.[14] In his statement introducing the bill for the Republican leadership, Rep. Goodling accused the DoL of being 'overzealous and misguided' in their promotion of ETIs. He went on to suggest that the DoL had become 'the chief promoter and apologist for social investments', and was, as a consequence, beholden to 'special interests'. He summarized the bill by arguing that ETIs were a 'scandal in-the-making', and that the DoL had been transformed from the 'Nation's Pension Watchdog, into a lapdog and huckster for special interests'. One implication to be drawn from these claims is that Reich and the Clinton administration had subverted the legitimate role of the DoL regarding the protection of the integrity of the pension system. A conspiracy was implied between 'special interests' and the Secretary of Labour. Rep. Knollenberg then linked up the DoL, Reich, and 'special interests' to suggest that ETIs 'are nothing more than a code word for pork barrel projects in urban areas' (2:15 p.m.).

Claims of virtue and vice added fuel to the emotional fire. On the Republican side, virtue was to be found in their 'protection' of ordinary 'American workers' and their pension benefits. Allusions were made to 'big' government and free-spending liberals who, 'like Willy Sutton' (the famous bank robber), were conspiring to rob employees of their pensions made through 'a lifetime of hard-earned wages' (Rep. Fawell, 1:30 p.m.; Rep. Stockman, 2:45 p.m.). A number of times, Secretary Reich was accused of conspiring to 'raid . . . private pension funds', to divert precious pension assets into risky 'pork-barrel spending on liberal social projects' (Rep. Salmon, 3:00 p.m.). Reich's vices were, apparently, many and very troubling. His liberal agenda had been noted by Saxton in earlier congressional debate, referencing his (1991) book *The Work of Nations* and its influence on Clinton's first election campaign. While being a liberal has its own disadvantages in US politics, Reich was accused of something far worse. His ultimate vice was the fact that his 'promotion of ETIs' meant that 'he doesn't believe in the free market' (Rep. Knollenberg, 2:15 p.m.). On many occasions, and in response to counter-moves by the Democrats to introduce regulation of pension funds' foreign investments into the bill, the Republicans proclaimed the virtues of the 'free market'.

Claims made by the Republicans with respect to protecting workers pensions, claims made against big government and liberal pork barrel

projects, and claims about the riskiness of ETIs in relation to the market
all based upon, in one way or another, deeply embedded political values
in the community at large. But this does not mean that these values are
*necessarily* widely shared. For the Republicans advancing the virtues of
their bill, legitimacy was claimed in more specific ways. To begin, Rep.
Fawell was noted as an expert on pensions and ERISA in particular.
Implied and, at times, displayed was Fawell's knowledge of ERISA's
fiduciary standards and prudential requirements. At the same time, the
Democrats failed to challenge the Republicans on their associated
claims about the inherent riskiness of ETIs, as if risk itself was antithetical to ERISA and modern portfolio theory. The Republicans also
used the same examples throughout the debate to 'show' that ETIs were
prone to failure. Backing these examples were references to other
studies that 'showed' that ETIs cost pension fund beneficiaries with
claims of rates of return significantly below average rates of return.
More complex but conventional issues, like the choice of benchmarks
against which to evaluate rates of return, went unacknowledged.

Attempts by the Democrats to legitimize ETIs, by referring to vague
instances of support for pension fund investment in urban infrastructure by the Reagan and Bush administrations, embarrassed the Republicans. But this counter-attack was not sustained.[15] The initiative was
held by the Republicans whose strongest rhetorical weapon was an
appeal to the commonplace. Early in the debate, Saxton suggested that
the basic issue was the protection of workers' pensions. He identified
three kinds of ordinary workers: (1) factory workers who talk in the
factory lunch room every day 'about their plans for retirement and their
retirement fund'; (2) 'a clerk in a department store' who talks with
his/her spouse every evening about when they will 'retire and about
their retirement fund'; and (3) 'the parcel delivery person who works
hard all day and hustles around town in the little brown truck'
(1:45 p.m.). He evoked their dreams of retirement and their dependence
upon retirement funds. He said their dreams were threatened by 'risky'
investments, investment failures, and lower rates of return. And he
invoked examples of ETI failures, and studies of low rates of return for
ETI. A more subtle racial association was suggested by other Republican speakers. Jesse Jackson had backed ETIs in the past; therefore,
ETIs were for 'social experiments' in American cities (Fawell, 2:00 p.m.).

Later, Rep. Green (a Democrat from Texas) was to remark that he
represented 'the beer and barbecue crowd', and while they were also
concerned about pensions, they were also concerned about the flow of
pension fund assets overseas (3:15 p.m.). In direct response, Fawell
argued that the DoL ETI initiative was led by Reich, who was 'from

Harvard' with 'elite views' (3:15 p.m.). In general, the Democrats simply reacted against the Republicans' rhetoric. As noted above, they reacted against the redescription of ETIs as social investments, accusing the Republicans of 'hysteria', and of engaging in 'dumb-agoguery' (Rep. Clay, 1:16 p.m.). Pomeroy said in response to Fawell that 'I resent . . . the misinterpretations and mischaracterisations of the investment bulletin' (2:00 p.m.). They also argued that the bill was unnecessary; that the Republicans had created a fictitious problem which required no solution (Rep. Martinez, 1:30 p.m.). Their strategy was to reiterate the unchanged status of ERISA, the continued necessity of prudence, and the conventional standards of risk assessment. ETIs were defended with the facts, and with the actual circumstances of pension fund investment policy. To add legitimacy, they quoted private institutions, including the Council of Institutional Investors, similarly concerned the Republican use of 'inflammatory language and baseless allegations' (Rep. Owens, 2:15 p.m.). Nevertheless, they were forced time and again to reiterate the benefits of ETIs for communities against claims that the ETI policy was 'socialism 101' (Rep. Hefley, 2:45 p.m.).

About halfway through the debate, however, the Democrat minority changed tactics. Instead of responding to Republican rhetoric, which was framed for the external media, the Democrats used the legislative process to claim back the initiative. Amendments were introduced to regulate the overseas investment of pension funds, sustained by arguments to the effect that Republican opposition to ETIs would promote a greater volume of overseas investment. Rep. Green (D, Tex.) introduced a new amendment that would have added a Section 5 to the Saxton bill. Section 5, according to Green, was intended to ensure that domestic investments would have the same status as foreign investments. He summarized the logic of his amendment as follows: 'I want them (pension funds) to build those houses in Houston, TX, or Cleveland, OH, or anywhere else if the risk is the same as going overseas' (3:30 p.m.). The argument put to the Republican majority was superficially simple: why oppose an amendment that formally sought equal status for domestic and foreign investment? (See Rep. Traficant, 3:45 p.m.). Fawell responded with an obvious retort: the amendments were designed to distract attention from the core logic of the Republican bill (3:45 p.m.). The Green amendment was lost, 192 to 217 (Table 10.1, Roll No. 649).

While the Democrats persisted with a series of amendments introducing other issues like infrastructure investment into the debate, it was clear that the Republicans were in control of the proceedings and retained control of their rhetorical strategy returning at every opportunity to the 'under-performance of ETIs' (Saxton, 5:45 p.m.). This would then force the Democrats back to the 'facts' about ETIs, returning again to their attempt to link up public unease with international financial flows and pension funds' domestic investments. By the time the debate closed and the last vote was taken, the Republicans had comprehensively reasserted control over the legislative process and had refocused debate on their agenda: the de-legitimization of ETIs. Indeed, the final amendment offered by Rep. Andrews (Democrat, NJ) virtually accepted Republican claims about the nefarious nature of ETIs. He sought to allow ETIs to remain legitimate pension investment products by explicitly recognizing the prudent man rule as applicable to all investments regulated by ERISA. To sustain his position, however, he abandoned Reich (6:15 p.m.). The final vote was taken around 7:00 p.m. and was won by the Republicans, 238 to 180 (Table 10.1, Roll No. 652).

## Contested Principles and Workers' Pensions

One implication to be drawn from House debate over ETIs is that it was all about politics: being caught up in conflict between the President and a hostile House, defeat was inevitable. Any policy that sought to mobilize pension fund investment for urban infrastructure would have to wait for another more advantageous political moment. While plausible, there was more to the ETI debate than a ruthless quest for political power. Lurking behind the debate were a set of unresolved issues of 'principle', hinted at, but mostly unrecognized in the debate. By 'principles', I mean abstract claims about proper conduct that appeal to standards set outside the immediate context. These principles could also be understood as 'essentially contested concepts', made so because of deep, genuinely held disagreements over their meaning (Gallie 1956).[16] In summary terms, these issues were (and remain) the proper *status of pension fund assets* as workers' deferred income; the proper *roles and responsibilities of pension fund trustees* with respect to fund assets; and, the proper *nature and management of risk* in the context of funds' investment portfolios. In this context, even if Democrats controlled Congress and held the Presidency, any ETI-like initiative would be contentious within and without Congress.

Unresolved issues of principle inevitably reinforce the power of rhetoric as a mode of persuasion. In this respect, Bender and Wellbery (1990*b*: 23) suggest rhetoric is part and parcel of contemporary cultural and discursive pluralism, affecting all kinds of institutions, including the law.[17] To the extent that rhetoric is designed to appeal, however obliquely, to prior beliefs, it may be more effective than 'unanchored' rhetoric. Yet rhetorical appeal to principle is bound to be less rewarding than hoped, if the target principle is not as it is presumed to be—an unambiguous trump card. Eliding the ambiguity of principles, and making the jump between general claims and specific circumstances in the context of competing interpretations of principle, are the essential tasks of rhetoric.[18] Recall that Reich's political agenda included the 'crystallisation' of basic issues about the status of markets with respect to social solidarity. His agenda was played out against the Republicans, but had as a crucial audience White House Presidential advisers who sought time and again to distance Clinton from the values Reich believed important. Reich was not successful in his political strategy. Nevertheless, to the extent that there were, as Reich hoped, issues of principle to be found in the ETI debate, these issues remain embedded in political argument, and are recurrent reference points about the proper design of American institutions.

To illustrate, consider the status of workers' pension fund assets. As we have seen, Rep. Saxton justified the Pension Protection Act of 1995 by invoking ordinary workers' dreams and aspirations about retirement. Prefacing remarks about their dreams, he said 'this debate is about workers' savings, workers' savings for their retirement years' (1:00 p.m.). In a similar vein, Rep. Fawell said soon after that IB94-1 sought to justify the unjustifiable: the 'stealing' of 'working Americans' 'hard-earned after-tax savings' for 'social experiments' (2:00 p.m.). A basic claim of principle seems to have been embedded in these phrases. Most obviously, they suggested a direct equivalence between individuals' savings and pension fund assets. Just as workers own their savings, they also own their share of pension fund assets. Therefore, pension fund assets are workers' savings. In effect, Saxton and Fawell implied that institutional differences between individual retirement savings accounts and employer-sponsored pension plans do not matter. Going further, Fawell managed to imply that workers have a direct economic (ETIs as a form of taxation) interest, and possibly a political (ETIs as inner-city social experiments) interest in the investment strategies of their pension funds. Claimed lower ETI rates of return would be translated into lower retirement income.

There is no doubt that, in the end, pension plan assets are the basis of participating workers' retirement income. Both sides of the debate would also surely agree that the link between plan assets and an individual worker's retirement income depends upon plan rules regarding eligibility and benefit entitlements mediated by state and federal laws.

Furthermore, I suppose both sides would agree that worker contribution rates to employer-sponsored pension plans depend on the nature
of the plan, the institutional context in which plans were established,
and the income of plan participants. Unionized workers commonly
participate in employer-sponsored defined benefit plans and rely upon
contract negotiations to set employers' contributions on their behalf.
Promised benefits are set in accordance with years of service and wages.
But employers bear the long-term liability of those benefits. By contrast,
many salaried workers participate in employer-sponsored defined
contribution plans. The final retirement benefit is a product of the
investment performance of accumulated employer and the flow of contributions. To the extent that non-unionized workers in retail and service
sectors participate in employer-sponsored pension plans, most contribute their own gross income to individual 401(k) plan accounts
(Logue and Rader 1998).[19]

In this context, Saxton's invocation of the commonplace was quite
problematic. His three ordinary workers were particular slices of a much
larger and diverse institutional universe, and more or less relevant to
his argument. Would his 'factory worker' be covered by a defined
contribution plan or, more likely, a defined benefit plan? Would his
department store clerk be covered by a pension plan? As for his 'delivery person', presumably such a worker would be a participant in the
company profit-sharing programme as a co-contributor to a defined
contribution plan and other individual retirement accounts. Simply
put, Saxton's rhetoric was either misleading in its claimed scope of
significance or largely irrelevant in the face of the diversity of institutional arrangements of pension plans. Here, of course, my objection is
grounded in the diversity of pension fund schemes. But surely, as R. A.
Posner (1997) suggests, rhetoric is a form of selective information, as
well as a means of persuasion. Most participants in pension plans are
unsure of the precise status and scope of their benefits. It is widely recognized that educating plan participants is both expensive and often
unreliable (Logue and Rader 1998). Saxton was effective because he
used public ignorance of different pension schemes to gloss over incon-
sistencies internal to his basic claim of principle.

We can take another, deeper step into the issue. Imagine that an
employer-sponsored defined benefit plan was in surplus (the current
value of assets being in excess of expected long-term liabilities). If,
according to Saxton, workers own their share of the plan's assets, would
they also own a proportionate share of the plan surplus? It is unclear
who owns the assets of such a plan, let alone its surplus. Two recent cases
illustrate this point. In *Lockheed* v. *Spink* (1996), the US Supreme Court

reversed a lower court decision, holding that the plan sponsor was entirely justified in making acceptance of an early retirement deal conditional on forsaking future claims of employment on the employer.[20] Spink (an employee) had contended that the plan sponsor (his employer Lockheed Corp.) was a fiduciary within the terms of ERISA and, hence, had to observe the relevant statutory obligations—being an agent of Spink's and other similarly situated plan participants with regard to their vested pension entitlements. In effect, Spink asserted Saxton's claim. Whatever the interests of the employer in managing the reduction of its workforce and forestalling possible future claims of employment, the employer as plan sponsor could not use plan assets to benefit itself and thereby 'injure' the plan or a beneficiary (see the majority opinion, p. 1788). Therefore, the plan sponsor could not vary the design of a plan and offer conditional retirement benefits.

In setting out the majority opinion, Justice Thomas observed that Congress does not require that employers offer pension plans, nor does Congress mandate the level or nature of pension benefits. Rather, a basic objective of ERISA is to ensure that promised pension benefits are actually realized (protecting the plan beneficiary from fraud, corruption, bankruptcy, etc.). In doing so, the majority opinion noted that employers offer pension plans for many reasons, including some related to the management of labour resources.[21] Therefore, there was nothing wrong, in principle, in a company attaching conditions to early retirement benefits: as in other aspects of labour relations, there is bound to be a 'quid pro quo' in any agreement between an employer and its employees (p. 1791). In doing so, the majority opinion returned to the historical roots of private pension plans, recognizing the intimate connection with collective bargaining and labour relations in the USA (Clark 1993*b*).

It could be argued, of course, that being an employer-contribution defined benefit plan, the firm had a legitimate interest in the nature and allocation of pension assets. Would this argument work if the plan was a joint contribution defined benefit plan? In *Jacobson* v. *Hughes Aircraft* (1997), a US Court of Appeals (9th Cir.) decided that Hughes had an ERISA case to answer; the facts being different from the *Lockheed* case.[22] As in *Lockheed*, the firm had amended the plan to take advantage of the plan surplus. It offered an early retirement benefit to existing employees, and introduced a non-contribution plan for the willing remaining and all new employees funded from the surplus of the previous plan. The plaintiffs contended that, in effect, the firm had not simply amended the plan, but had actually terminated the plan, using surplus assets to its own benefit. In this respect, Hughes claimed that it was covered by *Lockheed*; it had not acted as a fiduciary in amending the plan. However, because at least a portion of the surplus was owed to employee contributions, the court decided that the plaintiffs had 'cognizable claims under ERISA' (p. 1292).

At the same time, the minority opinion argued that Jacobson et al. could not claim 'ownership' of a portion of the surplus. Judge Norris contended that any 'surplus' is only an actuarial statement of current circumstances, the implication being that a contributor to a plan has no special legal status with respect to its assets.[23] This argument was then taken up, in part, by the US Supreme Court in their 25 January 1999 opinion reversing the Appeals court decision cited as 1999 WL 24546 (US Cal.). In brief, the Supreme Court argued that the change in plan structure did not violate ERISA, since pension plan assets were not used in a manner to enrich either the company or its shareholders. Therefore, the change of plan did not violate expectations regarding fiduciary duty. Moreover, because the firm was ultimately responsible for any shortfall in plan assets, it could also claim any surplus even if participants were also contributors to the plan. In summary terms, the Court held that the '[r]espondents' vested-benefits and anti-inurement claims proceed on the erroneous assumption that they had an interest in the Plan's surplus . . .' (p. 5).

Notwithstanding this recent decision, the status of defined benefit pension plan assets remains highly contested.[24] For Ambachtsheer and Ezra (1998), amongst others, this is yet another reason why employers have systematically shifted towards defined contribution plans and 401(k) plans. Whereas twenty years ago defined benefit plans dominated defined contribution plans, the latest US DoL (1994*b*) data indicates that defined contribution plans now have the majority of covered private employees, even if defined benefit plans still hold the majority of pension plan assets. And within the defined contribution category, 401(k) plans are increasingly important options. Defined contribution plans allocate the risk of the ultimate retirement benefit value to the employee. The employer does not guarantee the value of the retirement benefit. The employee relies upon the flow of contributions and investment performance to determine that value. The employer may, nevertheless, have considerable fiduciary obligations, especially if the employer, as plan sponsor, manages the investment process, including asset allocations (amongst other related responsibilities). In this respect, however, an increasing number of employers have sought refuge from exacting fiduciary obligations by establishing 401(k) options which rely upon plan participants to make their own asset allocation decisions in relation to the available investment vehicles.

As is widely recognized, the core legal institution linking the plan sponsor with the plan beneficiary is the pension fund trustee (Langbein 1997). With few exceptions, private plans are administered by boards of trustees appointed by the plan sponsor. In some cases, including multi-employer industry plans and public sector plans, trustees may also be nominated by employees or their representatives. Whereas plan sponsors have considerable fiduciary obligations, so too do fund trustees matching, in substance, inherited English and US common law traditions and statute (e.g. ERISA). See Note (1975) for a summary of the links between tradition and statute regarding ERISA. By statute, trustees are required to administer pension plans in accordance with plans' terms and conditions, and act in accordance with the 'exclusive interest' of plan beneficiaries. Trustees may have significant responsibilities, including management of the investment process. However, trustees may also delegate many administrative and management functions to specialized third-party service providers on a fee-for-service contractual basis. In doing so, contracted third-party providers may also be fiduciaries, by virtue of the inclusive functional nature of fiduciary definitions.[25] As a consequence, there is an enormous, variegated market for financial services located in the major national and international financial centres, involving a myriad of large and small service providers (Chapter 4).

In Saxton's world, however, there appear to be two kinds of trustees. Principled trustees act in accordance with the exclusive interest of plan beneficiaries, whereas unprincipled trustees take into account all kinds of interests, including those of local development coalitions. In the first instance, the trust relationship is unproblematic in that underlying principal–agent fiduciary relationships function as idealized in trust law (notwithstanding theoretical and empirical arguments to the contrary; see Cooter and Freedman 1991). In the second instance, his targets were state and local public sector pension plans. Time and again Saxton and his colleagues drew two implications from public sector pension plan investments in local economic development projects. One implication was that ETIs or PTIs are 'risky'. The second implication was that, as a result, pension plan beneficiaries end up with lower pension benefits. I focus here on the second implication (the first being dealt with below). For this to be true, Saxton must have assumed local and state public pension plans offer defined contribution benefits. In fact, most offer defined benefit plans. Therefore, plan participants do not bear the risk of ETIs. It could be argued, however, that lower returns translate into lower offered benefits in that taxpayers are limited in terms of their capacity to pay pension benefits. But it could also be argued that, notwithstanding the risks involved, ETIs contribute to local economic growth and an expanded tax base promising an opportunity for higher levels of retirement benefits.

But there is a deeper issue, one that has been previously identified as problematic in the exclusive benefit rule. Fischel and Langbein (1988: 1107) observed that the 'central concept of ERISA fiduciary law, the exclusive benefit rule, misdescribes the reality of the modern pension and employee benefit trust'. As I have suggested above, with respect to the interests embedded in different kinds of employer-sponsored pension plans, Fischel and Langbein pointed to the diverse but legitimate nature of employer interests in plan design. They also argued that focus on the exclusive benefit rule muddles ERISA fiduciary law, creating uncertainty about the proper roles and responsibilities of plan trustees across 'a remarkable array of the main issues of modern pension trust administration', including plan termination, surpluses, ESOPs, social investing, etc. (p. 1107). In sustaining their case, they also pointed to profound but entirely plausible differences of interests between older and younger plan participants, between retired plan beneficiaries and current employees (future plan beneficiaries). In fact, there are so many stakeholders in employer-sponsored pension plans that simple rules like the exclusive benefit rule fail to do justice to the inevitable conflicts between principals over the principles of trustee fiduciary duty. No simple reading of the exclusive benefit rule could hope to deal with these kinds of internal and external conflicts over competing interests.

As important to Saxton's argument was the assertion that ETIs are PTIs. Embedded in ETIs are nefarious interests sustained by the (sometimes) local economic development political coalitions. For Saxton and others, local economic development projects are the breeding ground for corruption (Romano 1993). Celebrated instances of pension fund trustee involvement in Mafia-controlled construction projects have been generalized to all kinds of related investments. Whether such generalizations are empirically warranted, given the overarching principal–agent problems that characterize the investment management process, cannot be resolved here. It is sufficient to observe that the potential for corruption in local economic development projects is a common observation, made by left of centre academics and right of centre politicians. It is important to acknowledge, however, that a close relationship between trustees and those who benefit from development projects is not, in itself, a sufficient reason to dispute the virtues of pension fund investment. This point was made in *Donovan* v. *Walton* (1985).[26] The DoL believed that close relations between trustees and the union executive was reason enough to dispute the integrity of pension fund investment. However, the court held that the crucial object of analysis ought to be the investment decision making process not the existence (or non-existence) of related political interests. If trustees properly assess the risks of investment, drawing upon the appropriate expertise inside and outside of the fund, then they have discharged their fiduciary duties whatever the outcomes of investment.

With respect to the status of ETIs as legitimate or illegitimate investments, it could also be contended that Saxton and his colleagues appealed, in part, to a quite outmoded notion of fiduciary duty— referred to by Gordon (1987) and others as the 'constrained' prudent man rule. Narrowly interpreted, the constrained prudent man rule required trustees to avoid risky investments, thereby idealizing risk aversion and disregarding the opportunity costs of conservative investment strategies. For Gordon, the constrained prudent man rule in effect 'discourag[ed] trustees (and other fiduciaries) from making many investments now regularly favoured by prudent investors, including start-up enterprises, many kinds of real estate-based investments, foreign stocks, short sales, options, and futures' (pp. 52–3). Gordon also contended that the constrained prudent man rule was antithetical to modern portfolio theory, focusing as it does upon individual investments, as opposed to the place of those investments in a diversified investment portfolio, differentiated by risk-and-return. In this respect, the obsession of the Republican majority with the riskiness of ETIs implied a theory of prudential behaviour overtaken by new protocols in the legal community, and new theoretical principles of investment (see Halbach 1990 on the Restatement Third of the Law of Trusts sponsored by the American Law Institute). If ETIs are risky compared to other investment products, then they may be desirable for any pension fund concerned to diversify its portfolio of investments.

## Reframing Pension Fund Community Investment

In large part, the Republican position on ETIs was negative. They declared the DoL policy to be illegitimate, thereby denying the Clinton administration a low-cost opportunity to promote community development. While ETIs are still on the policy agenda, especially at the level of state public pension funds, Republican rhetoric has 'chilled' the development of third-party intermediaries like clearinghouses for the communication of information on ETI performance and design.[27]

Industry media also have remained concerned about ETI-like experiments, raising questions about the appropriateness of public sector pension fund investment in urban and regional economic development. In a few cases, states have even introduced 'exclusive benefit' rules to shore up perceived weaknesses in the governance of their public pensions systems. Consequently, industry consultants have had to reassure clients about the logic of economic development projects, and the place of such projects in the context of broader investment strategies— witness the briefing produced by Economic Innovation International Ltd. (1997*b*) on 'prudent' ETIs.

Basically, the ETI debate brought out into the open the general issue of pension fund investment in urban development. Given Republican rhetoric about the 'riskiness' of ETIs, how might pension fund community investment be justified? There are some ad hoc reasons, and some arguments of principle. Let us begin with an obvious trend in pension fund investment strategy. It is apparent from industry sources that many larger pension funds are very interested in AIPs (Greenwich Associates 1996*b*). While the proportion of assets allocated to AIPs remains small compared to the dominant asset classes, the total volume of funds is increasing rapidly. Yet AIPs seem very similar to ETIs. For example, jurisdiction-focused venture capital investments are now commonly labelled as AIPs, just as they could have been labelled as ETIs according to the DoL rubric. Perhaps the crucial difference between ETIs and AIPs is the fact that AIPs are chosen for their contribution to a portfolio of investments, irrespective of their contribution to other social or community objectives like long-term economic development and the growth of tax revenue. In this respect, urban and regional development may be thought of as an investment opportunity, just as other investment products compete for assets. Therefore, assigning a label consistent with current investment industry practice may reasonably circumvent any legacy owed to Robert Reich's attempt to engage in debate about our community obligations.

We should recognize, of course, that urban and regional AIPs are, inevitably, highly specific. Not only do they cream-off the most valued urban environments and related functional systems, their time horizons are often limited and comparable to the time horizons of competing asset classes. For instance, the risk-and-return profile of a major urban land development project and its related access routes, is commonly compared with the risk-and-return profiles of market-traded securities in the light of expected plan liabilities (if a defined benefit plan). To the extent that participants in defined contribution plans are preoccupied with long-term, as opposed to short-term, risk-and-return, offered AIPs may or may not be valued as complements to other commitments within diverse portfolios. In this sense, relabelling would be a first step in any strategy of resuscitating pension fund investment in urban life. But given the costs of developing AIPs, and given the need to match or mimic the logic of risk-and-return that underpins other, more accepted, asset classes, much of the urban and regional landscape will be excluded from the investment process. Worse, apparent community needs will remain unmet in a world in which governments, banks, and second-order financial intermediaries are increasingly in retreat from any commitment to community development.

Notwithstanding the virtues of ad hoc arrangements, the question remains: how could community investment be justified, in principle, given the risks and limits of practice? Assuming we retain a commitment to customary interpretations of fiduciary duty, three plausible and intersecting claims can be drawn from the preceding discussion. First, as there are a variety of different models of pension plans, some are more consistent with community development than others. Following on from the discussion of who owns the surplus of defined benefit plans, I would argue that non-contributory defined pension plans could be encouraged to invest in urban development, even if trustees incur long-term risks. By design, any such risks are incurred by plan sponsors, not plan participants. This assumes plan sponsors delegate responsibility for investment management to trustees, and plan sponsors have a right to review trustee actions and to terminate appointments. To the extent that plan participants contribute to defined benefit plans and share in the risk of under-performance, then they also should be entitled to appoint trustees and join any review of trustee behaviour. There would be, however, a moral hazard problem embedded in any governance system that would allow plan participants a voice in investment decision making if they do not share equally in the risks of resulting investment performance.

There are, of course, many more defined contribution plans than defined benefit plans. In some cases, employers are the sole contributors. Here plan participants have a profound economic interest in the integrity of the investment decision making process, whereas plan sponsors have an interest in the extent to which plan sponsorship reflects upon their management of human resources and reflects upon their reputations as fiduciaries. Nevertheless, because employers as plan sponsors offer plan participation as part of their employment contract and incur the administrative and legal costs of such arrangements, sponsors and participants are best understood as equal partners in the enterprise. This is a little different, actually, from instances where plan participants also contribute their own wages to defined contribution plans. The issue here is the extent of delegation of investment decision making, given that plan participants bear the entire risk of the final value of the retirement benefit. As a matter of fact, some plan sponsors claim the right to govern the pension plan and the investment process; delegation is presumed by virtue of plan participants' acceptance of the tendered employment contract. In other cases, plan participants nominate or elect trustee representatives on trustee boards. Recognizing that participants' trustees may be more risk-averse than trustees representing plan sponsors, and more hesitant in accepting long-term risk as embodied in urban development projects, the crucial reference point may become the investment strategy of a fund, rather than its 'ownership.'

Notice one further observation I would make about the integrity of defined contribution plans. Just as plan participants have an economic interest in trustee investment decision making, they also have an interest in the scope of investments. While we would no doubt criticize a fund that 'over-invested' in long-term community development, we should also be critical of plan sponsors that promote self-investment. In some cases, plan sponsors so control offered defined contribution 401(k) plans that their actions in promoting self-investment run grave risks of impoverishing their plan participants. In essence, all plan participants have an interest in diversification. Put slightly differently, all participants in defined contribution plans have an interest in the diversity—design and management—of plan portfolios, as opposed to individual investments. This is also true of sponsors of defined benefit plans, whether contributory or non-contributory. Diversification in this context has three elements: (1) diversity of asset allocation between assets classes; (2) diversity within asset classes; and (3) diversity over time and space. This is a lesson derived from modern portfolio theory. And it is also the lesson to be drawn from jurisdictions that have regulated the scope of investments, limiting the allocation of assets to products offered within state or national borders, specific types of assets (like bonds, as opposed to equities), and time horizons (short-term, as opposed to long-term).

Portfolio diversification can be achieved in many different ways. At this point I do not mean to suggest that long-term urban development projects are the only way to achieve diversification. Recent studies of AIPs suggest that pension funds have considered a wide range of potential investment opportunities, including private placements, venture capital investments, and infrastructure financing. These may, or may not, have direct community development pay-offs, and may, or may not, meet community needs, as opposed to exploiting existing context-specific urban values. As I have suggested elsewhere, the development of these kinds of investment products depends a great deal on the innovativeness of the investment management industry (Chapter 8). At the same time, it must also be acknowledged that these kinds of investments are relatively few in number (compared to the available volume of assets), and lack the kind of established track records characteristic of investment products derived from the conventional asset classes. In this context, the existence of the municipal bond market in the USA is a significant investment option; the tax preferred status of municipal bonds, combined with the relevant guarantee corporations, are vital public subsidies of urban development unavailable to investors in most other Anglo-American countries. Notwithstanding the Savings and Loan debacle, it is important to retain these institutional foundations for urban investment.

One implication to be drawn from Saxton and others' arguments in Congress is that risk in itself is undesirable. But modern portfolio theory demands a differentiated set of risk-and-return profiles. In this context, urban investment, being normally a long-term investment product, could command an important place in any portfolio. However, in recent years, given the run-up in Western equity markets and the declining yields from government bond offerings, many trustees and plan sponsors have tended to forget this aspect of fiduciary duty. At the same time, the lack of regulatory oversight of plan trustees and sponsors, except in cases of extreme prejudice, has meant that the asset allocations of many defined contribution plans have been increasingly concentrated on short-term domestic traded equities. There may be serious, but long-term consequences for plan participants of such a narrowing of focus. In this context, society at large bears the risk of poorly performing, short-term focused equity investment strategies. Indeed, it is not an exaggeration to argue that the current preoccupation with equity markets is a massive instance of moral hazard: given a presumption amongst many people that governments will make up the difference between an adequate retirement income and the cumulative performance of short-term equity strategies, the shift of assets towards equities in defined contribution plans exploits society's apparent willingness to bear that risk.

In summary terms, then, the case for pension fund community investment can be made on three grounds. One is entirely pragmatic and reflects the variety of current investment practice, notwithstanding the exaggerated claims made by the Republicans of the inevitable 'risks' of AIPs and similar kinds of investment products. Another is more principled and reflects the variety of institutional forms, recognizing the

*Contested Terrain*

diversity of pension plans ignored and elided by Republican rhetoric. There are strong reasons to respect and enhance the commitment of public sector pension plans to urban development when they also may benefit from supervisor performance and bear the risks of poor fund performance. At the same time, of course, not all pension funds can be relied upon to have an interest in urban development. A third, important, reason for promoting pension fund urban investment reflects the necessary commitment of all pension fund trustees to portfolio diversification. Instead of evaluating individual investments according to their risk-and-return profiles, the most appropriate investment policy is to evaluate investments in relation to the risk-and-return profile of whole portfolios. In this context, it is important to have a differentiated set of investments with variable risk profiles, time horizons, and geographical sensitivities. To think otherwise is to ignore basic lessons from modern portfolio theory, and accentuate an existing unfortunate trend of asset allocation to equities.

Having suggested reasons why pension funds should consider urban investment, it should also be acknowledged that the design and implementation of such an investment strategy remains problematic. There are a variety of issues to be considered in detail, including the design of investment products with respect to the potential for corruption that, in the end, will affect the take-up of urban and community development as an investment product. These issues are considered in more detail in another chapter. Here, I have been most concerned to re-establish the legitimacy of pension fund urban investment, and contribute to Reich's project of reexamining the bases of socio-cooperation in the context of an accelerating movement to redefining community relations in terms of market exchange.

## Conclusions

Looking back on the political events of 1995, including the Republican stage-managed budget crisis of the last months of the year, the ETI initiative had no chance of success, once it became enmeshed in the escalating conflict between the Republican Congress and the Clinton administration. Not only had Reich been forewarned of the decline of bipartisanship, making compromise impossible within the House, and between the House and the Executive branch, the Republican majority pursued a strategy aimed to de-legitimize the President's claim on the domestic policy agenda. On the other side of the House, Reich (1997) suggests that the morale of the Democrats had been seriously weakened by their minority status, their independence and imagination compromised by reliance on corporate America for campaign funding, and their capacity to act, constrained by internal divisions over the policy agenda, including the balanced budget and welfare reform. Even traditional supporters like the AFL-CIO were wary of public commitment, in part because of NAFTA, which was widely perceived as a Clinton victory at their political expense.

Analysis of the ETI debate focused on rhetoric and principle. In this respect, my goals were threefold. First, I sought to suggest that rhetoric has a legitimate place in policy analysis. Whereas many analysts decry rhetoric, believing it (at best) distracts attention from the crucial issues or (at worse) subverts reason, it was shown that rhetoric is an essential weapon of political persuasion. In general, the identification of rhetorical tropes allows us to better appreciate the leverage gained by political claims and, in particular, the logic underlying arguments deployed by the Republican majority to de-legitimize the Clinton administration's ETI policy. Second, I sought to establish the basic claims of principle that informed Republican rhetoric. This does not mean that rhetoric is always informed by principle, nor does it mean that rhetoric is necessarily coherent with respect to hidden claims of virtue. Rhetoric may be superficial, but none the less significant. In this case, I believe the Republican case against ETIs can be shown to be problematic once we pull apart their claims of principle. Third, I sought to establish the grounds on which pension fund investment in communities might be reasonably justified. In this respect, my case was empowered by claims of principle embedded in Republican rhetoric.

It must be clear, however, that the ETI policy initiative was, for all intents and purposes, fatally compromised by the Republicans. I do not believe that another debate on the virtues of ETIs would be able to overcome the impression of illegitimacy so craftily developed by the Republican leadership. Even if there were to be a Democrat majority with a sympathetic executive branch, ETIs are unlikely to recover their claimed status. Indeed, I would suggest that the failure of the ETI policy has robbed many governments of the chance to assert a legitimate interest in the community consequences of pension fund investment strategies. Whereas it might be argued that the debate was really limited to US federal policy, it seems that the scope of state and local public pension plans' investments have also been affected by the debate. Just as importantly, other Anglo-American governments have also taken the debate seriously, recognizing that US pension law is an essential cornerstone of pensions policy in many other countries. There is a real danger that just as banking systems have become more concentrated in terms of their ownership and their control, eschewing traditional concerns for geographical access to capital in favour of credit rationing by individual attributes irrespective of location, pension funds' investment strategies may also be increasingly distant from their members.

My argument here was less about reclaiming the lost status of ETIs than it was about reframing the more general issue of pension fund investment in community development. Recognizing there is a danger that the rhetoric of the ETI debate has affected the legitimacy of community development as an asset class, it is possible that the ETI debate will chill the emerging market for urban and regional economic development. In this respect, my strategy has been to reassert the interests of pension funds in objectives which go beyond a narrow reading of 'exclusive benefit', while reinforcing the theoretical and practical importance of plan diversity and asset diversification. Here, my claims of legitimacy are based upon the diversity of interests in employer-sponsored retirement vehicles, and the importance of modern portfolio theory for pension fund investment. In doing so, I do not believe my strategy is especially radical or contentious. Indeed, many of my points regarding the diversity of interests embodied in pension funds have been made by those opposed to ETIs (see Fischel and Langbein 1988). Likewise, my appeal to modern portfolio theory is hardly original— notwithstanding the apparent reference by Republicans to the 'constrained' prudent man rule, modern portfolio theory is the essential reference for all Anglo-American pension funds in structuring investment portfolios (Ambachtsheer and Ezra 1998). In this respect, my case will disappoint those concerned with gaining control of workers' pension assets for community good.

However, at the dawn of the twenty-first century we have to rethink what is politically feasible. Likewise, we have to scrutinize carefully what private financial institutions can accomplish and cannot accomplish in terms of community welfare. While the ETI debate failed to advance the cause of community welfare, just as pension funds may not make a substantial difference to the poorest of our communities, the need for community economic development has hardly retreated as a significant political issue. Paradoxically, the ETI debate has reintroduced the issue of community development into political discourse. Where it has been implicitly ignored as either a racial issue or an issue of class and social exclusion, at the heart of Republican rhetoric were fears about redistribution. Simple solutions, like pension fund investment, have been ruled out. More difficult political issues like what we owe those least well-off in the community have been placed back on the agenda. Indeed, social exclusion with respect to pension entitlements based upon race and class will haunt Anglo-American pensions policies. The ETI debate is just a beginning of a debate about pension welfare that is bound to last at least a generation.

## Notes

1. See the manifesto of the Industrial Heartland Labor Investment Forum Working Group prepared for a meeting held in Pittsburgh in June 1996 sponsored, in part, by the United Steelworkers of America. The document is available from the office of the Secretary-Treasurer of the union (5 Gateway Plaza, Pittsburgh).
2. These are the comments of Rep. Saxton (Republican, NJ) introducing H4551 The Pension Protection Act of 1995 into the House on 9 May 1995 (Cong. Rec. 141, 270324).
3. Examples are not hard to find. Debates about welfare, race, and urban crime seem to be ridden with rhetoric. On one side, there are those who believe that the only option is a harsher regulatory regime, whereas, on the other side of the debate, there are those who believe that the interdependence between poverty and welfare institutions is the key to tackling these and other related problems (see Bane and Ellwood 1993).
4. In Clark (1985: ch. 5), this claim is illustrated by reference to a judicial dispute involving construction contractors and the City of Boston. The City had instituted a resident-preference hiring scheme, requiring City-funded contractors to set aside a proportion of their resulting work for local residents. Initially, the issue had been framed around race—the access of blacks to white work. Subsequently the mayor reframed the issue, focusing upon residents' access to the available local work as a means of cross-race coalition formation. Ultimately, the resident-preference policy was upheld by the US Supreme Court. As a lawyer for the contractors observed, the City's constitutional expert won the framing competition, 'painting' a picture of local unemployment and poverty thereby displacing opposition to the policy on other grounds.
5. Compare with Rescher (1987) who argued that idealism is deliberately emancipatory, eschewing the current 'real' world for something that may be just out of reach, even unattainable.
6. See Sperber and Wilson (1990: 154) where they argued that '[r]hetoric has no proprietary subject matter to study because the phenomena and issues it claimed as its own make up a disparate collection rather than an autonomous category'. I think they are mistaken in the scope of their conclusion even if I have some sympathy with their observation about rhetoric as a 'disparate collection' of tropes. See immediately below.
7. I tend to agree with de Man (1984: 3) where he noted '[i]n everyday use words are exchanged and put to a variety of tasks, but they are not supposed to originate anew; on the contrary, one wants them to be as well known, as "common"

as possible, to make certain that they will obtain for us what we want to obtain [efficient communication].'

8. The available evidence suggests that pension fund investment in ETIs has been restricted to public pension plans, and in that domain ETIs are very limited in scope and significance. The Riverside Economic Research (1994) survey of ETIs for The Brancato Report focused upon the largest 20 US public state and local pension plans. They found very low rates of ETI investment, accounting for just 3.6% of all assets (in total $23.5 billion). Of the identified ETI investments they found that ETIs were overwhelmingly mortgages, mortgage-backed securities, and real estate equity (86% of all ETI assets).

9. At much the same time, the Governor of New York also established a Task Force on Pension Fund Investment (1989) chaired by Ira Millstein. The Task Force documented the emerging significance of pension funds in the US economy and in New York in particular, and assessed the proper roles of trustees with respect to corporate governance, mergers and acquisitions, and the like. The Report was also concerned with the internal governance of New York state public sector funds, and commented favourably on the role that funds could play in stimulating local economic development. A separate report was issued in 1993 by the New York State AFL-CIO. It was very critical of the use of public sector funds in making-up shortfalls in state budgets and was not nearly as enthusiastic about ETIs.

10. In this report, Porter was much less equivocal about the 'efficiency' of US capital markets. In fact, it is clearly suggested that US markets are the most efficient in the world. The problem, however, is that efficiency need not translate into long-term investment strategies, especially if there are imperfections due to government tax policies, principal–agent conflicts, and informational asymmetries. Issues related to the efficiency of capital markets are embedded in debate about ETIs (compare Hylton and O'Brien 1992 with Zelinsky 1995, 1996).

11. The relationship between minimum wages and employment is quite problematic. In theory, assuming perfect markets and negligible transaction costs, increased wage costs ought to decrease demand. In fact, as was argued at the time on the basis of empirical evidence from New Jersey, increased minimum wages could actually promote employment depending upon the initial level of those wages in relation to the structure of employment and the subsequent distribution of income between consumption and investment.

12. It might be reasonably argued that Reich had lost his control over Clinton's domestic policy agenda once Clinton was elected. Woodward (1994: 69–70) recounts a meeting Clinton held with Greenspan immediately after his election but prior to his inauguration. At that meeting, Greenspan convinced the President-elect that the crucial issue was the budget deficit. Thereafter, while clearly influenced by Reich on a variety of issues, Reich's (1991) agenda for infrastructure investment was fatally compromised.

13. Remarkably, Reich's (1997) diary of his time as Secretary of Labor has no entry for the passage of the Saxton bill. On 12 Sept. he was in New York City meeting large clothing retailers about evidence collected by the DoL regarding the use of sweat-shops and illegal immigrants in clothing manufacturing. He had authorized the DoL to publish the names of the retailers, and had set up the meeting to pressure them to change their procurement policies.

14. Skinner (1996: 126) notes that at about the time of Hobbes it was common to suppose that the right mix of words and phrases could arouse dormant but highly volatile emotions. Indeed, there seemed to be genuine concern that in using emotive language, people could easily become 'inflamed'. Of course, it is true that emotive language need not only arouse passions of hatred and contempt. It is equally possible that other more congenial emotions could be aroused including love and compassion. The Republicans used emotive language to heap scorn and contempt upon the Secretary of Labor and the DoL.
15. Rep. Owens (Democrat) managed to associate Reagan with Jackson and Bush, arguing that they all had, in one way or another, directly or not, encouraged the development of ETIs (2:15 p.m.).
16. Gallie has a complicated set of criteria he uses to identify 'essentially contested concepts'. In large part, these criteria are linguistic in that they refer to the constitutive elements of whole ideas, arguing that those elements are not simply added up to create the whole. He uses notions such as context and circumstances to show that constitutive elements may change thereby affecting how different people value the whole and how they assess value.
17. In his recent (1998) H. L. A. Hart Lecture at the University of Oxford Justice Stephen Breyer of the US Supreme Court argued that one characteristic of the principles embodied in the US Constitution is their open-texture (or indeterminacy). In a society characterized by significant differences over basic moral values, it should not be surprising that appeals to 'objective' and 'independent' principles may leave many issues unresolved. He illustrated this argument with a number of cases, showing that no method of fixing meaning can hope to claim dominance. Compare with Scalia (1997).
18. See also R. A. Posner (1997: 500) who develops an argument in favour of rhetoric based upon rudimentary notions of the economic costs of information. He suggests that by supplying information (some true and some false), the speaker seeks to alter the audience's beliefs thereby altering how they assess the available options. Of course, the audience will recognize that the supplied information is part of a strategy of persuasion. It would be wrong to presume a naive audience. On the other hand, the audience commonly relies upon speakers to provide the information necessary to make a decision. The costs of independent information can be high (in terms of time and effort).
19. Data on US coverage rates by income, plan type, and industry and gender are to be found in US DoL (1994*b*). It is important to note that public sector coverage rates are much higher than private sector coverage rates, and tend to offer defined benefit plans rather than defined contribution plans.
20. *Lockheed Corp.* v. *Spink*, 116 S.Ct. 1783 (decided June 1996). Justice Thomas wrote the opinion for the majority. Justices Breyer and Souter dissented in part.
21. The court noted that employers use pension plans to attract and retain workers, to pay increased wages in tax-preferred ways thereby contributing to workers' long-term income, to encourage harmonious labour relations, and to adjust their workforces by offering inducements for retirement. The Court noted that Spink's also acknowledged these were important albeit incidental benefits to employers of pension plans (p. 1791).
22. *Jacobson* v. *Hughes Aircraft Company*, 105 F.3d 1288 (1997) as amended 128 F.3d 1305 (1998).

23. Norris suggests, in fact, that the existence of a surplus has to be judged against the long-term performance of a fund's investments. If a plan were to become underfunded, the employer would have to make up the difference. Ultimately, the employer guarantees solvency. In this sense, Norris argues that employees can hardly claim their share of a current surplus.

24. This issue has been widely debated inside and outside of Congress. An interesting related but earlier exchange is to be found in the debate over the Balanced Budget Reconciliation Act of 1995 (1995 WL 631244 Cong. Rec.) involving (amongst others) Senators Kennedy and Kassebaum. In debate over issues related to pension fund surpluses and corporate restructuring Senator Roth (Republican, Del.), a ranking Republican senator, contended (with respect to defined benefit pension plans) 'excess pension assets do not belong to employees'.

25. See *Lockheed* v. *Spink*, n. 2 above, where the ERISA definition of a fiduciary is quoted by the court. The scope of the definition is broad and inclusive, being focused on functional aspects of the administrative and management processes of pension funds and their service providers.

26. *Donovan* v. *Walton*, 609 F.Supp. 1221 (D. C. Fla. 1985). Donovan, the then Secretary of the DoL went to court, arguing that fund trustees had 'breached their fiduciary duties' by constructing an office building and then leasing it on favourable terms to the union that (together with industry firms) sponsored the pension plan.

27. See Levine (1997) on recent Wisconsin programmes.

# 11

# Community Solidarity

WHEREAS twenty years ago the financing of local economic development was a combination of direct government spending and community lending by banks, pension funds are seen by many as the only institutions capable of filling the gaps left by the retreat of the state and first-order intermediaries.[1] In this respect, it could be argued that pension funds have, in effect, promoted US regional economic development. See Black and Gilson (1997) and Gilson (1998) on the significance of pension fund investment in high-risk low-cap stocks and initial public offerings for the development of Silicon Valley. Venture capital firms, in particular, have relied upon the positive and reinforcing agglomeration economies evident in the Silicon Valley innovation process to capture and sustain high rates of return. But private pension plans rarely use geographically targeted investment strategies. To the extent such plans deliberately hold 'local' assets, those assets are typically traded property portfolios or (less commonly) development partnerships. As we have seen attempts to validate broader community-based investment criteria through the federal regulatory process have failed—witness the fate of economically targeted investments during the Clinton administration (Chapter 10).

By marked contrast, many US state and local government pension plans have community development programmes. In some jurisdictions, public pension funds have intervened in corporate restructuring in the interests of stabilizing local employment. In many cases, pension funds have established long-term investment partnerships, linking with existing institutions and investors to develop local venture capital groups. A vibrant consulting industry has grown to match the expanding state-by-state demand for related expertise.[2] However, given the diversity amongst states regarding regulation of fiduciary duty, funding levels, and asset allocation formula, leading analysts contend that public pension fund 'investments are frequently subject to non-financial criteria' (Mitchell 1998: 13). In abstract, there are two basic and opposing views about these institutions and policies. One view, dominating mainstream law and economics, is that pension funds are properly and only the agents of individual plan beneficiaries; public or private they owe nothing to the community and have as their mandate the maximum welfare of plan participants. This is the exclusive benefit view. On the other side, there is the view that as pension funds were conceived for social purposes they embody reciprocal obligations even if, in the final analysis, benefits flow to individuals. I refer to this as the reciprocal benefit view. Compare Fischel and Langbein (1988) with AFL-CIO (1993).

A great deal of academic research justifies the former view, supposing that political interests have no place in pension funds and in financial markets in general (see Romano 1993). In this chapter, however, I set out a two-pronged argument justifying the second view. This is largely a theoretical claim, about general principles and proper practices. It is based upon empirical observations about the nature of pension fund investment decision making gleaned from related research on pension investments, and a principled argument about social institutions and social obligations gleaned from contemporary social contract theory. This does not mean that I am indifferent to the political subversion of pension fund decision making nor does it mean that I am naive when it comes to the nature of social obligation. Pension plan beneficiaries have legitimate legal and moral rights to their promised benefits. But I show that these rights are inevitably embedded in complex sets of institutions and reciprocal obligations. Relying upon contemporary moral philosophy, I suppose that rights (in a broad sense) are made via social contracts and are not simply handed down from some deity or likewise unencumbered soul (Hampton 1991). To illustrate my argument, in a subsequent section of the chapter I show what is right and wrong about the West Virginia's state legislature's directive to their public pensions' investment management board to invest in the state corrections' authority.

## Market Form and Functions

To set the context for subsequent analysis, we should start with the ideal investment management model underpinning the exclusive benefit view. Rather than identify a specific theorist to represent that view, believing such a strategy may be at once misleading about the scope of their opinions and limiting in terms of the permissible scope of my own argument, let me summarize the dominant model utilizing the logic established in

Chapter 4. Nominated trustees are delegated to serve the interests of plan beneficiaries, regulated by statute and through case-by-case adjudication in the courts with respect to fiduciary duty. Trustees basic-ally oversee the flow of funds, beginning with plan participants' and plan sponsors' contributions all the way through to the disbursement of benefits to eligible recipients. In between, they rely upon a wide range of market-based service providers, selected on the basis of the cost, quality, and performance of their services. Market agents like con-sultants may be responsible for allocating the flow of funds between agents, and they may be responsible for asset allocation decisions, the placement of tranches of assets to particular investment managers, and the assessment of managers' performance against a priori benchmarks. In some jurisdictions, service providers may share trustees' fiduciary duty.

This model is a reasonable proxy for the complex set of relationships that are part and parcel of the institutional investment industry. There are, of course, other important elements like the decentralized map of pension funds in relation to the more centralized map of service providers. Understanding the spatial organization of the industry in relation to the universe of different types of pension funds requires an appreciation of issues like the scale economics of processing money, the contractual relations between service providers and their employees, as well the relative efficiency of competing finance markets. The exclusive benefit view takes this functional map of services and advances a set of claims: as trustees are properly independent of plan sponsors, they are properly reliant upon the investment management industry for expert advice on the investment of plan beneficiaries' assets. The alternative is intrusion by external political interests into trustee decision making, and the arbitrary assessment of complex financial matters and relationships best left to market agents. In the end, it is supposed that 'political' invest-ment decisions are avoidable costs borne plan beneficiaries. Not only are 'political' investment decisions likely to be more risky with lower rates of return, the whole web of financial services are likely to be per-meated with costly inefficiencies (relationships).

Advocates of the exclusive benefit view idealize unencumbered trustees reliant upon the (efficient) market for financial services.[3] They denigrate political interests emphasizing the capriciousness of political decision making, the effects of inappropriate (even pernicious) com-mitments, and the costs of limited expertise. Is this combination of idealism and realism warranted? I think not. To explain my view requires a couple large sets of argument. In this section, I rewrite the functional model noted above incorporating empirical evidence gleaned from the pensions project and elsewhere regarding trustee decision making and the market for financial services. The picture that emerges is far from the ideal. The philosophical or dark side of realism is more complicated and is tackled in subsequent sections.[4]

However trustees are appointed, all the evidence from the Anglo-American world is that most trustees begin their term relatively ignorant of investment theory and practice. Even if experienced, the trustee institution is not now usefully circumscribed by nineteenth-century common law notions of fiduciary duty (a common initial reference point for theorists when analysing the contemporary world; see Langbein 1995). Complex statutes, and even more complex rules and regulations regarding proper standards of behaviour interact with case law to set the stage for decision making (see Logue and Rader 1998 for an introduction to related issues relevant to trustees). The legal imperatives notwithstanding, actual trustee decision making is rarely studied. What has been established in previous chapters is that trustees' behaviour is framed in two interrelated ways. First, and in order of significance, by reference to habits of prudence, rules of proprietary conduct, and the norms of relationships. Second, and again in order of importance, by reference to trustees' social identity, the inevitable collegiality involved in collective decision making, and the necessity of justification. The first set of elements are especially important for coping with risk and uncertainty while the second set of elements are especially important in understanding the formal patterns of decision making. In Chapter 7, I also show how the social frames can be used to understand the systematic corruption of collective decision making.

The point here is simple but important. Advocates of the exclusive benefit view look through the trustee decision making process to beneficiaries' interests believing (or hoping) that legal imperatives are sufficient or legal sanctions so significant to ensure implementation of the simple recipes of finance theory like modern portfolio theory. Behavioural issues are eschewed in favour of external imperatives (a common methodological presumption shared by all kinds of social and economic theorists; compare D. Hirshleifer 1995). Looking through the trustee institution, however, misses important frames of reference that internally structure decision making. Some of these elements may be consistent with finance theory, but many are tangential (at best) and antagonistic (at worst) to its imperatives. In response, it could be argued, of course, that poor performing trustees and their advisers would not survive the wrath of their plan beneficiaries. But short of the most obvious egregious conduct, there are few 'tests' of performance sufficient to dislodge incompetent trustees. Indeed, beneficiaries are so ignorant of the nature and conduct of trustee behaviour that boards of trustees are more properly thought of as insulated self-regarding clubs.[5]

This is not to say that trustees are isolated from market agents. Quite the contrary. Recognizing their ignorance, trustees often contract with consultants for advice on decision making, and contract with all kinds of service providers who share the burden of investment management. In this sense, trustees are at the centre of a vast web of agency relationships. Ambachtsheer and Ezra (1998: 8–9), well known and respected industry consultants, are especially concerned about the efficacy and integrity of such relationships. They note that lacking sufficient accountability and transparency, these agency relationships can easily degenerate into rent-seeking behaviour exploiting the ignorance and passivity of distant principals (plan beneficiaries). Previously I have set out in detail the various models of investment management, establishing how and why agency relationships are at once so important for trustees and so contested. By my assessment, agency relationships oscillate between contending ideal forms: on one side, there are the economies of distrust and, on the other side, there are the virtues of commitment. The former sustain recurrent rounds of mandate switching between multiple investment managers and service providers orchestrated by consultants who are, themselves, rarely trusted. The latter promise more stable relationships, hence lower long-term costs and more reliable information directed at trustees subject, of course, to satisfactory performance.

The problem with investment management, however conceived, is that the very idea of predictable long-term investment performance is implausible. Ideally, managers ought to be compared against commonly accepted benchmarks, and mandates and services allocated to the best performer. Ideally, the best performer or performers come to dominate the market, raising the entry barriers for the small and inept and forcing the exit of lower than average and inefficient producers. But the production of investment value is quite unlike conceptions of output production we have inherited from studies of manufacturing. We would argue that performance is highly dependent upon market conditions. What is a winning strategy in one period is hardly ever a recipe for winning in subsequent periods. For the most part, investment managers can only approximate underlying causal processes, and are very poor in anticipating other market agents' actions (Shleifer 1998). Only in retrospect can the average manager out-perform the market. And if we take into account the costs of management, the average manager always lags behind overall market performance (measured by the Dow Jones index etc.). Notwithstanding the extraordinary concentration of assets amongst a relatively few number of investment managers in each market, there is always room in the market for new players.

So far, I have stressed the problematic nature of agency relationships between sets of market (firms) and non-market (trustees) institutions. But it also must be acknowledged that agency relationships within investment service providers are also highly contested. At base, there is an unresolved tension between the firms who claim responsibility for any added value over and above that attributed to the market and their employees who are often paid on the basis of their individual perform-ance. Firms claim any added value according to their particular theory of the market or their internal organizational structure. Individual investment service managers claim any added value by virtue of their responsibility for the day-to-day operation of portfolios. In play are the formal attributes of the firm set against or set alongside the virtues of particular star performers. The competition for investment and service mandates in the industry is often a competition between firms that stress their internal structure (discounting the short-run effects of staff acquisitions and losses) and rival firms that stress their human capital. Given the chronic problems of predicting returns year-to-year (in rela-tion to commonly accepted benchmarks), and the unresolved tension within and between firms about the origin of added value, there are always reasons for trustees to switch mandates to other players, and newly favoured managers.

Here, I have stressed an ever-present reality: the widespread distrust between trustees and their agents over the responsibility for perform-ance. New products, new managers, and new promises of superior per-formance come and go. Even the most well-meaning consultant is often compromised by the poor relative performance of chosen previously highly-rated managers. In these circumstances, it is not surprising that motives are questioned, incentives reviewed, and client lists scrutinized for special favours not shared or for secret alliances that 'explain' the seemingly arbitrary choice of investment and service managers. Cor-ruption or influence-peddling is not far from the surface of otherwise assumed benign market transactions. In these circumstances, it might be supposed that trustees are simply the creatures of their advisers—paralysed by uncertainty and therefore captured by the intrigue of the industry. But the reality is far more complicated. The ideal of looking through trustee decision making to the industry is hardly credible. It serves as a justification for a particular kind of public policy favouring the market against other non-market agents rather than being a real-istic depiction of the actual organization of the industry and its various agency relationships.

In my opinion, this ideal is silent on the nature and imperatives structuring behaviour in the industry. While not especially consistent with finance theory, my critical perspective is not particularly radical. Industry analysts are similarly concerned about these issues. Ambachtsheer and Ezra (1998: 9) highlight the costs of inadequate levels of transparency and accountability in the industry, believing these costs could undermine 'twenty-first century democratic capitalism'. I return to this issue in the last sections of the chapter.

## Possessive Individualism and Exclusive Benefit

In the previous section, I raised doubts about the idealism of the market implied by the exclusive benefit view. I turn now to a more complicated theoretical issue: the philosophical status of the exclusive benefit view. Put simply (perhaps too crudely), my goal here is to show that the logic underpinning the exclusive benefit view is inadequate in the face of the more robust theory of social contract which underpins the rival reciprocal benefit view. I aim to show that as the exclusive benefit view relies upon the theory of possessive individualism it is an inadequate model of the complex set of reciprocal relationships between plan beneficiaries and their constituent communities. Of course, I am not about to invent anew either the critique of possessive individualism, or the theory of social contract. Here I will rely upon others more knowledgeable, including Macpherson (1962) and Sandel (1998) for the critique of possessive individualism and Gauthier (1986) and Lear (1998) for versions of social contract theory. With appropriate adjustments, I think their arguments can be shown to have relevance for understanding the relative merits of the two opposed views.

Let me remind the reader about the basic claim essential to the exclusive benefit view. It has two parts. The first is clear. Plan beneficiaries are not only entitled to their promised retirement benefits, they have a right to those benefits unencumbered by any other consideration. The second is less clear but nonetheless commonly implied by many analysts. Plan beneficiaries are entitled to the maximum value of those benefits. Put plainly, it is supposed that plan beneficiaries maximize their expected long-term welfare. By virtue of post-World War II legislation in Anglo-American economies, and the leading role played by the US Employee Retirement Income Security Act (ERISA) of 1974 in that regard, plan beneficiaries normally have a legal right to those benefits. As well, employees have a right to be treated equally with respect to establishing their entitlement to offered retirement benefits and with respect to any subsequent assessment of their benefits (matching in substance the intent of other anti-discrimination legislation). In effect, and often in fact, pension benefits are a property right protected by the state. To be denied one's promised benefits, to be disadvantaged with respect to the value of benefits compared to others similarly placed, or to be paid less than the expected maximum value of those benefits is to contravene the basic claim governing the exclusive benefit view (and its analogous legal rule).

This model of pension rights is so commonplace that we run the risk of ignoring its peculiar connection to the history of liberal political philosophy. The connection I have in mind can be found in Macpherson (1962: 3). Recognizing difficulties in the practice of modern liberal democracies, he located the origin of these problems in seventeenth-century 'possessive individualism'. In summary terms, he argued that the 'possessive quality' of liberal theory he alludes to is 'its conception of the individual as essentially the proprietor of his own person or capacities, owing nothing to society for them.' This argument is derived from what he identified as a Hobbesian 'model' of market society. This model relies upon two sets of assumptions or conditions that combine economic freedom within the framework of state-enforced contracts, and individual utility maximization within the context of diverse individual resources and capacities. From these initial conditions, Macpherson shows the significance of market competition for the allocation of resources between individuals and for the establishment of a hierarchy of social relations between differentially endowed individuals. The market is the institutional means of exchange, and the means by which the relations between people are defined. Macpherson's logic has become the reference point for many other studies of contemporary market exchange and contractual relations in law and economics (see Trebilcock 1993).

Of the various implications that could be derived from this model of society, with respect to the issues of this chapter a couple are worthy of emphasis. By this logic, individuals (plan beneficiaries) should be understood to be rational, calculating agents who maximize their welfare. If they are concerned about the social effects of their actions, they are far more concerned with the maintenance of the legal framework which protects their property rights (broadly understood). Furthermore, as they owe nothing to society individuals are not entitled to social resources if those resources are expropriated by the state from other individuals. In terms of contemporary debate over the use of pension fund assets for community welfare, this means that whatever the social consequences of limiting assets to the exclusive benefit of plan beneficiaries any tax, regulation of funds' investment strategies, or directed allocation of those assets for community purposes would be an illegitimate expropriation of individuals' assets. Equally, any policy that intervened in the market for investment services would be an unwarranted intrusion into the institution designed to allocate resources between individuals. In a principled sense, therefore, it is possible to see now why the Congressional Republican majority were so antagonistic to the US Department of Labor's proposals for economically targeted investments. Their implied moral mandate was Hobbesian.

Over the years, a variety of objections have been lodged against this model. Most objections attack the heroic individualism at the centre of the model, and how that analytical focus has spilled over into the practice of policy making in liberal democracies. A recent version of that critique can be found in the claims made by communitarians against the unencumbered individual psychology that seems at the heart of the model (see Kymlicka 1990). Here, however, I want to identify three types of objections, all of which undercut the conclusiveness of the model without necessarily denying the virtues of individual rights. In this particular context, my critical strategy is more cautious than some (but see Sandel 1998). Most importantly, if we are to find room for the community interest in pension fund investment, we must do so in a way that advances a positive claim for due regard while not denying individuals' legitimate interests in their long-term welfare. To suppose otherwise, to imagine that pension fund assets are properly only community assets, would be to deny the historical roots of pension entitlements deeply embedded in Anglo-American political and financial institutions. We must show how in principle the community interest can be related to individuals' interests, even if we must also recognize the fact that there will be instances where these interests clash in the formation of specific policies.

The first objection is obvious, but important. The underlying logic of the model is all about setting a framework for economic freedom. Individuals are given the opportunity to achieve their desires, and to do so in accordance with their abilities and capacities. Justice is to be found in the combination of the initial framework and the subsequent actions of individuals, not the state. But it is, unfortunately, only half a model of society. It is a model that allows for economic freedom without providing a mechanism or a benchmark by which to correct 'unjust' or wrong outcomes. To illustrate, I have noted previously that Charles Booth and his middle-

class allies were successful in promoting UK state-provided social security in the late nineteenth century because they could sustain the argument that many older-aged people were impoverished by no fault of their
own. In essence, the nineteenth-century framework of individual economic freedom, embodying various voluntary and collective market-
based retirement institutions, had left many people in urban society
(particularly London) in poverty notwithstanding their best attempts to
provide for retirement. Booth did not challenge the integrity of possessive individualism. But he did question whether it was an adequate
institution in the face of the deserving poor. He put into political play
moral sentiments as a benchmark against which to judge justice—what
we owe others, given their best efforts to look after themselves.

It is possible to argue that as moral sentiments are irrelevant to the
initial framework of economic freedom any *ex post* adjustment for
moral reasons would be arbitrary and unjust. But there is a further
objection that makes this argument less than compelling. Actually
embedded in the initial model are a set of moral sentiments: a commitment to formal equality between individuals (denying the claims of
slavery etc.), a sense of tolerance for others' different life projects, and
a sense of mutual regard and advantage in circumstances where life projects conflict. On the face of it these sentiments may be rational in that
they sustain individuals' separate interests within the chosen model of
society. But to set the model in place requires the prior existence of
these sentiments; it would be impossible to evaluate the virtues or
otherwise of the model prior to its implementation without these sentiments being explicitly factored into the model. The objection here is
that the model relies upon the prior existence of moral sentiments and
then limits the scope of those sentiments to that consistent with the logic
of economic freedom. But, in this respect, it seems unlikely that these
(and other) moral sentiments could be so limited given their external
location in the hearts and minds of people (and their society) who may
have chosen a certain organization of economic freedom to accomplish
certain goals. Booth's moral claims on behalf of the deserving may properly transcend the inherited model of society.

Recognizing that the model has the virtue of liberating people from
limits imposed by community, it is oddly anti-social. In terms of modern
economic theory, it is a discrete choice model of exchange relations.
Two implications follow from this observation. First, any 'relationship'
is axiomatically pareto optimal: no one would, presumably, enter into
an agreement that would make him or her worse off. Such a relationship would be irrational. Second, each relationship is evaluated on its
own terms, in accordance with the set of available alternatives (and their

expected pay-offs) including autarky. Each relationship is a short-term relationship, its benefits calculated and recalculated every day and, if found wanting by virtue of changed circumstances, abrogated at will. Of course, to abrogate an agreement would incur costs not least of which would be the damages due to other involved contractual parties that may have relied upon the agreement. Costs of abrogation would not be so large to be a barrier to re-contracting. Embedded in the modern version of this model is a presumption in favour of system-wide efficiency; sets of pareto optimal relationships (discrete contracts) which culminate in the highest overall benefit to all (see J. L. Coleman 1992).

The shift from relationships to agreements to contracts in the modern idiom discounts the social nature of individuals. Others have hardly any virtue except that found in their instrumental quality—what they can offer to an individual in achieving selfish ends. Lost is any sense of emotional bonds, our commitment to others, and our need for moral regard. If these attributes of social life have any status in theory, they are reduced to the status of enabling exchange. This kind of reductionism runs a real danger of treating people in practice in profoundly inhuman ways. Furthermore, to treat relationships as discrete contracts means there may be no community, no moral sentiments, and no institutions capable of sustaining the framework of economic freedom. Possessive individualism is so ambivalent about the value of community that if individuals' separate rewards in sum favour autarky there may be no reasonable theoretical claim to hold the community together. In this sense, the whole theoretical edifice becomes self-defeating. One option, then, is to invoke social 'glue' like reciprocity to keep the model (society) together. But I cannot see how reciprocity could be limited to being the substance of last resort; to be effective, it would also have to have a separate (higher) status in the life of the community.

By itself, the exclusive benefit view relies upon an unsatisfactory model of social life. Possessive individualism assumes a great deal about the virtues of economic freedom in relation to the limits imposed by communities without an adequate explanation of the origin and status of moral sentiments. Possessive individualism promises a world of discrete contracts, a world in which moral sentiments are reduced to mere instruments of economic advantage. In this respect, we need an alternative view, one that can make sense of individual rights and social commitments. Here, we are led inexorably to social contract theory and the role and status of reciprocity (amongst other moral sentiments) in social relations. What is needed is a way of justifying community constraints on maximum individual advantage without invoking perverse psychology or local coercion.

## Social Contract, Reciprocity, and Obligation

So far, we have advanced two negative claims against the exclusive
benefit view. One was aimed at market idealism, showing that advocates
of the exclusive benefit view are silent on many shortcomings apparent
in the market for financial services. Agency relationships within the
market for investment and financial services are fraught with all kinds
of opportunities for hubris and self-serving deals. To the extent that
political agents have a role in public pension fund investment, any critique of their involvement would have to show that political agents are
more susceptible to hubris than market agents. Notwithstanding my own
research on trustee investment decision making in community economic
development, there is no evidence to justify such a claim. The second
negative claim has been to suggest that advocates' reliance on possessive individualism as a moral rationale justifying the exclusive benefit
view is misplaced. What I have been able to show, theoretically if not
practically, is that there are good reasons to suppose that moral sentiments in favour of community solidarity necessarily undercut any claims
about the hegemony of the exclusive benefit view.[6]

In this section, I advance the positive case in favour of the social contract view. In doing so, I make the following claim: that pension fund
trustees are justified in believing that plan beneficiaries would willingly
accept a less than maximum pension benefit given the web of reciprocal relationships that define the community and sustain community
solidarity.[7] Now, I should be clear that this claim is theoretical, advancing a claim of principle; its plausibility in particular cases has to be
judged by the circumstances of those cases. Hubris can be found in community relationships as it can be found in market agency relationships
(compare Roll 1986 and Romano 1993). To make this argument requires
a theoretical device, notably the notion of social contract. But my notion
of social contract is distinctive, and in some respects basically different
than related notions found in modern political philosophy. Therefore, to
make my argument I have to first set out this model of the social contract before, in the second stage of the argument, demonstrating how
and why it may be relevant to the issue of pension fund investment in
community economic development.

There are all kinds of social contracts, in theory and practice.[8] Rawls
(1971) is often cited as the canonical version. He used a veil of ignorance, the threat of inequality, and rational self-interest to show why
individuals might reasonably choose a regime consistent with social

justice for those least well-off. Gauthier (1986) turned that logic on its head, invoking full information and bargaining theory to achieve much the same result. Generally, social contract theory is a device for showing how and why cooperation is possible, given individuals' separate and competing interests. In the discussion that follows, I rely on a less formal model. In essence, like J. S. Coleman (1990) and others writing in the social-theoretic tradition, I assume the social contract is representative of the web of reciprocal obligations and expectations that define individuals' relationships with one another. It is also a reference point in political negotiations over the proper form of a society. In this sense, it represents an implicit constitution as well as a means of assessing the value or 'teasing out the implications' of current arrangements in relation to possible alternatives (Kymlicka 1990: 60). This analytical device allows for a comparative perspective on the world as we know it rather than having to imagine a 'society' made up of unencumbered individuals. See Dworkin (1977) and Gauthier (1986), and compare with Rawls (1971).[9]

Reciprocal obligations and expectations can be defined a variety of ways.[10] For Becker (1990) reciprocity is a moral virtue. It is less about the advantages of mutual exchange than it is about how we ought to treat others. Reciprocity means 'that we should return good for good, in proportion to what we receive; that we should resist evil, but not do evil in return; that we should make reparation for the harm we do; and that we should be disposed to do those things as a matter of moral obligation' (p. 4). Hence, reciprocity as a moral virtue exists prior to any discussion of the nature and proper form of the social contract. Of course, reciprocity has an important instrumental value, facilitating social relationships and market exchange. But the functional value of reciprocity does not, in itself, exhaust the value of reciprocity. J. S. Coleman (1990: 306) goes a step further, providing a working model of reciprocity. He said, in part, 'if A does something for B and trusts B to reciprocate in the future, this establishes an expectation in A and an obligation on the part of B to keep the trust.' In this respect, the moral virtue of reciprocity is intimately related to the institution of trust. He then suggested that obligations are a form of relational credit, which can be redeemed by members of society if and when needed. In this sense, reciprocity is also a form of social capital which is 'embodied in the relations among persons' (p. 304).

Coleman's (1990) working model emphasized the bilateral relations between pairs of individuals (A and B). Actually, reciprocity as social capital is an essential ingredient sustaining the complex web of community multilateral relationships. Whereas most models of bilateral relations rely (implicitly or explicitly) upon pareto optimality logic, the complex web of reciprocal relations may contain stable non-pareto agreements as well a myriad of second-best solutions to common problems. In many formal bargaining theories, non-pareto optimal agreements would be either abrogated or renegotiated in accordance with the immediate interests (in time and space) of the affected parties. By contrast, if we take seriously the web of reciprocal relations community participants may have a variety of options. For instance, they could balance their immediate interests across large sets of agreements, relying upon the community web for overlapping value. Alternatively, they may use their relational credits to compensate for immediate less than satisfactory outcomes without necessarily disrupting their inherited obligations. As well, they could plan to adjust agreements for future benefits, relying upon the continuity of community relationships to accomplish desired outcomes that cannot be achieved immediately. Reciprocal relationships have a past, present, and future.[11]

Now there are clearly important potential threats to the continuity of those relationships. Most obviously, inherited obligations are only well defined and deserve immediate respect if the whole web is to be sustained over the long term. At the same time, it is possible that the burden of those obligations at any point in time may fall heavily on a small set of participants. The community at large has an interest in ensuring that the execution of those obligations is not so destructive of their welfare that the future of the reciprocal web is put into jeopardy. Equally important is the fact that future expectations may not be realized. There will always be great uncertainty over the fulfilment of legitimate expectations, especially in circumstances of sacrifice by a few on behalf of the whole community. Here, those reliant upon expected benefits rely upon the continuity of relationships, and rely upon the community as a whole in case legitimate but unfulfilled expectations may require compensation in some manner. Furthermore, all agents must rely upon the good will of the community (web of reciprocal relations), recognizing that compensation is rarely, if ever, equivalent to that lost. Thus, there is an ever-present threat: that individual agents will defect from the web of reciprocity believing rightly or wrongly that their interests are better served in the unencumbered market for goods and services. The community has a legitimate interest in overseeing the justice of whole sets of agreements that if not immediately optimal for the parties concerned nevertheless sustain the integrity of the whole web of relations.

The social contract, then, is a commitment by individual agents to the institutions sustaining the web of reciprocal relations. This commitment has two overlapping and constraining dimensions. One concerns the integrity of the underlying moral sentiments that sustain reciprocity. A core function of the state is to protect and enhance those sentiments, subject to individual assessments of the virtues of the subsequent collective outcomes. The other dimension concerns the virtues of outcomes. A related core function of the state is to ensure that relationships are not systematically exploitative, subject to the importance of facilitating the web of reciprocity that sustains interrelational balance, compensation, and credit. The social contract is vulnerable to defection, and is always evaluated against the long-term welfare of individuals in the whole community. It is not, however, a set of institutions that can guarantee equality of outcomes nor is it a set of institutions that can, once and for all, set the terms of exchange. The state is neither the embodiment of moral sentiments nor the only stage on which bilateral agreements are negotiated. Nevertheless, there is a significant danger that the state could replace moral sentiments and be called to intervene in the terms of exchange. In either case, the web of reciprocity may be threatened by an acquisitive and interventionist state.

My argument for the social contract as a web of reciprocal relations could be dismissed as fanciful and implausible. It could be allied with related work on norms and conventions and ridiculed for its supposed idealism. In a related context, Richard Posner (1998: 560) has suggested that only 'a handful of saints' are motivated by what is right. He might be correct. But I should make it clear that I am not arguing for an impossible world or for exacting high moral standards. In fact, aspects of my argument can be found in contemporary accounts of economic geography (in general) and regional economic development (in particular). In this respect, I would argue that the social contract view is consistent with the actual world of economic institutions and communities (although not exhaustively so; see also L. Cao 1998).

To illustrate, let us begin with Storper and Salais's (1997) account of the development of the region commonly identified in the literature as the third Italy (what they actually identify as northeast-central Italy). Having noted the significance of brand names, global markets for specialized consumer goods, and the local networks of related producers, they go on to suggest that the labour market of the region was characterized by a high level of coherence being neither a spot market for labour nor being dominated by firm-specific labour markets. They argue that the local labour market has been dominated by region-specific conventions drawing upon a civic culture of close and long-term interpersonal ties. See R. Putnam (1993) for a related assessment of the significance of local political cultures in Italy, set against the weakness and incoherence of the nation-state. Storper and Salais suggest, in effect, that local civic culture in the third Italy is a form of social capital, sustained by local economic institutions that reinforce the virtues of reciprocity. The resilience of community-based social capital has had important positive effects for local economic growth in the context of global economic volatility. It has been a vital mechanism 'regulating' the flow of skilled labour within and between local firms over the business cycle.

By contrast, the story told by Saxenian (1994) and others about the growth and development of Silicon Valley (California) emphasizes the flow of individuals between firms within the region rather than local economic or political institutions. In effect, the rapid flow of skilled people between competing firms has promoted the transfer of knowledge between firms within the region, but then the isolation of outside firms from the catalytic forces of local knowledge spill-overs. The ability of local employees to step outside of firms and set up their own enterprises combined with the financial resources of venture capital firms has meant that the effects of wealth creation have been spread down the local employment hierarchy. As well, the cycle of small firms that become larger firms and employees who become entrepreneurs before starting the cycle again has created sets of expectations that have functioned as career norms. Reinforcing these norms have been networks of similarly placed individuals who, over their career cycles, draw upon the talents of colleagues inside and outside of local firms. Social capital in this region is quite literally the intra-regional flow of individuals and knowledge, sustained by discrete exchange contracts. Gilson (1998) suggests that the success of Silicon Valley (compared to Route 128 in Massachusetts) can be partly explained by the informality of the process as well as the geographical localization of its positive effects.[12]

These two stories are very different from one another. But they share one basic assumption: that economic geographers' agglomeration economies are constituted, in part, by community-specific social capital. Terms like norms and conventions, reciprocity, obligations and expectations are simply ways of representing decentralised mechanisms of economic regulation. They are different in form from legal structures but act at the local level to sustain the continuity of economic relations in ways beneficial to the local community. In this context, the social contract view juxtaposed against the exclusive benefit view attempts to fill in the details of how and why geography matters for the performance of local economies.[13] At the same time I must make it clear that not all local economies are so dependent upon the web of reciprocity. There are other kinds of local economies that are less reliant upon agglomeration than others. Indeed, there are many economies that are simply sets of isolated production sites linked into the global economy through their reliance upon multi-location firms. These economies do not rely upon the web of reciprocity. Their 'value' is their internal coherence and vulnerability to external exploitation (see Clark 1993*a*) and B. Harrison (1998).

## Public Pensions and Community Development

There is a vibrant industry in community economic development, linking public pension fund investments with local projects. This industry has grown significantly over the past twenty years, bypassing the banking sector as the principal source of development financing. Even so, it is not often studied except when it intersects with the study of the venture capital industry (B. Black and Gilson 1997) and the local politics of project selection and investment (Romano 1993).[14] While public pension funds often rely upon venture capital firms for project selection and management expertise, many other forms of financial intermediation have evolved to cope with the risks and uncertainties of characteristic of community investment (see Chapter 8 for an assessment of the principles underlying their design). More often than not community investment is focused on either the retention of employment in large, often failing, plants of multi-locational firms or on facilitating the growth of small and medium enterprises in specific industry-region niches. The former strategy is, by necessity, short-term in orientation whereas the latter is, hopefully, long-term in orientation.[15]

In large part, the community development industry and its investment products are quite separate from the global asset management firms whose conventional financial products dominate most pension funds' (public and private) asset allocation formula. Whereas most funds' investment products are transparent in design, price, and execution, community development investment products are not. These products tend to be relatively opaque, there being significant informational asymmetries favouring the designers and managers of specific projects and products. As well, there is commonly great uncertainty over the costs of execution and the benchmarks against which to evaluate returns. Nevertheless, the US community investment industry has flourished. In part, its growth has been driven by the demand of public pension plans for local investment opportunities as well as the 1979 revisions to the US Department of Labor's trustees' investment standards explicitly allowing private pension fund investment in small-cap, venture capital enterprises characterized by higher than average risks. Notwithstanding the recent congressional debate over the virtues and vices of economically targeted investments, pension fund investment in local economic development has had a profound impact on the map of investments.

Public pension funds have tended to select between two types of local economic development strategies. For many, project-specific investment in advantageous locations has been a standard strategy. In the industry, this kind of investment is sometimes identified as a private placement or as an alternative investment product, and is closely related to property portfolios and real estate investment trusts. The terms and standards of such investments are widely known, and rely very much on specialized contracts managed by large and small investment companies. The rate of return is a product of the intrinsic functional value of the project and, in some cases, the extent to which it is able to reap the unmanaged externality benefits of geographically adjacent land uses. The other kind of strategy is less common, being focused upon the social capital of industry-regions. In these kinds of deals, pension funds invest in venture capital firms that are able to capitalize and mobilize the talent and networks of local entrepreneurs. The long-run rate of return is therefore determined, in part, by the ensemble or thickness of industry-region networks. Valuing a specific investment requires valuing the likely inter-firm local transfer of information and innovation. In the end, pension funds may earn enormous pay-off through initial public offerings.

If these kinds of investments are controversial in the academic literature, more controversial have been public pension fund investments in social infrastructure. A recent instance was the action by the State of West Virginia requiring their public pension Investment Management Board (IMB) to invest in twenty-five year bonds issued by the State's Regional Jail and Correctional Facility Authority (corrections authority). In summary terms, West Virginia is a small and relatively poor state (see Hovey and Hovey 1998). Historically reliant upon the coal industry, metals processing, and manufacturing, for much of the past fifty years it has experienced economic and demographic stagnation. High rates of unionization, and a labour relations environment more consistent with northern states than southern states has sustained the dominance of the Democratic Party in the state legislature even if, at times, Republicans have controlled the governorship. As Barone et al. (1998:

383) indicate, the 'legislature is overwhelmingly Democratic' (and has been for many years). In the legislature, the Republicans are weak, although radical Democratic governors tend to be rejected in favour of mainstream Republicans.

In terms of per capita real income, state revenue and expenditure on most functional items, West Virginia ranks towards the bottom of the 50 states (Council of State Governments 1998: 259–60). About two-thirds of the state's 1997 revenue was derived from two sources, personal income taxes and consumer sales taxes ($1.6 billion out of $2.4 billion) while more than three-quarters of the state's expenditure was allocated to education and health services ($2.0 billion out of $2.4 billion). Federal transfers were $1.5 billion of which about $1.2 billion were allocated directly to health and human resources. When the state's supreme court mandated additional spending to upgrade the standards of prisons, the Republican governor and the state legislature passed a law to require the IMB to buy the corrections authority's extraordinary bonds. House Bill 4702 directed the IMB to invest $150 million of its funds in the authority over twenty-five years. The bill required that any funds 'must earn an annual return equal to the five year annualised rate of return earned by the core fixed-income portfolio of PERS, plus one tenth of one per cent, and such a rate of return shall not be less than five per cent.' The investment is protected by an insurance policy, linked to a special state fund guaranteeing payment of its obligations. In effect, the state bypassed other financing options like a tax increase or the issuing of a traded bond.

Recognizing the controversy surrounding the legislation, a 'friendly suit' was brought before the state supreme court to test its constitutionality.[16] The majority opinion held the legislation valid, referencing conventional standards of trustee fiduciary duty and state obligations to protect the pension rights of its plan beneficiaries established in a previous decision *Dadisman* v. *Moore*.[17] Nevertheless, the investment directive attracted considerable criticism. For some, it promised a poor rate of return when compared to equities. For others, the rate of return was to be judged against an inappropriate benchmark when compared to US Treasury bills. And some contended that the fund would be 'trapped' in the investment. None of these criticisms are especially compelling. In a fund worth more than $4.9 billion (November 1998) paying defined benefits to retirees, diversification of investment between asset classes and within asset classes is an important strategy but conditional upon the fund's expected long-term liability profile.[18] In that respect, a minimum 5 per cent return compares very favourably with post-1945 US experience across a couple of asset classes (see Cochrane 1997) and

would be consistent with expected liabilities. The fact that the rate of
return is guaranteed means that the investment is practically risk-free,
especially if compared to the short-term riskiness of stocks and many
corporate bonds; witness the October 1987 crisis and the gathering
global financial crisis.

Behind these criticisms is a hidden contestable supposition: the
market for investment services is the best place for investment decisions
to be made. It contends that traded liquidity is the ultimate test of virtue,
and it assumes the highest rates of return are always best notwithstanding the need to take account of plan-specific interests in managing
short-term and long-term risks. At stake, it seems, was a more general
debate about the slowness of many public pension funds to embrace the
market equity culture of the 1990s rather than the particular circumstances of the IMB's long-term liabilities. In earlier sections of this
chapter, I argued against market idealism. I noted that investment managers' performance in market-traded balanced portfolios is highly contingent on circumstances, and very difficult to predict year-to-year. I also
noted that most managers do not consistently out-perform the market,
once fees and transaction costs are taken into account. Indeed, last
year's winning manager is often this year's poorest performer. While
not disputing the importance of a diversified portfolio, in this case
the investment directive was an entirely reasonable investment when
assessed against the long-term risk-and-return objectives of the fund. It
was also remarkably inexpensive to execute in terms of the costs of
issuing market bonds. In effect, it seems that many criticisms of the
investment directive were of the fact that it bypassed the market (for
investment products and services).

Because the state supreme court decided that the directive was not
inconsistent with plan beneficiaries' interests, the exclusive benefit rule
was largely deemed irrelevant to the debate. Nevertheless, some analysts contended that the directive violated the exclusive benefit principle
even if in law the majority opinion effectively muted opposition.[19]
Their argument has had a number of related parts. Some contended that
the state's interest in the investment of IMB assets meant that it was
not a neutral agent of plan beneficiaries' interests. Linked to this argument has been a second strand to the effect social infrastructure is not
a conventionally accepted investment product, being more properly
thought of as a public responsibility. The third strand of argument was
that individual plan beneficiaries' assets had been hijacked by the legislature. Implied by these related arguments were a couple of underlying assumptions or propositions. Most obviously, many analysts have

assumed that the state is only the conduit for plan beneficiaries' assets notwithstanding its status as plan sponsor. Less obviously, it was also implied that the market for services and investment products is neutral with respect to contested values regarding the proper role of government. In this sense, those who objected in principle to the directive seem to have held a philosophical position not dissimilar to that summarized by Macpherson as 'possessive individualism'.

Yet again, idealization of the market was clearly an important part of the debate. But this time market idealism was allied with a strong claim of neutrality sustained by a presumed separation between the public and private realms and the location of 'rights' with the private realm. In fact, underpinning the exclusive benefit argument against the directive is an assumption that individual pension rights must inevitably 'trump' public policy. Here, their views appear to be also entirely consistent with Ronald Dworkin's (1977) atomistic liberalism conceived to protect individual liberty from majoritarian claims in favour of the common good. Implied, it seems, is the supposition that individual rights-holders are entitled to veto state actions that are inconsistent with their own views regarding the proper role of government. At this point, the philosophical roots of the exclusive benefit view re-emerge as very strong political (normative) claims about the proper limits of government policy. My own view is that these types of claims are an implausible recipe for democratic government policy making, and more significantly reflect a mistaken methodological priority assigned to individuals as the primary political unit of social analysis. At the same time, given the march of history, it is unlikely that these types of claims are going to simply evaporate in the face of academic logic.

So, let us return to the reciprocal benefit view and make a positive argument in favour of the West Virginia directive. The first point to be made in this context is to reiterate the claim that rights are best understood as social constructs—that individual rights embody social interests, and are formulated for public purposes. Pildes (1998) makes this argument in the context of American jurisprudence and judicial decision making quoting Raz (1995) against Dworkin (1977). His point is significant for this chapter. Instead of viewing rights as necessary constraints on the common good for individual advantage, it is better to understand rights as embodying and advancing common interests. This means that rights are designed to achieve certain goals, and are part and parcel of government decision making. The fact that they are enshrined (as pension rights are) in statute, and the fact that they have a linguistic or rhetorical power that is more than that found in customary policy making simply reflects the status of those rights relative to other competing policy interests. By this logic, individual rights are a means to a (social) end rather than a statement of absolute advantage. Extending this claim to the constitutional context, Pildes argues 'the justification for many constitutional rights cannot be reduced to the atomistic interest of the right-holder alone' (p. 731).

Clearly, this kind of claim is contentious—jurisprudence and political institutions are littered with the remnants of past debates over the legitimacy of this claim. But it is an open question whether it is more contentious than the absolute rights view underpinning the exclusive benefit rule. This is not the occasion to adjudicate that question. Rather, my argument is more straightforward. Once we realize the contingency of the exclusive benefit view, any compromise of individuals' pension rights (the maximum value of promised pension benefits) in the interests of community economic development should be justified with respect to the overall benefit to the community. Benefit may have many different measures, and may reasonably include investment projects that have a direct economic value like venture capital projects as well as social infrastructure projects whose economic value is found in the savings to the state government. Either way, directly or indirectly, the welfare of most citizens may benefit through economic growth or lower taxes or both. In this respect, there are a wide range of investment options going well beyond the conventional categories of stocks and bonds that currently dominate asset allocation formula in public and private pension funds.[20]

Note, however, that we must only account for the local value of a particular investment policy; we must also assess the harm done to the goal that pension rights embody. In the West Virginia case, of course, because state employees participate in defined benefit plans, it is difficult to sustain any argument that their welfare would be reduced if the investment were to fail. And because a minimum rate of return was guaranteed by state-funded insurance, it is highly unlikely that the investment would 'fail'. But what if state employees participated in a defined contribution plan, and the investment was not guaranteed? What if their maximum welfare was threatened by the risk of under-performance? Would the analysis above still hold true? Generally, the answer would be yes. While there may be difficulties in law given the state supreme court decision in *Dadisman*, defined contribution schemes allocate the risk of performance to individuals. Any decision to offer state employees a defined contribution scheme would be a policy decision of the state government, and thus any risk associated with community economic development would be added to the existing risk profile of the fund borne by individual participants. More abstractly, given the web of reciprocal obligations underpinning the entire community including collective responsibility for the welfare of prison inmates, why should the long-term well-being of state employees be sheltered from the potential costs of community development?

## Coda—Community and Democracy

There are, I think, two reasons to pause and consider the implications of this question. One reason state employees might be reasonably sheltered from the long-term costs associated with community development is that too high a burden could affect the integrity of the retirement plan. The community also has an interest in protecting the retirement system, in part because impoverishing state employees could mean shifting the retirement burden back to the state. At this point, the proper burden of community development risk is an empirical question to be assessed against the overall investment strategy of the fund rather than an issue of absolute principle. As I noted, referencing the work of Storper and Salais (1997) and Saxenian (1994) on industrial districts and my own work on spatially-elongated production networks (Clark 1993a), investing in local economic development may not always reap the rewards expected by advocates of community pension fund investment. Whereas recent arguments in favour of network-based economic development strategies idealize the local content of those networks (Porter 1998), in many cases the value of those networks may be limited to firms whose loyalty to local networks is open to question.

In essence, my point here is that community investment should be evaluated as other investment opportunities are evaluated. Even if risk and return profiles are very different, comparing the characteristics of conventional assets classes to so-called alternative investments, the logic of assessment ought to match or mimic accepted practices. Too often, pension fund community investment is seen as a subsidy for failing businesses and a gift for development projects that cannot attract private finance. While no doubt justified in some cases by virtue of 'gaps' in existing capital markets, the combination of 'special' criteria of assessment and 'special' interests apparent in notable failures suggests that pension fund community investment is too often deemed a 'special' case rather than being seen as a legitimate option set within the terms and conditions of any assessment of investment options. It is also clear that those investment consultants specializing in community economic

development are most successful when they are able to link pension
fund investment to the private capital market. My opinion in this
matter may dismay those who believe pension fund assets are an essential weapon in community development. But it seems clear that the
subsidy of community development cannot be justified as an investment
goal.

Even more significant, however, is the issue of representation. There
must be mechanisms through which state employees are protected from
exploitation. Under-represented minorities should not be required to
bear the entire risk burden of community development. Here, then, is
the basic problem with the West Virginia investment directive. Notwithstanding the risk-free nature of the investment, *in principle* a comparatively small group of citizens were required to bear the entire burden
properly shared (if not equally) by the community. This was made possible because the state governor has two overlapping mandates. He or
she is a political agent, acting on behalf of state political interests. The
governor is also chair of the IMB, acting on behalf of plan beneficiaries.
There is a real risk that the first set of interests may overwhelm the
second set of interests.[21] In the main, this kind of arrangement is justified
by reference to the practice of delegation, characteristic of Anglo-
American institutional politics (see Kiewiet and McCubbins 1991). But
in this case delegation runs the risk of exploitation because the confu-
sion of political representation with interest representation allows the
former to overtake the latter without any means of redress.

In this respect, we need to reconsider the democratic integrity of the
mechanisms by which pension fund beneficiaries' interests are represented in pension fund investment decision making. This point was
made some time ago by Ely (1980), although about a more general issue
that goes to the heart of US politics and jurisprudence. He asked the
question about the representation of minority interests in systems of
representation that promote the interests of the majority. In this respect,
he was most concerned about issues of discrimination (race, gender,
sexual orientation, etc.) wherein minorities are held hostage to majority values. But it seems to me that his argument is also applicable to the
topic considered here: reciprocal obligation should not be an excuse for
the majority to exploit the minority. Ely argued that the courts ought to
scrutinize government decision making with respect to the interests
of minorities, and in effect enhance the process of representation of
minorities' interests. By this logic, the virtues of community investment
ought to be justified and defended. More generally, plan beneficiaries
ought to have broader rights of representation.

## Conclusions

In this chapter, and throughout the book, I have argued against those who believe that pension funds have no role in community economic development. For all kinds of reasons, there are many academic and industry commentators who distrust pension fund investment programmes that have either a local component or betray a willingness to entertain so-called alternative investment products like regional venture capital programmes. Too often, these policies appear to critics as unjustified 'raids' on public employee funds (see *Pensions & Investments*, 2 Nov. 1998, 12). On the other side of the equation, I have sought to show there are good reasons to support pension fund investment in community economic development. Not only are there sound financial reasons to invest in regional growth, there are also many instances where investment in social infrastructure may reap appropriate risk-adjusted rewards to both pension fund beneficiaries and the communities to which they belong. To think otherwise is to unnecessarily narrow the legitimate range of investment options.

To make these arguments has required a two-pronged analytical strategy. On one hand, I have advanced a set of negative arguments against those who idealize the market and the theory of possessive individualism. Too often, those who dispute the value of pension fund investment in community economic development and advance the cause of the exclusive benefit rule make unjustifiable assertions about the virtues and the neutrality of the market for investment services and products. On the other hand, I have argued for a rather different view believing that the reciprocal benefit view is a useful way of understanding the links between plan beneficiaries and their communities. My argument relied upon a broad reading of the notion of social contract, and the significance of social capital for regional economic development. But I did not suggest that all regions should be characterized in these terms.

Like Romano (1993) and others, however, I have also suggested that there remain important issues concerning the relationship between the political sphere of the state legislature and the investment board—the trustees normally charged with the responsibility of acting on behalf of the state government (as plan sponsor) and plan beneficiaries. In the West Virginia case, the overlap between the state government executive and the board of trustees is at once efficient in the sense of sustaining the interests of the plan sponsor but runs the risk of dominating the board of trustees which ought to be independent. For some, the exclusive benefit rule would be the right method of dealing with these issues. In effect, it would simply and directly rule out any consideration not clearly in the best interests of plan beneficiaries. But as I have suggested, I am not convinced the exclusive benefit rule is adequate to the task in theory or in practice. It presupposes a theory of society that is contentious, at best. And it fails to recognize the deeply embedded reciprocal relationships that sustain communities. Given those relationships, it is hard to accept any argument to the effect that on one issue (pension entitlements), a set of citizens are to be privileged over all others including others less privileged of the current generation and the next generation.

While this argument has been made with respect to public pension fund investment in community development, it may also be relevant to private firm-sponsored pension funds. These types of funds have escaped the obligations attached to banks, and related financial institutions for community investment. At the same time, private pension funds have played a crucial role in providing retirement incomes for a significant portion of Anglo-American societies. They have done so with the blessing and tax advantages of each country, and they have benefited enormously from regulatory structure policed by the respective federal governments. Commonly, they rely upon legal formality—pension rights attached to eligible individuals and protected by statutes that treat pension entitlements as a form of property. As we noted above, however, this kind of regulatory regime is neither absolute nor necessarily exclusive of other competing social interests. With the slow demise of banks as important sources of local finance, and with the retreat of the state from any significant involvement in the provision of social infrastructure, pension funds will become increasingly vulnerable to political pressures to play an active role in community development.

Pension fund capitalism carries with it a basic unresolved issue. Ideally, plan sponsors offer pension benefits to those eligible to participate and, in doing so, undertake to manage the accumulated funds in a manner consistent with beneficiaries' best interests. Plan sponsors have two roles in this world. They are at once principals in their own right and agents on behalf of beneficiaries. But it is also true that plan sponsors are agents of society, administrating systems of retirement provision that have been actively supported by Anglo-American governments since the early years of the nineteenth century. At the other end of the system are many, many service providers who are also the agents of plan sponsors. There are then many principals and many more agents all caught up in interlocking obligations and commitments. As I noted, above, however, there are important instances where agents' interests overlap and compete for priority. And, more generally speaking, there are many instances where agents conspire against principals.

But lost in this maze are plan beneficiaries' voices, and community interests. The associated exclusive benefit view seems to legitimize the maze, is silent on what voice plan beneficiaries should have, and is antagonistic to the web of reciprocal obligations that sustain people's place in society. An ideal vision of the individual and the market stands in place of a recognition of the complex social and political life of people inside and outside of their communities. This ideal vision cannot be a bulwark against society. In this respect, the governance of pension funds, and their regulation in relation to social interests will be of profound importance over the coming century.

## Notes

1. It is widely believed that US federal regulation of banks' community lending practices failed to live up to the expectations of its original advocates. In two influential studies of the Community Reinvestment Act (1988 and 1991), G. P. Miller (1992) and Macey and Miller (1993) argued that the Act only imposed more costs on the regulatory system without basically changing the access of depressed communities to development capital. They went to some length to indicate that urban redevelopment is a worthy and important goal. And they were aware of the value of the Act for specific cases. But their assessment of the Act's lack of overall success was compelling. In conjunction with state-by-state deregulation and geographical consolidation of the banking industry, many communities have become increasingly isolated from development finance. Attempts to resurrect local economic development financing through federal initiatives such as the Community Development Financial Institutions (CDFI) fund have not been yet proven effective. See the recent evaluation of the General Accounting Office (1998). Martin (1999a) deals in more detail with the local implications of the retreat of banks from local economic development, providing a useful cross-national comparison of recent trends in Europe and North America.
2. See the reference material on related investment services provided by Economic Innovation International Inc. (1997a,b).
3. For all the significance attached by critics of pension fund activism to the ideal of a perfect market, they are remarkably silent about its configuration and parameters. In this respect, critics share with some branches of law and economics what Schroeder (1998: 523) termed as 'acts of fantasy'. Even though some of the leading theorists of law and economics like Coase are hostile to such idealism, arguing that idealism has resulted in ignorance of how actual markets function, it remains a well-rehearsed rhetorical weapon of critics. Of course, in this chapter I do indulge in my own version of idealism, one which I hope is achievable.

4. There are, however, other significant problems with the logic and nature of arguments in favour of the exclusive benefit view. In large part, these arguments are characterized by a reductive idealism, simultaneously privileging the individual while denying the community any status. Inherent in these arguments is a once-and-for-all theory of the significance of individuals, and a clear antipathy to the world as we know it. Methodologically, a superior unencumbered vantage point is invoked to inform criticism which is necessarily separate from customary practice. That vantage point is then supposed to be the right reference point to anchor public policy. Nagel (1986) deals with this style of argument.

5. There has also been considerable debate over public pension fund activism regarding corporate governance. Del Guercio and Hawkins (1999) survey the reasons for activism, focusing upon CalPERS and CalSTRS who have used public campaigns and others like CREF who have resisted publicity. In the main they believe pension funds seek to improve long-term corporate performance believing this is in the best interests of all shareholders. B. Black (1998), however, argues that the effectiveness of such activity is muted by significant statutory impediments (compared to the UK, for example). Notwithstanding the publicity in the business press, he thinks pension fund activism is of limited importance when assessed against management entrenchment and has had few real successes.

6. It should be observed, of course, that my argument in favour of the social foundations of moral sentiments including reciprocity presupposes priority assigned to socialization (as opposed to individual identity). By contrast, much of economic theory begins with priority assigned to individual identity and works out to socialization as a problem of cooperation and coordination. The fable of Robinson Crusoe captures the spirit of that enterprise. As a matter of psychology, I think this fable and its methodological implications for the theory of social science and the practice of policy making are wrong. The best recent survey of the social psychology of the brain directly relevant to understanding why the fable is implausible is to be found in Brothers (1997). Whether the community is necessarily the proper location of social life is harder to assess. In the examples illustrating my argument, this does seem to be the case. But it is possible to argue that my community could have various scales, going from the local level to humanity in general. Recognizing the possibility of various forms and scales of reciprocity, citizens should have the means to indicate their loyalty to particular configurations. Otherwise, social psychology could easily become tyranny in the name of one version of the scale of human nature (see Plant 1998 for an assessment of the virtues of communitarianism).

7. My notion of community solidarity will not satisfy some commentators. For instance, Sennett (1998) disparages communitarianism, arguing it makes impossible assumptions about the need for, and possibility of, consensus. Communities, by his account, ought to be both more organic and capable of self-sustainment in the face of unresolved internal conflict. Perhaps so. But my point in making an argument for community solidarity in relation to pension fund investment is the need to begin from current circumstances and work towards a practical alternative. As a result, however, my notion of community may appear overly instrumental.

8. In Cooter's (1998) account of the relationships between law and social norms, a clear distinction can be made between conventional economic theories of behaviour and those that rely upon social values. By convention, law operates as a price or sanction, constraining behaviour to that mandated by the state. Alternatively, law could be thought of as representing social norms or obligations accepted by community members. In this respect, law need not have a price, since it simply expresses an accepted obligation. To illustrate he notes 'men regularly take their hats off in a boiler room from inclination, and men take their hats off in church from obligation' (p. 587).

9. Subsequently, I have come to realize that my functional model of the social contract overlaps and intersects with MacNeil's (1980) 'new social contract'. His argument is about the necessary relational structure of modern contract law, associating interdependence and mutual need with the contemporary world of agents rather than principals. To sustain his argument, he relies throughout upon a distinction between the discrete form of exchange contract that dominates neoclassical economics and the idea of contractual solidarity which can be found in Durkheim's notion of the social contract. Citing Durkheim's 'organic solidarity' MacNeil argues that the defining characteristic of modern capitalism is the 'common belief in effective future interdependence' (p. 91).

10. Compare with Williamson (1985: 33–4) where reciprocity is invoked as a means of sustaining bilateral exchange in the context of 'transaction-specific assets'. In another section, Williamson suggests reciprocity is a means of conditional exchange, in effect a means of bilateral exchange (see ch. 8, sect. 1, pp. 191–5). Williamson makes a great deal out of his close connection with MacNeil (1980) but does so by ignoring significant elements of MacNeil's argument related to solidarity, interdependence, and mutuality.

11. In theory, at least, this is a contentious argument. Half hidden in my discussion is a presumption in favour of what economists define as sunk costs: the costs of past investments. Many economists believe that people ought to let bygones be bygone. However, like Nozick (1993: 22–3) I believe that many people honour past commitments as a matter of principle. He says in part 'we do *not* treat our past commitments to others as of no account except insofar as they affect out future returns, as when breaking a commitment may affect others' trust in us and hence our ability to achieve other future benefits'. There are, however, dissenting views; see Steele's (1996) critique.

12. See also Pastor and Dreier's (1998) study of the positive reinforcing linkages between US regional economic growth and inner-city development. Their study combines econometric results with a case study of Los Angeles to argue the case for a social capital approach to local economic development. More generally, Schwartz (1994) argued that the success of Silicon Valley through its internalized 'social structure of innovation' and positive reinforcing links with the venture capital industry is a development recipe for many underdeveloped countries. Case studies of success based upon the assumed positive externalities of economic geography have been widely generalized (perhaps beyond credibility).

13. See also Scott (1998) on the significance of formal and informal networks in sustaining local economic development. He identifies similar issues, linking the institutions and related social practices that sustain Marshallian industrial

districts to the evolving global economy. Like Scott, I also recognize that idealized localized communities are hardly relevant to the new world of global capitalism. Any model of community solidarity must allow for spatially extensive
networks of affection and loyalty.

14. See Federal Register, Vol. 44 (No. 124), 26 June 1979 (p. 37222), where it is noted
    that the US Department of Labor does not rule out individual investments
    because of their relative riskiness and that the value of such an investment
    should be judged in relation to the 'overall plan portfolio'. The Department then
    notes that even though small or new firm securities may be riskier than large
    blue-chip stocks, these kinds of investments have a role to play in the whole
    portfolio of investments. Ronald Gilson drew my attention to this revision.

15. A related analysis of the structure and management of a state-based public
    sector pension fund system is to be found in Levine (1997). His summary of the
    Wisconsin system helps understand the nature and design of public pension
    systems, and the links between specific types of pension benefits and investment
    strategies. Notice, he is principally concerned with the system's investment in
    ETIs. The Wisconsin system is generally thought to be a well-managed and effec-
    tive system.

16. *State of West Virginia ex rel. West Virginia Regional Jail and Corrections Facility
    Authority v. West Virginia Investment Management Board* (No. 25134); decision
    filed 17 July 1998.

17. 384 S.E.2d 816 (W. Va. 1988). In *Dadisman*, the State was found to have failed
    'to properly fund' the public employee retirement system (PERS) thereby vio-
    lating statute, trust, and the state constitution (p. 825). During the 1980s, the
    State had failed to appropriate budgetary resources to match contributions by
    employees to the PERS. The state supreme court held that this was illegal, and
    concluded that 'the Legislature's improper expiration of the appropriations
    worked as an expropriation from the PERS trust funds' (p. 825). The court also
    concluded that the PERS trustees had not acted, as one would expect, in ways
    consistent with plan beneficiaries' interests. In fact, they had 'actually cooper-
    ated with the Legislature's invasion' of fund assets (p. 826).

18. Summary data on the West Virginia public pensions system is available through
    *Pensions & Investments*, 20 Jan. 1997 and 26 Jan. 1998. There it is shown that
    pension benefits offered are for defined (final salary) benefits allocated between
    a variety of fixed income products, cash, and mortgage products. Apparently, the
    pension fund system was given permission to shift assets towards equities in
    early 1998, now accounting for about 17 per cent of all assets. The shift in fund
    assets coincided, of course, with the end of the 1990s bull market (*Pensions &
    Investments*, 2 Nov. 1998).

19. Highly critical front-page articles and editorials in the financial press accompan-
    ied the West Virginia directive. See e.g. *Pensions & Investments*, 27 July and 10
    Aug. 1998.

20. It is clear that the State's management of pension fund assets was, for many
    years, narrowly focused upon fixed income products. Compared to most US
    public pension funds, the State's investment policy was conservative in the
    extreme. Only in 1997 was there a concerted attempt by the State to liberalize
    pension investments, explicitly embracing the rudiments of modern portfolio
    theory. Previously, investments in equities (company stocks) were deemed

unconstitutional. See the 12 Apr. 1997 amendment to the West Virginia Code (WV Statutes, Ch. 12, Art. 6) declaring (in part) that 'experience has demonstrated that prudent investment provides diversification and beneficial return not only for public employees but for all citizens of the state' (12-6-1c legislative findings).

21. The state governor is by statute, in fact, the major force behind the composition and management of the IMB. Of the thirteen members of the IMB, three are appointed by virtue of their office—the governor, the state treasurer, and the state auditor. The ten other trustees are appointed by the governor for terms of six years providing that they have relevant experience and providing that no more than six of the ten appointed members come from the same party. The governor also has the power to remove any trustee for gross misconduct and replace that person with another trustee. While quarterly meetings are open to the public and plan beneficiaries, the appointment process does not take into account the representation of plan beneficiaries nor does it provide for legislative scrutiny of the appointed trustees. The governor serves as chair of the IMB, and is supported by a deputy chair whose term only lasts for two years. The chief executive officer of the IMB is appointed by the board of trustees, and is subject to appropriate qualifications and experience (12-6-4). These kinds of arrangements are problematic; see Clark (1998c) on the power politics in boards of trustees where chairs have such wide-ranging powers.

# BIBLIOGRAPHY

AARONSON, D., and SULLIVAN, D. (1998). 'The Decline of Job Security in the 1990s: Displacement, Anxiety, and their Effect on Wage Growth'. *Economic Perspectives*, 22(1): 17–43.

ABEL-SMITH, B. (1994). 'The Beveridge Report: Its Origins and Outcomes', in J. Hills, J. Ditch, and H. Glennerster (eds.), *Beveridge and Social Security: An International Retrospective*. Oxford: Clarendon Press, 10–22.

ABOLAFIA, M. (1996). *Making Markets: Opportunism and Restraint on Wall Street*. Cambridge, Mass.: Harvard University Press.

AFL-CIO (1993). 'Pensions in Changing Capital Markets: A Report and Guidelines for International Investment Issues'. Washington, DC: Pension Investment Committee.

ALCHIAN, A. (1950). 'Uncertainty, Evolution and Economic theory'. *Journal of Political Economy*, 58: 211–22.

ALLEN, F., and GALE, D. (1994a). *Financial Innovation and Risk Sharing*. Cambridge, Mass.: MIT Press.

————(1994b). 'A Welfare Comparison of the German and US Financial Systems'. Philadelphia: Rodney White Center for Financial Research, Wharton School, University of Pennsylvania.

————(1997). 'Financial Markets, Intermediaries and Intertemporal Smoothing'. *Journal of Political Economy*, 105: 523–46.

——and SANTOMERO, A. M. (1996). 'The Theory of Financial Intermediation'. Philadelphia: Financial Institutions Center, Wharton School, University of Pennsylvania.

ALSTON, L. J., EGGERTSSON, T., and NORTH, D. C. (1996) (eds.). *Empirical Studies in Institutional Change*. Cambridge: Cambridge University Press.

AMBACHTSHEER, K., and EZRA, D. (1998). *Pension Fund Excellence: Creating Value for Stakeholders*. New York: Wiley.

AMIN, A. (1994) (ed.). *Post-Fordism: A Reader*. Oxford: Blackwell.

——and THRIFT, N. (1992). 'Neo-Marshallian Nodes in Global Networks'. *International Journal of Urban and Regional Research*, 16: 571–87.

ANAND, P. (1993). *Foundations of Rational Choice under Risk*. Oxford: Clarendon Press.

ANDERSON, R. W., and HARRIS, C. J. (1986). 'A Model of Innovation with Application to New Financial Products'. *Oxford Economic Papers*, 38: 203–18.

APPADURAI, A. (1996). *Modernity at Large: Cultural Dimensions of Globalisation*. Minneapolis: University of Minneapolis Press.

ARMSTRONG, M. (1997). 'Competition in Communications'. *Oxford Review of Economic Policy*, 13: 64–82.

ARTHUR, W. B. (1986). 'Industry Location and the Importance of History', Palo Alto, Calif.: Stanford University.

——(1994). *Increasing Returns and Path Dependency in the Economy*. Ann Arbor: University of Michigan Press.

ATIYAH, P. S. (1995). *An Introduction to the Law of Contract*. Oxford: Oxford University Press.

AUDRETSCH, D. B., and FELDMAN, M. (1996). 'Knowledge Spillovers and the Geography of Innovation and Production'. *American Economic Review*, 86: 630–40.

AXELROD, R. (1984). *The Evolution of Cooperation*. New York: Basic Books.

BAERT, P. (1996). 'Realist Philosophy of the Social Sciences and Economics: A Critique'. *Cambridge Journal of Economics*, 20: 513–22.

BAIER, A. (1994). *Moral Prejudices*. Cambridge, Mass.: Harvard University Press.

BANE, M. J., and ELLWOOD, D. (1993). *Welfare Realities: From Rhetoric to Reform*. Cambridge, Mass.: Harvard University Press.

BARCET, A. (1991). 'Production and Service Supply Structure: Temporality and Complimentarity Relations', in P. Daniels, and F. Moulaert. (eds.), *The Changing Geography of Advanced Producer Services*. London: Belhaven Press, 59–69.

BARNES, T. (1996). *Logics of Dislocation: Models, Metaphors, and Meanings of Economic Space*. New York: Guilford Press.

BARONE, M., LILLEY, W., and DELFRANCO, L. J. (1998). *State Legislative Elections: Voting Patterns and Demographics*. Washington, DC: Congressional Quarterly.

BARRO, R., and SALA-I-MARTIN, X. (1995). *Economic Growth*. New York: McGraw-Hill.

BASU, S., and FERNALD, J. G. (1997). 'Returns to Scale in US Production: Estimates and Implications'. *Journal of Political Economy*, 105: 249–83.

BAUMOL, W. (1991). 'Towards a Newer Economics: The Future Lies Ahead!' *Economic Journal*, 101: 1–8.

BAXTER, C. I. (1994). 'Canals Where Rivers Used to Flow: The Role of Mediating Structures and Partnerships in Community Lendings'. *Economic Development Quarterly*, 10: 44–56.

BEBCHUK, L. A., and ROE, M. J. (1998). 'A Theory of Path Dependence in Corporate Governance and Ownership'. New York: Columbia Law School.

BECKER, L. C. (1990). *Reciprocity*. Chicago: University of Chicago Press.

——(1996). 'Trust as Non-Cognitive Security about Motives'. *Ethics*, 107: 43–61.

BELL, J. (1989). 'The Effect of Changes in Circumstances on Long Term Contracts', in D. R. Harris, and D. Tallon (eds.), *Contract Law Today*. Oxford: Clarendon Press, 195–220.

BENDER, J., and WELLBERY, D. E. (1990*a*) (eds.). *The Ends of Rhetoric: History, Theory, Practice*. Palo Alto, Calif.: Stanford University Press.

————(1990*b*). 'Rhetoricality: On the Modernist Return of Rhetoric', in J. Bender, and D. E. Wellbery (eds.), *The Ends of Rhetoric: History, Theory, Practice*. Palo Alto, Calif.: Stanford University Press, 3–41.

BERG, O. (1993). Speech before the AFL-CIO asset managers conference. Washington, DC: US Department of Labor, Pension and Welfare Benefits Administration.

BERGER, A. N., DEMSETZ, R. S., and STRAHAN, P. E. (1998). 'The Consolidation of the Financial Services Industry: Causes, Consequences, and the Implications for the Future'. New York: Federal Reserve Bank of New York.

BERKOWITZ, E. D. (1991). *America's Welfare State: From Roosevelt to Reagan*. Baltimore: Johns Hopkins University Press.

——(1997). 'The Historical Development of Social Security in the United States', in E. R. Kingston, and J. H. Shulz (eds.), *Social Security in the 21st Century*. Oxford: Oxford University Press, 22–38.

BERLIN, M., and MESTER, L. J. (1998). 'Intermediation and Vertical Integration'. *Journal of Money, Credit, and Banking*, 30: 500–19.

BEYERS, W., and LINDAHL, D. (1997). 'Strategic Behaviour and Development Sequences in Producer Service Businesses'. *Environment and Planning A*, 29: 887–912.

BIKHCHANDANI, S., HIRSHLEIFER, D., and WELCH, I. (1998). 'Learning from the Behavior of Others: Conformity, Fads, and Informational Cascades'. *Journal of Economic Perspectives*, 12: 151–70.

BLACK, B. (1992). 'Agents Watching Agents: The Promise of Institutional Voice'. *UCLA Law Review*, 39: 811–93.

——(1998). 'Shareholder Activism and Corporate Governance in the United States', in P. Newman (ed.), *The New Palgrave Dictionary of Economics and Law* (forthcoming).

——and GILSON, R. J. (1997). 'Venture Capital and the Structure of Capital Markets: Banks Verses Stock Markets'. Palo Alto, Calif.: School of Law, Stanford University.

BLACK, F. (1985). 'The Future for Financial Services', in R. P. Inman (ed.), *Managing the Service Economy: Prospects and Problems*. Cambridge: Cambridge University Press, 223–30.

——(1986). 'Noise'. *Journal of Finance*, 43: 529–43.

BLACKBURN, R. (1999). 'The New Collectivism: Pension Reform, Grey Capitalism and Complex Socialism'. *New Left Review*, 233: 3–65.

BLAKE, D. (1995). *Pension Schemes and Pension Funds in the United Kingdom*. Oxford: Clarendon Press.

——LEHMANN, B., and TIMMERMAN, A. (1997). 'Performance Measurement Using Multiple Asset Class Portfolio Data: A Study of UK Pension Funds'. London: Centre for Economic Policy Research.

BLUME, M. (1997). 'An Anatomy of Morningstar Ratings'. Philadelphia: Rodney White Center for Finanancial Research, Wharton School, University of Pennsylvania.

BODENMAN, J. E. (1998). 'The Suburbanization of the Investment Advisory Industry: Metropolitan Philadelphia 1983–1993'. *The Professional Geographer*, 50: 112–26.

BODIE, Z., and CRANE, D. B. (1998). 'The Design and Production of New Retirement Savings Products'. Boston: Division of Research, Harvard Business School.

BODIE, Z., and MERTON, R. (1993). 'Pension Benefit Guarantees in the United States: A Functional Analysis', in R. Schmitt (ed.), *The Future of Pensions in the United States*. Philadelphia: Pension Research Council, Wharton School, University of Pennsylvania, 194–234.

——and PAPKE, L. E. (1992). 'Pension Fund Finance', in Z. Bodie, and A. Munnell (eds.), *Pensions and the Economy: Sources, Uses and Limitations of Data*. Philadelphia: University of Pennsylvania Press, 149–80.

Boice Dunham Group Inc. (1993). 'The Nature and Scale of Economically Targeted Investments by the 104 Largest US Public Pension Plans'. Report prepared for Goldman Sachs. New York.

BONDI, L. (1997). 'In Whose Words? On Gender Identities, Knowledge and Writing Practices'. *Transactions, Institute of British Geographers*, NS 22: 245–58.

BOOT, A. W., and THAKOR, A. V. (1997). 'Financial System Architecture'. *Review of Financial Studies*, 10: 693–733.

BOURDIEU, P. (1990). *In Other Words: Essays Towards a Reflexive Sociology*. Cambridge: Polity Press.

BOWERS, L. A. (1993). *The Fiduciary Duty Aspects of Economically Targeted Investments*. Washington, DC: Center for Policy Alternatives.

BOYER, R., and DRACHE, D. (1997) (eds.). *States Against Markets: The Limits of Globalisation*. London: Routledge.

BRAITHWAITE, J. (1989). *Crime, Shame and Integration*. Cambridge: Cambridge University Press.

BRENNAN, G., and PETTIT, P. (1993). 'Hands Invisible and Intangible'. *Synthese*, 94: 191–225.

BRONFMAN, C., and FERGUSON, M. (1995). 'Would Greater Transparency Increase or Decrease Contracting Costs?' *Journal of Financial Engineering*, Vol. 4(2), pp. 115–24.

BROTHERS, L. (1997). *Friday's Footprint: How Society Shapes the Human Mind*. Oxford: Oxford University Press.

CAMPBELL, J. Y., LO, A. W., and MACKINLAY, A. C. (1997). *The Econometrics of Financial Markets*. Princeton: Princeton University Press.

CAO, C., CHOE, H., and KHO, B.-C. (1997). 'Does the Specialist Matter? Differential Execution Costs and Inter-Security Subsidization on the NYSE'. *Journal of Finance*, 52: 1615–40.

CAO, L. (1998). 'Looking at Communities and Markets'. Durham, NC: Duke University School of Law.

CARHART, M. (1997a). 'Mutual Fund Survivorship'. Los Angeles: Marshall School of Business, University of Southern California.

——(1997b). 'On Persistence in Mutual Fund Performance'. *Journal of Finance*, 52: 57–82.

CARLTON, D., and PERLOFF, J. (1994). *Modern Industrial Organization*. New York: Harper Collins.

CARR, E. H. (1961). *What is History?* London: Macmillan.

CARTWRIGHT, J. (1991). *Unequal Bargaining: A Study of Vitiating Factors in the Formation of Contracts*. Oxford: Clarendon Press.

CASSON, M. (1991). *The Economics of Business Culture*. Oxford: Clarendon Press.

CAVE, T. (1995). 'Fictional Identities', in H. Harris (ed.), *Identity*. Oxford: Clarendon Press, 99–128.

CHANDLER, A. (1977). *The Visible Hand: The Managerial Revolution in American Business*. Cambridge, Mass.: Harvard University Press.

CHEN, Z., and HUANG, H. (1995). 'Investment Trap'. London School of Economics, Financial Markets Group.

CHOE, H. K., KHO, B.-C., and STULZ, R. M. (1998). 'Do Foreign Investors Destabilise Stock Markets? The Korean Experience in 1997'. Cambridge, Mass.: National Bureau of Economic Research.

CIALDINI, R. B. (1993). *Influence: The Psychology of Persuasion*. New York: Quill.

CLARK, G. L. (1985). *Judges and the Cities: Interpreting Local Autonomy*. Chicago: University of Chicago Press.

——(1986). 'Towards an Alternative Conception of Job Search Theory and Policy: Information as an Indeterminate Process'. *Environment and Planning A*, 18: 803–25.

——(1990). 'The Virtues of Location: Do Property Rights "Trump" Workers' Rights to Self-Organization?' *Environment and Planning D: Society and Space*, 8: 53–72.

——(1992). 'Real Regulation: The Administrative State'. *Environment and Planning A*, 24: 615–28.

——(1993a). 'Global Interdependence and Regional Development: Business Linkages and Corporate Governance in a World of Financial Risk'. *Transactions, Institute of British Geographers*, NS 18: 309–26.

——(1993b). *Pensions and Corporate Restructuring in American Industry: A Crisis of Regulation*. Baltimore: Johns Hopkins University Press.

——(1994). 'Strategy and Structure: Corporate Restructuring and the Scope and Characteristics of Sunk Costs'. *Environment and Planning A*, 25: 9–32.

——(1997b). 'Rogues and Regulation in Global Finance'. *Regional Studies*, 31: 221–36.

——BURKETT, J., CALDOW, W., and JOBLING, M. (1996). *Australian Superannuation: The Anatomy of an Industry*. Melbourne: Australian Housing and Urban Research Institute.

——and DEAR, M. J. (1984). *State Apparatus: Structures and Language of Legitimacy*. London and Boston: Allen and Unwin.

——and EVANS, J. (1998). 'The Private Provision of Urban Infrastructure: Long Term Contracts as Financial Intermediation'. *Urban Studies*, 35: 301–19.

————(1999). 'Competition and Innovation in the Anglo-American Investment Management Industry'. Oxford: School of Geography, University of Oxford.

—— GERTLER, M. S., and WHITEMAN, J. (1986). *Regional Dynamics: Studies in Adjustment Theory*. London: Allen and Unwin.

—— and O'CONNOR, K. B. (1997). 'The Informational Content of Financial Products and the Spatial Structure of the Finance Industry', in K. Cox (ed.), *Spaces of Globalization*. New York: Guilford Press, 89–114.

—— and WRIGLEY, N. (1995). 'Sunk Costs: A Framework for Economic Geography'. *Transactions, Institute of British Geographers*, NS 20: 204–23.

—— —— (1997). 'The Spatial Configuration of the Firm and the Management of Sunk Costs'. *Economic Geography*, 73: 285–304.

CLARK, N., and JUMA, C. (1988). 'Evolutionary Theories in Economic Thought', in G. Dosi, C. Freeman, R. Nelson, and L. Soete (eds.), *Technical Change and Economic Theory*. London: Pinter, 197–217.

CLARK, R. C. (1975). 'The Federal Taxation of Financial Intermediaries'. *Yale Law Journal*, 84: 1603–82.

—— (1976). 'The Soundness of Financial Intermediaries'. *Yale Law Journal*, 86: 1–102.

—— (1981). 'The Four Stages of Capitalism: Reflections on Investment Management Treatises'. *Harvard Law Review*, 94: 561–82.

COASE, R. H. (1937). 'The Nature of the Firm'. *Economica*, NS 4: 386–405.

—— (1974). 'The Lighthouse in Economics'. *Journal of Law and Economics*, 17: 357–76.

COCHRANE, J. H. (1997). 'Where is the Market Going? Uncertain Facts and Novel Theories'. *Economic Perspectives*. 21(6): 3–37.

—— (1999*a*). 'New facts in finance.' *Economic Perspectives* 23(3), 36–58.

—— (1999*b*). 'Portfolio advice for a multifactor world.' *Economic Perspectives* 23(3), 59–78.

COLEMAN, J. L. (1992). *Risks and Wrongs*. Cambridge: Cambridge University Press.

COLEMAN, J. S. (1990). 'Norm-Generating Structures', in K. S. Cook, and M. Levi (eds.), *The Limits of Rationality*. Chicago: University of Chicago Press, 250–272.

Commonwealth of Australia (1966). '21st Report of the Senate Select Committee on Superannuation: Investment of Australia's Superannuation Savings'. Canberra.

COOTER, R. (1998). 'Expressive Law and Economics'. *Journal of Legal Studies*, 27: 585–608.

—— and FREEDMAN, B. J. (1991). 'The Fiduciary Relationship: Its Economic Character and Legal Consequences'. *New York University Law Review*, 66: 1045–75.

—— and RUBINFELD, D. L. (1989). 'Economic Analysis of Legal Disputes and their Resolution'. *Journal of Economic Literature*, 27: 1067–97.

Council of the State Governments (1998). *The Book of the States. 1998–99 Edition*. Lexington, Ky.

CRAGG, J. G., and MALKIEL. B. (1982). *Expectations and the Structure of Share Prices*. Chicago: University of Chicago Press.

CRAIG, P. P. (1990). *Public Law and Democracy in the United Kingdom and the United States of America*. Oxford: Clarendon Press.

——and DE BURCA. G. (1995). *E.C. Law: Text, Cases and Materials*. Oxford: Oxford University Press.

CRANE, D. W., FROOT, K., MASON, S. P., PEROLD, A., MERTON, R. C., BODIE, Z., SIRRI, E., and TUFANO, P. (1995). *The Global Financial System: A Functional Perspective*. Boston: Harvard Business School Press.

DALTON, C. (1986). 'An Essay in the Deconstruction of Contract Doctrine'. *Yale Law Journal*, 94: 997–1114.

DANIEL, K., HIRSHLEIFER, D., and SUBRAHMANYAM, A. (1998). 'Investor Psychology and Security Market Under- and Overreactions'. *The Journal of Finance*, 53: 1839–86.

DAVIS, E. P. (1993). 'Theories of Intermediation, Financial Innovation and Regulation'. *National Westminster Bank Quarterly Review*, May: 41–53.

——(1995). *Pension Funds: Retirement Income Security and Capital Markets: An International Perspective*. Oxford: Clarendon Press.

DEBONDT, W. F. M., and THALER, R. J. (1994). 'Financial Decision-Making in Markets and Firms: A Behavioural Perspective'. Cambridge, Mass.: National Bureau of Economic Research.

DEL GUERCIO, D., and HAWKINS, J. (1999). 'The Motivation and Impact of Pension Fund Activism'. *Journal of Financial Economics* (forthcoming).

DELONG, J. B., SHLEIFER, A., and SUMMERS, L.(1990). 'Noise Trader Risk in Financial Markets'. *Journal of Political Economy*, 98: 703–38.

DEMAN, P. (1984). *The Rhetoric of Romanticism*. New York: Columbia University Press.

DEMIRGUC-KUNT, A., and MAKSIMOVIC, V. (1998). 'Law, Finance, and Firm Growth'. *The Journal of Finance*, 53: 2107–38.

DEMSKI, J. S., and SAPPINGTON, D. (1987). 'Delegated Expertise'. *Journal of Accounting Research*, 25: 68–89.

DENHAM, R., and PORTER, M. (1995). 'Lifting All Boats: Increasing the Payoff from Private Investment in the US Economy'. Washington, DC: Capital Allocation Subcouncil.

DE RYCK, K. (1996). *European Pension Funds: Their Impact on European Capital Markets. An International Perspective*. Brussels: EFRP.

Deutsche Bank AG (1997). *Aspiring Equity Culture in Germany*. Frankfurt am Main: Deutsche Morgan Grenfell European Equity Research.

DIAMOND, D. W. (1984). 'Financial Intermediation and Delegated Monitoring'. *Review of Economic Studies*, 60: 393–414.

DIAMOND, P. (1994). 'Privitisation of Social Security: Lessons from Chile'. *Revista de Analisis Economico*, 9: 21–53.

DISNEY, R. (1996). *Can We Afford to Grow Older? A Perspective on the Economics of Ageing*. Cambridge, Mass.: MIT Press.

DOBRIS, J. (1986). 'Arguments in Favour of Fiduciary Divestment of "South African" Securities'. *Nebraska Law Journal*, 85: 209–41.

DOSI, G., and ORSENIGO, L. (1988). 'Coordination and Transformation: An

Overview of Structures, Behaviours and Change in Evolutionary Environments', in G. Dosi, C. Freeman, R. Nelson, and L. Soete (eds.), *Technical Change and Economic Theory*. London: Pinter, 13–37.

Dow, S. (1997). 'Mainstream Economic Method'. *Cambridge Journal of Economics*, 21: 73–93.

Doyle, C. (1989). 'Strategy Variables and Theories of Industrial Organization', in F. Hahn (ed.), *The Economics of Missing Markets, Information, and Games*. Oxford: Clarendon Press, 149–62.

Drache, D., and Gertler, M. (1991) (eds.). *The New Era of Global Competition: State Policy and Market Power*. Kingston and Montreal: McGill-Queens University Press.

Driver, J. (1996). 'The Virtues and Human Nature', in R. Crisp (ed.), *How Should One Live? Essays on the Virtues*. Oxford: Clarendon Press, 110–30.

Drucker, P. (1993). *Post-Capitalist Society*. Oxford: Butterworth–Heinemann.

Duff, R. A. (1990). *Intention, Agency and Criminal Liability*. Oxford: Blackwell.

Dunn, J. (1990). 'Introduction', in J. Dunn (ed.), *The Economic Limits of Modern Politics*. Cambridge: Cambridge University Press, 1–13.

Dworkin, R. (1977). *Taking Rights Seriously*. Cambridge, Mass.: Harvard University Press.

Easterbrook, F., and Fischel, D. (1991). *The Economic Structure of Corporate Law*. Cambridge, Mass.: Harvard University Press.

Economic Innovation International Inc. (1995). *Michigan Private Equity Market Evaluation*. Boston.

——(1997a). *Enterprise Southern California: Towards Increasing the Equity Flows for Emerging and Expanding Enterprises in Los Angeles and Southern California*. Boston.

——(1997b). *Thinking about Prudent Economically Targeted Investment*. Boston.

Economic Planning Advisory Commission (1995). *Private Infrastructure Task Force Report*. Canberra: Australian Government Printing Service.

Edison, H. J., Luangaram, P., and Miller, M. (1998). 'Asset Bubbles, Domino Effects and "Lifeboats": Elements of the East Asian Crisis'. *International Finance Discussion Paper*. Washington, DC: Board of Governors of the Federal Reserve System.

Edwards, J., and Fischer, K. (1994). *Banks, Finance and Investment in Germany*. Cambridge: Cambridge University Press.

EFRP (European Federation for Retirement Plans) (1996). *European Pension Funds: Their Impact on European Capital Markets and Competitiveness*. London: EFRP.

Eggertsson, T. (1996). 'A Note on the Economics of Institutions', in L. J. Alston, T. E. Eggertsson, and D. C. North (eds.), *Empirical Studies in Institutional Change*. Cambridge: Cambridge University Press, 6–24.

Ehring, D. (1997). *Causation and Persistence: A Theory of Causation*. Oxford: Oxford University Press.

EINHORN, H., and HOGARTH, R. M. (1986). 'Decision Making under Ambiguity'. *Journal of Business*, 59: S225–49.

ELLISON, G., and GLAESER, E. L. (1997). 'Geographic Concentration in US Manufacturing Industries: A Dart-Board Approach'. *Journal of Political Economy*, 105: 889–927.

ELLSBERG, D. (1961). 'Risk, Ambiguity and the Savage Axioms'. *Quarterly Journal of Economics*, 75: 643–69.

ELTON, E. J., GRUBER, M. J., and BUSSE, J. (1995). 'The Persistence of Risk-Adjusted Mutual Fund Performance'. New York: Stern School of Business, New York University.

ELY, J. H. (1980). *Democracy and Distrust: A Theory of Judicial Review*. Cambridge, Mass.: Harvard University Press.

EMERSON, R. M., FRETZ, R., and SHAW, L. (1995). *Writing Ethnographic Field-notes*. Chicago: University of Chicago Press.

EMMONS, W. R., and GREENBAUM, S. (1996). 'Twin Information Revolutions and the Future of Financial Intermediation'. St Louis: Olin School, Washington University in St Louis.

ESPING-ANDERSON, G. (1990). *The Three Worlds of Welfare Capitalism*. Oxford: Polity Press.

European Commission (1997). *The Single Market Review*, Subseries III. *Dismantling of Barriers*, 5. *Capital Market Liberalisation*. Brussels.

——(1997). 'Supplementary Pensions in the Single Market: A Green Paper'. Brussels: DG XV.

FAMA, E. (1970). 'Efficient Capital Markets: A Review of Theory and Empirical Evidence'. *Journal of Finance*, 25: 383–417.

——(1991). 'Efficient Capital Markets: II'. *Journal of Finance*, 46: 1575–617.

——(1996). 'Discounting under Uncertainty'. *Journal of Business*, 69: 415–28.

FARRAND, J. (1996). 'Farrand's First Year', in A. Phillips (ed.), *Pension Funds and their Advisors*. London: AP Information Services, 53–6.

FELDMAN, M., and FLORIDA, R. (1994). 'The Geographical Sources of Information: Technological Infrastructure and Production Innovation in the United States'. *Annals, Association of American Geographers*, 84: 210–29.

FERLAUTO, R. (1993). 'Putting a Sharp Pencil to ETIs: Economic Buoyancy or Hopes about to Pop'. *Pensions World*, No. 24.

——and CLABOURN, J. (1993). *Economically Targeted Investments by State-Wide Public Pension Funds*. Washington, DC: Center for Policy Alternatives.

FISCHEL, D., and LANGBEIN, J. (1988). 'ERISA's Fundamental Contradiction: The Exclusive Benefit Rule'. *University of Chicago Law Review*, 55: 1105–60.

FOGELSON, R. (1984). *Pensions: The Hidden Costs of Public Safety*. New York: Columbia University Press.

FOX, C. R., and TVERSKY, A. (1995). 'Ambiguity Aversion and Comparative Ignorance'. *Quarterly Journal of Economics*, 110: 585–604.

FROUD, J., HASLAM, C., JOHAL, S., WILLIAMS, J., and WILLIAMS, K. (1997). 'From Social Settlement to Household Lottery'. *Economy and Society*, 26: 340–72.

GAGNIER, R. (1991). *Subjectivities: A History of Self-Representation in Britain*. Oxford: Oxford University Press.

GALBRAITH, J. K. (1967). *The New Industrial State*. London: Andre Deutsch.

GALLIE, D. (1956). 'Essentially Contested Concepts'. *Proceedings of the Aristotelian Society*, 56: 167–98.

GAMBETTA, N. (1988) (ed.). *Trust: Making and Breaking Cooperative Relations*. Oxford: Blackwell.

GAO, *see* General Accounting Office.

GARUD, R., and SHAPIRA, Z. (1997). 'Aligning the Residuals: Risk, Return, Responsibility, and Authority', in Z. Shapira (ed.), *Organizational Decision Making*. Cambridge: Cambridge University Press, 238–56.

GAUTHIER, D. (1986). *Morals by Agreement*. Oxford: Clarendon Press.

——(1990). *Moral Dealing: Contract, Ethics, and Reason*. Ithaca, NY: Cornell University Press.

GEERTZ, C. (1983). *Local Knowledge*. New York: Basic Books.

General Accounting Office (1993). 'The Business Environment in the United States, Japan, and Germany'. Washington, DC.

——(1995). 'Private Pension Plans: Efforts to Encourage Infrastructure Investment'. Washington, DC.

——(1996*a*). 'Airport Privatization: Issues Related to the Sale or Lease of US Commercial Airports'. Washington, DC.

——(1996*b*). 'Public Pensions: State and Local Government Contributions to Underfunded Plans'. Washington, DC: General Accounting Office.

——(1998). 'Community Development: Early Results of the Community Development Financial Institutions Funds Programmes'. Washington, DC.

GERTLER, M. S. (1993). 'Implementing Advanced Manufacturing Technologies in Mature Industrial Regions: Towards a Social Model of Technological Production'. *Regional Studies*, 27: 259–78.

——(1996). 'Worlds Apart: The Changing Market Geography of the German Machinery Industry'. *Small Business Economics*, 8: 87–106.

GETZLER, J. (1996). ' "Gentlemen Do Not Collect Rents": Fiduciary Obligations and the Problem of Delegation'. Oxford: St. Hugh's College.

GHILARDUCCI, T. (1992). *Labor's Capital: The Economics and Politics of Private Pensions*. Cambridge, Mass.: MIT Press.

GIBBARD, A. (1990). *Wise Choices, Apt Feelings: A Theory of Normative Choice*. Cambridge, Mass.: Harvard University Press.

GIBSON-GRAHAM, J. K. (1996). *The End of Capitalism (As We Knew It): A Feminist Critique of Political Economy*. Oxford: Blackwell.

GILL, S. (1997). 'Transformation and Innovation in the Study of World Order', in S. Gill, and J. H. Mittelman (eds.), *Innovation and Transformation in International Studies*. Cambridge: Cambridge University Press, 5–23.

GILSON, R. J. (1998). 'The Legal Infrastructure of High Technology Industrial Districts: Silicon Valley, Route 128, and Covenants Not to Compete'. Stanford Calif.: Stanford Law School.

—— and ROE, M. J. (1998). 'Lifetime Employment: Labor Peace and the Evolution of Japanese Corporate Governance'. New York: Columbia Law School.

GLYN, A. (1996). 'Taxing and Spending'. *Imprints*, 1: 48–58.

GOETZMANN, W. N., INGERSOLL, J., and ROSS, S. A. (1998). 'High Water Marks'. New Haven: Yale School of Management.

Goldman Sachs (1997). 'Report on Alternative Investment by Tax Exempt Organizations'. New York.

——and Frank Russell Capital Inc. (1995). 'Executive Summary: Survey of Alternative Investments by Pension Funds, Endowments and Foundations'. New York.

GOMPERS, P. A., and METRICK, A. (1998). 'Are the Hundred-Million-Dollar Managers just like Everyone Else? An Analysis of Stock Ownership, Concentration, and Trading by Large Institutions'. Boston: Division of Research, Harvard Business School.

GOODE, R. (1993). *Pension Law Reform: The Report of the Pension Law Review Committee*. London: HMSO.

——(1994a). 'Defining and Protecting the Pension Promise'. *Journal of the Institute of Actuaries*, 121: 161–77.

——(1994b). 'Occupational Pensions: Securing the Pension Promise'. *The Denning Law Journal*, 15–25.

GOODMAN, R. B. (1995) (ed.). *Pragmatism: A Contemporary Reader*. London: Routledge.

GORDON, J. (1987). 'The Puzzling Persistence of the Constrained Prudent Man Rule'. *New York University Law Review*, 62: 52–114.

GRANT, W. (1997). 'Perspectives on Globalisation and Economic Coordination', in J. R. Hollingsworth, and R. Boyer (eds.), *Contemporary Capitalism: The Embeddedness of Institutions*. Cambridge: Cambridge University Press, 319–36.

GRAVES, W. (1998). 'The Geography of Mutual Fund Assets'. *The Professional Geographer*, 50: 243–55.

GREEN, M. (1995). 'The Geography of US Institutional Investment, 1990'. *Urban Geography*, 16: 46–69.

Greenwich Associates (1996a). 'Investment Management: Statistical Supplement'. Greenwich, Conn.

——(1996b). 'New Paradigm, New Potency'. Greenwich, Conn.

——(1998). 'What Now?' Greenwich, Conn.

GREGORY, D. (1996). *Geographical Imaginations*. Oxford: Blackwell.

GRIFFIN, J. (1993). 'On the Winding Road from Good to Right', in R. G. Frey, and C. W. Morris (eds.), *Value, Welfare, and Morality*. Cambridge: Cambridge University Press, 158–79.

GROSSMAN, S. (1989). *The Informational Role of Prices*. Cambridge, Mass.: MIT Press.

——(1995). 'Dynamic Asset Allocation and the Informational Efficiency of Markets'. *Journal of Finance*, 50: 773–87.

——and STIGLITZ, J. (1980). 'On the Impossibility of Informationally Efficient Markets'. *American Economic Review*, 70: 393–408.

GRUBER, M. J. (1996). 'Another Puzzle: The Growth of Actively Managed Mutual Funds'. *Journal of Finance*, 51: 783–810.

GRUNDGER, F. (1994). 'Beveridge Meets Bismarck: Echo, Effects, and Evaluation of the Beveridge Report in Germany', in J. Hills, J. Ditch, and H. Glennerster (eds.), *Beveridge and Social Security: An International Retrospective*. Oxford: Clarendon Press, 134–53.

HABERMAS, J. (1984). *The Theory of Communicative Action*. Boston: Beacon Press.

HAHN, F. (1989) (ed.). *The Economics of Missing Markets, Information and Games*. Oxford: Oxford University Press.

——(1989). 'Information Dynamics and Equilibrium', in id. *The Economies of Missing Markets, Information and Games*. Oxford: Clarendon Press, 106–28.

——(1991). 'The Next Hundred Years'. *Economic Journal*, 101: 47–50.

HALBACH, E. (1990). 'Redefining the Prudent Investor Rule for Trustees'. *Trusts & Estates*, Dec.: 14–22.

HAMEL, G., and PRAHALAD, C. K. (1994). *Competing for the Future*. Boston: Harvard Business School Press.

HAMPTON, J. (1991). 'Two Faces of Contractarian Thought', in P. Vallentyne (ed.), *Contractarianism and Rational Choice: Essays on David Gauthier's Morals by Agreement*. Cambridge: Cambridge University Press, 31–55.

HANNAH, L. (1986). *Inventing Retirement: The Development of Occupational Pensions in Britain*. Cambridge: Cambridge University Press.

HARDIN, R. (1996). 'Trustworthiness'. *Ethics*, 107: 26–42.

HARRÉ, R. (1993). *Social Being*. Oxford: Blackwell.

HARRISON, B. (1994). *Lean and Mean*. New York: Basic Books.

——(1998). 'It Takes a Region (or Does It?): The Material Basis for Metropolitanism and Metropolitics'. New York: Milano Graduate School of Management and Urban Policy, New School.

——KELLY, M., and GANT, J. (1996). 'Innovative Firm Behavior and Local Milieu: Exploring the Intersection of Agglomeration, Firm Effects, and Technological Change'. *Economic Geography*, 72: 233–58.

HARRISON, D. (1995). *Pension Fund Investment in Europe*. London: Financial Times Publishing.

HARVEY, D. (1982). *The Limits to Capital*. Chicago: University of Chicago Press.

——(1985). *Consciousness and the Urban Experience*. Oxford: Blackwell.

——(1989). *The Condition of Post-Modernity*. Oxford: Blackwell.

HAWLEY, J. P., and WILLIAMS, A. T. (1996). 'Corporate Governance in the United States: The Rise of Fiduciary Capitalism'. Moraga, Calif.: St Mary's College of California.

HAYES, S. L. (1993) (ed.). *Financial Services: Perspectives and Challenges*. Boston: Harvard Business School Press.

HELM, D., and JENKINSON, T. (1997). 'The Assessment: Introducing Competition into Regulated Industries'. *Oxford Review of Economic Policy*, 13: 1–14.

HENDRICKS, D., PATEL, J., and ZECKHAUSER, R. (1991). 'Hot Hands in Mutual Funds: Short-Run Persistence of Performance, 1974–88'. *Journal of Finance*, 48: 93–130.

HILLS, J., DITCH, J., and GLENNERSTER, H. (1994) (eds.). *Beveridge and Social Security: An International Retrospective*. Oxford: Clarendon Press.

HIRSHLEIFER, D. (1995). 'The Blind Leading the Blind: Social Inference, Fads, and Informational Cascades', in *The New Economics of Human Behaviour*. Cambridge: Cambridge University Press, 188–215.

——and WELCH, I. (1994). 'Institutional Memory, Inertia and Impulsiveness'. Los Angeles: Graduate School of Management, University of California.

HIRSHLEIFER, J. (1971). 'The Private and Social Value of Information and the Reward to Inventive Activity'. *American Economic Review*, 60: 561–74.

HIRST, P., and THOMPSON, G. (1997). 'Globalisation in Question: International Economic Relations and Forms of Public Governance', in, J. R. Hollingsworth, and R. Boyer (eds.), *Contemporary Capitalism*. Cambridge: Cambridge University Press, 337–60.

——and ZEITLIN, J. (1997). 'Flexible Specialisation: Theory and Evidence in the Analysis of Industrial Change', in J. R. Hollingsworth, and R. Boyer (eds.), *Contemporary Capitalism*. Cambridge: Cambridge University Press, 220–39.

HM Treasury (1995). *Private Opportunity, Public Benefit: Progressing the Private Finance Initiative*. London: HMSO.

HOBSBAWN, E. (1994). *Age of Extremes: The Short Twentieth Century, 1914–1989*. London: Michael Joseph.

HOLLINGSWORTH, J. R., and BOYER, R. (1997). 'Coordination of Economic Agents and Social Systems of Production', in J. R. Hollingsworth, and R. Boyer (eds.), *Contemporary Capitalism*. Cambridge: Cambridge University Press, 1–48.

HOUTHAKKER, H., and WILLIAMSON, P. J. (1996). *The Economics of Financial Markets*. Oxford: Oxford University Press.

HOVEY, K. A., and HOVEY, H. (1998). *CQ's State Fact Finder: Rankings across America*. Washington, DC: Congressional Quarterly.

HUTTON, W. (1995). *The State We're In*. London: Jonathan Cape.

HYLTON, R., and O'BRIEN, M. (1992). 'Socially Responsible Investing: Doing Good Versus Doing Well in an Inefficient Market'. *American University Law Review*, 42: 1–44.

Institute of Economics (1936). *The Recovery Problem in the United States*. Washington, DC: Brookings Institution.

Investment Property Forum (1996). *Property for UK Pension Funds*. London: National Association of Pension Funds.

JACKSON, H. (1994). 'The Expanding Obligations of Financial Holding Companies'. *Harvard Law Review*, 107: 507–619.

——(1997). 'The Regulation of Financial Holding Companies'. Cambridge, Mass.: Harvard Law School Center for Law, Economics and Business.

JENSEN, M. (1978). 'Some Anomalous Evidence Regarding Market Efficiency'. *Journal of Financial Economics*, 6: 95–101.

JESSOP, B. (1994). 'Post-Fordism and the State', in A. Amin (ed.), *Post-Fordism: A Reader*. Oxford: Blackwell, 251–79.

JOBLING, M. (1994). 'A Legal Perspective on Targeted Superannuation Fund Investment: A Comparison between the United States and Australia'. Melbourne: Australian Housing and Urban Research Institute.

Joint Economic Committee (1985). 'Venture Capital and Innovation'. Washington, DC: US Congress, 98 (2).

JONES, G. STEDMAN (1971). *Outcast London: A Study in the Relationship between the Classes in Victorian Society*. Oxford: Clarendon Press.

KAHNEMAN, D., and LOVALLO, D. (1993). 'Timid Choices and Bold Forecasts: A Cognitive Perspective on Risk Taking'. *Management Science*, 39: 17–31.

——and TVERSKY, A. (1979). 'Prospect Theory: An Analysis of Decision under Risk'. *Econometrica*, 47: 263–91.

KALDOR, N. (1985). *Economics without Equilibrium: The Arthur Okun Memorial Lectures*. New York: M. E. Sharpe.

KANE, E. (1988). 'How Market Forces Influence the Structure of Financial Regulation', in W. S. Haraj and R. M. Kushmeider (eds.), *Restructuring and Financial Services in America*. Washington, DC: American Enterprise Institute, 343–82.

——(1991). 'Financial Regulation and Market Forces'. *Swiss Journal of Economics and Statistics*, 127: 325–42.

——(1993). 'Reflexive Adaptation Business to Regulation and Regulation to Business'. *Law and Policy*, 15: 179–89.

KAPLAN, A. (1993). *French Lessons*. Chicago: University of Chicago Press.

KEYNES, J. M. (1921). *A Treatise on Probability*. London: Macmillan.

——(1936). *The General Theory of Money, Interest and Employment*. London: Macmillan.

KIEWIET, D. R., and McCUBBINS, M. D. (1991). *The Logic of Delegation: Congressional Parties and the Appropriations Process*. Chicago: University of Chicago Press.

KINDER, P. D., LYDENBERG, S. D., and DOMINI, A. L. (1992) (eds.). *The Social Investment Almanac*. New York: Henry Holt.

KING, R., and LEVINE, R. (1993). 'Finance and Growth: Schumpeter Might be Right'. *Quarterly Journal of Economics*, 108: 717–38.

KLEIN, B. K., and LEFFLER, K. (1981). 'The Role of Market Forces in Assuring Contractual Performance'. *Journal of Political Economy*, 89: 615–40.

KNIGHT, F. (1921). *Risk, Uncertainty and Profit*. Boston: Houghton Mifflin Company.

KNOLL-SHAFFER, C. (1993). 'Pennsylvania's Public Pension Funds: The Needs for a New Consensus'. Harrisburg: Commonwealth of Pennsylvania, Bipartisan Commission.

KRUEGER, A. O. (1996). 'The Political Economy of Controls: American Sugar', in L. J. Alston, T. Eggertsson, and D. C. North (eds.), *Empirical Studies in Institutional Change*. Cambridge: Cambridge University Press, 169–218.

KRUGMAN, P. (1991). *Geography and Trade*. Cambridge, Mass.: MIT Press.

——(1996). *The Self-Organizing Economy*. Oxford: Blackwell.

KUHN, T. (1970). *The Structure of Scientific Revolutions*. Chicago: University of Chicago Press.

KUTTNER, R. (1997). *Everything for Sale: The Virtues and Limits of Markets*. New York: Knopf.

KYMLICKA, W. (1990). *Contemporary Political Philosophy: An Introduction*. Oxford: Clarendon Press.

LA PORTA, R., LOPEZ-DE-SILANES, F., SHLEIFER, A., and VISHNY, R. W. (1996). 'Law and Finance'. Cambridge, Mass.: National Bureau of Economic Research.

—————————(1997). 'Legal Determinants of External Finance'. *Journal of Finance*, 52: 1131–50.

LAKONISHOK, J., SHLEIFER, A., and VISHNY, R. W. (1992). 'The Structure and Performance of the Money Management Industry'. *Brookings Papers: Microeconomics*, SISI: 339–91.

LAMOND, G. (1996). 'Coercion, Threats, and the Puzzle of Blackmail', in A. P. Simester and A. T. H. Smith (eds.), *Harm and Culpability*. Oxford: Clarendon Press, 215–38.

LAMONT, M. (1992). *Money, Morals, and Manners: The Culture of the French and the American Upper-Middle Classes*. Chicago: University of Chicago Press.

LANGBEIN, J. (1995). 'The Contractarian Basis of the Law of Torts'. *Yale Law Journal*, 105: 625–75.

——(1997). 'The Secret Life of a Trust: The Trust as an Instrument of Commerce'. *Yale Law Journal*, 107: 165–89.

LATOUR, B. (1986). *Science in Action*. Milton Keynes: Open University Press.

LAULAJAINEN, R. (1998). *Financial Geography—A Banker's View*. Gothenburg: School of Economics and Commercial Law.

LAUMANN, E., GAGNON, J., and MICHAEL, R. (1994). *The Social Organisation of Sexuality*. Chicago: University of Chicago Press.

LEAR, J. (1998). *Open Minded*. Cambridge, Mass.: Harvard University Press.

LEIBFRITZ, W., ROSEVEARE, D., FORE, D., and WURZEL, E. (1995). 'Ageing Populations, Pension Systems and Government Budgets: How Do They Affect Savings?' Paris: Economics Department, OECD.

LEVINE, M. V. (1997). *The Feasibility of Economically Targeted Investing: Wisconsin Case Study*. Brookfield, International Foundation of Employee Benefit Plans.

LEWONTIN, R. C. (1995). 'Sex, Lies, and Social Science'. *New York Review of Books*, Apr. 20: 24–9.

LEYSHON, A., THRIFT, N., and PRATT, J. (1998). 'Reading Financial Services: Texts, Consumers and Financial Literacy'. *Environment and Planning D: Society and Space*, 16: 29–55.

LIGHT, J. O., and PEROLD, A. (1987). 'The Institutionalisation of Wealth: Changing Patterns of Investment Decision Making', in S. Hayes (ed.), *Wall Street and Regulation*. Boston: Harvard Business School Press, 91–118.

LOGAN, J., and MOLOTCH, H. (1987). *Urban Fortunes: The Political Economy of Place*. Berkeley: University of California Press.

LOGUE, D. E., and RADER, J. S. (1998). *Managing Pension Plans: A Comprehensive Guide to Improving Plan Performance*. Boston: Harvard Business School Press.

LOWENSTEIN, G., and PRELEC, D. (1992). 'Anomalies in Intertemporal Choice: Evidence and an Interpretation'. *Quarterly Journal of Economics*, 107: 573–98.

LUHMANN, N. (1979). *Trust and Power*. New York: Wiley.

LUTTWAK, E. (1998). *Turbo-Capitalism: Winners and Losers in the Global Economy*. London: Weidenfield & Nicolson.

McDOWELL, J. (1994). *Mind and World*. Cambridge, Mass.: Harvard University Press.

McDOWELL, L. (1992*a*). 'Doing Gender: Feminism, Feminists and Research Methods in Human Geography'. *Transactions of the Institute of British Geographers*, 17: 399–416.

——(1992*b*). 'Valid games? A Response to Erica Schoenberger'. *The Professional Geographer*, 44: 212–15.

——(1997). *Capital Culture*. Oxford: Blackwell.

MACNEIL, I. R. (1980). *The New Social Contract: An Inquiry into Modern Contractual Relations*. New Haven: Yale University Press.

MACPHERSON, C. B. (1962). *The Political Theory of Possessive Individualism: Hobbes to Locke*. Oxford: Clarendon Press.

MACEY, J. R., and MILLER, G. P. (1993). 'The Community Reinvestment Act: An Economic Analysis'. *Virginia Law Review*, 79: 291–348.

MACHINA, M. (1991). 'Dynamic Consistency and Non-Expected Utility', in M. Bacharach and S. Hurley (eds.), *Foundations of Decision Theory*. Oxford: Blackwell, 39–91.

MAILLOUX, S. (1989). *Rhetorical Power*. Ithaca, NY: Cornell University Press.

MAJESKI, S. J. (1990). 'Comment: An Alterntive Approach to the Generation and Maintenance of Norms', in K. S. Cook and M. Levi (eds.), *The Limits of Rationality*. Chicago: University of Chicago Press, 273–83.

MALKIEL, B. (1990). *A Random Walk Down Wall Street*. New York: Norton.

MARDEN, P., and CLARK, G. L. (1994). 'The Regulation of Private Pensions (Superannuation) and Strategic Unionism in Australia: Learning from the United States'. *Monash Publications in Geography and Environmental Science*, 44.

MARKOWITZ, H. M. (1952). 'Portfolio Selection'. *Journal of Finance*, 7: 77–91.

MARTIN, R. L. (1999*a*). 'The New Economic Geography of Money', in id. (ed.), *Money and the Space Economy*. New York: J. Wiley, 3–27.

——(1999*b*). 'Selling of the State: Privatization, the Capital Market and the Geography of Share Ownership', in id. (ed.), *Money and the Space Economy*. New York: J Wiley, 261–83.

MARTIN, R. L. and MINNS, R. (1995). 'Undermining the Financial Bases of Regions: The Spacial Structure and Implications of the UK Pension Fund System'. *Regional Studies*, 29: 125–44.

——and SUNLEY, P. (1996). 'Paul Krugman's "Geographical Economics" and its Implications for Regional Development Theory: A Critical Assessment'. *Economic Geography*, 72: 259–92.

————(1997). 'Slow Convergence? The New Endogenous Growth Theory and Regional Development'. University of Cambridge.

MEHTA, J., STARMER, C., and SUDGEN, R. (1994). 'The Nature of Salience: An Experimental Investigation of Pure Co-ordination Games'. *American Economic Review*, 84: 658–73.

MERTON, R. C. (1994). 'Influence of Mathematical Models in Finance on Practice: Past, Present and Future'. *Philosophical Transactions, Royal Society*. London. 347: 451–63.

——and BODIE, Z. (1995). 'A Conceptual Framework for Analyzing the Financial Environment', in D. B. Crane (ed.), *The Global Financial System: A Functional Perspective*. Boston: Harvard Business School Press, 3–31.

MILHAUPT, C. J. (1995). 'A Relational Theory of Japanese Corporate Governance: Contract, Culture, and the Rule of Law'. St Louis: Olin School, Washington University in St Louis.

MILLER, G. P. (1992). 'Legal Restrictions on Bank Consolidation: An Economic Analysis'. *Iowa Law Review*, 77: 1083–131.

——(1998). 'Political Structure and Corporate Governance: Some Points of Contrast between the United States and England'. *Columbia Business Law Review*, 1998 (1): 51–78.

MILLER, J. H. (1987). *The Ethics of Reading*. New York: Columbia University Press.

MILLER, M. (1986). 'Financial Innovation: The Last Twenty Years and the Next'. *Journal of Financial and Quantitative Analysis*, 21: 459–71.

MILLSTEIN, I. (1989). 'Our Money's Worth'. Albany, NY: Governor's Task Force.

MINNS, R. (1980). *Pension Funds and British Capitalism: The Ownership and Control of Shareholdings*. London: Macmillan.

MISHKIN, F. (1998). 'Financial Consolidation: Dangers and Opportunities'. Cambridge, Mass.: National Bureau of Economic Research.

MISZTAL, B. A. (1996). *Trust in Modern Societies*. Oxford: Polity Press.

MITCHELL, O. S. (1996). 'Administrative Costs in Public and Private Retirement Systems'. Cambridge, Mass.: National Bureau of Economic Research.

——(1998). 'Developments in Pensions'. *NBER Reporter*, Spring: 12–15.

——and HSIN, P. L. (1994). 'Public Pension Governance and Performance'. Philadelphia: Pension Research Council, University of Pennsylvania.

——and ZELDES, S. P. (1996). 'Social Security Privatisation: A Structure for Analysis'. *American Economic Review, Papers and Proceedings*, 86(2): 363–7.

MOFFAT, G. (1994). *Trust Law: Text and Materials*. London: Butterworths.

MOON, J. J., PIZANTE, L. R., STRAUSS, J., and TUKMAN, J. (1998). 'Asset Management in the 21st Century: New Rules, New Game'. New York: Goldman Sachs Investment Management Group.

MORROW, R., and BROWN, D. (1994). *Critical Theory and Methodology*. London: Sage Publications.

MUNNELL, A. (1983). 'The Pitfalls of Social Investing: The Case of Public Pensions and Housing'. *New England Economic Review*, Sept./Oct.: 20–40.

——(1990) (ed.). *Is There a Shortfall in Public Capital Investment?* Boston: Federal Reserve Bank of Boston.

NAGEL, T. (1986). *The View from Nowhere*. Oxford: Oxford University Press.

NELSON, R. (1994). 'The Co-Evolution of Technology, Industrial Structure, and Supporting Institutions'. *Industrial and Corporate Change*, 4: 47–63.

——(1995). 'Recent Evolutionary Theorizing about Economic Change'. *Journal of Economic Literature*, 33: 48–90.

——and WINTER, S. (1982). *An Evolutionary Theory of Economic Change.* Cambridge, Mass.: Harvard University Press.

NEVIN, J. A. (1995). 'Contingencies of Reinforcement and Behavioural Momentum: Research and Applications'. Manchester, NH: Department of Psychology, University of New Hampshire.

New York State AFL-CIO (1993). 'It's Still Our Money (What's Left of It)'. Albany, NY: Task Force on Public Employee Pensions.

NOBLES, R. (1993). *Pensions, Employment and the Law.* Oxford: Oxford University Press.

Note (1975). 'Fiduciary Standards and the Prudent Man Rule under the Employment Retirement Income Security Act of 1974'. *Harvard Law Review*, 88: 960–79.

NOTTAGE, R., and RHODES, G. (1986). *Pensions: A Plan for the Future.* London: Anglo-German Foundation for the Study of Industrial Society.

NOYELLE, T. (1991). 'Transnational Business Service Firms and Developing Countries', in P. Daniels and F. Moulaert (eds.), *The Changing Geography of Advanced Producer Services.* London: Bellhaven Press, 177–96.

NOZICK, R. (1981). *Philosophical Investigations.* Cambridge, Mass.: Harvard University Press.

——(1993). *The Nature of Rationality.* Princeton: Princeton University Press.

NUSSBAUM, M. (1996). *Poetic Justice: The Literary Imagination and Public Life.* Boston: Beacon Press.

——(1990). *Love's Knowledge: Essays on Philosophy and Knowledge.* Oxford: Oxford University Press.

O'BARR, W., and CONLEY, J. M. (1992). *Fortune and Folly.* Homewood, Ill.: Business One Irwin.

O'CONNOR, J. (1973). *The Fiscal Crisis of the State.* New York: St Martin's Press.

OECD (1997). *Economic Outlook.* Paris: OECD.

ORDESHOOK, P. (1986). *Game Theory and Political Theory: An Introduction.* Cambridge: Cambridge University Press.

ORLOFF, A. S. (1993). *The Politics of Pensions: A Comparative Analysis of Britain, Canada, and the United States, 1880–1940.* Madison: University of Wisconsin Press.

PAIN, N., and YOUNG, G. (1996). 'The UK Public Finances: Past Experience and Future Prospects'. *National Institute of Economics Review*, 158: 27–35.

PAINE, T. (1993). 'The Changing Character of Pensions: Where Employers are Heading', in R. V. Burkhauser and D. L. Salisbury (eds.), *Pensions in a Changing Economy.* Washington, DC: Employee Benefit Research Institute, 33–40.

PALMER, K., OATES, W. E., and PORTNEY, P. (1995). 'Tightening Environmental Standards: The Benefit-Cost or the No-Cost Paradigm'. *Journal of Economic Perspectives*, 9: 119–32.

PASTOR, M. J., and DREIER, P. (1998). 'The "New Regionalism" and Community

Development'. Santa Cruz, Calif.: Latin American and Latino Studies, University of California.

PEIRCE, N. R. (1995). 'Challenge for Pension Fund Trustees'. *National Journal*, 27: 1671.

——BERGER, R., PETERS, F. M., and STEINBACH, C. F. (1994). 'Market Standards, Community Standards: Economically Targeted Investments for the 1990s'. Washington, DC: National Academy of Public Administration.

PERLOFF, M. (1996). *Wittgenstein's Ladder*. Chicago: University of Chicago Press.

PETERSON, V. S. (1997). 'Whose Crisis? Early and Post-Modern Masculinism', in S. Gill and J. H. Mittelman (eds.), *Innovation and Transformation in International Studies*. Cambridge: Cambridge University Press, 185–205.

PHILLIPS, W. (1957). *Pension Scheme Precedents*. London: Sweet and Maxwell.

PIERCE, J. L. (1995). *Gender Trials: Emotional Lives in Contemporary Law Firms*. Berkeley: University of California Press.

PILDES, R. H. (1998). 'Why Rights are not Trumps: Social Meanings, Expressive Harms, and Constitutionalism'. *Journal of Legal Studies*, 27: 725–64.

PIORE, M. J., and SABEL, C. F. (1984). *The Second Industrial Divide: Possibilities for Prosperity*. New York: Basic Books.

PLANT, R. (1998). 'Antinomies of Modernist Political Thought: Reasoning, Context and Community', in J. Good and I. Velody (eds.), *The Politics of Postmodernity*. Cambridge: Cambridge University Press, 76–106.

PLOUG, N., and KVIST, J. (1996). *Social Security in Europe: Development or Dismantlement*. London: Kluwer Law International.

PONTIFF, J. (1996). 'Costly Arbitrage: Evidence from Closed-End Funds'. *Quarterly Journal of Economics*, 111: 1135–52.

PORTER, M. (1992*a*). 'Capital Choices: Changing the Way America Invests in Industry'. Washington, DC: Council on Competitiveness.

——(1992*b*). 'Capital Disadvantage: America's Failing Capital Investment System'. *Harvard Business Review*, 70: 65–82.

——(1998). 'Clusters and the New Economics of Competition'. *Harvard Business Review*, 76(6): 77–91.

——and VAN DER LINDE, C. (1995). 'Towards a New Conception of the Environment Competiveness Relationship'. *Journal of Economic Perspectives*, 9: 97–118.

POSNER, E. (1996). 'The Regulation of Groups: The Influence of Legal and Non-Legal Sanctions on Collective Action'. *University of Chicago Law Review*, 63: 133–97.

POSNER, R. A. (1997). *Overcoming Law*. Cambridge, Mass.: Harvard University Press.

——(1998). 'Social Norms, Social Meaning, and Economic Analysis of Law: A Comment'. *Journal of Legal Studies*, 27: 553–66.

PRATT, J., and ZECKHAUSER, R. (1985) (eds.). *Principals and Agents: The Structure of Business*. Boston: Harvard Business School Press.

PRYKE, M. (1994). 'Urbanising Capitals: Towards an Integration of Time, Space and Economic Calcuations', in S. Corbridge, R. L. Martin, and N. Thrift (eds.), *Money, Power and Space*. Oxford: Blackwell, 218–52.

——and LEE, R. (1995). 'Place your Bets: Towards an Understanding of Globalisation, Socio-Financial Engineering and Competition within a Financial Centre'. *Urban Studies*, 32: 329–44.

PUTNAM, H. (1992). *Renewing Philosophy*. Cambridge, Mass.: Harvard University Press.

PUTNAM, R. (1993). *Making Democracy Work: Civic Traditions in Modern Italy*. Princeton: Princeton University Press.

——(1994). 'Between the New Left and Judaism', in G. Borradori (ed.), *The American Philosopher*. Chicago: University of Chicago Press, 55–69.

QUEISSER, M. (1996). 'Pensions in Germany'. Washington, DC: World Bank.

RADNER, R. (1997). 'Bounded Rationality, Indeterminancy, and the Managerial Theory of the Firm', in Z. Shapira (ed.), *Organizational Decision Making*. Cambridge: Cambridge University Press, 324–52.

RAKOFF, T. (1993). 'Social Structure, Legal Structure and Default Rules: A Comment'. *Southern California Interdisciplinary Law Journal*, 3: 19–28.

——(1994). 'The Implied Terms of Contracts: Of Default Rules and "Situation sense"', in J. Beatson and D. Friedman (eds.), *Good Faith and Fault in Contract Law*. Oxford: Clarendon Press, 191–228.

RAWLS, J. (1971). *A Theory of Justice*. Cambridge, Mass.: Harvard University Press.

RAZ, J. (1986). *The Morality of Freedom*. Oxford: Clarendon Press.

——(1995). *Ethics in the Public Domain*. Oxford: Clarendon Press.

REICH, R. (1991). *The Work of Nations*. New York: Vintage Press.

——(1997). *Locked in the Cabinet*. New York: Vintage Press.

RENO, V. (1993). 'The Role of Pensions in Retirement Income', in R. V. Burkhauser and D. Salisbury (eds.), *Pensions in a Changing Economy*. Washington, DC: Employee Benefit Research Institute, 19–33.

RESCHER, N. (1987). *Ethical Idealism: An Inquiry into the Nature and Function of Ideals*. Berkeley: University of California Press.

RHODES, G. (1965). *Public Sector Pensions*. London: Allen & Unwin.

RICHARDSON, G. B. (1972). 'The Organization of Industry'. *Economic Journal*, 82: 883–96.

RIFKIN, J., and BARBER, R. (1978). *The North Will Rise Again: Pensions, Politics, and Power in the 1980s*. Boston: Beacon Press.

RIGHTER, W. (1994). 'The Origins of Endogenous Growth'. *Journal of Economic Perspectives*, 8: 3–22.

Riverside Economic Research (1994). 'The Brancato Report on Institutional Investment: Patterns of Institutional Investment and Control in the USA'. Fairfax: The Victoria Group.

ROBINSON, P. (1996). 'Competing Theories of Justification: Deeds v. Reasons', in A. P. Simester and A. T. H. Smith (eds.), *Harm and Culpability*. Oxford: Clarendon Press, 45–70.

ROE, M. (1994). *Strong Managers, Weak Owners: The Political Roots of American Corporate Finance*. Princeton: Princeton University Press.

——(1998a). 'Backlash'. *Columbia Law Review*, 98: 217–41.

320                          *Bibliography*

ROE, M. (1998*b*). 'German Codetermination and German Securities Markets'. *Columbia Business Law Review*, 1998: 167–83.

ROLL, R. (1986). 'The Hubris Hypothesis of Corporate Takeovers'. *Journal of Business*, 59: 197–216.

ROMANO, R. (1993). 'Public Pension Fund Activism in Corporate Governance Reconsidered'. *Columbia Law Review*, 93: 795–853.

ROSE-ACKERMAN, S. (1991). 'Risk Taking and Ruin: Bankruptcy and Investment Choice'. *Journal of Legal Studies*, 20: 277–310.

ROSECRANCE, R. (1996). 'The Rise of the Virtual State'. *Foreign Affairs*, 75: 45–61.

ROSS, S. (1989). 'Institutional Markets, Financial Marketing, and Financial Innovation'. *Journal of Finance*, 46: 541–56.

ROY, A. D. (1950). 'Safety First and the Holding of Assets'. *Econometrica*, 20: 431–49.

RUDDEN, B. (1989). 'The Domain of Contract', in D. R. Harris and D. Tallon (eds.), *Contract Law Today*. Oxford: Clarendon Press, 81–113.

SAMUELSON, W., and ZECKHAUSER, R. (1988). 'Status Quo Bias in Decision Making'. *Journal of Risk and Uncertainty*, 1: 7–59.

SANDEL, M. J. (1998). *Liberalism and the Limits of Justice*. Cambridge: Cambridge University Press.

SASS, S. A. (1997). *The Promise of Private Pensions: The First Hundred Years*. Cambridge, Mass.: Harvard University Press.

SAXENIAN, A. (1994). *Regional Advantage: Culture and Competition in Silicon Valley and Route 128*. Cambridge, Mass.: Harvard University Press.

SAYER, A. (1995). *Radical Political Economy: A Critique*. Oxford: Blackwell.

SCALIA, A. (1997). *A Matter of Interpretation: Federal Courts and the Law*. Princeton: Princeton University Press.

SCHAUER, F. (1991). *Playing by the Rules: A Philosophical Examination of Rule-Based Decision Making in Law and in Life*. Oxford: Clarendon Press.

SCHEPPELE, K. (1988). *Legal Secrets: Equality and Efficiency in the Common Law*. Chicago: University of Chicago Press.

SCHERER, F. M., and ROSS, D. (1990). *Industrial Market Structure and Economic Performance*. Boston: Houghton Mifflin.

SCHMALENSEE, R. (1982). 'The New Industrial Organization and the Economic Analysis of Markets', in W. Hildenbrand (ed.), *Advances in Economic Theory*. Cambridge: Cambridge University Press, 253–85.

SCHOENBERGER, E. (1991). 'The Corporate Interview as a Research Method in Economic Geography'. *The Professional Geographer*, 43: 180–9.

—— (1992). 'Self-Criticism and Self-Awareness in Research: A Response to Linda McDowell'. *The Professional Geographer*, 44: 215–18.

—— (1996). *The Cultural Crisis of the Firm*. Oxford: Blackwell.

—— (1998). 'Discourse and Practice in Human Geography'. *Progress in Human Geography*, 22: 1–14.

SCHROEDER, J. L. (1998). 'The End of the Market: A Psychoanalysis of Law and Economics'. *Harvard Law Review*, 112: 484–558.

SCHWARTZ, L. W. (1994). 'Venture Abroad: Developing Countries Need Venture Capital Strategies'. *Foreign Affairs*, Nov./Dec.: 14–18.

SCOTT, A. (1988*a*). *Metropolis*. Berkeley: University of California Press.

——(1988*b*). *Regions and the World Economy: The Coming Shape of Global Production, Competition, and Political Order*. Oxford: Oxford University Press.

SEARLE, J. R. (1995). *The Construction of Social Reality*. London: Allen Lane.

SENNETT, R. (1980). *Authority*. New York: Knopf.

——(1998). *The Corrosion of Character: The Personal Consequences of Work in the New Capitalism*. New York: W. W. Norton and Co.

SHACKLE, G. L. S. (1972). *Epistemics and Economics: A Critique of Economic Doctrine*. Cambridge: Cambridge University Press.

SHARPE, W. (1964). 'Capital Asset Prices: A Theory of Market Equilibrium under Conditions of Risk'. *Journal of Finance*, 19: 425–42.

——and ALEXANDER, G. (1990). *Investments*. Englewood Cliffs, NJ: Prentice Hall.

SHKLAR, J. (1984). *Ordinary Vices*. Cambridge, Mass.: Harvard University Press.

SHLEIFER, A. (1985). 'A Theory of Yardstick Competition'. *Rand Journal of Economics*, 16: 319–27.

——(1998). *Market Inefficiency*. Oxford: Clarendon Press (forthcoming).

——and VISHNY, R. (1997). 'The Limits of Arbitrage'. *Journal of Finance*, 52: 35–55.

SHONFIELD, A. (1965). *Modern Capitalism*. Oxford: Oxford University Press.

SIEBERS, T. (1992). *Morals and Stories*. New York: Columbia University Press.

SIEGEL, J. J. (1994). *Stocks for the Long Run: A Guide to Selecting Markets for Long-Term Growth*. Homewood Ill.: Irwin Professional Publishing.

SILVER, W. (1983). 'The Process of Financial Innovation'. *American Economic Review*, 73: 89–95.

SILVERMAN, C., and YAKOBOSKI, P. (1994). 'Public and Private Pensions Today: An Overview of the System', in D. Salisbury and N. Jones (eds.), *Pension Funding and Taxation: Implications for Tomorrow*. Washington, DC: Employee Benefit Research Institute, 7–42.

SIMESTER, A. P. (1996). 'Why Distinguish Intention from Foresight?', in A. P. Simester and A. T. H. Smith (eds.), *Harm and Culpability*. Oxford: Clarendon Press, 71–102.

SIMON, H. (1961). *Administrative Behavior*. New York: Macmillan.

——(1984). 'On the Behavioral and Rational Foundations of Economic Dynamics'. *Journal of Economic Behavior and Organization*, 5: 35–55.

——(1986). 'Rationality in Psychology and Economics'. *Journal of Business*, 59: S209–S224.

SIRES, R. (1954). 'The Beginnings of British Legislation for Old-Age Pensions'. *Journal of Economic History*, 14: 229–53.

SIRRI, E., and TUFANO, P. (1993). 'Buying and Selling Mutual Funds: Flows, Performance, Fees, and Services'. Boston: Division of Research, Harvard Business School.

SKINNER, Q. (1996). *Reason and Rhetoric in the Philosophy of Hobbes.* Cambridge: Cambridge University Press.

SKOCPOL, T. (1990). *Protecting Soldiers and Mothers: The Political Origins of Social Policy in the United States.* Cambridge, Mass.: Harvard University Press.

SLOTE, M. (1989). *Beyond Optimizing.* Cambridge, Mass.: Harvard University Press.

SMITH, J. G. (1997). *Full Employment: A Pledge Betrayed.* London: Macmillan.

SOBEL, J. (1997). 'A Re-examination of Yard-Stick Competition'. La Jolla: Department of Economics, University of California at San Diego.

SPENCE, N. (1992). 'Impact of Infrastructure Investment Policy', in P. Townroe and R. L. Martin (eds.), *Regional Development in the 1990s.* London: Jessica Kingsley, 229–37.

SPERBER, D., and WILSON, D. (1990). 'Rhetoric and Relevance', in J. Bender and D. Wellbery (eds.), *The Ends of Rhetoric: History, Theory, Practice.* Palo Alto, Calif.: Stanford University Press, 140–55.

STANLEY, L., and WISE, S. (1993). *Breaking Out Again: Feminist Ontology and Epistemology.* London: Routledge.

STAW, B., and ROSS, J. (1989). 'Understanding Behaviour in Escalation Situations'. *Science*, 246: 216–20.

STEAD, F. (1909). *How Old-Age Pension Began to Be.* London: Methuen.

STEELE, D. R. (1996). 'Nozick on Sunk Costs'. *Ethics*, 106: 605–20.

STORPER, M. (1989). 'The Transition to Flexible Specialization in the U.S. Film Industry: the Division of Labour, External Economies, and the Crossing of Industrial Divides'. *Cambridge Journal of Economics*, 13: 273–305.

—— (1991). 'The Limits to Globalisation: Technology Districts and International Trade'. *Economic Geography*, 67: 60–93.

—— and SALAIS, R. (1997). *Worlds of Production: The Action Frameworks of the Economy.* Cambridge, Mass.: Harvard University Press.

SUMMERS, L. (1986). 'Does the Stock Market Rationally Reflect Fundamental Values?' *Journal of Finance*, 41: 591–601.

SUNLEY, P. (1996). 'Context in Economic Geography: The Relevance of Pragmatism'. *Progress in Human Geography*, 20: 338–55.

TAYLOR, M., and THRIFT, N. (1983). 'Business Organization, Segmentation and Location'. *Regional Studies*, 17: 445–65.

TERRY, F. (1996). 'The Private Finance Initiative: Overview Reform or Policy Breakthrough?' *Public Money and Management*, Jan./Mar.: 9–15.

THALER, R. H. (1980). 'Toward a Positive Theory of Consumer Choice'. *Journal of Economic Behaviour and Organization*, 1: 39–60.

—— (1991). *Quasi-Rational Economics.* New York: Russell Sage Foundation.

—— (1993) (ed.). *Advances in Behavioral Finance.* New York: Russell Sage Foundation.

THRIFT, N. (1996). *Spatial Formations.* London: Sage.

—— and OLDS, K. (1996). 'Refiguring the Economic in Economic Geography'. *Progress in Human Geography*, 20: 311–37.

TILOVE, R. (1976). *Public Employee Pension Funds.* New York: Columbia University Press.

TREBILCOCK, M. J. (1993). *The Limits of Freedom of Contract.* Cambridge, Mass.: Harvard University Press.

TUFANO, P. (1989). 'Financial Innovation and First-Mover Advantage'. *Journal of Financial Economics*, 25: 213–40.

TVERSKY, A., and KAHNEMAN, D. (1974). 'Judgement under Uncertainty: Heuristics and Biases'. *Science*, 185: 1124–31.

——— (1986). 'Rational Choice and the Framing of Decisions'. *Journal of Business*, 59(S): 251–79.

TYRIE, A. (1996). *The Prospects for Public Spending.* London: Social Market Foundation.

UNGER, R. M. (1996). *What Should Legal Analysis Become?* London: Verso.

US Congress (1985). *Venture Capital and Innovation.* 98th (2nd session). Washington, DC: Government Printing Office.

—— (1993). 'Financing Future Connections'. Washington, DC: Commission to Promote Investment in America's Infrastructure.

US Department of Labor (1994a). 'Interpretive Bulletin Relating to the Fiduciary Standard under ERISA in Considering Economically Targeted Investments'. Washington, DC: Pension and Welfare Benefits Administration.

—— (1994b). 'Pension and Health Benefits of American Workers: New Findings from the April 1993 Current Population Survey'. Washington, DC: Pension and Welfare Benefits Administration.

US Department of Labor Work Group on Economically Targeted Investments (1993). 'A Clearinghouse Network for Economically Targeted Investments'. Washington, DC: Advisory Council on Pension Welfare and Benefit Plans.

US Department of Labor Work Group on Pension Fund Investments (1992). 'Economically Targeted Investments: An ERISA Policy Review'. Washington, DC: Advisory Council on Pension Welfare and Benefit Plans.

VALDES-PRIETO, S. (1997) (ed.). *The Economics of Pensions: Principles, Policies, and International Experience.* Cambridge: Cambridge University Press.

VAN HORNE, J. (1985). 'Of Financial Innovations and Excesses'. *Journal of Finance*, 40: 621–31.

VITTAS, D. (1996). 'Private Pension Funds in Hungary: Early Performance and Regulatory Issues'. Washington, DC: World Bank.

—— and MICHELITSCH, R. (1995). 'Pension Funds in Central Europe and Russia: Their Prospects and Potential Role in Corporate Governance'. Washington, DC: World Bank.

VON NEUMANN, J., and MORGENSTERN, O. (1944). *Theory of Games and Economic Behaviour.* Princeton: University of Princeton Press.

WAHAL, S., and McCONNELL, J. J. (1997). 'Do Institutional Investors Exacerbate Managerial Myopia?' Atlanta: Goizueta Business School, Emory University.

WEBBER, M. J., and RIGBY, D. (1996). *The Golden Age Illusion: Rethinking Postwar Capitalism.* New York: Guilford Press.

William Mercer (1996). 'Key Terms and Conditions for Private Equity

Investing'. Boston: Pension Reserves Investment Management Board of Massachusetts.

WILLIAMS, B. (1995). 'Identity and Identities', in H. Harris (ed.), *Identity*. Oxford: Clarendon Press, 1–12.

WILLIAMSON, O. (1985). *The Institutions of Capitalism*. New York: Free Press.

WOODWARD, R. (1994). *The Agenda: Inside the Clinton White House*. New York: Simon and Schuster.

WOOLLEY, F. (1993). 'The Feminist Challenge to Neoclassical Economics'. *Cambridge Journal of Economics*, 17: 485–500.

ZECKHAUSER, R., PATEL, J., and HENDRICKS, D. (1991). 'Nonrational Actors and Financial Market Behaviour'. *Theory and Decision*, 31: 257–67.

ZELINSKY, E. A. (1995). 'ETI, Phone the Department of Labor: Economically Targeted Investments, IB94-1 and the Reincarnation of Industrial Policy'. *Berkeley Journal of Employment and Labor Law*, 16: 333–55.

——(1996). 'Economically Targeted Investments: A Critical Analysis'. New York: Yeshiva University, Cardozo School of Law.

ZINGALES, L. (1998). 'Survivial of the Fittest or the Fattest? Exit and Financing in the Trucking Industry'. *Journal of Finance*, 53: 905–38.

ZYSMAN, J. (1994). 'How Institutions Create Historically Rooted Trajectories of Growth'. *Industrial and Corporate Change*, 3: 243–83.

# INDEX